SENSIBILITY AND ENGLISH SONG

Critical Studies of the Early 20th Century

1

SENSIBILITY AND ENGLISH SONG

Critical Studies of the Early 20th Century

1

STEPHEN BANFIELD

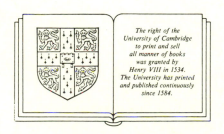

The right of the
University of Cambridge
to print and sell
all manner of books
was granted by
Henry VIII in 1534.
The University has printed
and published continuously
since 1584.

CAMBRIDGE UNIVERSITY PRESS

Cambridge
London   New York   New Rochelle
Melbourne   Sydney

Published by the Press Syndicate of the University of Cambridge
The Pitt Building, Trumpington Street, Cambridge CB2 1RP
32 East 57th Street, New York, NY 10022, USA
296 Beaconsfield Parade, Middle Park, Melbourne 3206, Australia

First published 1985

Printed in Great Britain at
the University Press, Cambridge

Library of Congress catalogue card number: 83–7801

British Library Cataloguing in Publication Data
Banfield, Stephen
Sensibility and English song.
1. Songs, English – History and criticism
2. Songs – HIstory and criticism – 20th century
I. Title
784   ML283/
ISBN 0 521 23085 3 volume 1
ISBN 0 521 30360 5 volume 2

This book is dedicated to the memory of
John Clough, whose hospitality at
13 College Green, Gloucester, was a
friendly and generous stimulus to
my Gurney research.

CONTENTS

vii

Song lists

PREFACE

Not long after commencing this project in Oxford in 1972, I more or less invited myself to visit Frank Howes, whose book *The English Musical Renaissance* was and still is the starting-point for the critical investigation of British music of the early part of this century. I enjoyed rural surroundings, fruitful conversation, and lunch at his home, Newbridge Mill near Witney. He was encouraging; however, he said that for years he himself had wanted to write a book on English song but did not know how to set about it. At the time, I who was one-and-twenty felt confident that I did know how to set about it; now I am not so sure.

The subject is potentially vast. Almost any second-hand book shop will contain a ragged pile of songs, normally stacked in such a position as to make systematic investigation impossible without abrasion of the hands and knees and a rush of blood to the head. And (unlike Novello's octavo cantatas and oratorios) it is not always the same few titles that meet one's gaze. Yet this book does not fully embrace such material, which future students will need to approach inclusively, with an eye on statistics, economics and social documentation, and with a mind better equipped than mine to define anew, or perhaps abolish, the perplexing distinction between 'popular' and 'art' songs.

But while this is not primarily a documentary study, neither is it intended to expound an aesthetic of song. This subject has been treated by a number of writers (see Clinton-Baddeley; Frye; Tippett, 1960; Pears, 1965; Ivey; and Stein) who, roughly speaking, have taken up one of two positions: either that there are 'words which have been deliberately written for music, and it is this which is the true and ancient art of song' (Clinton-Baddeley: 23), or that, since 'the moment the composer begins to create the musical verses of his song, he destroys our appreciation of the poem as poetry, and substitutes an appreciation of his music as song' (Tippett, 1960: 462), any words are fair game. The bias of this book is towards the second position, which if anything throws more of a spotlight on to the words, carrying as it does the implication that the composer had designs on the texts he set to music. It will be noticed that here I have moved into the past tense, as a recognition that the concerns of this book are primarily those of a historical critique. Why a composer or more than one composer was attracted in the first place to a poem, poet or group of poets; how he understood his text; and to what personal purpose he was, so to speak, quoting it by setting it to music when and in the way that he did – these are questions repeatedly asked in the course of this study. They lead to two further questions that are kept in mind, namely, how well did the composer succeed in conveying his textual designs, and how significantly can they be placed in both his personal history (as a composer and as a man) and that of his country and period. This last question gives rise to extended discussion of idiomatic influence, stylistic development, and tradition.

Like any historical perspective, this one is highly selective, and many readers will be disappointed to find no mention of figures in whom they are interested; this pertains to the problem of the size of the subject. The greatest degree of selectivity is probably in the treatment of composers active around the turn of the century: I have not covered Corder, Cowen, German, Liza Lehmann, MacCunn, McEwen, Mackenzie or Maude Valérie White, to name only eight prominent figures. Some may censure my avoidance of the issue of folksong, others my relative lack of concern with rescue from neglect, with the topical phenomenon of reassessment (or secondary assessment as I would prefer to call it), where later composers are in question: for example, I give no space to Bainton, York Bowen, William Busch, Rebecca Clarke, Robin Milford, Rootham or Felix White. I might have warmed to the investigation of these and similar figures had space and time permitted; but I hope that I have at least made out a case for (or against) the composers that I have treated, most of whom seemed to me still in need of a critical and technical gloss on their primary assessment (i.e. their historical reputation).

Both the book's title and its shape require some explanation. I use the term 'sensibility' in its 18th- and early-19th-century sense, as defined by the *Shorter Oxford English Dictionary*, of a 'capacity for refined emotion; delicate sensitiveness of taste; also, readiness to feel compassion for suffering, and to be moved by the pathetic in literature or art'. This, it seems to me, is a property whose application to Romantic song bears close pondering. The 'refinement' of emotion, the codification and hence distillation of the emotional essence or overriding image of a poem, is perhaps the quality by which a Romantic song accompaniment, and indeed the song itself, stands or falls; if, however, the composer's 'compassion' becomes too self-regarding, the 'readiness . . . to be moved' too automatic and stereotyped, then sensibility needs replacing with some new quality in a song. Perhaps the life-cycle of taste always follows this pattern; if so, then this book is an account of one such historical life-cycle.

One further observation on the connotations of Romantic song and sensibility concerns the genre's essentially inward-looking, private and intimate nature. Many songs, like many lyric poems, are to be heard as serenades or read as love letters. This explains a number of things. Serenades and love letters are created only when the beloved is absent or in some way inaccessible; lovers have better things to do when they are in each other's arms. Sometimes the serenade is not heard or the love letter not posted, in which case the element of self-communion is paramount. Hence the reflective and reflexive role of the accompaniment in so many cases, hence the relative unimportance of questions of performance (which are hardly touched upon in this study), and hence the fact that, with many of the composers, we are dealing with a young man's art.

The book's shape, roughly that of two balancing *Stollen* and an *Abgesang*, was arrived at over a number of years. The central chapters in Part II were conceived early on and researched separately, the first drafts of Chapters XI and XIII belonging to 1973 and 1974 respectively. The treatment of the music of Ireland,

Gurney and Finzi and of the poetry of Housman, Hardy, the Celts and the Georgians in separate chapters reflects my estimation of their importance. Much of Part I of the book, on the other hand, leading up to this central plateau, was written straight off in 1975. Other material in Parts I and II was added subsequently, to complete the text of my Oxford DPhil thesis (Banfield, 1979). The Postscript in the thesis was very brief, and has recently been greatly expanded to give more adequate, if still restricted, coverage of figures and tendencies not accounted for by the book's main concerns. If, after revision, some of the older parts of the text still seem unduly to display the taint of Enthusiasm, I plead only an abiding love of the music (or dislike of it, as the case may be) in their defence.

A great many people have helped in the preparation of this book. Of those who have read parts of it in typescript, I must particularly thank Hugh Macdonald, who as my research supervisor at St John's College, Oxford, offered encouragement, criticism and a good deal of time from the start of the project. Thanks are also due to Geoff Hutchings, who read nearly the entire book and made many comments; to Bernard Rose and Arthur Hutchings, who as my DPhil examiners patiently corrected my grammar and pointed out errors of fact and conception; and to John Carey, Joy Finzi, Lewis Foreman, Stephen Jackson, Diana McVeagh, Christopher Palmer, Eric Sams, Tom Shippey and Ursula Vaughan Williams, all of whom read chapters and offered helpful critical comments. Lewis Foreman, with his unrivalled knowledge of many aspects of the period, also kindly agreed to read the whole text for obvious inaccuracies and inconsistencies; for any that remain I alone am responsible. As for the song lists, I am all too aware that their details are not exhaustive; but some limits had to be put on investigation in the attempt to catalogue 54 composers.

The following people have all willingly and generously given me information, and a number of them, in circumstances delightful to recall, have also given me food and drink: Sir Thomas Armstrong, Malcolm Arthur, Mr C. R. L. Avenell (Alfred Lengnick & Co), Richard Austin, Mr H. Baron, John Barrow, Trudy Bliss, the late Sir Adrian Boult, Malcolm Boyd, Trevor Bray, Alan Bush, Nancy Bush, Roger Carpenter, Hugo Cole, Justin Connolly, Brian Rayner Cook, Ian Copley, Noel Cox, Dr and Mrs A. J. Croft, Sir Mordaunt Currie, Bart, George Dannatt, Brian Daubney, Michael Dawney, Peter Dennison, Jeremy Dibble, Peter Dickinson, John Dodd, Leslie East, Peter Evans, Sir Keith Falkner, Joy Finzi, John Fisher, Lewis Foreman, John Eliot Gardiner, John Gardner, Bryan Gooch, Robert Gower, Andrew Guyatt, Marvell Hart, Graham Hatton, Trevor Hold, Katharine Howard, the late Herbert Howells, the late Frank Howes, Frederick Hudson, Garry Humphreys, Michael Hurd, David Josephson, Ian Kemp, Karl Kroeger, Margaret Lambart, Robin Langley (OUP), Joan Littlejohn, Stephen Lloyd, Odean Long, Sheila MacCrindle (J. & W. Chester), Rhoderick MacNeill, Diana McVeagh, Charles Moore, Adrian Officer, the late C. W. Orr, Graham Parlett, Robert Pascall, Mary Peppin, Peter Pirie, Gordon Pullin, Philip Radcliffe, Arthur Rankin, Mark Raphael, John Rippin, Gregory Roscow, Mark Rowlinson, Edmund Rubbra, Mr and Mrs Lyndon Rust, Mrs M. Hartston Scott, Hugh Taylor, Rev. Kenneth Thompson, Graham Titus, Peter Todd, Fred Tomlinson, William Tortolano, Peter Tranchell, Leslie Walters, Judith Williams and

John Wilson. If there are others whom I have failed to mention, I offer them my sincere apologies. I also apologise to those of the above who supplied information which it was not possible to incorporate.

I should like to thank the following libraries and their staff for their co-operation: The British Library (Hugh Cobbe); Bodleian Library, Oxford (Margaret Crum, Peter Ward Jones); Music Faculty Library, University of Oxford; Cambridge University Library (Derek Williams, Hugh Taylor); Pendlebury Library, Cambridge (the late Charles Cudworth); Fitzwilliam Museum, Cambridge; Parry Room, Royal College of Music (Watkins Shaw, Joan Littlejohn); Royal Academy of Music Library (Miss M. J. Harington); BBC Music Library; British Institute of Recorded Sound (Timothy Day); Royal Northern College of Music Library (Anthony Hodges); Scottish Music Archive (Paul Hindmarsh); Music Department Library, University of Edinburgh; Music Library, University of Birmingham (Paul Wilson); Balliol College Library, Oxford (Mr E. V. Quinn); Eton College Library (Jeremy Potter); Britten-Pears Library (Sir Peter Pears, Rosamund Strode); Gloucester City Library; Dorset County Museum; Library of Congress (Wayne Shirley); Music Department Library, University of Hawaii at Manoa.

I gratefully acknowledge the award of small research grants from the British Academy and the University of Keele in connection with this project.

Finally I extend my eager thanks to Cambridge University Press: to Michael Black, who offered enthusiastic encouragement and critical advice; to Clare Davies-Jones, who disentangled much of my prose; to Rosemary Dooley, who took over Clare Davies-Jones's burden of tactful patience with an unproductive author and continued to shoulder it magnificently for an inordinate length of time; and to my dextrous, clear-minded and infinitely painstaking subeditor, Ruth Smith. I must add that were it not for the granting of a term's leave of absence from Keele University and the willingness of my colleagues in the Music Department there to reorganise their teaching while I was away, this book might never have been finished at all.

STEPHEN BANFIELD

London, 5 December 1982

ACKNOWLEDGEMENTS

The author and publisher are grateful to the following for permission to reproduce copyright material:

The Trustees of Sir Arnold Bax's Estate (chap. XII, exx. 1 and 2, and extracts from *Farewell, My Youth*)

John Bishop (chap. IV, exx. 6–8)

Lady Bliss (Postscript, exx. 31–4 and extracts from *As I Remember*)

Boosey & Hawkes Music Publisher Ltd (chap. III, exx. 1–12, 16–22, chap. VI, exx. 7–30, Postscript, exx. 16–18, 46–8, 51)

Mr Benjamin H. Burrows (chap. X, ex. 10 and chap. XI, exx. 1–3)

Chappell Music (chap. XII, ex. 5 © 1924 Murdoch & Co. Ltd. Assigned Chappell & Co. Ltd, ex. 10 © 1922 Murdoch Murdoch & Co. Ltd. Assigned Chappell & Co. Ltd, exx. 11–12 © 1922 Murdoch Murdoch & Co. Ltd. Assigned Chappell & Co. Ltd)

Chester Music (chap. VIII, exx. 11–14, chap. XII, exx. 3(b), 4, 6–9, chap. XIV, exx. 1–6, Postscript, exx. 41–5)

The Trustees of Sir Walford Davies's Estate (chap. III, exx. 13–15)

Mrs Joy Finzi (chap. XIII, exx. 1–14, and extracts from the writings of Gerald and Joy Finzi)

John Eliot Gardiner (excerpts from the letters of Grainger to Rolf Gardiner and from Grainger's *Henry Balfour Gardiner, Champion of British Music*)

J. R. Haines (chap. IX, exx. 1–3, 14, 15(b-d), chap. X, ex. 9, and extracts from Gurney's letters to Marion Scott)

Mrs Marvell Hart (Postscript, ex. 27)

David Higham Associates Ltd (extracts from C. Hassall's *Edward Marsh, Patron of the Arts: A Biography*, and from Edith and Osbert Sitwell's *Collected Poems* and *Left Hand, Right Hand*)

G. & I. Holst Ltd (Postscript, ex. 8 = BL Add. MS 57876)

The Society of Authors as the literary representative of the Estate of A.E. Housman and Jonathan Cape Ltd publishers of A.E. Housman's *Collected Poems* for A. E. Housman's Poems II, IX, XX, XXIX, XL and 'The lads in their hundreds' and extracts from Poems I, XXIII, XXV and XXXIX. In the USA *The Collected Poems of A. E. Housman* are copyright 1939, 1940, © 1965 Holt, Rinehart and Winston. Copyright 1967, 1968 by Robert E. Symons. Reprinted by permission of Holt, Rinehart and Winston, Publishers.

The John Ireland Trust (chap. VIII, exx. 2 and 5–10)

The executors of the James Joyce Estate (excerpts from 'Chamber Music' from *Collected Poems* by James Joyce. In the USA copyright 1918 by B. W. Huebsch, Inc. Copyright 1927, 1936 by James Joyce. Copyright 1946 by James Joyce. Reprinted by permission of Viking Penguin Inc.)

The Literary Trustees of Walter de la Mare and The Society of Authors as their representative for 'Silver' and extracts from 'The ghost' and 'The song of the mad prince'

Methuen London Ltd, extracts from Humbert Wolfe's *The Unknown Goddess*

Mrs Helen Orr (chap. XIV, exx. 1, 3–6, and quotations from letters)

Oxford University Press (chap. VIII, exx. 21, 24, 25, chap. IX, exx. 5–6, 9–13, 16 and Postscript exx. 1, 35–40 and extracts from M. Kennedy's *Portrait of Elgar* and *The Works of Ralph Vaughan Williams*, M. Hurd's *The Ordeal of Ivor Gurney* and G. Richards's *Housman 1897–1936*)

Mrs Ann Rust (chap. X, exx. 5–8 and 11–12)

Stainer & Bell Ltd and Galaxy Music Corporation (chap. VIII, exx. 1, 15–20, 23, Postscript exx. 19–21)

Mrs R. Vaughan Williams (chap. IV, exx. 10–23 and Postscript, exx. 3–4)

Michael and Anne Yeats for W. B. Yeats's 'The coat' and extracts from *Ideas of Good and Evil*, and 'The hosting of the Sidhe', and Macmillan Publishing Co. Inc. for 'The coat' in the USA

Chap. IV, exx. 1, 5 and chap. VI, ex. 3 are Royal College of Music, Parry Room, MS nos. 4526, 4525 and 4428 respectively; Postscript exx. 12–13 are BL Add. MS 50221; chap. XII, exx. 26–8 are Fitzwilliam Museum, Hadley MSS MU 29.

EXPLANATION OF
BIBLIOGRAPHICAL SYSTEM
AND SONG LISTS

In order to avoid footnotes, bibliographical sources have been cited in the text, in abbreviated form. Where necessary for identification the author's name is given, and/or the date of the item referred to; the page number(s) follow(s), after a colon. The letters a, b, c etc. appearing after the date distinguish between different works by the same author dating from the same year; they are similarly used in the bibliography itself.

In addition to books and articles, sources listed in the bibliography include record sleeve notes, periodicals, unpublished typescripts, collections of letters, letters to the author, and conversations with the author. Books of verse are not included, references to them in the main text being considered self-sufficient. The bibliography is highly selective of published writings, particularly where journalistic material is concerned, and it consists solely of items which have been found helpful. Editions other than the first are mentioned only when use has been made of them.

For references to the bibliography by subject, see entries in the index.

The song lists present, as far as it has been possible to ascertain, each composer's output in full. Accordingly in the main text of the book details of songs are kept to a minimum, except when the composer is not represented in the song lists, in which case details of authorship of the words and dates of the song follow the title in brackets. Throughout the book dates of songs in roman type are those of composition or completion, dates in italics those of publication or, to be precise, copyright (which may have preceded publication by a few months).

Each individual song carries a number, used to identify it in the index. The lists are set out, as far as possible, chronologically and/or by opus number, the latter taking precedence. Where there is a complex of dates within one work, the earliest takes precedence for chronological listing. Within the confines of chronology titles are arranged alphabetically. Songs comprising a set or cycle, whether so designated by the composer or by the publisher, have in general not been broken up (Gurney is a slight exception to both these procedures, as the notes preceding his list explain).

All works for solo voice are counted as songs; duets are included only where they seem to have been conceived for two solo voices rather than massed voices. Unison songs are listed only where there is doubt about the original conception, or where (as with Warlock) they have also been published as solo songs. Children's songs have not been listed where class rather than solo performance seems to have been envisaged. Cycles for SATB and piano, which may have included solo numbers, are not listed (there were a number of these in the period, including Somervell's *Wind Flowers*, Liza Lehmann's *In a Persian Garden* and *The Daisy-Chain*, Stanford's *Cycle of Songs from 'The Princess'*, Harold Darke's *Youth Rides Forth*, Walford Davies's *Six Pastorals* and *Noble Numbers*, and Ernest Walker's *Five Songs from 'England's Helicon'*). In general carols are not listed. Arrangements and collections of folksongs are not listed when (arguably) they form a substantially separate part of the composer's output. Songs composed as incidental music in a theatrical production or film are listed, but solo items extracted from an existing larger musical work, such as an opera or oratorio, in general are not. For composers born before 1900 complete lists are given; for those born after 1900 there is a postwar cut-off point (Finzi, Head and Sykes excepted, on stylistic grounds), or later works are listed summarily or selectively if germane to this study (Britten, *Winter Words*; Berkeley, de la Mare and Auden settings). Songs to non-English texts are listed in most cases; exceptions are made of the two 'cosmopolitans', Delius and van Dieren. Works which require a chorus are not listed, though exceptions are made of Stanford's *Songs of the Sea* and *Songs of the Fleet*. However, it must be stressed that each composer has had to be regarded as a separate case, and with many of them the policy is outlined in a prefatory note.

All items are for voice and piano unless otherwise indicated. 'Also with' and 'or' indicate alternatives to the piano accompaniment; 'with' means the specified instrument(s) in addition to piano; 'piano quintet' means piano and string quartet.

The poet's name or other source of the words is given in brackets, if known. Poetic attributions and spelling follow those in *Granger's Index to Poetry* (Smith, 1973). Surnames only are given where the poet is well known; the index usually furnishes the full name as well as aliases.

Speculative datings are marked *ca*. A song without a publication (copyright) date is still in manuscript.

The exact wording of a dedication is given in inverted commas when it seems significant, such as when 'for . . .' indicates a singer for whose repertoire the song was commissioned or envisaged.

Details of first known performance are given in the order: singer, other soloist(s), accompanist or orchestra and conductor, venue, date. Venue is London except where otherwise stated.

Principal bibliographical sources for the song lists are mentioned immediately after the composer's name and dates; however, many of the lists in their final form owe a great deal to information collated from first-hand study of the published scores and manuscripts as well as from Hull (1920), Blom (1954) and Sadie (1981). In addition many people, mentioned in the Preface, have helped by supplying needed details.

ABBREVIATIONS

acc.	accompanied	RAM	Royal Academy of Music, London
BBC	British Broadcasting Corporation	RCM	Royal College of Music, London
BPL	Britten–Pears Library, Aldeburgh, Suffolk	RNCM	Royal Northern College of Music, formerly the Royal Manchester College of Music
GSM	Guildhall School of Music, later Guildhall School of Music and Drama, London		
OUP	Oxford University Press	SO	Symphony Orchestra
perf.	first known performance	unacc.	unaccompanied

Library sigla

DK-Ku	University Library, Copenhagen	-Gu	University Library, Glasgow
EIRE-C	Bax Memorial Room, Music Department, University College, Cork	-Lam	Royal Academy of Music, London
		-Lbbc	BBC Music Library, London
		-Lbl	British Library, London
GB-Bu	Music Library, Barber Institute of Fine Arts, University of Birmingham	-Lcm	Parry Room, Royal College of Music, London
-Cclc	Fellows' Library, Clare College, Cambridge	-Lcs	Cecil Sharp House, London
		-Lu	Senate House Library, University of London
-Cfm	Fitzwilliam Museum, Cambridge	-M	Royal Northern College of Music, Manchester
-Cgc	Gonville and Caius College, Cambridge	-Ob	Bodleian Library, Oxford
		US-NH	Osborn Collection, Yale University
-Cu	University Library, Cambridge	-NYp	New York Public Library
-En	National Library of Scotland, Edinburgh	-PHf	Philadelphia Free Library
		-Wc	Library of Congress, Washington DC
-Gm	Mitchell Library, Glasgow		

I

THE GROWTH OF SENSIBILITY

I

The condition of English song in 1900

The turn of the century was a crucial period in the growth and rebirth of English music. The renaissance, which had been gathering impetus and self-respect throughout the 1880s and 1890s, reached maturity around 1900. Elgar was the key figure: the *Enigma Variations* were instantaneously successful at their first performance, at St James's Hall, London, on 19 June 1899, and, more important perhaps, established themselves in the orchestral repertoire by further performances later in the same year ('the 1st time anything by an Englishman has been done twice!!', as Elgar pointedly remarked in a letter to Troyte Griffith (Kennedy, 1968: 62)). Sixteen months later, on 3 October 1900, *The Dream of Gerontius* suffered an unfortunate première at Birmingham, but it redeemed itself at Düsseldorf the following year and was soon accepted as an English choral masterpiece of unprecedented stature. Elgar had stood indigenous English choral and orchestral music on its feet single-handed, and continued to strengthen its position throughout the pre-war period with his subsequent oratorios, the two symphonies, the Violin Concerto, the overtures, the marches, the Introduction and Allegro and *Falstaff*.

Other genres developed less noticeably. English opera was not a strong force until after the second world war, Boughton's *The Immortal Hour* (1912–13), which was given its first London production in 1922, remaining an isolated repertorial success and Holst's *Sāvitri* (1908) an equally isolated aesthetic one. Chamber music, like keyboard music, partly because of its less spectacular nature, tended not to draw attention to itself, though with the stimulus of W. W. Cobbett's and others' patronage a remarkable corpus of chamber works was gradually built up, and is still, if one considers the works of Bax and Bridge, being rediscovered or even recognised for the first time today. Church music, which was less in need of revivification than other genres, because its flame, tended by S. S. Wesley, Stainer, and some fine hymn-writers, had never died, retained a comfortable if sometimes maudlin level of competence, and provided at least one composer, Standford, with a major outlet for his lyrical inspiration. Ballet was not considered as a self-sufficient genre until the arrival of Diaghilev's Russian Ballet in London in 1911, and produced no noteworthy native works until well after the first world war.

But what of song? Publishers' and library catalogues show that there was an enormous market in both royalty ballads and 'art songs' – the distinction was not always clear, as we shall see – from the mid-Victorian period into the 1930s, without giving any obvious indication that the turn of the century was climac-

1

teric. Nevertheless, beyond the relatively stable commercial success of song-writing throughout this 60-year period there was, roughly in the middle, a radical transformation in the aesthetic status of English song. In the 1870s and 1880s no composer was likely to feel proud of concerning him- or herself overmuch with the genre; by 1914, however, song was beginning to flaunt its rediscovered pedigree. How was this transformation effected?

Five events around 1900 can be seen as historically important. Two of them reflected changing attitudes and sensibilities with respect to English song, a further two were prophetic of future developments and perhaps also productively influential, and the fifth was something of an enigma. Their significance will, it is hoped, become clear when placed in context in the course of the following chapters, but they can be enumerated here. The enigma, as we might expect, came from Elgar: *Sea Pictures*, his cycle of five songs for contralto and orchestra, was first performed at the 1899 Norwich Festival on 5 October by the 26-year-old Clara Butt, who, 'dressed like a mermaid', as Elgar described her, 'sang *really well*' (Kennedy, 1968: 71). It was highly acclaimed, but spawned no worthy progeny by Elgar or anyone else, and stands, in its subtle orchestral garb, as a curiously isolated *fait accompli*, owing nothing to English or continental traditions of song composition and reminding one only of the song-cycles of Mahler, which Elgar surely did not know. The two representative events of around 1900, by contrast, stand respectively at the head of two song-composing careers of considerable importance; they are the first performance of Sir Arthur Somervell's Tennyson song-cycle, *Maud*, by Lawrence Rea at the Salle Érard in London on 2 November 1899, and that of Roger Quilter's *Four Songs of the Sea*, op.1, by Denham Price at the Crystal Palace late in 1900. Of the two prophetic occasions, one, the Delius concert at St James's Hall on 30 May 1899 (his first hearing in London), was of symbolic rather than real importance and none of his English songs was performed in the programme; the other, rather later, was the founding in April 1902 of *The Vocalist*, a monthly periodical supposed to be exclusively concerned with English solo song and its exponents. *The Vocalist* had been preceded by *The Dome: An Illustrated Monthly Magazine and Review of Literature, Music, Architecture and the Graphic Arts*, which ran from 1897 to 1900 and displayed something of the panache of the nineties. In May 1898 Yeats had contributed three poems, under the title *Aodh to Dectora*, which were later to appear in *The Wind Among the Reeds*, and one of these, 'Half close your eyelids', was reprinted in the January 1900 issue set to music by Thomas Dunhill; earlier issues included songs by Coleridge-Taylor, Delius, Dunhill, Liza Lehmann, [Martin] Fallas Shaw and Elgar, the second of whose *Sea Pictures*, 'In haven', was printed there with its original title, 'Love alone will stay (Lute song)'. *The Vocalist*'s cultural pretensions were far lower than this, but it was nevertheless significant, partly because it presented an Edwardian reaction to the royalty ballad, and in retrospect because it entertained angels unawares, in the forms of Vaughan Williams, Frank Bridge and Gustav (von) Holst. It scooped 'Linden Lea', the song which was to earn Vaughan Williams more money than any other of his works (Kennedy, 1964: 51), for its first issue, as well as his first published article, 'A school of English music'; later numbers included, as supplements to be sold separately, his settings of 'Blackmwore by the Stour' and 'Whither must I wander' (which were best-sellers, according to an editorial of March 1903), 'Boy Johnny', 'If I were a queen', 'Tears, idle tears' (the latter 'in great demand' (*Vocalist* II, 1903: 66)), two duet arrangements of old songs ('Think of me', 'Adieu'), 'The winter's willow', 'The splendour falls' and 'The Virgin's cradle song', before the periodical finally ceased in December 1905. Bridge entrusted five early songs to *The Vocalist* late in 1905 ('The Devon maid', 'Go not, happy day', 'Dawn and evening', 'E'en as a lovely flower' and 'So perverse'), and Holst was represented by 'Invocation to the dawn', the first of his Vedic Hymns and also one of the earliest foretastes of his mature idiom, issued in January 1903. Most of these songs did not achieve regular publication until much later – Vaughan Williams's in 1912, Bridge's in 1916, and Holst's in 1920.

These five landmarks by no means tended in the same direction and can hardly be seen to have been interconnected at all. But they did constitute minor eruptions of creativity at a time when a fresh approach to the setting of the English language to music was long overdue. Beneath the surface a whole new literary sensibility was generating in composers' minds: to the five events outlined above one might add a sixth, possibly more far-reaching, namely the publication of A. E. Housman's first volume of poems, *A Shropshire Lad*, in 1896. This sharpening of their literary sensibility coincided with a rapid widening of their technical resources, and by 1914 the isolated upheavals had joined up to form an unmistakable eminence, an impressive mass of English song which provided the foundation for the technically mature inter-war achievements.

A backward glance at English song before 1900 is necessary. A vast and facile productivity is amply evident, and, by comparison with the *Lieder* of Schumann, Brahms and Wolf, the *mélodies* of Bizet, Fauré, Duparc and Debussy, and the songs of Grieg, the overall impression is one of worthlessness. Whole volumes of mid- and late-Victorian songs and ballads by various composers are indistinguishable, showing a uniform lack of musical imagination. Even an apparently serious attempt to set up a *Lied* tradition in England, Sullivan's cycle *The Window or The Loves of the Wrens*, published in 1871 as settings of poems especially written by Tennyson in 1866, can hardly be exempted from this censure. Not that the poverty of invention is simply a manifestation of English sterility; the disease is rather one of cosmopolitan convention, from which continental composers such as Franz Abt, Charles Gounod and George Henschel enjoyed no exemption. It was the attitude of Victorian England to music as an exportable or importable – and on occasions expendable – commodity based largely on proven international standards of design and dimension which led to the ballad style, immediately recognisable by its very lack of distinction, in which personality was submerged, the influence of the text upon the music was at best pedestrian and at worst nonexistent, the texture of the flowing accompaniment was uniformly 'pianistic', and the general idiom was such that procedures of Schubert, harmonies of Schumann, histrionics of Liszt, echoes of Grieg and foretastes of Fauré were alike reduced to a level of mediocre unmemorability. Its reliance upon stereotyped figures has never been better characterised than by Plunket Greene. He is writing (with illustrations) about vamped repeated chords:

> The old series of repeated chords . . . forms the main accompaniment of three-quarters of all British so-called 'ballads'. It is the *vade-mecum* of the popular composer, and the old, old friend of the sloppy sentimentalist. No doorstep on a winter's night is complete without it. It has discovered more orphans than the combined force of the Metropolitan Police; it has saved more children's lives than the whole of the Country Holiday Fund.
>
> In its extended triplet form it is the only authorised ladder to heaven; the self-respecting Organ Obbligato would faint at the suggestion of supplementing any other style; it can play Ercles rarely, or roar you like any sucking dove; it is the embodiment of self-satisfaction, but is capable of fierce passion. Its love is like anything from a red, red rose to a Tannhäuser Venus. It has no particular drive in its rhythm, no imitation of the voice, no melodic figure, no atmospheric suggestion – just a good roast-beef, up-and-down, accommodating set of plain chords. Does the tenor want to stay in 'Heaven' on that top A? – it is delighted to oblige; does he wish to hurry over the ineffective middle notes? – nothing could give it greater pleasure than to hurry along after him. He has the melody, it has the harmony; what more can any one want? Rhythm? Balance? What will you ask for next? (1912: 54–6)

The ballad mentality did not die with Victoria; many English songs of the 1920s and 1930s and even later display a similarly low common denominator, amounting to a stylistically updated equivalent of the ballad's mindless facility. Composers – a musical counterpart to poetasters is meant by the term here – such as Alec Rowley and Eric Thiman show in their style a continuation of the ballad's musical complacency, associated more with the classroom and nursery than with the drawing room but still an unhealthy twilight zone between the artistic and the commercial from which English music has already more than once needed rescuing.

Technically the royalty ballad was simply a song for which the publisher paid royalties, not just to the composer but also, or perhaps only, to the professional singer who promoted it at concerts; the sheet music would be headed 'sung by . . . '. Since these songs often carried prominent dedications as well (normally to a friend or relative of the composer, opposed to the non-royalty practice of strategically dedicating the song to its singer), and since the names of the composer, author of the words, and (a frequent complication) translator also had to be mentioned, title-pages were apt to become cluttered.

The workings of the royalty ballad system seem to have varied. Percy Scholes's account of 'the paying of a fixed sum to vocalists for the introduction and every repetition of a new song' (:292) suggests a method of payment different from that described in a *Musical Times* editorial in 1867:

> A fixed sum is paid upon each copy sold to the vocalist who will push a composition by introducing it at every concert at which he or she is engaged, where the nature of the programme will not positively forbid it (XIII, 1867: 72; Scholes: 293).

The writer goes on to demonstrate how the system was advertised:

> The columns of the daily newspapers must have enlightened the public upon the manner in which this system is worked. 'Miss — will sing the successful new ballad, "My Mother's Voice," at Greenwich on the 4th inst., at Croydon on the 8th, at Worcester on the 11th, at Hereford on the 14th,' etc., etc.

It is uncertain when the practice of paying royalties to singers began, but on 8

January 1866 (not 3 January, as in Scholes, or 1867, as in Turner: 13) John Boosey consolidated the system by coining the term 'ballad concert' to describe a programme, in this case a concert given by Charlotte Sainton-Dolby in St James's Hall (which was managed by Chappell's), 'exclusively or almost exclusively made up of items from [the publisher's] own catalogues' (Scholes: 292–3).

Had the status of the royalty ballad been simply that of commercial entertainment, and its methods of advertisement and presentation were not, after all, very different from those of the modern pop song, it could be dismissed forthwith from this survey. But there were several ways in which it was bound up with the history of serious song. It occasionally threw up a respectable work, such as Stanford's *An Irish Idyll*, written for Harry Plunket Greene, and often involved the setting of a serious text to trivial music or vice versa; some of Shelley's and Tennyson's most famous poems were used in this way. Further, if an item appeared in a programme *not* sponsored openly as a ballad concert by a publisher, the listener had no means of telling 'which songs are sung on their merits and which for a consideration', as a *Musical Times* editor complained as late as December 1917; he was worried that this put 'publishers and singers . . . morally in a false position, because their relations are secret' (Scholes: 293). The boundaries of taste always have a tendency to blur in the realm of song, because of the multiple considerations of music, text, singer and occasion, and this situation served to confuse them further. Another complication was that many composers tarred themselves with the ballad brush without necessarily writing for the royalty system, often in far more specific ways than the remarks above imply. Bantock's 'The blind man and his dog', 'The organ-grinder and his monkey' (both with words by L. Bantock, and the latter with a chorus) and 'The two roses' (Myrrha Bantock) are the most blatant music-hall effusions, perhaps undertaken as family affairs out of financial necessity; Stanford's 'The monkey's carol' is not dissimilar, though on the subject of organ-grinders it shows an attitude of indifference where Bantock's social conscience produces artistically disastrous sentimentality. Frederick Keel's 'My love and I went maying' (Elinor Sweetman) (*1901*) may be treasured for its bathos. As for Charles Wood's 'Life's memories', Ian Copley (1975b) is unable to believe that Wood wrote it; however, if Bantock could sink to such depths, so perhaps could Wood. The ballad twilight-land is in truth enormous; the style is sensed in some of the songs of Elgar and Somervell (e.g. 'Sweet and low'), Gurney juvenilia ('I would my songs were roses', 'Dearest, when I am dead'), Holst's self-styled 'early horrors' (the worst of the published ones being 'Dewy roses'), the whole of Graham Peel's song output, Parry's 'Not unavailing', 'An evening cloud', 'When the dew is falling', 'Shall I compare thee', 'Music' and 'There be none of Beauty's daughters', and Ireland's 'A song from o'er the hill'. Cyril Scott, who stigmatised the ballad concert as 'an institution, the unmentionable tastelessness of which no country in the world but England would tolerate' (1971: 123), maintained that Boosey ceased publishing his songs in 1904 because they were not in a lucrative ballad style (1969: 93), but many of them are, nevertheless. For some composers, like Elgar, song composition could be a way of making money by supplying what the public wanted, and in his case it was probably also a form of emotional relaxation necessary after completing a major work; however, it would be misleading to suggest that the bulk of Elgar's songs owe their weakness to these factors. For others, the ballad tradition was simply too strong to be avoided, especially if their technical facility tempted them into it. Bridge, for instance, even in his progressive songs never entirely abandoned the ballad mentality. It was a state of mind perplexing and saddening to the foreigner:

> . . . le succès de quelques–unes de ses [Frank Bridge's] mélodies comme *Isobel* ou *Love went ariding* est malheureusement dû aux ressemblances que ces mélodies offrent avec les 'ballads' chères au public anglais et qui sont assurément l'un de ses goûts les plus répréhensibles. Pendant trop longtemps (et même encore aujourd'hui) la plupart des compositeurs, en Angleterre, n'ont guère prêté d'attention aux textes qu'ils mettaient en musique: ils se contentaient de choisir quelques vers sentimentaux qui pussent permettre le déploiement de la plus facile émotion extérieure. On n'a pas idée en France de la pauvreté et de la niaiserie des poèmes que les compositeurs anglais, même les meilleurs, choisissent ordinairement pour en faire des chansons; et cela dans le pays le plus magnifiquement pourvu qui soit au monde d'œuvres lyriques admirables. Dans ce pays . . . on voit figurer, sur les programmes des concerts, des poèmes qui ne dépareraient pas un journal de modes dans une ville de province (Jean-Aubry: 213–14).

On the other hand, ballads were capable of rising above the system which produced them. Maude Valérie White (1855–1937) published well over 150 songs, at least 40 of them under the royalty ballad system, mostly in the last two decades of Queen Victoria's reign, though 'The exile' (Mary Boyle) (*1929*) and other late songs show her cultivating her lyrical muse unaltered well into the 20th century; they were sung by Helen d'Alton, Mary Davies, Harry Plunket Greene, Marguerite Hall, Cecilia Hutchinson, Liza Lehmann, Lena Little, Kirkby Lunn, Emma Osgood, Eugène Oudin, Mr J. Robertson, Miss Robertson (probably Fanny), Kennerley Rumford, Charles Santley, Edith Santley, Marcus Thomson, Zelia Trebelli and Mary Wakefield – a fair proportion of the recitalists of her time. Her songs, though often facile and superficial, rarely become fulsome, and her polished style, which often makes something interesting out of a drab *raison d'être*, was an important influence on Quilter (who dedicated his 'Oh, the month of May' to her), and on Bridge. Her list of works is almost a caricature of *fin-de-siècle* cosmopolitanism, in itself a peculiarly English trait, though she did have the excuse of having been born in Dieppe: she set English, French, German, Swedish, Italian, Sicilian, Latin and Scottish texts, and founded songs on French, German, Italian, Sicilian and Brazilian traditional melodies. Yet when she broke away from universal balladry, she produced one of the few Debussy-like songs by an English composer, 'Le foyer' (Verlaine) (no. 1 of *Two Songs*, *1924*), an effective attempt at cultivating an impressionistic sensibility, with a meticulous recitative setting of the French text. It can hardly be classed as an English song, however.

The ballad, calculated to grace social leisure and frivolity, was perhaps more a state of mind than a genre. Stainer gave an amusing account of it as a song,

> the words of which are a sort of three-verse epitome of a three-volume novel. The plot is often told without any preface, it begins by saying 'he' was a little somebody and 'she' a little somebody else; the next verse discloses the circumstances of their meeting; and in the last verse one or both of these interesting little creatures die and are beatified in an extended and *fortissimo* coda warranted to introduce the singer's favourite high notes (:21).

This is a caricature of its spirit rather than a description of its average form; the provision of three verses, categorically confirmed in *Grove 5* (Blom, 1954, I: 375), was immaterial. As its most recent historian has pointed out,

> efforts to define the Victorian ballad in histories and reference books have gener-
> ally been too restrictive. It had few limitations of mood or of subject matter:
> almost the whole range of human experience and emotion was covered, though,
> to be sure, the treatment was generally shallow, conventional, or even men-
> dacious. Not all ballads were sentimental: some were grisly, humorous, or cynical.
> Nor was there any set musical form (Temperley: 123).

Certainly the ballad had by this stage lost its implication of a strophic, narrative poem, and was, as Jean-Aubry pointed out further on in the passage quoted
above, often a less palatable equivalent of the sentimental French *romance*, the
two types of text being intertwined in Gounod's output. If the criteria for a
serious song are a sincere sense of identification with the text and a personal expression of it in a style which is worthy of it, of the period and of the composer,
then there are a great many English songs of the late 19th and early 20th centuries
which do not pass the test, the majority of them in the ballad category.

It was really a question of Victorian double standards, as the common term
'drawing-room ballad' implied: bad taste was admissible, if only in private. As
early as 1867 the anonymous *Musical Times* editor had recognised this:

> There is a great deal of nonsense talked and written in the present day about
> music for the 'domestic circle;' and in our late strictures upon 'drawing-room
> music,' we endeavoured to prove that no real difference exists between composi-
> tions suited for the drawing-room and those suited for a concert-room, save that
> difference which is obvious to all, viz., that certain works require large orchestral
> and choral resources, for which a small space is not suitable. If this title, there-
> fore, be really invented to pass off flimsy productions which are merely intended
> for the music-market, it would be a satisfaction to art-lovers to think that in
> public, at least, they are safe from the infliction of listening to them. Music writ-
> ten for 'home' should certainly stay there: like other home-made manufac-
> tures we could mention, they may be very apt to disagree with strangers . . .
> (XIII: 71).

As for the royalty system, it faded as obscurely as it had arisen. The ballad concert, in which four or five singers participated, was already giving way to the one-
voice recital before the first world war (Anon., 1913) and it did not survive to the
second. Exposure by broadcasting may have killed it, as Frank Howes suggested
(1972): the BBC at first sponsored ballad concerts (from 1922 onwards), and
'What radio did . . . was give the royalty-ballad public a chance to revise its preferences' (Mackerness: 256). As the literary awareness of composers developed,
and as public consumption turned to jazz and other forms of popular song which,
unlike the ballad, did not lose their appeal when transferred to a gramophone
record, the royalty ballad was left stranded. When, apparently at the suggestion
of Martin Shaw, who had earlier found it impossible to publish songs not in a
ballad style, Kenneth Curwen decided to publish a new series of English songs
after the first world war, he was proud to announce on the advertising page of the
copies that 'we pay no royalties or fees to singers for singing any of these songs.
When they are sung they are sung on their merits, and because the singer thinks
them better worth singing than other songs on which he might be paid a fee'
(Shaw: 55, 121–2; Curwen).

Before leaving the subject of ballads mention must be made of the folk ballad, for it needs to be distinguished from the royalty ballad, although Temperley's discussion (:124) shows that the distinction is difficult to uphold in the 19th century, particularly where collections such as Moore's *Irish Melodies* are concerned. The genuine folk ballad is of limited significance before 1900, when the revival of interest in folk music began to complicate the history of song in England. Scots folk tunes and poems, particularly the Border ballads, were in circulation throughout the 19th century, Walter Scott's *Minstrelsy of the Scottish Border*, a collection without tunes, having appeared in 1802–3; but these appealed more to the full-blooded Romanticism of the continent than to decorous English taste. Thus there are few British equivalents of Loewe's ballads before the 20th century. However, Coleridge-Taylor wrote a setting of 'The three ravens', Walford Davies one of 'The lawlands o' Holland' and Dalhousie Young a version of 'The twa corbies'; Somervell also arranged *Songs of the Four Nations* (*2/1892*) and MacCunn *Songs and Ballads of Scotland* (*1891*). Otherwise, Somervell's *The Dawyck Edition of Scottish Song* (*1911*) and the various settings of 'The twa corbies', 'Edward', 'The bonny Earl of Murray', 'Helen of Kirkconnell' and others belong to the present century, a consequence of the widening susceptibility to folk elements. There were also some imitations, such as Somervell's 'Young Sir Guyon', a strong, rough-cast setting in the Loewe mould, and Stanford's setting of Keats's 'La belle dame sans merci', a pale reflection of Schubert, in particular of *Der Erlkönig*. Professional interest in Irish balladry, a vast and confused topic (See Howes, 1969: 238–50 for a clarification) stretching back into the 18th century and receiving great impetus from Thomas Moore's *Irish Melodies*, which appeared from 1807 onwards (Clinton-Baddeley: 99–105), is best studied as it appears in the work of individual composers, notably Wood and Stanford. Welsh ballads seem to have been practically non-existent, though Somervell again contributed arrangements in his two sets of *Sixteen Welsh Melodies*, with J. Lloyd Williams (trans. A. P. Graves) (*1907* and *1909*).

In 1834 John Barnett (1802–90) had published *Lyric Illustrations of the Modern Poets*, a collection of 12 solo vocal compositions written variously for soprano, contralto, tenor and bass voices with an accompaniment which seems, from the surviving vocal score, to have been conceived in orchestral terms. The style is not particularly compelling but is at least liberal, in parts not unlike that of his contemporary, and later friend, Hector Berlioz; it is certainly more colourful than Mendelssohn's *Lied* style, which helped to stabilise too conventional procedures in England. The poems, by Byron, Shelley, Wordsworth and others, are varied and offer the composer a fairly wide range of expression. By the end of the century, however, settings of the Romantics had narrowed into a number of colourless, impersonal, stereotyped responses to stock poems, chosen for their lyrical ease, offering no resistance to the composer; any simple, well-made tune with a rippling accompaniment would fit. Longfellow, Shelley and Tennyson suffered most. Tennyson settings were at one time the virtual monopoly of John Blockley, who even obtained the poet's permission to alter *Enoch Arden* for his purposes (Disher: 122). Willson Disher has given a racy account of this urge for setting lyric poetry to music:

> . . . the Victorians had to sing. Tunes, in urgent demand, were wanted for the eloquence of Tennyson and Longfellow over chestnut tree, windmill, mountaineering, invitations to the garden, brook, breakers, Arab steed, departing swallows, and Queen of the May. Enraptured sopranos saw in all these the accepted notions of what had always been fit and proper excuses for straining after top notes. Composers, hurrying to please them, engaged in a wild free-for-all, since no copyrights existed to restrain them. All seized the same verse at the same time . . . (:117).

Settings of certain lyrics occurred so frequently that the poems may usefully be listed:

Byron	Stanzas for music ('There be none of Beauty's daughters')
Hood	A lake and a fairy boat
	The time of roses
Keats	The Devon maid
Christina Rossetti	A birthday ('My heart is like a singing bird')
	When I am dead
Shelley	I fear thy kisses
	The Indian serenade ('I arise from dreams of thee')
	Music, when soft voices die
	A song ('A widow bird') (from *Charles I*)
	To Jane ('As the moon's soft splendour')
Tennyson from *The Princess*:	
	As thro' the land
	Home they brought her warrior dead
	O swallow, swallow
	The splendour falls
	Sweet and low
	Tears, idle tears
from *Maud*:	
	Come into the garden, Maud
	Go not, happy day
	Crossing the bar
	What does little birdie say? (from *Sea Dreams*)
Wordsworth	Lucy ('She dwelt among th' untrodden ways')

Settings of these poems and others by the same authors, constituting a stream which flows on through the 20th century as well as the 19th, have been comprehensively listed elsewhere (see Gooch and Thatcher, 1979 and 1982). Most other late-18th- and 19th-century poets' work was little touched until the 20th century. It is worth noting that Christina Rossetti's poems were utilised far more than those of her brother, Dante Gabriel, though there are at least seven settings of the latter's 'Three shadows', one of them, by Somervell, published before the turn of the century. Most other D. G. Rossetti settings, including three of 'Silent noon' (by Vaughan Williams, Ernest Farrar and C. W. Orr), belong to the present century, though a notable exception is Bantock's 'The blessed damozel', for recitation with orchestra (1892), written four or five years after Debussy's cantata. Of Blake settings – and there are many – only a few by obscure composers plus Walford Davies's 'A song of innocence' and Somervell's five settings from the *Songs of Innocence* date from the Victorian period. Beddoes's poems were published in 1851 but most settings date from the 20th century. Burns, however, was increasingly set to music – by Mendelssohn, Sterndale Bennett, MacCunn,

Mackenzie, Coleridge-Taylor, Walford Davies, Ernest Walker, Sullivan and especially Somervell – as the 19th century wore on.

The poet most apposite to Victorian song, however, was not English. Fascinated though the ballad-writers may have been with blind men, lame girls, impoverished organ-grinders with monkeys, and the bloody deeds and blasted moors of the Border ballads, it was the simple, sentimental, domestic love-lyric, preferably making frequent reference to flowers, gardens, blackbirds, sunshine and spring, which unfailingly won the heart of the consumer and precipitated the discreet tear. The poetry of Heinrich Heine (1797–1856) succeeded in erecting a strong ironic superstructure on such conventional foundations. It appealed to the Victorians more for the foundations than the superstructure, however: it could be made to emphasise the approved ingredients, especially in translation; the 'precisely lyrical sense of both epigram and irony' (Foss, 1942: 237), which put settings by Schubert, Schumann and Brahms on a higher plane altogether, was ignored. 'Heine seen through English mid-Victorian spectacles, as in Bennett's setting of "Mädchen mit dem rothen Mündchen", is by no means a specially attractive vision', wrote Ernest Walker in 1907 (:277), though he himself had succumbed to setting Heine in three of his *Six Songs*, op. 3 (*1893*), in his *Duets for Contralto and Tenor* (1904), and elsewhere. So had Balfe ('The arrow and the song' (*1856*)), Coleridge-Taylor ('The arrow and the song' and *Three Songs of Heine*), Mackenzie (*Three Lieder*, op. 14 (1870s)), Maude Valérie White, Delius ('Der Fichtenbaum' (1886) and *Four Songs* (1890–1)), Holst ('Soft and gently') and Stanford (*Twelve Songs,* opp. 4 and 7, one song from op. 14, and op. 72). The lyrical impulse continued unabated into the 20th century, finding residually Victorian interpretations in Gurney's early 'I would my songs were roses' and in Bridge's first batch of songs, ten in all. Finally the reaction set in:

> *Du bist wie eine Blume! Jawohl!* One can see the elderly gentleman laying his hands on the head of the pure maiden and praying God to keep her for ever so pure, so clean, and beautiful. Very nice for him! . . . He knows perfectly well that if God keeps the maiden so clean and pure and beautiful . . . for a few more years, then she'll be an unhappy old maid, and not pure nor beautiful at all, only stale and pathetic. Sentimentality is a sure sign of pornography. Why should 'sadness strike through the heart' of the old gentleman, because the maid was pure and beautiful? Anybody but a masturbator would have been glad and would have thought: What a lovely bride for some lucky man! – But no, not the self-enclosed, pornographic masturbator. Sadness has to strike into his beastly heart! – Away with such love-lyrics, we've had too much of their pornographic poison, tickling the dirty little secret and rolling the eyes to heaven (Lawrence, 1929/1961: 75).

Lord Berners set the poem Lawrence mentions here, in German, in his *Lieder Album* of 1913, with an explanation:

> According to one of Heine's Biographers, this poem was inspired by a white pig that the Poet had met with in the course of a walk in the country. He was, it appears, for some time afterwards, haunted by the thought of the melancholy fate in store for it and the note of foreboding that runs through the poem is thus explained.
>
> . This fact does not seem to have been sufficiently appreciated by those who have hitherto set the poem to music and the present version is an attempt to restore to the words their rightful significance, while at the same time preserving the sentimental character of the German Lied.

The piano accompaniment is punctuated by repeated dissonant chords, marked *'schnauzend'* (snorting), while the voice part bears the directions *'innig'* (intimately), *'mit Gefühl'* (with feeling), etc. By this time, English composers had unwittingly made a closer approach to the spirit of Heine in their cult of Housman, whose verse owes a good deal to Heine's techniques of lyrical irony (Marlow: 64, 99).

Given a reliable sense of taste, the simple lyric was, and always will be, perfectly capable of inspiring a musical gem. John Ireland's 'Spring sorrow' (Rupert Brooke) is one. Nevertheless, the type of lyrical poetry outlined above involves an approach to song composition with severe limitations. The negative implication of this approach is that a song, consisting of music and text, should be a smooth, frictionless lyrical entity. What is said is of less importance than the slick, easily palatable way in which it is said. A song should titillate rather than disturb. A text should be chosen not through a sense of identity with or interest in the thought and personality of the poet but for functional reasons – because it offers no resistance but simply rhythmic flow and sensual ease. But if the marriage between words and music is to be without tension then it will also be without direction – there will be no sense of the music pointing the words or interpreting them – and it matters little whether music is added to existing words, or words are written around existing music. Indeed 'wandering melodies', as Frederick Sternfeld calls them (:17), whereby the poet writes 'words for music', having in mind a hypothetical or real melody as he writes his text, are an important traditional concept in Britain, accounting for many Elizabethan texts (no doubt including the songs of Shakespeare), for much of the poetry of Burns and Moore, for at least two of the popular poems listed earlier (Byron's 'Stanzas for music' and Shelley's 'The Indian serenade', first published as 'Song written for an Indian air'), for some of Stevenson's *Songs of Travel*, for Yeats's late volume of poems, *Words for Music Perhaps*, and, under the influence of Yeats, for an entire aesthetic of songwriting, expounded by V. C. Clinton-Baddeley in his book *Words for Music*.

This attitude, as is evident, has by no means died out in the present century. It has, rather, been responsible for a vast amount of song material, especially from composers with an eye on sales – Martin Shaw, Warlock, Armstrong Gibbs, Head and Quilter – who have in many cases kept the lyrical tradition youthful and spontaneous by the artful assimilation of modern techniques. Others, castigated above, have kept it styleless and stultified, sterile and degrading, in which state it languished at the end of Victoria's reign, when objectives in setting words to music in solo song were in urgent need of rejuvenation. English attitudes were too circumscribed. They were, in the first place, responsible for a good deal of undistinguished verse, not only by long-forgotten poetasters but also by great figures, such as Arnold:

> Come to me in my dreams, and then
> By day I shall be well again!
> For then the night will more than pay
> The hopeless longing of the day.
>
> Come, as thou cam'st a thousand times,
> A messenger from radiant climes,

And smile on thy new world, and be
As kind to others as to me!

Or, as thou never cam'st in sooth,
Come now, and let me dream it truth;
And part my hair, and kiss my brow,
And say: *My love! why sufferest thou?*

(repeat 1st stanza)

This kind of verse, though not exactly bad, is impossible to make fresh (see the settings by Bridge and Somervell, the latter published as late as 1935), and it persisted in poetry as well as music right through the age of Eliot and Pound. It was the sort of verse which composers snapped up. Yet it might just as effectively have been set to a hymn tune; it made no demands for advanced musical technique at all. Composers thus made no attempt at stretching the intellectual faculties, either musical or poetic, and had no use for a personal style in any way remotely contemporary. The resulting level of aesthetic tension was nil. Hence the whole German *Lied* tradition, which demanded much more, from *An die ferne Geliebte* onwards, was little understood in England, the approach to Heine notwithstanding. *Lieder* recitals were unknown in England before about 1880, when they were pioneered by the tenor Raimund von zur Mühlen and by George Henschel and his wife (Scholes: 285). But perhaps the most severe curb on the composer was that the very strength of the English lyrical tradition put him in a debased position, unworthy of the high flights of Romantic imagination so evident in other countries. However much the poet might complain, it had to be the composer's duty and only possible salvation to use the poetry for his own ends. There must be a compulsive 'chosen identification' (Finzi's phrase), the need to express something individual and personal in the composer's own imagination by linking it with the poet's. This need was crucial, because England, until about 1880, had lacked a musical response to almost the entire Romantic movement – whether the dearth of composers was cause or effect is immaterial – and if, now that stirrings were evident, composers were to bring the deadened imagination out of hibernation, where should they turn for inspiration? Technically there was so much to catch up on. What was the use of becoming Wagnerians when they had not yet assimilated Schumann? How were they to square the modern demands of technique with a lyrical convention which had no use for it and with the inherited memory of a native tradition which, they thought, stopped dead at Purcell? A start could only be made by the careful nurturing of a response which had not been forced upon the composer's sensibilities from some alien source but which was innate and could be personal, different for each individual: a response to literature, the only secure lifeline to the sources of English Romanticism. Thereby the composer could develop his 'chosen identification'. True, the manifestations which this rebirth of experience produced were often to be more quaint and exotic than convincing, especially during the Edwardian era: we shall find that shades of the nineties, of the Pre-Raphaelites, of symbolism and impressionism, of Gothick horror, of Olympian grandeur, of the cult of the East and of past ages all appeared in various composers, the more eccentrically through being a delayed reaction, out of phase with the other arts. However, the effort had at last been made, and at least some of the results were of great value.

Meanwhile, *The Vocalist* tried to inaugurate the new era, but did so on an entirely barren premise. It made the mistake of thinking that if you could apply a more stringent test of taste to the ballad tradition, and could rescue composers and poets from the cut and thrust of the big publishing houses, you could make song-writing both artistically respectable and commercially viable. This was a misguided prescription for a cure, even though the first editorial was accurate enough in diagnosing the disease:

> . . . it is impossible not to observe that real musical art, as it exists in modern songs and ballads, is becoming more and more subservient to the demands of what is correctly described as 'commercialism in art', and is therefore in danger of becoming almost extinct, or at least to be of so degraded a type as to be unworthy of the notice of refined instincts.
> . . . we seem to have drifted into a current of sentimentalism, which is manifest on even the merest acquaintance with that vast quantity of effusions called lyrics, and their musical companions called songs, which is week by week being poured forth from the workshops of the music-publishers.
> But we are told – 'it pays;' if we are to judge by the enormous profits made by publishers out of some of their songs, this is doubtless true; but is it also true that artistic songs cannot be made to pay in a business sense too? It is not quite easy to say that they would do so, but unfortunately in this country artistic songs rarely have the opportunity of fair trial (I, 1902: 2).

The second editorial had to admit that 'the consensus of opinion seems to be that our first four songs [April 1902] were almost too high-class to be popular' (I, 1902: 34), but the naïvety of good faith implicit in this admission is less staggering than the specification of the songs themselves, a list which reads extraordinarily today: Gounod: 'In the hour of trial' (J. Montgomery); Vaughan Williams: 'Linden Lea' (William Barnes); George S. Aspinall: 'A summer slumber song' (Alfred Hyatt); and Noel Johnson: 'Roses and lilies' (E. Teschemacher). Needless to say, what appeared to *The Vocalist*'s subscribers 'almost too high-class' seems to us, with the exception of 'Linden Lea' but not of Gounod's song, as banal and poverty-stricken as the effusions from which the editor was trying to rescue the public. But *The Vocalist* struggled on, still believing that if you could present a promising composer with a straightforward lyrical text he would come up with a master-piece, still trying to help desperate composers by instigating, for a fee, a postal service for tidying up and revising manuscripts, still not realising that Vaughan Williams's success was much more than a result of good taste and a certain (though limited) degree of technical suavity, still giving Bridge openings for the publication of songs which were probably doing his creative potential more harm than good, until publication of the journal suddenly and inexplicably stopped in December 1905. Whatever the reason, it was no loss to English song, whose pulse was to be felt elsewhere.

Earlier, in 1891, in one of these periodical bids to exalt song by commercial means, Sir Harold Boulton had edited and published an anthology, *Twelve New Songs: By Some of the Best and Best-Known British Composers*. In his preface, after giving a brief history of England's dearth of song since the Puritan movement, and a spirited account of the high hopes held for a renaissance of talent in 'our . . . sturdy band of minstrels' (:viii) now that foreign giants (e.g. Verdi and Wagner) are dead or lack successors, he expounds the current song-writing situation in the by now familiar economic terms of supply and demand:

> If our greatest poets have not sufficiently laid themselves out for fellowship with
> the sister art, and indeed some of them have, with occasional exceptions, signally
> failed in this respect, the deficiency may perhaps be attributed to the unnecess-
> arily low estimation in which song writing, pure and simple, has been held. Mu-
> sicians now complain that the supply of really good material for songs is not
> equal to the demand (:xi–xii).

These are terms which make poetry sound like a most ancillary occupation, and
one questions why either art had to be regarded in this way. Boulton himself then
increases 'the supply' by providing the words of the 12 songs which follow. There
are no outstanding contributions, and not one of the songs is remembered today.
The list of composers represented, however, does give some idea as to who was in
the ascendant at the time:

Barnby	C. H. Lloyd	Somervell
Alfred Cellier	Mackenzie	Stanford
Frederick Corder	MacCunn	Goring Thomas
Cowen	Parry	Charles Wood

Sullivan is the most notable absentee; Elgar's reputation in 1891 was still too
insecure to make his exclusion surprising. The three greatest figures represented
are undoubtedly Parry, Somervell and Stanford; since all three were in full
maturity in 1900 and continued writing well into the 20th century, an outline of
their individual achievements, with a consideration of Elgar, Wood, and Walford
Davies (too young for Boulton's anthology, although he was to write a remarkable work in 1894), will occupy most of the next two chapters.

Reticent Victorians: Elgar, Parry, Stanford and Wood

It will have become clear from the previous chapter that Elgar's position in the history of English song is not a simple one. Nor is it finally of great importance. *Sea Pictures* used the idea of a thematic web, and this was paralleled, as we shall see, in *Maud* and echoed elsewhere, but the motivic imagery itself was too personal, too originally orchestrated, too marine and too austere to appeal to the English generation which, on the whole, was to prefer inland, pastoral lushness as a background to its thoughts and a setting for its words, seascapes by Bax, Bridge, Vaughan Williams and Delius notwithstanding. The sad, sighing cry of the swell, the dragging of the waves, and the toss of the spray (Ex. 1 (a), (b) and (c)) bore significant offspring perhaps only in the Sea Interludes of Britten's *Peter Grimes* (1945). The structure of *Sea Pictures* is strengthened by these images. The overall form is like a rondo: two relaxed, delicately scored, episodic and (with a slight exception) thematically self-contained strophic songs separate the more organic unity of the other three, whose more complex poems are disposed into musical patterns analogous in approach to the mediaeval *formes fixes* and their settings. In the analysis that follows, the use of upper- and lower-case letters reflects Elgar's concern with two separate structural planes, the larger of whole sections and the smaller of thematic motives. Thus the first song, 'Sea slumber-song', moulds a continuous, short-lined poem into an apt ABCABC structure articulated by the use of motives Ex. 1 (a), (b) and (c).

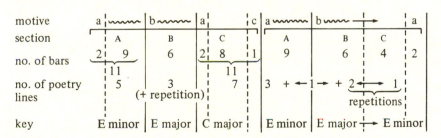

The various musical ways of achieving balance and contrast are shown in the diagram above. The use of two 11-bar sections (A and C) separated by a six-bar one (B) in the first half is striking. In the second half (basically a repetition of the first) sections A and C are more closely interrelated, since the two-bar opening statement of (a) in section A is not put on the other half of the scales, as it were, until the very end of the song, where, however, it is presented as an augmented

Ex. 1

version of just under *one* bar's worth of (a) – an uncompleted, notated final ritardando – which therefore can be seen to form, with B (six bars) and a truncated reprise of C (four bars), another 11-bar section. What is more striking, however, is that Elgar possesses the imagination to impose all this on a division of the poem into groups of lines which are totally asymmetrical and not even self-contained, inasmuch as one line from the second A section, 'Leave woes, and wails, and sins', reappears in the following B section, and the 'good night' refrain permeates the second B and C sections. This lack of self-containment in the second half itself parallels that of the musical 11-bar sections just described. Whatever its limitations, Elgar's approach to the setting of poetry was not facile. The third song and the fifth are not unlike the first in basic structure, and no less interesting. The third, 'Sabbath morning at sea', has five stanzas disposed in an ABCAC musical form. A at its first appearance and B are introduced by a new, spiritual rather than pictorial two-bar motive (Ex. 1 (d)), and c is heralded by its own thematic material. On its return c is heralded by (d), but A is not. Into this second c section, now extended musically (with verbal repetitions), both a diminished form of (d) and a Wagnerian surging sequence on (a) are incorporated. At the end (d) finally joins hands with c's theme in an elevating epilogue. More subtle, perhaps, is the way (b) is woven into both of the A sections and into B. The final song, 'The swimmer', again employs the basic binary ABCABC pattern, but with yet another variant. Of the five eight-line stanzas of the poem, 4 and 5 become a musical entity complementing that of 1 and 2. An A section covers the first four lines of stanza 1, a B section the last four, and a c section the first four of stanza 2. Stanza 4 looks as though it is going to instigate a repetition of this process (its first word, 'So', suggests the recapitulation), and its first four lines are duly set to A. Then, however, a transposition of sections occurs: the last four lines of the stanza are set to c, not B. This leaves B to take place in stanza 5; however, it is not set to the first four lines but to lines 3–6. Thus separated off, lines 1–2 and 7–8 of stanza 5 are set to a new thematic motive (Ex. 1 (e)) outside the ABC structure but in fact dominating the whole song. It first appears (as does (c)) in the orchestral introduction. In the last two, climactic, lines of the last stanza it is combined with (b) over an inspiriting tonic pedal. It also occupies lines 5–6 of stanza 2. Lines 7–8 of stanza 2 are disposed as part of a crucial middle section to the song, a six-line fulcrum completed by the first four lines (which are all he sets) of stanza 3. This fulcrum is a piece of Elgarian self-revelation, an indulgence in characteristically wistful nostalgia which is quite opposed to its spiritually aspiring surroundings. The predominant (e) in lines 5 and 6 of stanza 2,

> Love! when we wandered here together,
> Hand in hand through the sparkling weather,

effects the transition to the new section:

> From the heights and hollows of fern and heather,   [stanza 2]
>   God surely loved us a little then.

> The skies were fairer and shores were firmer –   [stanza 3]
>   The blue sea over the bright sand roll'd;
> Babble and prattle, and ripple and murmur,
>   Sheen of silver and glamour of gold.

This nostalgic retrospect is new and disturbing in the context. It is articulated by technical means similarly new to the cycle. So far all cross-references between the songs have involved only thematic motives. Here, however, Elgar looks back by quoting whole sections. The last two lines of stanza 2 are set to the music of stanza 3 of the fourth song, 'Where corals lie' (this is the only cross-reference to this song anywhere in the cycle, and the music quoted is in any case not part of the fourth song's otherwise strophic structure), then for the four lines of stanza 3 the c section of the first song returns. The two structural levels of sections and motives seem integrated by the reintroduction of (c) heralding the recapitulation described earlier.

This final song of *Sea Pictures* amalgamates the two strongly contrasted aspects of Elgar's personality, the outer love of invigorating, sometimes vulgar spectacle and bombast (matched in the verse by some crude gymnastics of alliteration), and the inner, private hypersensitivity to emotional influence, in this case personal nostalgia. Perhaps one reason why none of Elgar's other songs has managed to communicate much to posterity is that none of them shows both these sides. Some are occasional works of imperial character (mentioned in Chapter VII). In most of the others Elgar's inner feelings seem to retreat into the poem that expresses them. There is no question of an insensitivity to the verse or an arbitrary selection of it, but he seems too reticent, afraid of showing his personal identification too blatantly. The result is a communication barrier and, as Basil Maine says of the early songs later grouped into the *Seven Lieder*, a 'treatment which, in each case, is so severely simple as to be almost conventional' (:231). Certainly in 'The poet's life', the fourth of the *Seven Lieder*, conventionality protrudes as a debilitating mask. Both the poetic and the musical expression are fairly paltry, and the song is easily dismissed as a rather tasteless, unthinking ballad-romance. Only an informed acquaintance with, say, *The Music Makers* and its ardent personal endorsement of the poem's statements about the pain of artistic creation would cause one to sense, deep down under the drab execution, a similar testimony here:

> There fell a day when sudden sorrow smote
>   The poet's life. Unheralded it came,
> Blotting the sun-touched page whereon he wrote
> His golden song. Ah! then, from all remote,
>   He sang the grief that had nor hope nor name
> In God's ear only; but one sobbing note
>   Reached the world's heart, and swiftly in the wake
>   Of bitterness and passion and heartbreak,
>   There followed fame.

The work in which one most regrets this snail-shell retreat is the Gilbert Parker *Cycle*, op. 59. One may guess, from the way in which Parker's verse in these poems contrasts in mood with his imperialistic career and novels, that his problems of personality were similar to Elgar's. A potentially devastating sadness at the loss of love is held in check with a stiff upper lip. The implications are clearly of romantic love, but it would seem likely that, since the cycle was first performed at, and probably written for, the memorial concert to his friend Jaeger, Elgar was applying the emotions to his own loss of comradely friendship on which he had leaned heavily in the preceding decade. Perhaps this accounts for the reticence of treatment. Certainly his setting of the third song, 'Twilight', is far from being the paralysing Celtic depressant it would have become at the hands of Warlock or Delius:

> Adieu! – and the years are a broken song,
> The right grows weak in the strife with wrong,
> The lilies of love have a crimson stain,
> And the old days never will come again.
>
> Adieu! – Some time shall the veil between
> The things that are, and that might have been,
> Be folded back for our eyes to see,

And the meaning of all be clear to me.

Adieu! –

Yet there is a deep beauty in these three settings – in, for instance, the sagging rhythms of 'Twilight' and its inarticulate final cadence (Ex. 2), and in the tonally

Ex. 2

restrictive, repetitive little phrases of 'Was it some golden star?' In all probability they never received in their own time the intensely sympathetic attention they need to communicate that beauty in performance.

In his inaugural lecture as Peyton Professor of Music at Birmingham University, on 16 March 1905, Elgar mentioned the year 1880: 'Some of us who in that year were young and taking an active part in music – a really active part such as playing in orchestras – felt that something at last was going to be done in the way of composition by the English school' (P. M. Young, 1968: 33–5). It is probable that he was thinking of Parry's *Scenes from 'Prometheus Unbound'* (Shelley), a large choral and orchestral work performed, in all likelihood with Elgar in the audience, at the Three Choirs Festival, Gloucester, in 1880. Elgar's idiomatic debt to Parry has been constantly underestimated; *Prometheus* foreshadowed many of the distinctive features of his style (there was even an embryonic Demons' Chorus). More to our point, it showed the composer working in a refreshingly close relationship with an Olympian text. Never again did Parry achieve such sustained inspiration in a choral work (though even *Prometheus* has a number of weak points), for he veered away from Romantic poetry towards Biblical oratorio, in which he always became bogged down (the many fine passages in *Job* notwithstanding), and towards ethical oratorio, for which he supplied his own pseudo-Biblical texts and tried in vain to overstep his own creative confines. In the year following *Prometheus*, however, he wrote the earliest items in his series of solo songs, *English Lyrics*. Although there are some high peaks of inspiration in the *English Lyrics*, and the series is a monument remarkable for its sensitive presentation of a wide range of poetry, there is nowhere such vitality and tensile strength as the setting of the text in *Prometheus* promised. Sadly, Parry's potential as a composer was unfulfilled after *Prometheus*. To see why, it is necessary to look at his career and personality.

He was born at Bournemouth, but grew up in a family of landed gentry at Highnam, just outside Gloucester. Highnam is a bleak, forbidding estate, thickly surrounded with dark conifers, its stark, neo-Gothic parish church in the grounds isolated from any village and approached only by a dank, sunken path. It hardly seems to belong to Gloucestershire, a county of colourful orchards, stone cottages and precipitous hills with breathtaking views, and indeed Parry remained largely aloof from these rustic and open rural surroundings; not until he was nearly 20 did he visit Upton St Leonards, only five miles away, to obtain one of the famous views from the Cotswold escarpment, and then it was in a trap, not on foot. Gurney, to whom the Gloucestershire landscape meant everything, and who frequently tramped the hills all night long, would have found this incomprehensible. Parry seems to have spent more time steeped in the austere, sunless atmosphere of the Gothic revival, sitting as a model for one of the heads of the Genealogy while his father, Thomas Gambier Parry, a well-known ecclesiastical decorator, painted the frescoes on the roof of the nave of Ely Cathedral. A reserve of loneliness was built up, and from 1864 he kept a diary to which he confided many thoughts, particularly about religion.

When he went to Eton his circumscribed environment was violently counteracted. A hearty side to his character developed, perhaps a defence necessary in a school at that time completely unmusical, but never to be shaken off. He played sport with alarming violence, frequently suffering considerable injuries on the football field. (Later in life he tackled driving in an equivalent fashion, suffering a fair number of road accidents and speeding fines; similarly, his idea of a game of blind man's buff was 'fearfully rough', according to Edward Marsh's amusing account (Hassall: 91-2).) Whilst still at school he over-drank. Later, at Exeter College, Oxford, he fooled around in innumerable immature undergraduate pranks, drank and danced a lot, studied little, and went to the theatre not at all. Music was neglected. After his marriage (which, probably because of his solitary disposition, was not particularly happy) his sporting energy was channelled into sailing, which he undertook with his customary reckless vigour, and into the devastating but friendly slap on the back which the more delicate of his pupils came to dread in the corridors of the RCM. Few realised that behind the slap lay a hypersensitive nature and, in his son-in-law's words, 'a definite shyness which made words difficult at moments of deep feeling, when a pound on the back had to take the place of praise; a form of inhibition which made clubs of no account to him and kept him a lonely man all his life' (Greene, 1935: 119). His health was greatly troublesome during his final years, partly because of continual overwork, though he tried to shrug off even his frequent and very painful heart attacks with his usual bluster. His introspective side ultimately found sublimated expression in his metaphysical texts for choral works (of which the best and most extended is *A Vision of Life*, similar to Whitman in its humanistic aspirations but full of inhibitions), in the large prose work of his final years, *Instinct and Character*, which expounded his radical liberalism and which to his great disappointment he could not publish, and in his songs. Songs, 'like other great masters of this branch of music', he treated 'as a sort of private diary in which he expressed his most intimate thoughts . . . To this it may be added, in proof of the intimacy of these utterances, that they were occasionally dedicated to his most intimate friends' (Colles, in C. L. Graves, 1926, II: 168).

The two sides of Parry's character, strikingly similar to the two sides of Elgar's, have been dwelt upon at length because they are reflected in his music.

His life, while not schizophrenic, was made up of two contrasting impulses, one a haven from the other, neither capable of fulfilment on its own, and never finally integrated. His music can be hearty and blustering, thick and heavy, failing to get off the ground; at other times it is intensely lyrical, almost too sensitive and, in proximity to his robust mood, producing an effect of weak sentimentality. These two disunified aspects appear in almost all his works, especially the large-scale ones, where the conflicts are most exposed. They are certainly present as early as *Prometheus.* A creative crisis of some sort might have fused them in deeper unity, but that crisis never came, for in his life as in his composition Parry was, with his Victorian diligence, simply too busy and devoted to duty, especially after his appointment to an RCM composition professorship in 1883, to precipitate it. And he might not have had the strength to weather it. As far as the songs are concerned, most of them express either one side or the other, though there is one, the Mary Coleridge setting 'Three aspects', in which Parry leads us musically through his conflicting views of life: seen first as a 'royal game' and then a 'terrible fight', it is finally dwelt upon as 'a vision . . . of . . . deep happiness', and it is tempting to see the dramatised first-person form as a telling self-revelation.

Parry began composing at an early age. At Eton he took organ lessons from Elvey at St George's Chapel, Windsor, and seems to have been nurtured, in an all too English fashion, on S. S. Wesley (whom he later got to know personally), Mendelssohn and Handel. His earliest acknowledged song, 'Fair is my love', is very Mendelssohnian, as are the earliest chamber works and many of the surviving undated songs, probably belonging to this time, which are no more than well-written ballad-romances typical of their period. 'Why does azure deck the sky' is on a higher plane, but in general his attitude to his texts at this stage has little to distinguish it from that of any other ballad composer. In 'She thought by heaven's high wall that she did stray' he indulges in the worst Victorian religiosity, and in 'Miss Agnes had two or three dolls' he gives us a piece of *Struwwelpeter* moralising which to the Victorian mind was pert and, at least in Parry's setting, almost humorous, but to us just appears tasteless:

> But I took her home and the doctor soon came
> And Agnes I fear will a long time be lame
> And from morning to night she laments very much
> That now when she walks she must lean on a crutch.

In the early 1870s he was still writing songs, such as those of op. 12, in the ballad mould, but then in 1873 came the biggest musical experience in his life: Wagner. In this year he had already met Edward Dannreuther, a brilliant pianist of German extraction and a curiously evasive, unknowable personality who was nevertheless one of the greatest influences on Parry's life and one of his few close friends – they seem to have been similarly lonely by temperament. Dannreuther, besides introducing the piano concertos of Chopin, Grieg and Tchaikovsky to English audiences at this time, was a friend of Wagner's and his only significant champion in England other than Francis Hueffer. In November 1873 Parry had his first piano lesson with Dannreuther, and in the same month heard a concert performance of *Die Meistersinger* and succumbed to it. In 1875 he saw *Lohengrin*, and the following year Dannreuther got him a ticket for the second *Ring* cycle at the first Bayreuth Festival. Stanford was there too; their attendance is a fact worth remembering about two composers later denigrated as weak Brahmsians. Parry studied the tetralogy carefully, and was enormously impressed by it, before leaving for the Festival. Dannreuther went on ahead, but by the time Parry arrived he was on his way back to England, the emotional excitement having proved too much for him. The following year Wagner stayed at Dannreuther's house for the duration of Richter's concerts, and there Parry met him.

Wagner's music exerted a sudden broadening influence on his technique, which first bore fruit in his fine chamber works – the Nonet of 1877, the Piano Quartet of 1879, the Third String Quartet (1878–80), the String Quintet, the Cello Sonata (1880) and the three piano trios. It also gave him the courage and vision to wrestle with a large-scale dramatic subject in *Prometheus*. But perhaps the most significant effect of the Wagner experience was a more lively approach to word-setting. Previously Parry's musical approach to the English language had been circumscribed and flat: he seemed not to realise its rhetorical possibilities. He 'deplored the lack of lyrics, such as Heine's, in English suitable to set to music' (C. L. Graves, 1926, I: 150) and, possibly influenced by his two months' study with Pierson in Stuttgart in the summer of 1867, preferred to set German to music. He wrote in his diary of 'When in disgrace', the first of the four Shakespeare sonnets which he actually composed in Bodenstedt's German translation, that 'I found I could get along better with the German than the English words' (*ibid.*, I: 149); the songs were only later adapted to Shakespeare's English. Yet at least he realised that there were important differences between the two languages, and that the English adaptation would need a separate vocal stave, which it is given in the published edition. The main point about the sonnets is that in both languages their structural demands forced him out of the pedestrian, four-square phrases of ballads, and for a later consolidation of this achievement one may turn to his setting of Keats's sonnet 'Bright star'. Harmonic progressions were becoming more fluid, so much so that Macfarren complained of their unorthodoxy (*ibid.*, I: 154), and vocal lines had a more subtle sense of span, not always tied to two-bar phrases.

By 1880 Wagner's forthright, rhetorical *arioso* declamation, complete with appropriate reflective gestures in the orchestra, was absorbed and appeared unmistakably in *Prometheus*. Prometheus's opening monologue stamps him as a being of Wotan-like grandeur. Yet in the songs, except perhaps in the fine 'Soliloquy from Browning's *Saul*' and the finer scena 'The solider's tent', broad gestures of nobility and texts that would give rise to them are avoided. In *English Lyrics* the retreating personality is evident. The extrovert nature has hardened into heavy-handed, mock-archaic bluster for the treatment of lively Elizabethan poetry ('Love is a bable', 'Ye little birds'); the introvert side is often in danger of relapsing into the all too smooth and palatable romance sentiment. A less invigorating influence, that of Brahms, to which he did not yield fully until 1880, after hearing the Second Piano Concerto and the Requiem, has knocked off some of the earlier corners, and with them, one feels, some of the sincerity. It is clear right from the first volume, particularly in the opening line of 'Where shall the lover rest', which is borrowed from the second subject of the first movement of Brahms's G major Violin Sonata, published four years before the song was written. Sentimentality, of a sort that Quilter later played on so effectively, is never far beyond sensibility; one notices it particularly in the 16th- and 17th-century settings, for all their heart-warming intimacy, as in the wonderful song 'Take, O take those lips away', in 'To Althea' (which is especially Quilterian), in 'And yet I love her till I die', where it tends to expose the superficiality of the verse, and perhaps most in the Byron setting 'When we two parted', despite more solid hopes raised by its rhetorical introduction. Not that any of these songs are tasteless; Parry's vocal contours and accentuation, by now maturely responsive to verbal nuances, and his pianistic assurance, for all its textural limitations, guarantee a certain standard of excellence. In their own way they are in fact very attractive and occasionally fresh in a totally unsentimental manner, for example in the neo-diatonic song with flat-7th cadential touches, 'A lover's garland'. Moreover, Brahms occasionally appears as a strengthening influence, particularly in 'Lay a garland', 'Dirge in woods', 'From a city window' and 'Sleep', which avoid excesses of sentiment. But the overall impression is that Parry set his texts as studies in controlled lyricism rather than as compulsive responses to poetry. His biographer follows Mackenzie in acknowledging that he often penned a song as an act of relief after grappling with a big work (*ibid.*, II: 168). But song-writing did not always come easily to him: 'Crabbed age and youth', which finally appeared in 1902 in *English Lyrics V*, gave him a good deal of trouble, as is evident from a letter to Dannreuther as early as 1882:

> I have been wrestling with 'Crabbed Age and Youth', but it seems to be too much for me. The dramatic breaks of continuity at the end jump from one side to the other so abruptly, and all through the two-sided nature of the thoughts take it out of the province of pure lyric. I've tried over and over again. The last version I send you to look at . . . If I could get it into order I should have sufficient for a set. If not, the set must wait till I can find other words. (*ibid.*, II: 169).

There is nevertheless something suspiciously facile about his diary entry for 21 September 1888: 'After the family had gone to bed, I wrote several new songs: Herrick, Beaumont and Fletcher' (*ibid.*, I: 293).

Once or twice, however, he seems to have been gripped by his texts. A *Times* article published a few years after his death, entitled 'A great song-writer', 'contended that his motive in setting the words of Julian Sturgis and Mary Coleridge was that they gave him a better chance of being himself, of saying something in music which he had very much at heart, than he found in interpreting the thoughts of Milton and Shakespeare on whom it was impossible to impose his own personality' (*ibid.*, II: 168). This was certainly true of at least one of the nine Sturgis settings in *English Lyrics*. Julian Sturgis, brother of the novelist Howard Sturgis (once well known as the author of *Tim* and *Belchamber*), wrote the libretto for Sullivan's *Ivanhoe* and was himself a prolific novelist. A contemporary of Parry's in his house at Eton, he remained a friend. Friendship is the theme of 'Through the ivory gate', but although its poetic treatment is dangerously near to the religious platitudes of 'She thought by heaven's high wall that she did stray' it is redeemed from banality by Parry's serene, moving setting, less indulgent than many of his songs, sublimating the mood into one of deep idealism. There is no hint of the ballad-romance; *arioso* phrases rise and fall with studied, poised irregularity, underpinned by sensitive accompanimental reflections (Ex. 3). Later he generates a poignant sighing motive in Wagnerian fashion

Ex. 3

Ex. 4

under the voice's floating phrases (Ex. 4). The feeling of intimacy given to the words is so personal that one almost suspects undertones of homosexuality:

> And as he there did stand,
> With gesture fine and fair,
> He passed a wan white hand
> Over my tumbled hair

But whatever the poet's intentions, Parry no doubt wanted only to capture the reality of a dream of friendship which had nothing to do with sex, a friendship of which he seems to have felt a permanent need and a permanent lack. The sense of personal identification has given him a grasp of technical restraint, reflected in the simplest of diatonic settings, and the technical restraint has created the poise which keeps the dream suspended, captured before it fades.

Musically, this is satisfying; we may note with sympathy, however, that here, as so often, Parry seems compelled to express himself lyrically in terms of a vision or dream of happiness, or in eschatological terms. The songs 'Whence', 'There', 'Armida's garden' and 'When the sun's great orb', as well as the familiar choral *Songs of Farewell*, testify to this. Looking closer, we may find that in some of the posthumous songs from *English Lyrics XI* and *English Lyrics XII*, as well as in 'Looking backward', this tendency is connected with intensely personal statements about the loss of love: 'What part of dread eternity' (for which, it is thought, Parry wrote his own words), 'The faithful lover', 'If I might ride on puissant wing', 'Why art thou slow' and 'She is my love' are cases in point. When these songs were written, and why Parry did not publish them, is unclear. Perhaps they were too personal; they were certainly not inferior, and indeed one of them, 'From a city window', could be considered Parry's finest song, as well as a poignant testimony to his inner loneliness. He had shown this Brahmsian bleakness of style before, notably in 'Nightfall in winter', but not so powerfully.

No consideration of Parry's songs should overlook the scena for baritone and orchestra, 'The soldier's tent', first performed by Parry's son-in-law, Harry Plunket Greene, at the Birmingham Festival on 2 October 1900 (the day before the first performance of *The Dream of Gerontius*, in which he also sang). It is a setting of a Rumanian folk poem from Alma Strettell's collection *The Bard of the Dimbovitza* (from which Bax also later constructed a cycle), and far removed in content and atmosphere from most of the poems Parry set. Having distanced himself from his customary material, he excels himself precisely in the evocation of a distant atmosphere, in setting the scene and taking leave of it. After some darkly mysterious opening chords, probably suggested by death-announcing passages in Wagner's *Ring* and similar in effect to the opening of Parry's choral work, *The Love That Casteth Out Fear*, comes one of his warmest passages, which is repeated at the end. Wagner's *Waldweben* (see below, p. 164) are in evidence, and even *Verklärte Nacht* is not far away (Ex. 5). Yet even here the warmth, the intimate touch, is incapable of being sustained throughout and integrated into the narrative that follows, which tails off sharply in inspiration. The repetitive poetic formula, by which spirits of comfort which he withstands come one after the other to tempt the doomed soldier as he sleeps, is not treated with subtle nuances of vision, but heavy-handedly in clear-cut, prosaic sections which destroy the magical atmosphere of the opening. Once again Parry's public manner gets the better of his private feeling, and in this the work is an epitome of his life.

The stature and influence of Sir Charles Villiers Stanford have never been satisfactorily assessed. As a teacher he was crucial to the development of English music at the turn of the century, but his achievement as a composer is difficult to evaluate; his problems, though as severe as Parry's, were less tangible, while his output is more impressive on paper. Cycles and separate songs to a wide variety of texts were published from 1878 until well after his death in 1924, numbering

Ex. 5

almost 200, in addition to about 150 arrangements of traditional Irish tunes. Understanding his limitations will be helped by first considering his fellow Irishman, Charles Wood.

Born in 1866, Wood, like Somervell, was young enough to be taught by Stanford. While a pupil at the RCM, he accompanied Anna Russell in a performance of his 'At the mid hour of night' and 'Up-hill' before Queen Victoria at Windsor Castle in June 1887. A song written in the same year, 'Through the twilight', won a seven-guinea song competition sponsored by the *Musical World* (the text was a poem which had itself won a previous *Musical World* competition). The judges, Alfred Blume and Goring Thomas, were particularly impressed with the 'strict adherence to declamatory emphasis, the last being an especially important point in an English composer' (Copley, 1978: 101), though why careful declamation should be more important in English than in continental song, and whether that was what they meant, is not clear.

The careers of Wood and Stanford were to run strikingly in parallel. Wood taught harmony at the RCM from 1888, where his pupils ranged from Martin Shaw and Butterworth to Goossens and Tippett. Also from 1888 he was resident at Cambridge in a variety of academic capacities, culminating in the music professorship from Stanford's death in 1924 until his own two years later. At Cambridge he taught Bliss, Armstrong Gibbs and Vaughan Williams. Bliss holds the key to his self-effacing personality in his description of him as 'a gifted musician whose complete lack of ambition prevented his own music from gaining much of a hearing' (Bliss: 26). But he had a hearty sense of humour, and when Bliss took him to Henry Wood's first performance of the Schönberg Five Orchestral Pieces at a 1912 Promenade concert Wood's loud, irreverent laughter during the performance caused his pupil to disown him (*ibid.*).

Wood's retiring disposition, reflected in his compositional style, stood him in good stead in one branch of his art: church music. Like Stanford, he was an Irish Protestant whose contributions to the liturgy were fresh because restrained. In his many service settings lyricism was tempered by decorum, as it was in Stanford's unaccompanied motets and G major Evening Service. When he opted for more personal self-expression, as in the anthem *Expectans expectavi*, the result was faintly embarrassing because overtly indulgent. On the other hand, when applied to his 55 songs (as also to his eight string quartets), harmonic restraint and semi-modal politeness were more questionable virtues. Even in the many Irish arrangements, where the aharmonic nature of the folk tunes might call for such stylistic reticence, the overall impression of both his and Stanford's attempts at Celtic characterisation is of a spuriously insipid, watery musical landscape. Wood's sole venture into the realms of bawdy fertility ritual in 'The potato song' makes a pleasing contrast.

As a student, however, Wood discovered Whitman. So did many other composers, and this corner of English musical history is spattered with settings and impressions testifying to his inspiriting impact at the turn of the century. Composers were not interested in his celebration of (homo-)sexual liberation, preferring homosexual repression as found in Housman, though Ernest Walker, reading *Leaves of Grass* as a Balliol undergraduate in 1890, was shocked and fascinated enough by it to discuss it in a diary entry (Deneke: 17–18); they were more responsive to his intoxicated boldness in describing, in *Drum Taps* (1865), from which three of Wood's four solo settings are taken, contemporary scenes, particularly those of the American civil war, which accorded well with the Englishman's pre-war romanticising of military endeavour. Whitman tackled the themes of love and death in an affirmatory manner, with plenty of apostrophes to the 'Soul', a convenient new name for God that satisfied both Christian and agnostic. Whitman could be an Englishman's Nietzsche. Moreover his metrically free verse patterns, with their short, ejaculatory repetitions, were a gift to composers who wanted to make a rhetorical impact in their declamation.

Most Whitman settings are choral, naturally enough, in accordance with his democratic and world-embracing ideals. The two most durable by British composers are Delius's *Sea Drift* and Vaughan Williams's *A Sea Symphony*. Vaughan Williams came closest to Whitman in personal temperament, sharing the poet's infectious love of life and the periodic lapses of technique which result from such inebriation, and admitting late in life that Whitman was an influence he had never outgrown (Kennedy, 1964: 100). Of the other composers who fell under his spell, most of them before the first world war took the edge off such idealism, Bridge, Coleridge-Taylor, Farrar, Gurney and Cyril Scott did not find the experience catalytic; Stanford and Wood, both of a considerably older generation, did.

Wood's first extant attempt was a student sketch for 'As toilsome I wander'd Virginia's woods'. Nothing else until 'Darest thou now, O Soul' (1891) has come to light. His other three solo settings are 'By the bivouac's fitful flame', 'O Captain! my Captain!' and 'Ethiopia saluting the colours'. 'Ethiopia' was also arranged with orchestral accompaniment. Although his choral *Dirge for Two Veterans* met with success at the Leeds Festival of 1901, Wood remains, like Frederick Keel of 'Trade winds', a one-song composer. Stanford may have been 'bowled over' by 'O Captain!' even more than by 'Ethiopia' when he heard them performed together (Copley, 1978: 106), but 'Ethiopia' is the only masterpiece. 'By the bivouac's fitful flame' is strenuous and certainly not understated like so many of Wood's songs, but its wide chords conceal vacuity. 'O Captain!' likewise tries hard, but its strophic form, moving from major to tonic minor and from $\frac{3}{4}$ to $\frac{4}{4}$ for the doleful portions, weighs heavily on it; so does the effusive poetry.

'Ethiopia', according to Plunket Greene (1935: 252–3), was discovered by Stanford in a drawer in Wood's room where the composer had diffidently discarded it. Stanford insisted on immediate publication. (Armstrong Gibbs (1958: 28) cites the same story and states that the song was actually rescued from the wastepaper-basket.) What gave 'Ethiopia' the vibrancy lacking in Wood's other songs? Its evident qualities are an overflowing humanism and a dramatic, pictorial sense of occasion. The poem (written, unusually for Whitman, with regular metre and rhyme) relates an episode during the march of Sherman's army to help free the American South from slavery. A centenarian Ethiopian woman comes to her hovel door to greet the march-past, portrayed in the accompani-

Ex. 6

ment's continuous tramp, borrowed in all probability from the march tune in Chopin's F minor *Fantaisie* (Ex. 6). The vividness of the pictorial presentation owes its success to Wood's being prepared, for once, to use harmless harmonic indulgences such as the dominant 7th with 4–3 appoggiatura (Ex. 6, *x*), and blatant dominant and subdominant modulations, which are exactly what is needed to depict the band. After the second stanza this is directly opposite us, *forte*, and as though the work were by Ives, it 'misremembers *John Brown's body*' (Copley, 1978: 106) (Ex. 7). Then comes the magic touch: the poet disengages himself from the marching column and stops to receive the woman's reply to his questions. The band merges almost unnoticed into the background as she, in a single sentence with suggestions of pidgin English in the word order, tells of her origin. Her narrative becomes disjointed and the accompaniment more lush as she remembers her deportation, her welling emotion culminating with a gulp on a Wagnerian interrupted cadence (Ex. 8; cf. Somervell's 'The worst of it'

Ex. 7

Ex. 8

(Chapter III, Ex. 19)). That is all – no comment on why she is so respectful towards the white Americans whose ancestors made her suffer. The poet quickly rejoins the regiment and the band accompaniment is reinstated, and as it recedes into the distance in the last stanza we lose the first beats of each bar and the quaver subdivisions. The poet is left musing on the equivocal nature of experience:

> 'What is it, fateful woman, so blear, hardly human?
> Why wag your head with turban bound, yellow, red and green?
> Are the things so strange and marvellous you see, or have seen?'

Formally, 'Ethiopia' is perfect. The approaching and receding army provides for a simple pattern of arsis and thesis, with its sudden *arioso* contrast in the middle. The three-line stanzas are set to an appealing 12-bar structure whose ostinato bass has something of the effect of a jazz riff, lengthened by an extra bar at the end of the second line and also, in the final stanza, at the end of the last line. Within the scope of a single voice Wood achieves the depiction of a situation which in Vaughan Williams's MS sketches for a setting of the same poem (*ca* 1908 and *ca* 1957–8) required a soprano, narrator and humming chorus. But perhaps most remarkable is Wood's brilliant appropriation of an 'imperial' style which almost anywhere else, for instance in the numerous patriotic songs of the first world war, including his own 'Roll up the map of Europe' and 'The Munsters at Mons', spelt cheap jingoism.

That Wood's song technique really comes to life only in 'Ethiopia' is thrown into stronger relief when we return to Stanford; the same can, with reserve, be said of his 'Darest thou now' (Wood's setting of this is very drab by comparison). Stanford made only three solo settings of Whitman, in his second set of *Songs of Faith*. Of these, 'Tears' suffers from excruciating poetry. 'Joy, shipmate, joy!' has a beautiful ending, whose music he was later to echo in his opera *The Travelling Companion*; the words of the song's title are slowly repeated, sinking into almost Mahlerian serenity. But by far the best of the three, and perhaps the only one of Stanford's songs in which full-blooded technique goes hand in hand with passionate conviction, is 'Darest thou now' ('To the Soul'). The poem was set a number of times, and twice by Vaughan Williams: Stanford himself conducted the first London performance of Vaughan Williams's first version, *Toward the Unknown Region*, for chorus and orchestra, premièred at the Leeds Festival in 1907; the second version was a unison song, published in 1925. The text is Whitman at his most individual:

> Darest thou now, O Soul,
> Walk out with me toward the Unknown Region,
> Where neither ground is for the feet, nor any path to follow?
>
> No map there, nor guide,
> Nor voice sounding, nor touch of human hand,
> Nor face with blooming flesh, nor lips, nor eyes, are in that land.
>
> I know it not, O Soul;
> Nor dost thou, – all is a blank before us;
> All waits, undream'd of, in that region, – that inaccessible land.
>
> Till, when the ties loosen,
> All but the ties eternal, Time and Space,
> Nor darkness, gravitation, sense, nor any bounds bound us.
>
> Then we burst forth, we float,
> In Time and Space, O Soul – prepared for them;
> Equal, equipt at last (O joy! O fruit of all!) them to fulfil, O Soul!

With its many short-breathed phrases it is conveniently pliable for musical treatment. Stanford wisely and without difficulty spins out the last line through a broad climax to a quarter of the song's entire length. It is no accident that Stanford's and Vaughan Williams's fine settings date from the early years of the century; evolutionary optimism was still in the air. Yet while Vaughan Williams's 1907 setting is one of his first major works to open up new technical vistas in English music, Stanford opts to make his setting totally Brahmsian. This gesture is in itself touching: he has shown where his allegiance lies, and is prepared to be wholehearted about it. One looks in vain for such stylistic conviction in much of his other music. Moreover, he writes with not a note out of place. Like Wood in the last stanza of 'Ethiopia', he constructs a texture of crotchet chords in $\frac{4}{4}$ with the first beat missing. This throws a tremendous responsibility on the voice, but enables it, if it has great sustaining power, to fashion a continuous *cantabile* line whose slowness of motion and climactic smoothness provide an apt gloss on the poem. It is a texture which Brahms normally dared trust only to an instrument (for example in the first movement of the Horn Trio, or the last of the A major Violin Sonata), but Stanford in transferring it to a vocal context has created a demand worth striving to meet in performance. The interpretation of the text gains by the stretching of the medium. Particularly effective, too, are the points at which the pattern is broken, especially after 'nor voice sounding', where the voice, true to the text, leaves us with an uncanny first beat of complete slience, and at the awestruck passage 'all is a blank before us . . . that inaccessible land', where the roles are reversed, and the accompaniment's profound binding chords are contrasted with the more inarticulate vocal line.

The first set of *Songs of Faith* is disappointing in the light of 'To the Soul'. The three songs lack conviction, for the texts, by Tennyson (with whom Stanford was personally acquainted), are platitudinous. The first, 'Strong Son of God', is a setting of the first three stanzas of *In Memoriam*. The second, 'God and the universe', has a serene final section which opens breathtakingly, *pianissimo*, with the invocation 'Spirit, spirit, nearing yon dark portal . . .', but loses inspiration long before the end. The third, 'Faith', risks an anticlimax by repeating the opening line, 'Doubt no longer that the Highest is the wisest and the best', at the end. Of Stanford's remaining Tennyson settings, two more (from the *Four Songs*, op. 112) are from *In Memoriam*, but, deeply felt and serious as they are, they lack the technical conviction of 'To the Soul'. His own account of setting Tennyson to music further undermines our confidence:

> The secret of the harmony of his verse lay in his incomparable ear for the juxtaposition of vowels and the exact suitability of each consonant. This makes it difficult to set his poems adequately to music. The music is so inborn in the poetry itself that it does not ask for notes to make incompleteness complete, and music is set to it rather for additional illustration than from inherent necessity (1908: 95).

It is perhaps the *Five Sonnets from 'The Triumph of Love'* (Edmond Holmes) that most closely approach 'To the Soul' in serious grandeur. Of these the third, 'When in the solemn stillness of the night', is particularly impressive, and the continuity of the sonnet structure aids rather than hinders the music's own struggle to shape itself.

Most of Stanford's other songs show a creative personality which never found fulfilling self-expression. Standford did not have Parry's problem of how to imbibe influences beyond the narrow Germanic range. Nor was he ever wedded to the ballad. Even his earliest songs, the George Eliot and Heine settings, are free of Victorian sentimentality, possessing an assured eclecticism which was no doubt partly a result of his training in Berlin and Leipzig under Kiel and Reinecke; in a letter home from Leipzig, he wrote that his *Spanish Gypsy* songs had been sung to Schumann's friend Dietrich, who 'said the greatest compliment he could give me was that they were not Englisch but Deutsch' (Greene, 1935: 60). Schubert is much in evidence (as in his string quartets), though such otherwise successful songs as 'Blue wings' and 'Day is dying' are marred by over-thick piano parts which betray their later-Romantic origin. In time he economised his resources, in line with his precepts as a teacher and as an arranger of traditional tunes. At the same time, non-Germanic influences grew, perhaps reflecting his wide-ranging contacts as conductor of the RCM orchestra and the Cambridge University Musical Society, under whose auspices he engaged Boito, Bruch, Dvořák, Glazunov, Grieg, Saint-Saëns and Tchaikovsky. His Italianate sympathies were well known – he wrote essays on Verdi and an *Elegia maccheronica*, a cunning Verdian pastiche lamenting 'the passing of the old Italian opera'. He was by nature adept at witty parody: the Wagner and Strauss blasphemies in his *Ode to Discord* are convincing enough to make one wish he could take their idioms as serious models, and the last of the posthumous *Nonsense Rhymes* cocks an endearingly *risqué* snook at *Tristan*. He often chose texts for their satirical scope, such as the inconsequential numbers in the Irish song-cycles, for example 'The crow' and 'Daddy-long-legs' in *Cushendall*. ('Daddy-long-legs' quotes Brünnhilde's fire motive in the piano part at the lines 'You try to moderate your legs / In lamp or candle flame.') Mention of Saint-Saëns brings to mind the legitimate parallel between him and Stanford; both were trying to maintain a moderate, mainstream approach to compositional technique in the late-Romantic period when there was no longer any mainstream to follow. Neither was prepared to identify with a particular school, and both ended up with a curiously emasculated style that contrasted painfully with a sometimes venomous intellectual sharpness. In Stanford at least there is a pervasive lack of focus that often overrides the positive qualities.

Whether as cause or result of creative impotence, there was an underlying sense of bitterness, which certainly emerged in his teaching. It must have been aggravated by the fact that his compositions were written in a vacuum, many of them at great speed during RCM vacations. Natural fluency and the need for remuneration may often have been the sole sources of creative compulsion. Stanford belonged to no artistic fraternity, and was at loggerheads with Elgar and in only uneasy communion with Parry. His wife did not get on with Lady Parry or with Lady Somervell (Howard); he and Somervell took refuge in the Athenaeum and Savile Clubs respectively, but these were no equivalent of the European café as a source of artistic inspiration. Maybe the fact that, during his lifetime, his was always a name to conjure with, something *The Vocalist* proudly did on more than one occasion, fanned his sense of creative frustration, which he took out on his pupils.

The one fixed point in Stanford's career as a song composer, his attachment to Ireland, was more an evasion than a facing of personal identity. True, he was born in Dublin, but he left for Cambridge at the age of 18 and had previously frequented well-to-do, middle-class Protestant circles far removed from the peasant conditions encountered in his songs. He was always a city-dweller; his songs about the Irish countryside were written in comfortable Kensington. This does not necessarily amount to an accusation of insincerity, and his love of Irish melodies was genuine. However, there were economic considerations as well: he stood to gain considerably from his arrangements and his collaboration with A. P. Graves, whose son Robert Graves says of 'Father O'Flynn', 'the song for writing which my father will be chiefly remembered', that

> He had put the words to a traditional jig tune *The Top of Cork Road*, which he remembered from his boyhood. Sir Charles Stanford supplied a few chords for the setting. My father sold the complete rights for one guinea. Boosey, the publisher, made thousands. Sir Charles Stanford, who drew a royalty as the composer, also collected a very large sum. Recently my father has been sent a few pounds from gramophone rights (1929: 23).

Stanford's Ireland, primarily a geographical locality celebrated in poetry straightforwardly describing places or people, had nothing to do with the Celtic twilight, and was in fact much better suited to opera, namely to *Shamus O'Brien*, than to song. It was not the seat of spiritual yearning, of mystical vibrations. It was not even romantic, except in a down-to-earth, colloquially domestic, *verismo* sort of way. To Bax it was not the real Ireland at all:

> I like to dally with the fancy that the creative mind in mountainous and hilly countries tends to express itself almost exclusively through the medium of literature, leaving the arts of music and painting to the plains . . . The Irish . . . can point to C. V. Stanford, Charles Wood, and Hamilton Harty. Unhappily, these three undoubtedly proficient musicians were assiduous and dutiful disciples of the nineteenth century German tradition, even whilst clothing their native melodies in all too conventional dress. They never penetrated to within a thousand miles of the Hidden Ireland (1952: iii).

Bax was writing when it had become clear that Stanford's Irish settings, though they were widely known during his lifetime, died shortly after their composer. In the wake of later folksong settings they dated badly, and Howells's positive appreciation of their 'utter, fundamental simplicity' (1952: 28) has not been sufficiently shared to revive them securely.

In addition to his arrangements, Stanford wrote five Irish cycles and one Scottish one. From the first of them, *An Irish Idyll*, Plunket Greene, the dedicatee, singled out 'The fairy lough' for analytical treatment (1912: 67–70, 165–6; 1935: 206–13). One takes all his points about the craftsmanship in the word-setting and scene-painting, but these are ultimately superficial qualities with an unsettling lack of underlying stylistic integration. Moira O'Neill's poetry is in itself superficial: it makes no demands for anything deeper. As a result, the mildly pleasant touches of Dvořák-like nature-painting in the opening chordal shifts (Ex. 9) are imposed on a background of complacency which periodically shows through (Ex. 10), and the song has no more thrill of reality in it than a faded water-colour. Elsewhere in the cycle Moira O'Neill adopts colloquial native speech; the result has no humour and is little short of bathos;

> Sure he's five months old, an' he's two foot long,
>   Baby Johneen;
> Watch yerself now, for he's terrible sthrong,
>   Baby Johneen.

It is hardly surprising that Stanford can do nothing with this. The same applies to

Ex. 9

Ex. 10

'The crow' and 'Daddy-long-legs' in *Cushendall*, though elsewhere, notably in 'Ireland' and the song 'Cushendall' itself, the lyrical nostalgia of the poems finds satisfying expression in the melody and stamps a quality of seriousness on the cycle as a whole, which concludes in this vein with a tiny reminiscence of the rhythmic motive of 'Cushendall'. 'Cuttin' rushes' from *An Irish Idyll* is melodically a stronger song than any in *Cushendall*, however, showing an immaculate control of piano figuration akin to Fauré's, the figuration itself being, as with Finzi, a fingerprint of motivic significance, having appeared at the mention of the 'soft rain' in 'Corrymeela', the first song of the cycle. This control is also found in 'Cowslip time' and 'Blackberry time' from *A Fire of Turf*, whose final song, 'The west wind', which elusively avoids strophic form, just misses being very moving, as does the self-consciously homecoming ending of *An Irish Idyll*, a setting of the last poem in Moira O'Neill's *Songs of the Glens of Antrim*. *Songs of a Roving Celt* contains one song, 'The pibroch', of unusual emotional vividness; there is, however, nothing outstanding in *The Glens of Antrim*. Only 'Lookin' back' contains any measure of warmth.

In *A Sheaf of Songs from Leinster* Stanford's strengths and weaknesses are jumbled together more startlingly than anywhere else. Four of the six poems concern Irish peasant, or at least lower-class, domesticity and poverty. Stanford seems to make hardly any gesture of involvement in two of them, 'Thief of the world' and 'The bold unbiddable child', setting them as patter songs in the manner of Irish jigs. This sort of verse has worn very thin, and it is difficult to see how it ever appealed:

> Oh, it's little Rosanne is the rogue of the world!
> If it's villainy in it, Herself will be there,

An' it's like she'll begin it with time and to spare.
For she's pullin' my coat, or she's teasing the goat,
Or huntin' the chuckins, the little old dote. [etc.]

Wood's 'Tim, an Irish terrier' is tedious for the same reasons. But in 'Grandeur' and 'Little Peter Morrissey' Stanford is more deeply concerned with his subject-matter. 'Grandeur', indeed, has an uncanny unity with its poetry, due partly to the extremely careful and sensitive syllabic word-setting, and partly to the perfect match, for once, between the poetic portrait of an insignificant girl, now dead, whose emotions never obtruded publicly, and Stanford's restrained, understated harmonic vocabulary. The song is remarkably prophetic of Finzi's celebrated settings of Hardy's portraits of women, 'Amabel' and 'To Lizbie Browne', and may well have influenced them (all three are in E flat). In 'Little Peter Morrissey', a portrait of a penniless urchin, the essentials are whittled down to even barer bones, and the song is little more than extended recitative. The ambivalent reactions of the poet and composer to the boy's poverty are exquisitely managed in the final *tierce de Picardie* (Ex. 11). 'A soft day', the only conspicuously Brahm-

Ex. 11

sian song in the cycle, suffers from its subject-matter, the eulogising of a wet day. The watery harmonies are too neutral to make much impact. However, 'Irish skies' makes a virtue out of a similar text. In this wonderfully heartfelt final song, nostalgia is the main ingredient – the nostalgia of a Londoner for his native Ireland. Did Stanford feel this himself? Howells suggested that he did (1952: 19), but what matters artistically is that he knew how to identify with the 'wanderer' tradition in Romantic song and literature (as did Vaughan Williams in responding to Stevenson and Somervell in setting Housman). Stanford also plays upon the nostalgia of homecoming at the end of *Songs of a Roving Celt* and *An Irish Idyll*, and in the present instance his treatment elevates a plain, undistinguished text above its own poetic level. One cannot point to stylistic fingerprints as such, except perhaps the frequent oscillations between tonic minor and major for the contrast between London reality and Irish reverie. More noticeable is a stylistic foreshadowing, in the introductory accompanimental figure that begins to generate the vocal melody (Ex. 12), of Gurney's many similar figures (e.g. in 'I will go with my father a-ploughing', or 'Winter' (Ex. 13)). Much of the appeal of the song is due to the discreet use of secondary 7ths; Stanford extracts a remarkable amount of feeling from them, especially in the major transformation of the

Ex. 12

Ex. 13

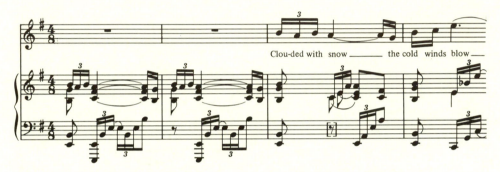

Ex. 14

introduction at the end (Ex. 14), but the most moving passage is the C major section of the last of the nostalgic dream-images, with its instantly soothing flat 7th (Ex. 15) and, later, its tiny scrap of Schumannesque piano *cantilena* to reflect the 'jewelled sky' (Ex. 16).

This song proves that Stanford could produce something personal from his vision of Ireland, but it does not alter the case. His Irish cycles failed, primarily perhaps through the shallowness of the poetry, most of which is now so dead that its public exposure causes embarrassment or even offence. However much Stanford played upon the nostalgia of the wanderer, his 'fundamental simplicity', encouraged by the poetry, amounted all too clearly to a lack of creative viewpoint, of commitment. This is why we cannot imagine him responding to Housman's

Ex. 15

Ex. 16

infinitely deeper poetry, whereas Butterworth could do so with a stylistic austerity almost identical to Stanford's own. The closest Stanford came to a creative viewpoint was in the development of motivically unified semiquaver or triplet figuration, at its best in 'Cuttin' rushes', to signify the soft rain or the wind or the streams of Ireland (Ex. 17, *x*), but he was unable to invest it with the breath of symbolism, to make it mean something more abiding than itself. In 'The west wind', the final song of *A Fire of Turf*, the poetry for once offers him this possibility:

> He bent Glencullen's tallest trees,
> His breath was rough on bird and beast,
> Across the mountain tops he flew
> To take his pleasure in the east.
> Oh, wild wind from the distant west,
> Be still again, [Be still, Be still,]
>   and give us rest.

Stanford set this in August 1912; we might hope that he would recognise in the wind the troubled political spirit of Ireland, or, Yeats-like, see it as his own spiritual restlessness, even homelessness. But somehow his music never quite invites us to do this.

Stanford enjoyed almost a monopoly as the teacher of young English composers. The following list is reduced from the longer one in Plunket Greene's biography (1935: 93):

Edgar Bainton	Thomas Dunhill	Gordon Jacob
Arthur Benjamin	George Dyson	Maurice Jacobson
Arthur Bliss	Ernest Farrar	Ernest Moeran
Rutland Boughton	Nicholas Gatty	Humphrey Procter-Gregg
Frank Bridge	Eugene Goossens	Cyril Rootham
Rebecca Clarke	Ivor Gurney	Marion Scott
Samuel Coleridge-Taylor	Gustav Holst	Martin Shaw
Harold Darke	Herbert Howells	Ralph Vaughan Williams
Malcolm Davidson	William Hurlstone	Charles Wood
Henry Walford Davies	John Ireland	

The fact that so many composers went to Stanford for lessons in no way implies that he represented a certain school – the problem was that he did not – but at this time the RCM had no real competition as a teaching institution. The RAM, with Frederick Corder as a prominent composition teacher, tended towards indiscipline, despite the efforts of its Principal, Sir Alexander Mackenzie; for their one notably successful composer, Bax, they produced a string of failures such as Holbrooke and Bantock. Thus good composition students were more or less obliged to pass through Stanford's hands, though Parry also shouldered some responsibility. (Vaughan Williams studied under both; later in life he was noticeably warmer in his admiration for Parry than for Stanford.) The English musical renaissance owes a good deal to the RCM, for it provided a lively community in which composers could exchange ideas, though there were lamentably few opportunities for them to hear their works played apart from the formal, overawing Patron's Fund concerts; little fraternities of budding composers flourished, in retrospect sometimes ill-assorted. Coleridge-Taylor, Fritz Hart, Holst, Hurlstone

Ex. 17

and Vaughan Williams formed one in the early 1890s; another, just before the first world war, included Benjamin, Bliss, Gurney and Howells. Stanford, how-ever, was at the centre only as a pedagogue, not as an inspiration.

He seems to have had no rigid teaching method, though he clearly put a high premium on song-writing as a craft, and according to James Friskin's description of his composition course (see Greene, 1935: 98–9) allowed his pupils to attempt songs only at the end of their period of tuition, presumably after two years or so. This seems strange, until one realises that to Stanford craftsmanship and polished neatness were everything in song. Greene's tribute unwittingly reveals how limited the criteria were:

> . . . in his knowledge of the handling of the voice he stands higher than any writer since Schubert. In all the years I have sung his songs I can never remember having had to ask him to alter a passage or note on account of technical difficulty. That knowledge was no doubt absorbed in his childhood from his father.
>
> In the wide range of Stanford's songs, from grave to gay, there is not one that is not ridiculously easy to sing, and that is the highest tribute you can pay to workmanship (*ibid.*: 204).

Similarly, in a letter to Greene on how to write a song, Stanford shows the bound-aries of his own considerations:

(1) Declaim your poem. If you can't do it silently, do it out loud.
(2) Find out the line or lines in it which give the central idea and fix the atmos-phere.
(3) Get a good voice part and a good bass part: the middle is texture and trim-mings, though very important ones.
(4) Write in one (not several) *tessitura*.
(5) Study your voice as carefully as a clarinet.
The rest is on the knees of the gods (*ibid.*: 242).

But why one should want to set a particular text in the first place, and what one is trying to do with it, other than 'fix the atmosphere', when one sets it – those questions he relegates to the deities. Where literary taste, personality, or any con-siderations other than craftsmanship were involved, he began to show that blind, irascible intolerance for which he is famous. This may or may not have been a self-consciously Irish pose. Dyson testifies that 'if he disagreed with a student's choice of a poem, he was not likely to see much sense in the setting of it' (*ibid.*: 105), and Bliss tells how, 'When I was a student, I had set to music one of [Hardy's] poems "The dark-eyed gentleman" from *Time's Laughingstocks*, and I remembered how Stanford had angrily told me to take what he considered a most unpleasant poem away from his desk' (:85). (However, since the poem is about a young virgin's seduction, Bliss's boldness in presenting it to Stanford is perhaps more surprising than his teacher's reaction.) Nearly all the reminiscences of Stanford by his pupils, including his invariable comment 'that's damned ugly, me bhoy!', show that, as Bainton pointed out (Greene, 1935: 96), in trying to keep his own personality in the background whilst teaching, he was betrayed into elevating subjective statements into rigid and often dismaying objectivity. Hence it is not surprising that, as Dyson confirms (*ibid.*: 95), those pupils who had the spirit to rebel against his narrowness and prejudices fared best. According to Howells (1974) one had to be able to manipulate Stanford to get something out of him, and for a worthless pupil he could do nothing. But Howells, who acknowledged that he was a favourite with Stanford (Palmer, 1978: 12–13), was always remarkably fluent as a student; Stanford was sufficiently impressed by his *Mass in the Dorian Mode*, composed before he took up his RCM scholarship, to promote it for performance at Westminster Cathedral during Howells's first year at college, in November 1912. Bliss, who was discouraged by the ease with which Howells composed, seems to have had a rough time:

> I prefer to forget the hours I spent with Stanford: they were not many and from the first moment when he scrawled on my manuscript 'He who cannot write anything beautiful falls back on the bizarre', I felt the lack of sympathy between us. He was a good teacher when in the mood: I felt that instinctively, and certain of his maxims, such as 'Let in air to your score', linger in the mind as truisms to be followed, but his own disappointments as a composer perhaps affected his outlook and he had a devitalising effect on me (:28–9).

Hurlstone, according to Fritz Hart's account, was given a vicious baptism by fire in his first lesson (Hurlstone: 99–100), more as a matter of policy than out of the conviction that his music was really bad; afterwards he turned out to be, in Stanford's opinion, his best pupil. Coleridge-Taylor, another favourite, was subjected to the 'hardening' treatment of having to write and copy three finales to his Symphony, each one rejected in turn by Stanford after trying it over with the RCM orchestra (Sayers: 36–7); Ireland suffered a similar experience (Schafer: 27).

Stanford was cruel to Coleridge-Taylor and Hurlstone because he believed in their potential, and he helped both of them in several ways. Whether he had faith in Rutland Boughton (after he had pulled strings with the Member of Parliament for Aylesbury to get his place at the RCM paid for) was another matter. Boughton recounted how, after rehearsing his *Imperial Elegy* on the death of Queen Victoria, Stanford 'told me that it was the ugliest thing he had heard, apart from the music of Richard Strauss. I tried to look unconcerned, but felt sick, for something more than my heart was in the work' (Hurd, 1962: 14). Once established as a musical journalist, Boughton was strongly critical of Stanford's position:

> . . . it seems likely that if a creative artist is forced to repeat very often the formulas he has derived from an analysis of his own unconscious work, he may come in the end actually to work upon them himself. On no other supposition can I account for the amazing number of bad songs written by Stanford . . . this statement . . . is due to my genuine admiration for those of Stanford's songs which bear with them evidence of having arisen in the deeps of his nature . . . evidence that the soul of him is still alive, in spite of the sins of his professorship . . . Will he not even now give up those wretched composition pupils and demand some life for himself? (1913: 65)

We are left to guess whether or not Boughton saw himself as one of those 'wretched composition pupils' whom Stanford should have given up.

Vaughan Williams claimed that 'Stanford was a great teacher, and like all great teachers he was narrow minded . . . To say that he was strict was to put it mildly . . . The only way to get good out of a teacher is to divest yourself entirely of your own personality and do what your teacher wants' (R. Vaughan Williams, 1952/1963: 197); but, with typical obstinacy and independence of spirit, he himself, as Michael Kennedy has commented, 'fought his teacher . . . he insisted upon obtruding his personality into the simplest harmony exercises' (1964: 19). As for Gurney, Stanford considered him brilliant but unteachable. Holst, 'Although he often disagreed with Stanford's opinions . . . was always grateful to him, especially for having taught him to become his own critic' (I. Holst, 1938: 11). Goossens thought Stanford a fine teacher. The young John Ireland wrote a string quartet especially for Stanford in the hope that he might be able to study with him, and did so from 1897 to 1901, though Stanford was not impressed with the quartet and Ireland himself became depressed and disillusioned by his cramping influence: 'Stanford always liked Dunhill better than me. He always seemed to write the sort of stuff Stanford wanted' (Longmire, 1969: 53).

Dyson's account of Stanford, with Howells's (1952) the most judicious and thoughtful, attributes his stature to 'qualities of mind and character of which he was probably never even conscious', including the eschewal of 'vagueness, shallowness, sentimentality, froth . . . the facile, the imitative, the popular, the best-seller' (:198); yet if Stanford had allowed himself more 'sentimentality' or more 'vagueness', he might have become a less emotionally inhibited, more compelling song composer.

In his old age Stanford softened towards his former pupils; we have two touching accounts. Goossens relates that Stanford was present at a performance of *Parsifal* which he conducted at Drury Lane in 1920 and went backstage afterwards to thank him for it, so moved that he burst into tears (:149). Benjamin, having returned from a sojourn in Australia, visited his old teacher in the following year:

> It looked as though he had had a stroke, and his speech was thick. He was touchingly pleased to see me, and thanked me for coming until I was embarrassed. With tears filling his eyes he said: 'All my lovely pupils – mad! They've all gone mad! Vaughan Williams, Holst, Howells, Bliss – all mad!' Then, looking very fixedly at me: 'Don't *you* go mad, me bhoy!' It was a change from that day when, on the announcing of the first Carnegie awards, he had sent a postcard with a scribble of a hen and lines leading to five eggs. On the hen were his initials, C. V. S., and on the eggs those of the five composers who had won awards – all five of them Stanford pupils (: 207).

Stanford's affection for his pupils was genuine; so, sadly, was his inability to grasp the necessity of the paths they had taken.

III

Narrative song-cycle and dramatic scena: Somervell and Walford Davies

Parry's style was wholly Germanic, based largely on Mendelssohn, Schumann, Wagner and Brahms. This in itself was no bar to the interpretation of English poetry, as his best songs show, and the same is true of Somervell, who was just young enough to have studied under both Stanford (at Cambridge) and Parry (at the RCM). He also received tuition from Kiel at the Berliner Hochschule. Somervell had a deeper love of English literature and a stronger response to its environmental associations than either Parry or Stanford. Born in 1863 at Windermere (his father founded the K shoe factory at Kendal), he was our only Lake composer and revelled in his surroundings, reading Wordsworth from an early age and walking a good deal. Later in life, in his *Intimations of Immortality*, he endeavoured to present one of Wordsworth's greatest works in music (Banfield, 1975), as Parry had done with Shelley in *Prometheus*. His other two poetic loves were Browning and Shakespeare.

Somervell undertook a considerable amount of arranging throughout his career, especially in collaboration with Sir Harold Boulton, partly as a side-issue of his job as Inspector of Music to the Board of Education. His collections were of 'national' and traditional songs rather than of more recently collected folksongs, and he argued with Cecil Sharp as to which were best for educational purposes. Somervell preferred the broader repertoire, and was in no sense a 'folksong composer'. His prime achievement was a large output of original songs, in particular the four song-cycles to be examined in this chapter, which witness to a remarkably suave technique drawing less on Wagner and more on Brahms than Parry's and owing most to Schumann; as with Parry, nationalistic influences passed him by, except perhaps in *A Shropshire Lad*.

The four cycles, *Maud*, *A Shropshire Lad*, *James Lee's Wife* and *A Broken Arc*, all tell a story. This in itself is unusual for the period, for after *An die ferne Geliebte, Die schöne Müllerin, Winterreise, Dichterliebe* and *Frauenliebe und –leben* composers tended to turn more to the presentation of anthologised or contrasted moods, impressions and pictures, and certainly most 20th-century English cycles and song sets are of this latter sort. Butterworth at first seems to have endeavoured to organise his Housman songs into a cycle with a narrative thread, but he abandoned the idea and changed the order of the songs, splitting them into two sets (see Banfield, 1981b). For Somervell, however, at least in *Maud* and *James Lee's Wife*, the need to tell a story arose from his choice of poetry. He coped successfully with its narrative aspects in these two cycles, and could apply similar treatment to *A Shropshire Lad* and *A Broken Arc*. His sole anthologised cycle, *Love in Springtime*, is insipid by comparison. He was the only composer to interpret mature works by Tennyson and Browning successfully in music (though Liza Lehmann's *In Memoriam* has its advocates). That he did so in a manner reflecting the stature of the works in question attests to the depth of his affinity with English Romantic poetry: the personal response was of a kind which Parry never achieved.

His *Maud* was a courageous undertaking. Balfe had set 'Come into the garden' in a manner which caused Tennyson to complain about the ineptitude of the declamation, which in the first line was the wrong way up (Stanford, 1911: 134) if not downright flippant, poisoning the poem for us ever since. Delius had written a cycle of songs from the poem in 1891 but it was never published, apparently at the composer's own request. *Maud* settings of no greater credibility, by Liszt, Massenet and Saint-Saëns, appeared in a volume of Tennyson songs published in 1880. Although the rugged modernity which critics disliked in the monodrama when it first appeared in 1855 was no longer alarming in 1898, the work was nevertheless potentially intractable to the composer: partly because of the overwrought language in which much of the hero's reflective monologue is couched – depicting his tendency towards madness, which is never far away; partly because of the thematic complexity of the work; and partly because of Tennyson's structural ingenuity, which casts the story in a series of 28 separate poems (grouped into three parts) of widely differing lengths, metres and number of stanzas, each presenting a mood, occasion or emotional impression experienced by the hero. The progression of the narrative often has to be deduced from chance comments in the course of a poem; links and explanations are avoided. Not that this structure is very far removed from the sort of poem-cycle with which composers such as Schubert had coped long before, but it has a mid-Victorian complexity, not to mention length, which could scarcely be cut down to the scope of a song-cycle without risking a complete loss of narrative coherence. Somervell's genius consists in being able to choose vital passages from a scheme which is already loose, present their emotional ambience immediately and vividly without any transitions, and leave the gist of the story just clear enough to make one eager to consult Tennyson for the details. What follows is largely an account of those details.

With Victorian earnestness, Tennyson weaves four Romantic motives into his monodrama: death, war, love and peace. In Somervell's first song, consisting of the first of the 19 stanzas which make up the first poem, we are plunged luridly into the atmosphere of death, which already obsesses the hero's mind, with plenty of dominant minor 9ths and diminished 7ths to reinforce the imagery of 'blood-red heath' and 'red-ribb'd ledges'. Much of this imagery may be unconsciously sexual (Wordsworth, 1974). The last word, 'Death', coincides with the strong dominant minor 9th arpeggio which opened the introduction, now in a tonic context. The hero hates 'the dreadful hollow' because there was found the body of his father, who had presumably killed himself, maddened by 'a vast speculation' which had failed yet left his fraudulent friend and business partner (owner of the nearby Hall) a comfortable profit. The hero is still haunted by the event and by his father's friend's inhumanity. This leads Tennyson to moralise on the brutality of commercial enterprise, and to condemn the complacency of the mid-Victorian notion of peace:

> Peace sitting under her olive, and slurring the days gone by,
> When the poor are hovell'd and hustled together, each sex, like swine.
> When only the ledger lives, and when only not all men lie;
> Peace in her vineyard – yes! – but a company forges the wine.

This, his second main theme, may have been Tennyson's chief motive for writing *Maud* in 1855, for he ends with a call to arms – prophetic, as it turned out, of the Crimean war. But the theme is at odds with the poem's literary essence as a Romantic monodrama which is almost melodrama, and Somervell was wise to ignore it, though it may leave one puzzled at the hero's change of heart in the last song. At this opening stage in the drama the hero's hatred of such false 'peace' leads him to intimate that he too may one day commit suicide as a way out.

The owner of the Hall, however, now a millionaire, is returning to it from abroad with his family. His daughter Maud is said to be very beautiful; the hero recalls playing with her as a child, but in Poem II, having seen her pass in her carriage on her return, he calmly assures us that her beauty is not of the sort which will affect him. In Poem III, however, it is clear that he has been affected, and the language of unbalanced emotion returns as he describes a sleepless night:

> Listening now to the tide in its broad-flung shipwrecking roar,
> Now to the scream of a madden'd beach dragg'd down by the wave . . .

In Poem IV he is still holding out against admiration for her, strengthened in this resolve by the appearance of her brother, a hard-hearted, proud character in the image of his father, unlike Maud, who inherits the innocence of her mother.

In Poem V, all three stanzas of which Somervell sets as his second song, Tennyson takes up the theme of war, already present in Poem I (and more fully treated later), as the necessary antidote to the hypocritical peace. The hero has heard Maud singing

> A passionate ballad gallant and gay,
> A martial song like a trumpet's call!

Somervell's setting is not very passionate, but it is gallant, with simple harmonies, octave bass support, and a swing which is presumably intended to convey martial associations (Ex. 1). The hero is still trying to convince himself that what he adores is

> Not her, who is neither courtly nor kind,
> Not her, not her, but a voice.

In Poem VI he has actually met Maud, and, the morning after, is suffering indecision and vacillations. The language softens as he muses that she *is* 'courtly' and 'kind', but the tone of imbalance returns as he contemplates the evil influence of the brother, who is the prospective Member of Parliament. He is still uncertain as to whether she is sincere. In Poem VIII, however, all doubt is at rest, for their eyes have met in church – a setting charmingly, if a little sentimentally, brought out in Somervell's short third song (see Greene, 1912: 191–2). In Poems IX and X a complication arises in the form of a rival suitor, the *nouveau riche* ennobled grandson of a miner, of whom the brother approves; his

> padded shape,
> A bought commission, a waxen face,
> A rabbit mouth that is ever agape

Ex. 1

stir the hero to show himself by contrast a man of warlike nobility:

> I wish I could hear again
> The chivalrous battle-song
> That she warbled alone in her joy!
> I might persuade myself then
> She would not do herself this great wrong,
> To take a wanton dissolute boy
> For a man and leader of men . . .
>
> And ah for a man to arise in me,
> That the man I am may cease to be!

By Poem XI the hero is recklessly craving and welcoming love ('O let the solid ground', Somervell's fourth song, is equally reckless and uncomplicated) and in a manner which causes madness now to appear of little consequence:

> What matter if I go mad,
> I shall have had my day.

Poem XII is the first song of triumph; the hero is successfully courting Maud in the woods, whilst the rival knocks bootlessly at the Hall door. Somervell leaves the rival out of his cycle altogether, but sets the first four stanzas and the sixth of this poem as his fifth song. Unfortunately the verse descends to bathos:

> I kiss'd her slender hand,
>   She took the kiss sedately;
> Maud is not seventeen,
>   But she is tall and stately

and Somervell, whose accompaniment to the first two stanzas seems somewhat heavy-handed, is likewise unable to rise to the level of lyric excitement the situation deserves, though his accompanimental motive in the second strophe, reminiscent of Kurvenal's bluffing figure in the third act of *Tristan*, adds an extra dimension (Ex. 2), and his subtle final cadence so nicely points the closing poetic conceit (Ex. 3) that it is difficult to realise that Tennyson's poem continues for a further two stanzas.

Ex. 2

Ex. 3

Poem XIII returns to a mood of dark brooding; the hero is worried by the figure of the brother, who scorns him, and the lurid poetic language returns:

> . . . his essences turn'd the live air sick,
> And barbarous opulence jewel-thick
> Sunn'd itself on his breast and his hands . . .

though he obviously enjoys his paranoia:

> [he,] curving a contumelious lip,
> Gorgonised me from head to foot
>   With a stony British stare.

In Poem XIV the hero returns to thoughts of Maud ('Maud has a garden'); her garden, with its passion-flower, is strongly symbolic of the garden of love (Wordsworth, 1974). Somervell seems to have set this poem at the same time as the others but he cut it out of his published version, only to reinstate it in the

1907 edition. In Poem XV madness is still hovering on the horizon; in XVI we learn that the brother is away in London for a week, and in XVII the hero indulges in an orgy of anticipation of Maud's accepting his proposal. Again the mood seems closer to bathos than ecstacy:

> Blush from West to East
>   Blush from East to West,
> Till the West is East,
>   Blush it thro' the West . . . [etc.]

Somervell's delicate setting, though, suggests a happier, unembarrassing middle ground of childlike bliss. Emotional equipoise is recovered in Poem XVIII ('I have led her home'), which is a central, in fact the only, point of repose in the drama:

> And never so warmly ran my blood
> And sweetly, on and on
> Calming itself to the long-wish'd-for end,
> Full to the banks, close on the promised good.

Somervell's delicate setting, though, suggests a happier, unembarrassing middle ground of childlike bliss. Emotional equipoise is recovered in Poem XVIII ('I have led her home'), which is a central, in fact the only, point of repose in the drama:

> Blest, but for some dark undercurrent woe
> That seems to draw – but it shall not be so:
> Let all be well, be well.

Ex. 4

This is explained in Poem XIX ('Her brother is coming back tonight'), where we learn that

> . . . Maud's dark father and mine
> Had bound us one to the other,
> Betrothed us over their wine,
> On the day when Maud was born

– a fact which had been hinted at, unexplained, as a sort of psychological premonition, in Poem VII. The hero sees the bond as cancelled by the suicide of his father, which thus continues to weigh on him with an inherited guilt. But he shrugs off his moroseness in Poems XX and XXI, and anticipates his meeting with Maud in her garden the following dawn, after an all-night dance which her brother is giving at the Hall and to which he has of course not been invited. Such are the circumstances of the joyful Poem XXII, 'Come into the garden, Maud', the climax of the romance of Part I, of which Somervell sets the first three and last three stanzas as his eighth song. This begins as an instrumental waltz with superimposed voice part, like Schumann's 'Das ist ein Flöten und Geigen' from *Dichterliebe*, but the ball is over by the first sectional modulation (to the subdominant), and from then on the music depicts not the band but the hero's enraptured expectation. It contains (p.24, final system, in the score) a slight reminiscence of the breathless accompaniment of his fourth song, gains more and more momentum as his heart beats faster and, we presume, he flies into the arms of his beloved, and ends with a triumphant metamorphosed statement of the opening theme in the piano.

Somervell opens Tennyson's Part II with sufficiently skilled mood-painting as to leave us in no doubt that we are now far away in time and place, and that a catastrophe has occurred. The title of his ninth song (Poem I in Part II of the monodrama) is, however, rather misleading. 'The fault was mine' is in fact the quotation of another's words, on which the hero is musing, and in the course of the poem, of which Somervell sets only the first five and last two lines of the first stanza, the details are filled in. The brother came rushing out of the house with the rival suitor and found the couple together: later (Poem V) the hero intimates, albeit incoherently, that it was the rival who betrayed them. In the altercation that followed the enraged brother struck the hero, with the result that the two fought a duel, inevitably in 'the red-ribb'd hollow behind the wood'. The brother was killed, and as he lay dying, '"The fault was mine," he whisper'd, "fly!"' But the hero, musing on the words, transfers the guilt to himself, for he is haunted by the 'cry for a brother's blood', the anguished cry of Maud which he imagined he heard as he killed his enemy and which continually sounds in his ears. He is eaten up with a mixture of self-reproach and pride, and the ambivalence consequent upon Tennyson's (and Somervell's) plunging into the first phrase prior to explanation is deliberate. However, Somervell weights the meaning on the side of self-reproach by means of his doleful introduction, with its skilfully cross-rhythmic sob of anguish, perhaps also meant to depict the brother's dying gasps (Ex. 5). The heavily descending octave scale passage in the last bar of Ex. 5 is a motive expressing the guilt-laden state of the hero's mind, used several times in the latter part of the cycle. It recurs in the next song, the tenth, a macabre masterpiece of Romantic melodrama in which the hero, apparently now entirely out of his right mind, imagines that he is dead, but, a lost soul (suicide?), can obtain no peace

Ex. 5

even in the grave. He still carries his guilt with him. The descending octaves first appear, after the diminished 7th arpeggios of the opening which recall his state of mind at the beginning of the cycle, in the vast sinking beneath the words 'Dead, long dead'. They recur in a transitional, fraught passage (Ex. 6), together with a

Ex. 6

motive reminiscent of the sob of anguish of the ninth song (Ex. 5) (and perhaps, by an emotional reversal, also reminiscent of the sigh of contentment of 'I have led her home' (ex. 4)) but now rising chokingly. (This motive is later echoed in the 12th song at the words 'haunts of horror and fear', as well as at similar points in *A Shropshire Lad* and *A Broken Arc*.) Finally the octaves subside into an effectively leaden, chaconne-like ostinato which continues below the words 'Ah me, why have they not buried me deep enough?' Previously, following the words '. . . is enough to drive one mad', there has been a direct reference to the introduction of the first song: the hero's mental imbalance and fantasies of death have returned. Somervell wisely sets only the first and last stanzas of the poem, which is 11 stanzas long and in places deliberately incoherent. Despite the bathos of the line 'To have no peace in the grave, is that not sad?', the poem is a powerful piece of imaginative writing stemming from, but on a higher plane than, the Victorian tradition of maniac songs; the passage in the first stanza

> The hoofs of the horses beat,
> Beat into my scalp and my brain

is supposed to have inspired the extraordinary pulsating section of the third movement of Elgar's Second Symphony (Kennedy, 1968: 206–7).

The burial in Poem V is symbolic; out of it the hero rises, a new being, in the one poem in Part III. The catharsis is effected by an archetypal Romantic vision of the hero's beloved, from whom he is now separated, not only by the English Channel but also by her death (of which we learnt in Poem III of Part II):

> She seem'd to divide in a dream from a band of the blest,
> And spoke of a hope for the world in the coming wars –
> 'And in that hope, dear soul, let trouble have rest,
> Knowing I tarry for thee,' and pointed to Mars
> As he glow'd like a ruddy shield on the Lion's breast.

Noble war is better than ignoble peace; he goes joyfully to prove his manhood and to rejoin his beloved in death. The 'blood-red heath' is now transformed into a triumphant image, 'the blood-red blossom of war'. In order to effect the catharsis not too abruptly in music, Somervell here for the only time sets an extract out of order: 'O that 'twere possible', his 11th song, comes before 'Dead, long dead' in the monodrama, as the first stanza of Poem IV, in which the hero is musing desolately on his separation; Somervell, however, turns it from an expression of forlorn longing into the beginning of a new hope, which, since he sets only isolated portions of Part III, he has little scope to fill out in his 12th and last song. This also gives him an extra theme with which to tie up his structural thoughts, by further cross-references, in the last song. It is an aspiring motive using Schubert's dactylic rhythmic fingerprint and modelled on the redemptive theme of Liszt's Piano Sonata – though probably unconsciously, for Somervell disliked Liszt's music (ex. 7); its upward striving effectively counteracts the downward tendency

Ex. 7

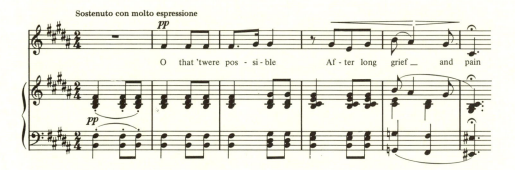

of all the preceding octave passages, especially when it returns in the 12th song with rising scales in the voice part. There are other appropriate thematic references in the 12th song. The setting of 'My life has crept so long on a broken wing' recalls the ostinato of the tenth song, now suitably limping in dotted notes. Then, as in the hero's dream Maud speaks 'of the coming wars', we are back with the martial air of the second song, discreet at first, then dominating the latter part of the song as the hero pledges himself to battle and death in a noble cause, ushering out the cycle in a confident show of courage that increases with the modulation through a variety of keys. The overall feeling of catharsis is reminiscent of Liszt's *Les préludes*: both compositions work through love to a military death symbolic of self-realisation.

This account has attempted to show that Somervell emphasises the archetypal Romantic elements in *Maud* – the horror of death and its glory in a worthwhile cause, fascination with martial music, with madness, with gardens and flowers, sentimentality over churches – underpinning them with a not extensive but perfectly adequate thematic structure, equally Romantic in its use of cross-references. It is the nearest an English composer ever came to writing a substantial Romantic song-cycle, though its technical resources are modest and its style conservative. While its subject-matter and presentation often verge on self-parody, it nevertheless succeeds overall and is continually enhanced by Somer-vell's command of technical nuances. The final cadence of the fifth song (Ex. 3) is one instance. Little vocal surprises are further examples, especially his predilection for emotionally charged turns of phrase onto a dominant, often by a downward 5th, for example in the third song (Ex. 8, *x*), where a counterbalance is provided at the end of the song by an upward 5th twist before the downward 5th is restated in the piano's Schumannesque postlude (Ex. 9, *x*).

In *A Shropshire Lad* these fingerprints are more common (e.g. Ex. 10, manuscript version), right from the opening (Ex. 11, *x*), and the style in general is more

Ex. 8

Ex. 9

Ex. 10

Ex. 11

refined; the melodramatic tendencies and heavy, octave-dominated piano writing of *Maud* have given way, at the prompting of the poetry's simplicity, to an intimacy closer to Schumann, at its most personal in 'Loveliest of trees'. Brahms's influence is restricted to that bleak, windswept side of him on which Parry and Stanford seemed largely incapable of drawing – particularly apparent in 'There pass the careless people', an austere study in 3rds (Ex. 12). Apart from these

Ex. 12

stylistic refinements the success of *A Shropshire Lad* is due to the poetry, which both released Somervell's remarkable gift for flowing and effortless melody and enabled him to impose an unobtrusive but significant story on the cycle. In the collection of poems as Housman presents it, narrative possibilities are perpetually just out of reach; Somervell draws some strands gently together.

His lad first appears enjoying the cherry blossom in springtime, realising that 20 of his 70 apportioned springs have passed; in 'When I was one-and-twenty' increased age has brought increased yearning – he has given his 'heart out of the bosom' and bitterly laments the fact in the third song. In 'Bredon Hill' he has more cause for bitterness, for his lover is dead. Then a march-past ('The street sounds to the soldiers' tread') and the sound of distant drumming ('On the idle hill of summer') prompt him to join up, but in the next song, 'White in the moon the long road lies', he is lonely and desolate as he leaves home, like Schubert's winter wanderer, in the middle of the night. However, in 'Think no more, lad' he heartily shrugs off morbid thoughts, although in the ninth song his monotone in the first stanza suggests that he is now at the point of death, his homeland vividly flashing upon his fading consciousness. This is the only point at which the technique of thematic cross-reference, developed in *Maud*, is used in this cycle. Somervell captures the poignancy of the poem, the quintessence of Housman –

> Into my heart an air that kills
>   From yon far country blows:
> What are those blue remembered hills,
>   What spires, what farms are those?
>
> That is the land of lost content,
>   I see it shining plain,
> The happy highways where I went
>   And cannot come again.

– by quoting his first song note for note, the cherry orchard evidently forming part of the lad's remembrance. It is now a semitone lower, and, a footnote tells us, 'the tempo . . . is much slower than that of No. 1'. While the piano plays the melody line, the voice, transfixed with longing, intones the first stanza on an inverted dominant pedal, then takes over the melody for the second. This flash-back technique, a stock-in-trade of the opera of the period, is also found in other song-cycles, such as Liza Lehmann's *The Life of a Rose* (*1905*), where the tempo is similarly slowed. Finally, in the tenth song, the young soldier has died, one of the 'lads . . . in their glory', far from home. Somervell has fashioned a narrative conclusion noticeably similar to that of *Maud*. The sentiment inspired by thoughts of soldiers languishing or dying in foreign fields was particularly dear to the late Victorians. Hardy, for instance, frequently played upon it in *The Trumpet-Major*, on the first such occasion actually using the cherry as his symbol:

> . . . the soldiers . . . caught the cherries in their forage-caps, or received bunches of them on the ends of their switches, with the dignified laugh that became martial men when stooping to slightly boyish amusement. It was a cheerful, care-less, unpremeditated half-hour, which returned like the scent of a flower to the memories of some of those who enjoyed it, even at a distance of many years after, when they lay wounded and weak in foreign lands (:21).

Housman's exquisitely formed verses certainly encourage Somervell's melodic warmth to glow as nowhere else. In 'Bredon Hill' and 'The lads in their hundreds', particularly, his affinity with 'national' and 'traditional' songs as opposed to orally transmitted folksongs is evident. 'Bredon Hill' mixes something of the rococo grace of Horn's 'Cherry ripe' with the lyrical intensity of Schubert's 'Mein'. 'The lads in their hundreds' is musically a curious cross between a drinking song (cf. 'Your hay it is mow'd' from Purcell's *King Arthur*) and a Sunday School hymn, which nevertheless suits the words. (The extension of the musical strophe in the repetition of the last line of the last stanza does not appear in the manuscript; it was evidently an afterthought.) These elements have an indefinably English flavour, yet in enabling Somervell to draw away from German influences, Housman unfortunately also caused him to betray the limitations of his poetic sensibility. Many composers have found difficulty in expressing opposing forces in Housman's verse, with its smooth surface and gritty underlying irony (Chapter XI devotes some space to the problem); Somervell's limitations are perhaps most apparent in 'Bredon Hill'. Too fond of a strophic approach, he cannot cope with the irony of the final stanza, pealing blithely on regardless of the bitterness in his protagonist's acceptance of fate; his only concession to the devastating ending is the careful avoidance of a return to *tempo primo* for this stanza.

For his last two cycles Somervell returned to mid-Victorian poetry, that of Robert Browning – more complex, obscure and, initially, intractable than Hous-man's, but more comfortably within the range of his susceptibilities. Within his lifetime Browning's verse was little set to music; Stanford's 'Prospice' (1884) is one of only a few significant instances. Later settings are diverse and largely peri-pheral. His massive, rugged optimism inspired American orchestral works by Ives and Ruggles, but English composers – Coleridge-Taylor, Gurney, Julius Harrison, Michael Head, Liza Lehmann, Mackenzie, Warlock, Maude Valérie White, Wolstenholme and others – generally drew on single lyrics for songs. Bridge set 'A lovers' quarrel', no doubt with tongue in cheek, as a recited dialogue with piano (given its style, it probably dates from around 1907); Parry, as might be expected, tried his hand at a more serious extract, a soliloquy from *Saul*. More significant was Bantock's attraction to Browning; he evidently felt an affinity with the extreme multifariousness which has caused the poet to be described as 'a strange blend of Victorian knowledge, Renaissance curiosity, and mediaeval pedantry' (Browning: 89). Bantock's insatiable curiosity and enthusiasm, which tended to spread themselves in place rather than time, particularly towards the Celtic fringes and the East, resulted in diffuseness, technical over-indulgence and a lack of concentration. *Fifine at the Fair* (1901, Tone Poem no. 3, later styled 'orchestral drama'), in which, as Harold Truscott suggested in a BBC radio talk in 1976, Bantock may have been reliving Browning's sexual guilt complex, makes a noisy assault on one of Browning's more obscure poems in an orgy of facile scene-painting. His general inability to get to the core of his subject-matter is perhaps why Bantock chose to respond to a number of Browning's poems in the form of impressions for the piano rather than solo songs. As for his song settings, even the best in his three sets of *Dramatic Lyrics*, 'By the fire-side' and 'Never the time and the place', violate Browning's Victorian integrity, by applying to it an anachronistic musical veneer of Edwardian opulence, stylistically just second-hand Wagner and Strauss without their tonal control and with saturations of added-note harmonies. The superficiality of his technique is evident by comparison with Somervell's where it most resembles his, as in 'Such a starved bank of moss' from *A Broken Arc*: Bantock's very fluency destroys the dramatic tension of Browning's monologues.

There is only one Browning setting that rivals, indeed surpasses, Somervell's: Walford Davies's 'Prospice'. This extraordinary work, now almost forgotten, is one of his few really powerful compositions. Like so many English composers, Davies devoted his mature faculties to other spheres, being first an organist, then an academic, lecturer and broadcaster. He was born at Oswestry in 1869, and at first had few cultural opportunities; though he was a chorister at St George's, Windsor, he did not hear a string quartet until he was 16, when the experience made a strong impression on him: 'I first went to Cannon Place and heard a real string quartet at the Hampstead Popular Concert . . . a tremendous event. I had never dreamt of such exquisite ensemble. And together with new dreams of music grew new love of poetry (Colles, 1942: 19). It is interesting that he already linked the quartet and poetry in his mind; he did so in practice five years later, in 'Prospice', and after him so did many English composers.

The love of poetry, and particularly of Browning, whose *Hervé Riel* and *The Pied Piper of Hamelin* he also set to music (both with solo and chorus), was fostered by his London landlady and mentor, Mrs Matheson, who frequently read aloud to him. In 1890 he suffered a long and serious attack of peritonitis which left him for a while a death-fearing hypochondriac, and it is not surprising that at this time he 'would constantly ask for "Prospice"' (*ibid.*: 37):

> Fear death? – to feel the fog in my throat,
>   The mist in my face,

When the snows begin, and the blasts denote
  I am nearing the place,
The power of the night, the press of the storm,
  The post of the foe;
Where he stands, the Arch Fear in a visible form,
  Yet the strong man must go . . .

Mrs Matheson 'would as constantly try gently to deflect his thoughts from it. He was too young; it was not for him. But despite this advice, perhaps because of it, she found him one day working at the sketch . . . She made no further protest, but quietly awaited the result, and the result justified his ambition' (*ibid.*). It would be difficult otherwise to account objectively for his fascination with the poem for, although popular, it is not one of Browning's greatest. The common Victorian literary topic of the courageous man facing death possesses only a latent grandeur, which Davies's music makes manifest. His use of the string quartet gives the setting an amazing breadth. Unlike Parry, Stanford, Somervell and the ballad composers, he is uninterested in the standard lyrical forms (the poem is through-composed) and the hackneyed harmonic formulae that tend to go with them. The work is in fact a scena rather than a song, a slowly developed conception of texture and instrumentation. The expansiveness of the fine prelude is due to the gradually unfolding string lines, fusing at A (Ex. 13) into a definite motive that reappears prominently later (Ex. 15), and culminating in the splendid entry of the voice (Ex. 14). (When in a later song, the Wordsworth setting 'Our birth is but a sleep', Davies uses a motive similar to that at A to achieve an equivalent effect, but with only piano accompaniment, the result is much less impressive.) The gradual attainment of serenity and fulfilment towards the

Ex. 13

Ex. 14

closing lines is likewise due to textural largesse, particularly after the words 'Shall become first a peace out of pain': a Mahlerian melody soars freely in the first violin part (Ex. 15), sinking onto a 6–4 chord in C major, whereupon the opening section returns with the final lines of the poem interposed in a moving vocal part. The placement of highly charged changes of chord and key on emotive words in the developmental penultimate section – 'glad', 'pain', 'darkness', 'cold', and then (see Ex. 15) 'rage', 'fiend', 'dwindle', 'blend' and 'peace' – is masterly. The

Ex. 15

Ex. 15 (cont.)

Ex. 15 (cont.)

whole formal idea is perhaps indebted to Brahms's *A Song of Destiny*: Davies was no exception to the Englishman's worship of Brahms, and actually journeyed to the Salzkammergut to meet him in August 1896. Apparently Brahms liked some of the works Davies showed him (*ibid*.: 42–3). 'Prospice', however, is no less intensely personal for the affinity.

Of Somervell's Browning settings, *James Lee's Wife* seems disappointing. It is the least interesting of his four important cycles. He too later felt the urge to write for string quartet, but his 1919 arrangement of the accompaniment does not alter what is essentially a pianistic conception, frequently thick in texture, and in any case he retains the piano in addition to the strings. Nor is it easy to see anything very orchestral in the writing, although the title-page of the autograph manuscript for voice and piano describes the work as being for contralto and orchestra. Given the genuine pathos with which Somervell later imbued the theme of lost love in *A Broken Arc* it is not difficult to see why he chose to set portions of this poem-cycle, with its similar subject matter, but it is not easy to do justice to Browning's poetic conceit in *James Lee's Wife*, and Somervell leaves much of it untreated and somewhat falsifies the whole. There are nine poems, each headed with a location. Somervell sets those marked with an asterisk:

     I   James Lee's wife speaks at the window*
    II   By the fireside (first three of four stanzas*)
   III   In the doorway (first and last of four stanzas*)
   IV   Along the beach
    V   On the cliff*

VI   Reading a book, under the cliff
VII   Among the rocks*
VIII   Beside the drawing board
IX   On deck

The predominant colour of the poem-cycle is grey: set in the autumn, it concerns a marriage which like the year is facing its winter, having grown old and cold. The protagonist's husband has lost his love for her, while she has lost her glamour. She muses on various aspects of the sterile relationship as she roams alone in the vicinity of their coastal home in France. There is only one ray of light in this sad situation: James Lee's wife cannot regret loving her cold of a husband, as she concludes in the seventh poem:

> That is the doctrine, simple, ancient, true;
>   Such is life's trial, as old earth smiles and knows.
> If you loved only what were worth your love,
> Love were clear gain, and wholly well for you:
>   Make the low nature better by your throes!
> Give earth yourself, go up for gain above!

But the marriage cannot survive, since the wife no longer has beauty by which to hold her husband, so she decides to leave him and sets sail, as we deduce from the cryptic title of the last poem, presumably for England. It is a depressing conclusion, for she admits to herself that she still loves him passionately:

> But did one touch of such love for me
>   Come in a word or a look of yours,
> Whose words and looks will, circling, flee
>   Round me and round while life endures, –
> Could I fancy 'As I feel, thus feels he';
>
> Why, fade you might to a thing like me,
>   Any your hair grow these coarse hanks of hair,
> Your skin, this bark of a gnarled tree, –
>   You might turn myself! – should I know or care
> When I should be dead of joy, James Lee?

The bitter lash of this ending is powerful and moving, but Somervell must have felt unequal to it, as he was to similar instances in Housman, for he ignores Browning's last two poems altogether. Instead he concludes with the seventh, forging it into a quasi-religious optimistic climax, not unlike the third and fifth songs of *Sea Pictures*, and certainly bearing a strong stylistic resemblance to other Victorian 'better land' songs, including his own *A Broken Arc* (VII) and the conclusions of *Maud* and *A Shropshire Lad*, as well as Parry's 'There' and Stanford's *Songs of Faith*. In itself it is tasteful and not fulsome, but as a corollary to the four preceding songs it is a puzzling reversal of mood, taken out of Browning's context, although it has been prepared for a little by the two upward emotional turns in 'On the cliff' – the one (the B major $\frac{9}{8}$ section, depicting the butterfly) reminiscent of the epilogue to *Dichterliebe* and the other, which draws the moral, of Walther's prize song in *Die Meistersinger* (Ex. 16). The other weakness of the cycle is the thematic structure. It relies more than *Maud* on motivic cross-reference, but the sombre tints of the emotional drama produce nothing strong enough for the weight it has to bear. Of the two significant motives,

Ex. 16

Ex. 17

Ex. 17 (a), which opens the cycle, is clotted, and Ex. 17 (b), which introduces 'On the cliff' but is first heard in the opening line of 'By the fireside', is colourless. The most attractive and musically positive song in the cycle is 'In the doorway', where, except for a tiny hint of (b), Somervell dispenses with borrowed material and relies instead on his flair for flexible compound-time melodic invention, here in $\frac{6}{8}$ three-bar phrases (compare the $\frac{15}{8}$ of 'The lads in their hundreds' and the $\frac{9}{8}$ of 'Meeting at night'). It is of course possible that the sombre character of the whole work, which is undoubtedly a deeply felt essay, might appear more positive in its orchestral version; should an orchestral score be found *James Lee's Wife* would make an interesting companion-piece to *Sea Pictures*.

Somervell's best cycle is *A Broken Arc*. Nothing is known about it except that it was published in 1923 and, according to Somervell's youngest daughter, received a favourable performance by Hervey Alan in the Wigmore Hall (Howard), though this can hardly have been the first, since Alan was only 13 at the time of publication. It may well be that most of the cycle was compiled from earlier songs written individually. It consists of the following:

1   Such a starved bank of moss (introduction to *The Two Poets of Croisic*)
2   Meeting at night (from *Dramatic Lyrics)*
3   My star (from *Dramatic Lyrics*)
4   Nay but you, who do not love her ('Song', from *Dramatic Lyrics*)
5   The worst of it (1st, part of 5th, and 19th (final) stanzas; from *Dramatis Personae*)
6   After (from *Dramatic Lyrics*)
7   From 'Easter Day' (Stanza XXXI)
8   The year's at the spring (from *Pippa Passes*)

Strictly speaking, the story-telling part of the cycle is confined to nos. 5 and 6, though thematic cross-reference also extends to no. 7. This song, like the fourth in *James Lee's Wife*, functions as a brightening transition to the inevitable happy ending, which, removed from the context of the play from which its poem is taken, is dangerously trite, and forms the weakest part of the cycle. The first four songs simply serve to introduce the singer's lover and to extol her (she is the 'star' in no. 3).

In the two outer songs, settings of two of Browning's most celebrated lyrics, Somervell's harmonic boundaries are reached. Both make much use of lush Wagnerian appoggiatura figurations borrowed from the *Waldweben* (see below, p. 164); for once Somervell is enjoying an impressionistic play of light and colour. In 'Such a starved bank of moss' he also introduces a harmonic sideslip on the world 'flash' which, though not impossible in Schumann's day, is more closely akin to the young Vaughan Williams's fondness for harmonic 'fault lines'. Similar shifts of harmonic centre, through mediant relationships, recur in 'My star'.

'The worst of it' plunges us into the heart of the cycle; it is Somervell's best song. In this and the next two songs he draws on his previous dramatic experience in *James Lee's Wife* and *Maud*. In 'The worst of it' the man speaks a monologue to his (presumably) absent lover, as the woman does in *James Lee's Wife*, but with added sorrow and poignancy, for here the loved one has actually been unfaithful. The song has much the same inexorable sadness as King Mark's monologue in *Tristan*, though the chromatics are closer to Schumann than Wagner. The thematic structure is subtle and tightly woven. The general ambience of the monologue demands *arioso*; in the first section fragments of rich harmony are periodically arrested for passages of vocal declamation, necessary because of the far from simple poetic diction (Ex. 18). The same harmonic

Ex. 18

My swan, that a first fleck's fall On her won-der of white must un-swan, un - do!

fragments are knitted together and elevated into a more eloquent elegy in the final stanza. In between, the fragment of the fifth stanza is set to music which provides reusable material of three motives (Ex. 19, *a–c*), the voice ceasing at one of Somervell's masterly vocal touches, an arresting enharmonic twist at the word 'love'. Ex. 19 *c*, with its poignant appoggiatura, returns at the close of the song. In 'After', which follows, Somervell leaves us to deduce a narrative link with the preceding song (as he had done in *Maud*). Evidently the woman was unfaithful with the man's friend, whom he has shot in a duel. (The duel is prepared for in Browning's poem 'Before', paired with 'After' in *Dramatic Lyrics*.) Now the man surveys his dead friend's face. The song opens with a choking, disjointed motive not unlike the interlude in the tenth song of *Maud* and clearly related to the less plastic Ex. 19 *a* and *b*, and later, as the 'change' of death is contemplated, its phrases are filled out and joined up (Ex. 20, *d*). But first the nobility of death is

Ex. 19

Ex. 20

Ex. 21

depicted in a solemn, march-like ostinato (Ex. 21, *e*). When the man begins to recollect his happy childhood with the friend, poignant pathos returns, and with it the intimate motives *a* and *b* from the fifth song. At the lines 'I would we were boys as of old / In the field, by the fold' Somervell indulges in a little self-plagiarism, quoting in the accompaniment the main theme, that of childhood's past happiness, from his *Intimations of Immortality* of 1907, with a new vocal counter-melody. The effect is moving, even if one has no idea where the tune comes from. Then *b* reappears, followed by the inarticulate *d* – now sinking rather than rising, as the hero looks his last on the corpse. Somervell directs that the final words, 'Cover the face!', be muttered 'with a shudder' (which can be made surprisingly effective), and the ostinato *e* closes the song, transformed from nobility to bleak emptiness by the exchange of its 6–3 chords for hollow 5th-filled octaves without 3rds. In the seventh song motivic reminiscences, as in *Maud*, help to effect the catharsis. The reappearance of the sadness motives *b* and *c* at the words 'Be all the earth a wilderness' leads into a more optimistic section, where *e* is transformed into an accompaniment of gentle but resolute tread (Ex. 22) rising

Ex. 22

to a climax, just within the limits of good taste, on the words 'To reach one eve the Better Land!' In the last song we are assured, with a further cushion of *Waldweben* appoggiaturas, that 'God's in his heaven – / All's right with the world!', and the catharsis is complete.

To the Victorian artist a painting could be used to tell a story or expound a moral, and so to Somervell could a song-cycle. In that approach lies his importance as a song composer. He saw it as his prime function to look square in the face two archetypal issues, love and death, and he did so not only with an earnestness born of his century but with an honesty and detachment which have not reappeared in English song. For later composers, more in tune with impressionist and symbolist aesthetics, pure sensation rather than dramatic development became the norm. Story-telling, and with it motivic cross-reference, largely disappeared. The residual exceptions will be noted as they arise.

IV

Three post-Victorians: Hurlstone, Bridge and Vaughan Williams

Stanford's pupils began to 'go mad', as he saw it, in the first decade of the 20th century. By examining the songs of three of them we can build up a telling picture of broadening stylistic sensibility in the years leading up to the first world war. Although the colourful Edwardian *Zeitgeist* appears in none of them as strongly as in the subjects of the next chapter, in Vaughan Williams at least the solidity of achievement will be seen to surpass the often ephemeral music of Bantock, Quilter and Scott, and to presage more fruitful inter-war developments.

Samuel Coleridge-Taylor and William Hurlstone, Stanford's model pupils, show us the sort of music he wanted his protégés to write. In the case of the Negro Coleridge-Taylor it was sterile: in stylistic terms, weak Dvořák with an ethnic admixture, of some historical and sociological interest today (see Tortolano) but lacking idiomatic freshness. Perhaps Coleridge-Taylor merits some rehabilitation on the basis of such instrumental compositions as the Clarinet Quintet and the Violin Concerto or the delightful choral work, *A Tale of Old Japan*, but the *Hiawatha* trilogy is now irrevivably dead, though kept embalmed by scattered choral societies, and so are his songs. Coleridge-Taylor's misfortune was an inflated sense of inspiration: whenever he read a poet for the first time he was convinced that he or she was the greatest ever, and was seized with a compulsive desire to set the verse to music, apparently unaware that the results were often indistinguishable from ballads. His settings of the black American poet Paul Dunbar are cases in point. A sociological study of the material circumstances of English artists at the turn of the century might suggest that, had Coleridge-Taylor been born or absorbed into an affluent or leisured class and, like Haydn, been 'forced to be original', his career might have turned out very differently. As it was, he was caught up in a perpetual frantic round of teaching, adjudicating, festival conducting and composing to commissions, writing songs for money and eking out a terraced-house existence to support his family in Croydon. His hyperactive temperament resembled Mendelssohn's, and like Mendelssohn he died young, of overwork and pneumonia, at the age of 37. His close friend and contemporary Hurlstone was even poorer, fighting a losing battle to support a widowed mother in South London and dying of consumption in 1906, barely 30 years old. Yet though cast in the Stanford mould and never openly rebellious, he possessed innate individuality which even in his pitifully stunted career kept pushing up through the Brahmsian foundations. His tiny song output offers more than the whole of Coleridge-Taylor's.

What one might call Hurlstone's 'abstract' personality emerges clearly in his

65

chamber music. His Phantasie for String Quartet, which won first prize in the first Cobbett competition (1906), manages to absorb Liszt, modality and possibly Strauss into a delightful and original framework of thematic metamorphosis. In his songs, his 'applied' personality – i.e. his way of responding to poetry – always evinces both fertility and polish, and much more warmth than Stanford's tendency to whittle down the means to the bare bones, though the verse he chooses to set has little bearing on the spirit of his time and may rather reflect Stanford's recommendations. He is not afraid of exploring his emotions. Although in 'The blind boy' this produces dire sentimental bathos, in 'A litany' it gives rise to a starkly serious and heartfelt setting, whereas in 'Tell me, thou star' it results, very differently, in a charming ballad-romance which is not unlike Parry's lyrical pieces, – though it has a resourceful neatness of effect which Parry would have outlawed as bordering on the sensuous and hence the unethical (e.g. in the third stanza, where the piano plays on stock emotions by taking over the melody (Ex. 1)). This sort of artlessness heralds a new phase in English song com-

Ex. 1

position and looks forward in particular to Quilter. Chromaticism is introduced in a similarly heart-easing (rather than disturbing) fashion, as in the introductions to 'A litany' and 'That time is dead'. These and other little touches are indications of a changing aesthetic, one which was beginning to prize suggestiveness of sound, in verse and music, for its own sake – a somewhat belated parallel to French symbolism. Indeed, the elements beginning to open interesting vistas in Hurlstone's *Four Songs* seem French, though no definite influences can be asserted. The aeolian modality of the Phantasie crops up again in the first line of 'Thou hast left me ever' and, enticingly, in 'Cradle song', where it is followed by a pair of modulations through flattened 7ths (Ex. 2), an indulgence used much more blatantly in 'A croon', which at one point sideslips quite simply from F major down to E flat and then on down to D major. This song, in both music and words, even though the latter are traditional, is well on the way to our more recent conception of light music (Ex. 3). Chromatics are also prominent in this group, ushering in 'My true love hath my heart', whose agile voice part and opulent though tasteful accompaniment amount to a lyric stylistically and emotionally midway between Parry and Quilter. The opening of 'Cradle song',

Ex. 2

Ex. 3

Ex. 4

however, is more innovatory, and would make one suspect the influence of Delius, were it not unlikely that Hurlstone ever heard any of his music (Ex. 4). Grieg, always a force to be reckoned with when considering minor composers of this period, may well have been the missing link.

Ex. 5

Hurlstone possessed a strong technique and, unlike Stanford, was not afraid to assert it. 'In spite of all', a passionate love-sonnet by Surrey (of which he omits one line), is indeed almost too vehement for its content. It foreshadows the reckless brilliance of Bridge's 'Love went a-riding', and the ending, with its tonic major/minor alternations, is particularly forceful (Ex. 5).

A *Times* review (16 January 1937) of Newell's pamphlet on Hurlstone saw a parallel between Hurlstone and Chausson or Lekeu, pointing out that they, who also died young and full of promise, were well known, but Hurlstone, alas, was not. The parallel is justified, but an even closer English equivalent of the French sub- and post-Franck school on stylistic grounds is Frank Bridge, whose early works often resemble Hurlstone's.

Of Bridge's 60-odd solo songs, as many as 38 may be regarded as the fruits of his student days or of a student mentality. He studied with Stanford at the RCM from 1899 to 1903, and although nothing survives prior to April 1901 the next two years saw a fair amount of song-writing. Stanford, as we have seen, schooled his more advanced composition pupils in song, and presumably the occasional pencil emendations that appear in the earliest Bridge manuscripts, such as the altered vocal ending of the Shakespeare sonnet 'When most I wink', which is an obvious magisterial improvement, are Stanford's. Like Hurlstone's, many of Bridge's texts – translations of Heine, famous lyrics of Shelley, Tennyson and Arnold, a smattering of Shakespeare and Herrick – were no doubt suggested by

Stanford or at least chosen to meet with his approval; they certainly do not give the impression of a selection prompted by wide reading and personal identification. In fact Bridge probably never read widely, having the least literary sensibility and education of several generations of English composers. He was aware of this lack and accommodated to it, for conversely he was in terms of purely musical technique by far the most professional of his peers. Writing to thank Elizabeth Sprague Coolidge in September 1922 for a timely holiday in France, he commented:

> If there were ever a human being less equipped with the art of expression in words, then he must indeed have been completely hopeless. Everything I put down reads at least 100% cooler than I intend it. At last, after a long apprenticeship, I think I know just when and how to put a few cellos and violas and wood-wind together, and even to add trombones at the right moment – but in words! No, they stump me. After this confession of weakness I am sure you'll know exactly where you have to transpose everything up at least an octave and a half.

Bridge's pride at having attained professional excellence as a composer provoked critical disapproval and neglect (no doubt exacerbated by jealousy of the concomitant reward of Mrs Coolidge's patronage) at a time when most of his English colleagues were feeling their way back from their torpor of deadened imagination into a state of musical awareness via the broad gates of humanistic expression, often, as this study aims to show, through literature. Bridge's pupil Britten was the first English composer since Purcell who could display technical brilliance with literary sensibility in a secure and acceptable combination.

Consequently Bridge can hardly be considered a song composer of major importance. In the early songs one scarcely ever feels that he has something to say and that it can be said only with the help of a particular poem. One senses instead that he is producing finely tailored exercises in small-scale composition, well written for voice and instruments with plenty of effective orchestral accompaniments and obbligato lines as well as grateful piano parts, and not obviously violating the poems set, but not exploring any deep recesses in poet or composer either. Text and music never seem to enlarge each other, at least not before 1908, when he appears to have ceased writing songs for four years; everything till then sounds like good student work, with its attendant obsolescence. Yet his chamber works of the same years, particularly the First Quartet and the Three Idylls, despite their occasionally glib facility, were seminal.

However, there are some positive elements in the early songs. Three of them have an obbligato viola part (Bridge was a professional viola player), and they are fertile textural essays in playing off two interacting melodic lines against a slowly unravelling harmonic framework, but one admires them accordingly, as vocal chamber music, not as settings of poetry. In 'Music, when soft voices die' the persistent little repeated figure of the piano part, squeezed into spacious lines in the voice and viola, is similar in its rather anxious effect to the texture of the Phantasie Piano Trio, which dates from the same year as the song's revised version. But although the literary and musical contexts for this sort of writing are well chosen, they exist in an atmosphere of sad lethargy, encountered again and again in these early songs, which proves very limiting. Many of them, particularly those written between 1903 and 1908, are full of yearning or are downright dismal. Bridge's creative nature was naturally melancholy, sometimes frighteningly so in the un-compromising later works, such as the Third Quartet and *Oration*, but here the impression is more of a linguistic convention he is unable to overcome, a *fin-de-siècle* dying fall of phrase extending to inform the whole structure. It stamps him as wholly Edwardian, more so perhaps even than Quilter, whose songs he loved (Raphael, 1974–7), or Maude Valérie White, whose 'I sometimes hold it half a sin' from the four Tennyson *In Memoriam* songs (*1886*) is obviously the model for 'Where is it that our soul doth go?'; and it caused some head-shaking even over his more mature songs (Jean-Aubry: 213–14). We may also sense in it an af-finity with Rachmaninov, for example in the sudden outflow at the end of 'When most I wink'. The measured descent of lines such as the viola part on the last page of 'Where is it that our soul doth go?' (Ex. 6) is supplemented all too often with

Ex. 6

minor $^{9-8}_{6-5}$ cadences such as those in 'Fly home my thoughts' (Ex. 7) which give an ambience of watery-eyed platitudes in both music and verse. The setting of Tennyson's 'Tears, idle tears' reaches the limits of expansion in this vein, but although the music is well wrought it certainly does not convince us that the tears are really 'from the depth of some divine despair'. Much more arresting is 'Far, far from each other', an Arnold setting with viola obbligato. The phrase to which the first line is set, again a heavy, falling one, permeates the opening section (especially the viola part), which builds to an impassioned climax. Then, after the climax has died down, a beautiful passage emerges, remarkably simple and diatonic for three bars after the preceding chromatic inflections, as the soul seeks repose in nature (Ex. 8). The opening phrase tentatively reappears, but this time its effect is not of expressing the sundering of the two spirits but of gently embrac-ing the overwrought soul (Ex. 8), cradling it through a series of modulations and offering it consolation in the last two lines, whose music repeats the opening paragraph of the song. This is one of the few instances in the early songs where Bridge seems to grasp his responsibility to the poem: he transcends it, making it

Ex. 7

Fly home my thoughts that fret-ting in a - lien worlds all day＿

Have longed for the sun's＿ set - ting And wished all words a - way.＿

Ex. 8

Fold close-ly, O

na - ture! Thine arms round thy child.

Ex. 8 (cont.)

sound more expansive than it does when read, by worthy exploitation of purely musical material. The message is an early example of one frequently met with in Bridge's finest works: the power of nature to sadden yet console the lonely spirit.

Wit is not a quality much in evidence in these songs, or indeed anywhere in Bridge's music. 'The Devon maid' and 'Go not, happy day' both have a certain ingenuous charm, which in the former includes a rhythmic sequence characteristic of the composer, for whom the ardour of the waltz was never far away (Ex. 9), and in the latter, which is a continuous cross-rhythmic dynamo, lends apt

Ex. 9

expression to Tennyson's hero's heady lovesickness; but in the end they do not rise far above the triviality mindlessly courted in 'So perverse', a song which is best forgotten. It is thus not surprising that the Heine settings largely miss the point. Some of the translations are bad to begin with, overwritten and sentimentalised, without Heine's flashes of irony. 'Where is it that our soul doth go?', 'Night lies on the silent highways' and 'All things that we clasp' sound excessively lugubrious, especially the last, in which for some reason Bridge states the text twice – presumably because he knew he was unable to match Heine's cruel curtness. In three of the settings, however, he understands Heine better and produces perhaps his strongest early songs. In 'Lean close thy cheek' the teardropped atmosphere is delicately expressed in the piano introduction. Heine is passionate and sincere when he says

> And while in my arms I clasp thee tight
> I will die with love and yearning.

So is Bridge, with a broad climax (implying a sexual one) that subsides in repeated throbs on his favourite dominant minor 9th chord. In 'The violets blue' a Chopinesque *cantilena* introduces heart-warming modulatory inflections at the lines

> The violets blue of the eyes divine,
> And the rose of the cheeks as red as wine,
> And the lilies white of the hands so fine
> They flourish and flourish from year to year . . .

This is achieved with an economy of writing which, despite a brief thickening of the texture '*con passione*' prepares us for the tight-lipped setting of the final line, 'And only the heart is withered and sore', after which the *cantilena* finally returns with accusing eloquence. 'Dear, when I look into thine eyes' is less successful. Schumann set the same text in *Dichterliebe* (no. 4, 'Wenn ich in deine Augen seh''), and the two composers' different interpretations can be seen to arise from their different formal readings of the poem:

> Dear, when I look into thine eyes
>   My deepest sorrow straightway flies
> But when I kiss thy mouth, ah, then
>   No thought remains of bygone pain
> And when I lean upon thy breast
>   No dream of heaven could be more blest
> But when thou say'st thou lovest me
>   I fall to weeping bitterly.

Both convey an overall bitter-sweetness, a mingling of pain and joy, in their basic material: coaxing G major repeated chords in Schumann, tender G flat major arpeggio harmonies in Bridge, who intermittently etches inner and upper lines which are themselves Schumannesque. However, Schumann treats each of the four couplets as following from the previous one, and keeps the vocal delivery flowing evenly through rationally modulated phrases (G, C, E minor, A minor, G), so that the sentiment of the last couplet as well as its music has the effect of the inevitable destination of a cyclic progression. Love's sorrow flows from love's joy with no clear dividing line; by moving away from sorrow one returns to it. Bridge, on the other hand, polarises the two emotions by creating a pair of musical stanzas. The parallelism is suggested in the text by the repeated word 'But' ('Doch' in the German) at the beginning of the third and seventh lines, and causes Bridge to break into a blissful piano interlude at the end of the first stanza, representing the banishment of 'bygone pain' with considerable finality; then, of course, exactly the same music represents the 'weeping bitterly' as an epilogue. This is perhaps too cruel, a level of irony that Heine himself for once avoids, according to Schumann's interpretation. Moreover, in order to make the correspondence effective, Bridge has to break the otherwise unruffled calm halfway through his second stanza, and the suddenly rough harmonic treatment of 'thou lovest me' seems rather too dramatic for the reflective context. Perhaps the ideal setting would combine Schumann's and Bridge's approaches.

Technically some of the early songs are more interesting than this. In the middle stanza of Shelley's poem 'On a faded violet', having prepared an agitated little thematic cell, he rises with it through three modulatory steps of a minor 3rd, then falls again through four major 3rds, thus ending a 5th lower, a quite powerful effect in the highly charged context of frustrated love. 'Lament' contains sinuous lines foreshadowing the Second Quartet, and its companion, 'Fly home my thoughts', matches it in a number of enterprising passages. The setting of Dorothy Wordsworth's 'Berceuse' is a good essay in orchestration. But Bridge only found his feet as a song composer, suddenly, after he returned to the medium in 1912. 'Isobel' still breathes a heavy atmosphere, with a most awkward terminal attempt at relative-major catharsis demanded by the rather tedious poem, but in the Arnold setting 'Strew no more red roses' he breaks out of the languor of his earlier songs with a new, agile vocal range, and in the famous 'Love went a-riding' all at once his muse, like Pegasus in the poem, takes wing. Somehow he has at last been stirred. How he came to be triggered off by Mary Coleridge's verse, which he had first approached the previous month in a charming, intimate song 'Where she lies asleep', is not obvious, for it has none of the intoxicating energy that Bridge hangs on it. But here for the first time is a level of technical involvement worthy of his development in other genres, making for a virtuosic showpiece; and it is refreshing to see an Englishman's music high-handedly mastering the verse. However, it is an isolated phenomenon; the first world war soon intervened.

We must bear in mind that Ralph Vaughan Williams's output in the Edwardian era was only the first phase of a life's work spanning a whole epoch in English song. But at the same time we should remember that he was born earlier than most of the composers whose style survived the Edwardian decade, and his relatively slow development gave his first published songs an air of maturity and authority. They began to appear in considerable numbers in *The Vocalist* from 1902 onwards, and captured a large market. *Songs of Travel*, following strategically, placed Vaughan Williams in the forefront of critical and appreciative notice; they were to be seen on every piano (Bliss: 26), fresh in matter and manner yet seeming to bear a consoling weight of Romantic experience. *On Wenlock Edge*, regarded with some justification as a direct outcome of his study with Ravel in France in 1908, caused raised eyebrows by apparently consorting with foreign gods; its passionate response to Housman's dramatising verse was both admired and execrated by contentious critics long afterwards. Never again did Vaughan Williams create song history, but his occasional excursions into the domain of the solo voice, particularly in conjunction with the exploration of solo instruments at the expense of the piano, showed a seriousness of purpose which, the older he became, increasingly precluded taking any parameter in song composition for granted. Whether consciously or not, between and even after the wars he countered the luxuriousness of other song composers with the asceticism of a sage. The progression of his textual concerns parallels this: beginning, almost with the unresisting involvement of a 19th-century contemporary, by setting Coleridge, Browning, Tennyson, Swinburne and the Rossettis, he graduated through the pastoral immediacy of Stevenson and Housman to the sharp freshness of Chaucer, the religious fervour of Fredegond Shove, the metaphysical poets and Bunyan, and, at the end, the visionary assurance of Blake and the gentle classicism of his own wife's verse.

Like Tippett after him, he was not easily satisfied with his education. Having gained a degree in history at Cambridge in 1895 he returned to the RCM (where he had previously studied with Parry) as a pupil of Stanford. In between he wrote his first song of any consequence, the July 1895 setting of Herrick's 'To daffodils'. Its style bears similarities to Schumann's and Chopin's, the winged group of five upbeat quavers (Ex. 10, *a*) in particular being a reliable Romantic device, later put to further use in the setting of Swinburne's 'Rondel' and in *The House of Life*, and the Brahmsian cycle-of-5ths 3rds (Ex. 10, *b*) also providing an expansive opening gesture to the possibly somewhat earlier 'Summum bonum'. But there are touches of originality as well. The first vocal phrase, apostrophising the daffodils, reappears embedded in the accompaniment at 'We will go with you along' (Ex. 10, *c*), whereupon the music cadences, somewhat unexpectedly, in E minor, – a hint of Vaughan Williams's later use of modality. Some lighter attempts followed, including the three *Rumpelstiltskin* settings, which have delicacy and

Ex. 10

already, in the third, a folksong simplicity. Vaughan Williams was also already learning some tricks of the English madrigalists, and before the turn of the century he recreated the English ayre in his setting of Thomas Vaux's 'How can the tree but wither?', which is full of elastic phrase-lengths, hemiola, *style brisé* embellishments, interrupted cadences (Ex. 11) and a period melancholy that suggests he may have written it for incidental performance in a play.

Ex. 11

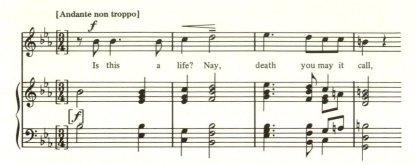

Little else followed until 1901, when a crucial but in some ways perplexing phase in Vaughan Williams's development began. There were no more Elizabethan songs until the Shakespeare set of 1925, with the exception of the over-popular 'Orpheus' (surely his weakest song), and Heywood's 'Ye little birds', which was included in Plunket Greene's Aeolian Hall recital in February 1905 with *Songs of Travel* but later, it seems, destroyed. Folksong was looming larger on Vaughan Williams's horizon, although at first with a certain ambivalence. Indeed, in his *Vocalist* article on 'A school of English music' he voiced more than reservations:

> Now, English composers do not spring from the peasantry. Indeed, in England there are [sic] no true peasantry for them to spring from. Why then, should an English composer attempt to found his style on the music of a class to which he does not belong, and which itself no longer exists? (1902 a: 8)

Therefore, he argues, an English musical nationalism along the lines of Russia's and Bohemia's is not within the bounds of sincerity: 'the national English style must be modelled on the personal style of English musicians'. Yet later in the same year, in one of a series of six Oxford University extension lectures on folksong which he gave in Bournemouth, he urged that the very sincerity of the folksinger should provide the vital spark of inspiration to English composers:

> The reason why those early musicians sang, played, invented and composed was simply and solely because they wanted to; and I think the lesson we can learn from them is that of sincerity. When English musicians learn to do that – to write and play for the sake of the music and for the sake of nothing else, then I think that the music which is latent amongst us will come to the front (Kennedy, 1964: 32).

At this stage he still refers to folk art in the past tense: it was not until December of the following year that the realisation that folksong was still a living art further complicated the issue for him – when he encountered, at a vicarage tea-party near

Brentwood, his first genuine folksinger, and collected 'Bushes and briars' from him.

His songs reflect this transitional state. William Barnes, though he wrote poems in Dorset dialect, was not a yokel but a Cambridge theologian and philologist (folk movements throughout the European Romantic epoch were similarly products of disguised scholarship), and when Vaughan Williams's setting of Barnes's poem 'Linden Lea' appeared 'on the strong recommendation of Professor Stanford' in *The Vocalist*'s first number (:4), the appreciative public was faced with a song which for all its simplicity still swung to the dominant and subdominant in the expected places. 'Blackmwore by the Stour' in the following month's issue, another Barnes setting, was described by *The Times* as the 'cleverest imitation of a genuine folk song' (Kennedy, 1964: 53), whereas 'Whither must I wander', issued in June, clearly marked a retreat to less consciously 'folk' poetry. It was these later offerings, not 'Linden Lea', that *The Vocalist* specified in March 1903 as having been amongst its best-selling songs during its first year (I: 389).

Different concerns were emerging, while folksong and Tudorisms were transferred to other media, (e.g. the orchestra, in the *Norfolk Rhapsodies* and *In the Fen Country*), and did not noticeably reappear in his songs until *On Wenlock Edge*. Even then folksong had to wait for Butterworth for its full assimilation into art song. Vaughan Williams was after all a child of his century, and we should not be surprised to find him early on making two inconsequential Tennyson settings, 'Crossing the bar' and 'Claribel', followed by a third, 'Tears, idle tears'. This last is not a very good song, heavy in texture and as maudlin as Bridge's marginally later setting, yet when, in the second and fourth stanzas (Ex. 12, from the second), he abandons himself to Tchaikovskian throbs of pathos,

Ex. 12

propelled by a 'symphonic' four-note motive which recurs in many of his later works, he seems for the first time to master the Romantic dialectic, even to the rising series of 6–4 chords heralding the final Wagnerian climax. Does it withstand his own test of sincerity? The question is best answered with reference to what followed: after some settings of slight poems by Christina Rossetti, he tackled the far more daunting verse of her brother Dante Gabriel, in two related cycles of sonnets from his sequence of 101, *The House of Life*, and made his own not entirely successful but unique contribution to the Pre-Raphaelite movement.

The impression made by these two cycles can be felt in lines from the second of the four *Willow-Wood* sonnets (the centrally placed sonnets which form a bitter-sweet core to Rossetti's *House of Life* sequence and were set by Vaughan Williams in his cantata of that name):

> his was such a song,
> So meshed with half-remembrance hard to free,
> As souls disused in death's sterility
> May sing when the new birthday tarries long.

Vaughan Williams's new musical birthday tarried for a number of years after *Willow-Wood* and *The House of Life*, arguably until 1908, but the mesh of half-remembrance, particularly of Schumann and Wagner, has a power of its own apt for the frequently retrospective pondering of love in these sonnets. Here for the first time Vaughan Williams attempts the expression of love's sorrows as well as its ecstasies. *Willow-Wood* is a text of gloomy imagery wringing sadness out of 'soul-struck widowhood' (willow is a symbol of mourning), and although it seems unlikely that Vaughan Williams had any personal cause for identification with Rossetti's moods, his capacity for empathy in its fullest sense, here as in the later Stevenson and Housman settings, is his greatest quality as a song composer. Musical success, however, is intermittent. The *Willow-Wood* sonnets, bound together in a closely thematic continuous setting, with frequent chains of augmented triads and a general lack of contrast, are too gloomy and intense for his musical capabilities. The dark and the bright sides of love are far better balanced in *The House of Life*, in which, although – or perhaps because – the songs are not linked continuously, there is a more satisfying web of themes and references.

The tenderness of love is presented at the outset, in a motive rising against a subdominant cycle of 5ths of Schumannesque intimacy (Ex. 13, *a*). The 'death-in-love' aspect is immediately counterstated, with a motto (Ex. 13, *b*) that becomes

Ex. 13

more explicit later on. This settles into a quaver accompaniment figure which, as in many of Vaughan Williams's songs of this period, notably 'Youth and love' from *Songs of Travel*, offsets the care and beauty of the vocal melody with a cushioning effect. As in the last song of the cycle, the harmonic impact of the figuration is of a coruscation borrowed from Wagner's *Waldweben* (compare Somervell's similar borrowing in *A Broken Arc*). It is allowed to expand harmonically only, as it were, with the modesty of a Rossetti portrait, while the voice part very slowly builds upwards in a line extended from Ex. 13, *a* to the note e″ . Here, however, the eyes of the beloved seem suddenly to be downcast, as the harmony evades us (Ex. 14). In coping with sonnet structure Vaughan Williams recognises not only the major division into eight lines plus six lines (octave and sestet) but also a less finite halving of the octave, and we reach a form of half-close at the end of the fourth line. What emerges in the music is, appro-

Ex. 14

priately, a somewhat disguised bar form (AAB), also employed for similar circum-stances in the fifth song, 'Death-in-love'. In each case the form is only recognised through matching cadence material. Here, after a further four lines of love-charged gentleness, the 'downcast eyes' moment returns, now in the dominant, having been prepared for by more explicit reference to *a* in its original form, which now soars rather than gradually climbs to the e″. The B section of the bar from, which follows, has to be both longer and emotionally less assured than A, for the inevitability of love ending in death is suddenly brooded upon. In a cor-respondingly sudden break to E flat, the overworked 'mourning' motive of a rising 4th and falling semitone from *Willow-Wood* anxiously flits across the lover's mind (Ex. 15, *c*) even though it is without the augmented-triad harmony of its original context. Its fourth statement dovetails with the typically Pre-Raphaelite line 'Nor image of thine eyes in any spring', couched in evocatively limpid piano chords with their 3rds in the voice only. Death imagery further

Ex. 15

darkens the lover's thoughts, until at the word 'death' itself the *b* motive of descending 3rds blazes out uninhibited, in a manner which leaves its lineage, from the 'downfall' motive in *Götterdammerung*, in no doubt at all (Ex. 16). It is revealing to see Vaughan Williams learning modes of expression from Wagner. After this, in the piano epilogue, the tenderness-of-love motive somewhat shyly reasserts itself: the juxtaposition of sweetness and menacing shadow is a curious one, but faithful to the poem's own progressions of thought and the essential theme of the whole cycle.

The second song, 'Silent noon', until recently the only one from the cycle that was at all well known, had in fact been completed and publicly performed while Vaughan Williams was still composing the rest of the work. Its position in the cycle, capturing a 'wing'd hour . . . dropt . . . from above', is in any case somewhat episodic, though deliberately and hauntingly so, especially at the end when the description without warning switches to the past tense: with a masterstroke characteristic of the composer (compare the first song) the melody hangs motionless on an upward octave, creating the realisation of a moment held for ever in the present tense of memory. The effect is similar to that of the concluding 'c'est l'heure exquise' of Fauré's 'La lune blanche', in *La bonne chanson*. Technically 'Silent noon' shows a grasp of old and new modes of expression to be consolidated further in *Songs of Travel*. The first four lines end traditionally enough with a strong modulation to the dominant, but the B flat chord switches with a thrill of heightened awareness to G, a mediant relationship exploited for sudden changes of consciousness throughout Vaughan Williams's music, as also in the works of Puccini, Debussy and most other post-Wagnerians. (Wagner,

Ex. 16

through his own development of the procedure, had given tonality a new, more existential lease of life, vital in early 20th-century developments.) The effect is later paralleled in 'Youth and love'. Here it is also followed through, for more mediant shifts ensue. A transitional cadence at the words 'far as the eye can pass' is repeated, in B major rather than minor, in the next line. After a semitonal slip into C minor a balancing submediant onto A flat at 'still as the hourglass' is achieved, followed by another onto F. But by this time it is as though, while the piano motive rises higher and higher, the acute awareness of the objects of nature which it represents is evaporating into love's ecstasy. With an inspired nakedness, as the spirit soars, the 'tenderness-of-love' motive *a* swells into a final section of caressing intimacy.

The most difficult song for the listener to grasp is the third, 'Love's minstrels', for Rossetti's imagery is elliptical and self-conscious, but it is the most obviously Pre-Raphaelite of the six, and helps to answer the question of what effect, if any, the Pre-Raphaelite movement had on English music, allowing for a delay of 40 years or so. The movement itself rejected the conventions of artistic representation of the previous three and a half centuries, and found in both mediaeval images and thoroughly contemporary subjects a straightforwardness and truth impossible in renaissance and later styles. In this poem Rossetti uses two symbols, the oboe (love's passion) and the harp (love's worship), and in representing them in the piano part Vaughan Williams himself rejects two comparably long-established musical conventions: four-part voice-leading harmony, and classical tonality. For the latter, he substitutes modality and block chord-shifts involving mediant relationships such as we have already encountered. His alternative to the former, though perhaps not so obvious, is here first explored in a manner highly significant to the development of his later style. The music is no longer concerned with harmonic or melodic development – a bold way of turning one's back on the 19th century. Instead there is a pure stasis: in the setting of the first six lines of the poem one dorian plagal cadence alone constitutes the harmony. The melodic lines in both accompaniment and voice, and the way in which they intertwine at certain points, are similarly inorganic: there is no concept of stress or growth through counterpoint and dissonance. The melisma on the word 'lady' and the triplet at 'Bid him depart', both ubiquitous fingerprints in later works, evoke instead a sense of timelessness borrowed from both plainsong and folksong. And in the two-part texture there is a new feeling for space and silence (Ex. 17).

The fourth song, 'Heart's haven', is curiously unstable. The opening gesture on which it is based, a contrary-motion scale ostinato unafraid of resulting dissonance, is bold in the manner of Holst. But it turns out to support a tonal and melodic structure with Puccinian chordal textures that is akin to the Romantic ballad, despite such sophisticated touches as the closely argued withholding of the cadence into G sharp minor at '. . . averted face, / Inexplicably filled with faint alarms' – a subtlety more readily associated with Brahms, Wolf or Strauss than with an English novice. Further careful manipulations of the material include the sudden flattened 7th at the words 'counter charms' and the subsequent beautifully compassionate voice part at 'And Love, our light at night', once again framed by the upward octave and cradled in a newly tender metamorphosis of the accompanimental figure. Nevertheless, there is an uncomfortable incongruity be-

Ex. 17

tween the blatancy of the musical structure's recapitulation of its first section in the last two lines and the private sensitivity of Rossetti's sonnet.

'Death-in-love', which follows, seems inevitable after the linking of the two themes in the first song, and the thematic processes are similar. A jaunty, heraldic motto reminiscent of Schumann darkens again into the *Willow-Wood* motive *c* at the holding up of the feather to the breathless lips, and at the final words 'and I am Death' we have the *fff* shock of the most blatant Wagnerism to be found in Vaughan Williams, a modified minor 9th subsiding, with the *Götterdämmerung* motive *b*, into a minor and similarly *Ring*-like version of the heraldic theme. Yet this does not only look back to Wagner: in its brutality it also foreshadows the moments of force and terror in Vaughan Williams's later music, such as the outburst as the sleeping city awakes in the *London Symphony*.

Death does not have the last word, however: in both the poetry and the music of the final song a new theme is introduced: 'love's last gift', symbolised by the laurel, is the creative faculty of immortalising memory in art. The motives representing love's tenderness (*a*) and death (*b*) are crystallised in this new permanence as they become a new theme, one of attained spirituality, to which Vaughan Williams returned throughout his life in various contexts in various works (Ex. 18, *d*). As it develops it shows correspondingly an attained freedom from harmonic constraint (Ex. 18, *e*) foreshadowing Vaughan Williams's mature style, but it also breathes a harmonic sweetness which pervades the song, culminating in a rising sequential shift at the words 'flowers to lure the bee'. The mood is peaceful, notwithstanding the strange harmonic oscillations expressing dark images of 'strange secret grasses' which 'lurk inviolably' under the sea. The last lines consolidate this peace. After an interruption of the flow of the song by the only open reference to *Willow-Wood* (dwelt on perhaps too melodramatically for this context of conquered rather than threatening anxiety), various earlier moments in the cycle pass before us: first the opening of 'Lovesight', with both the *a* and the *b* motives, then the opening of this final song, *d* presented in essence with the rising sequence mentioned above, then, growing out of it, *b* as it was used to

Ex. 18

cadence the repeated A section from 'Death-in-love', and finally *d* again, returning to its home key, F major, by a last mediant shift, and echoing itself in the
bass with Vaughan Williams's characteristic directness.

As we have seen, Vaughan Williams accomplished a good deal of stylistic
groundwork in *The House of Life. Songs of Travel*, which must have been composed soon after if not simultaneously (apart from the earlier 'Whither must I
wander') and was first performed in the same concert, achieves more by risking
less. The dominant impression is one of absolute integrity to the spirit of Stevenson. Vaughan Williams's capacity for empathy, which we have already observed
in relation to Rossetti, blots out the obvious dissimilarity between the frail, tuber-
cular, restlessly wandering and sensitively observing poet and the stolid, slowly
achieving, upper-middle-class composer, and produces instead a work as fertile in
its Romantic wayfaring images for early-20th-century England as was *Die
Winterreise* for early-19th-century Vienna. The images are different –
Edwardian and inter-war England dreamt of open roads, gently flowing rivers,
thatched cottages, Irish country lasses and gipsy caravans with canaries (presented with particular affection in *The Wind in the Willows*) rather than frozen
streams, linden trees and hurdy-gurdies – but the Wanderer impulse, associated
with both joy and sorrow, pervades Somervell (in the *Shropshire Lad* story) and
Vaughan Williams, Schubert and Schumann alike. Perhaps it is part of an
escapist dream; perhaps it stems from a desire to experience all things, to observe
rather than judge.

Like Schubert, Vaughan Williams sets store by his musical tramping figures as a force running through the cycle; the pulse of 'The vagabond', which Stevenson actually composed 'to an air of Schubert', is instantly memorable. Even more than in *The House of Life*, mediant relationships govern the tonal structure, and in a rougher manner that indicates deepening contact with folksong, with an ascetic, mystic impulse such as is expressed, if only later, in Holst's music, and perhaps with Puccini. Stevenson's ending, with a repetition of the second stanza after the third, is a boon, for its corresponding musical recapitulation (making the overall form AABA) gives a sense of the endless plod of the traveller. The text of the second song, 'Let beauty awake', is in one of the springing dactylic metres at which Stevenson excelled; Vaughan Williams renders it with surprising grace in $\frac{9}{8}$ over a buoyant accompaniment. The musical beauty is very selfconscious, including one figure which sounds like Butterworth (Ex. 19), but it is finally left

Ex. 19

hanging in the air by the dorian modality of the figure, which ends on F sharp in a key signature of four sharps; there is surely an erotic stress in the last lines of the second stanza which the composer either failed to notice or deliberately left unpointed. 'The roadside fire', which follows, is technically effortless in a manner rare in Vaughan Williams. The wayfaring figuration in the accompaniment has speeded up from a plod in the first song to a jog-trot: we are evidently in a landscape of ponies and gipsy caravans. We are also now in an immediately attractive harmonic world which verges on decadence: such effects as the added-6th harmony at 'toys for your delight', the intermediate dominant 9th in the next line (Ex. 20) (which Parry would have censured, judging from his remarks on Grieg in *The Art of Music*), and the boogie-woogie bass accompanying the second stanza,

Ex. 20

Ex. 21

especially where it varies the pattern under the former added-6th chord (Ex. 21, third bar), all tend in that direction, but are fabricated with a fastidiousness unusual in Vaughan Williams and look directly forward to some of the best songs of Ireland and Warlock. It seems a pity that the momentum of these first two stanzas, intercepted for the more lyrical third, is never fully regained, despite a short reference to it in the piano epilogue. 'Youth and love' contains the emotional core of the cycle. One of Vaughan Williams's later fingerprints, triplets continually alternating with duplets, appears in the accompaniment with affecting fluidity (Ex. 22), under a vocal line of great beauty (or above it, if the voice is male).

Ex. 22

Again the upward octave ('Nestle in orchard bloom') stands out; so do other turns of phrase, especially at the line 'Call him with lighted lamp'. Then at the *animando* section, where the wayfarer's eternal predicament of allegiance to lovers or to freedom is stressfully expounded, heavily transformed versions of the opening lines of 'The vagabond' and 'The roadside fire' are heard in the piano. The whole treatment verges on the maudlin as the second reference lapses into a cycle-of-5ths sequence, but it evaporates just in time and the song ends touchingly with its initial figuration and the repetition of 'is gone'. The next song, 'In dreams', is something of a chromatic experiment, too overlaid with self-pity to be an entirely successful reading of the poem; it is difficult to see where Vaughan Williams may have got this style from. 'The infinite shining heavens', however, perfectly transmits the beauty of the poem's conceit, combining a harp-like melodic and harmonic simplicity with considerable sophistication of phrasing: the poem's metre, the poem's phrasing, the music's metre and the music's melodic phrase structure (itself somewhat irregular, partly owing to the placing of the triplets) all pull in slightly different directions, and are different again for the musical recapitulation in the final stanza. The effect of the ending is perfectly gauged; it sounds right, even though it is difficult to explain why the music has to go up as the star comes down.

'Whither must I wander', though probably composed two or more years before the other songs, is surely the finest. Maybe its success was what prompted Vaughan Williams to build a cycle around it. The style, resembling that of 'Linden Lea', is clearly of Germanic parentage (Jacobs: 158), and borrows (as does Stanford's, e.g. in 'La belle dame sans merci') the austere folk-ballad textures of Schubert and Brahms, with their bare 3rds and horn-calls in the accompaniment. The song's strength lies in its entirely unsentimental approach to Stevenson's poem, which music could so easily have made into a nostalgic epitaph to the poet's sadness in life, in the manner of some of Schumann's Heine settings:

> Fair the day shine as it shone on my childhood;
> Fair shine the day on the house with open door.
> Birds come and cry there and twitter in the chimney –
> But I go for ever and come again no more.

But the music turns its back on these memories with firm finality: there is no musing piano epilogue. 'Bright is the ring of words' is built on a downward chiming motive (Ex. 23) which is a variant of Vaughan Williams's favourite

Ex. 23

motto (Ex. 18, *d*); it is an early example of a song by him with a rather heavy-textured religious atmosphere, perhaps too moralising in tone to be comfortable in this cycle. However, the drawing out of a piquant point in the harmony of the *Ur*-motive at the end of the second stanza has the apt and touching effect of twisting the song from the tone of an epitaph to that of a memento of love (Ex. 24). The epilogue, 'I have trod the upward and the downward slope', seems to have been composed half a century after the other songs, with rather less thematic summary than in *The House of Life* (or with different purpose, for there is no cathartic theme here). It looks gently back over the wanderer's episodes, starting in a chant-like, catechismic manner, and quotes themes from 'The vagabond', 'Whither must I wander' and 'Bright is the ring of words'. In the last three bars the slower tempo of the tramping bass from 'The vagabond' may seem to make it

Ex. 24

rather too loose an evocation of the original context to be wholly effective. However, the point is perhaps to suggest a broader spiritual perspective for the traveller's journey, one that has links with the close both of Part 1 of Elgar's *The Dream of Gerontius* and of Act IV of Stanford's opera *The Travelling Companion*. Edward Dent would have ascribed the inspiration for all three works to the transformation music in *Parsifal*, Act I, to judge from his astute comment on Holst's 'Saturn' (Carey: 97).

Songs of Travel, with its rather naïve outdoor youthfulness, and the heavily draped, elegiac outpourings of the early Frank Bridge were equally children of their diffuse decade. The Bridge songs were not forward- or outward-looking. In *Songs of Travel* Vaughan Williams at least took the opportunity to enlarge his harmonic palate and communicate a number of accessible poetic images to a large public; yet he did not explore new emotional areas, being more polished but rather less ambitious in this respect than he was in *The House of Life*. His emotional watershed came only after his two years' work on the *English Hymnal* and his study with Ravel. 'I . . . wrote . . . a song cycle with several atmospheric effects', he admitted (1963: 191) – somewhat modestly, for the 'atmospheric effects' of *On Wenlock Edge* are part of a radically altered approach to technique.

V

The Edwardian age (I)

When Queen Victoria died, twelve days into the 20th century, the mounting tension which had accompanied the final years of an extraordinarily long era snapped. Few were naïve enough to plunge into the new century with unqualified optimism, for Victorian stability had been waning since 1870, the year of the Franco-Prussian war, referred to by Tennyson in his preface to Sullivan's song-cycle *The Window* as 'the dark shadow of these days'. Bismarck's threatening consolidation of Germany and the grim business of the Boer war (1899–1902) had undermined confidence in the political field, whilst 19th-century ideology and practical ethics had been repeatedly challenged by aesthetic developments. As far back as the late 1840s the Pre-Raphaelite Brotherhood had promulgated a style of living whose second phase, led by William Morris and Edward Burne-Jones, continued to be felt well into the 1900s. From about 1870 the French literary and artistic movements of symbolism and impressionism, anglicised in the 'aesthetic movement' which began around 1880, and in the last decade of the century the arrival of Ibsen's plays, with their neurotic and rebellious heroines, fuelled a vigorous reaction against all Victoria stood for. 'Aestheticism' soon disintegrated, taking on the elements of tragedy in its final disastrous crisis, the trial of Oscar Wilde (1895). Already in the early 1890s a lethargic, languishing pessimism and sensual decadence had descended on those of aesthetic sensibilities, and Wilde's imprisonment caused a feeling of tiredness and collapse; 'Our unfortunate century was born middle-aged', to quote William Gaunt (1945: 182), who also describes how the trial hastened a selfconscious return to normality:

> An exaggerated robustness was one of the consequences. Poets, no longer velvet-collared, absinthe-sipping, were now a hearty and virile race, tweed-clad, pipe-smoking, beer-drinking, Sussex-downs-tramping. They broke into rousing choruses, discarded subtlety for the sake of a cheery lilt, and proclaimed that Philistines could also sing.
> The subject of sex was buried beneath fresh layers of discretion (*ibid.*: 180).

Much of this reaction was to be strongly reflected in music; Percy Grainger is a case in point (though he was hardly discreet about sex). On the other hand, to those whom the subversive odours of aestheticism had never permeated, the death of Victoria brought a feeling of relief; the rigid moral codes with which she was identified could at last be discarded, and in their place came a sense of irresponsibility, fostered by the reputation of Edward VII. At last people could be 'amused'.

Thus reactions polarised. One man's irresponsibility might be counterbalanced by another's apprehension, as experienced by Cyril Scott:

... the news of her [Queen Victoria's] passing produced in me a curious sensation, which might best be described as a feeling of insecurity ... I was a little apprehensive as to the future of England under the next sovereign ... I have a vague premonition that something dire *might* happen when she had gone. Is it far-fetched to say that thirteen years later my premonition proved correct? (1924: 51)

Everywhere there was the recognition that time would not wait and technology was advancing relentlessly; the Edwardian holiday must be enjoyed to the full, for it would not last; the things one loved must be savoured before they disappeared. John Middleton Murry's account of his reaction to the *Poems* (1906) and *The Listeners* (1912) of Walter de la Mare gives us a vivid impression of the spirit in which such verse was imbibed:

... in those far-off days, the sadness of de la Mare's poems was sweet indeed ... The peace of eternity is a thought not unwelcome to those who feel themselves fairly secure in time; to contemplate the transience of youth and beauty adds a precarious and subtle, but very real overtone of delight, to those who still possess them ...

It may be that there was in those years, – though my conscious mind had no inkling of it – some deep premonitory perturbation by the havoc to come which gave an added reverberation to the poet's silvery pipings of fragile mortality, so that they searched our souls. But they performed their office tenderly, and if they disquieted us, the unease was within our range of comprehensible and tenable emotion. It roused tremors within the frame of our experience; it did not shake and shatter the very frame itself ... Life's brevity, for those who had, as most had in those days, what the insurance companies call the normal expectation of life – was but a mote to trouble the mind's eye. But when, in a few years, Death's steady but almost homely scythe was changed into a combine harvester, the emotional pattern established through generations was crazed: the old rhythm of human experience was disrupted.

To this old and precious emotional pattern de la Mare's poetry belongs ... But the time came when, for millions of men and women there was precious little journeying towards the bourne of death. They were blown and blasted into it, burned into it, liquefied into it, starved into it ...

That will explain the feeling, now so strong in me, that de la Mare's poetry before 1914 was the last modern poetry that I could entirely and unfeignedly enjoy (1948: 45–7).

It is just this sense of precariousness that is shown in the attitude of the folksong collectors. 'Whatever is done', wrote Vaughan Williams to the *Morning Post* on 1 December 1903, 'must be done quickly. Every day some old village singer dies, and with him there probably die half a dozen beautiful melodies which are lost to the world for ever; if we would preserve what still remains we must set about it at once' (Kennedy, 1964: 36) – though his anxiety was not entirely justified, for 80 years later some of the songs, including industrial lyrics which he and Cecil Sharp, with their pastoral preoccupation, never noticed, are still being sung. But in other respects the undermining of traditional values was not illusory. English Liberalism, weakened by the suffragette movement and the industrial strikes of 1910–14, could not long survive. Germany's growing and restless bellicosity soon had international ramifications (encapsulated in Thomas Mann's *The Magic Mountain*), however blind to them the English populace at large may have remained right up to 1914. Within this multifarious picture of movement the British empire could be seen to be at once in expansion and decline; this was felt in Elgar's music, and was made cruelly vivid to popular consciousness when, within one month in the spring of 1912, Captain Scott perished in conquering the Antarctic and 1500 perished when the Arctic conquered the *Titanic*. Both events were commemorated in music, the former in the 'Thalassa' Symphony of Somervell (whose granddaughter was to marry Scott's song), the latter by numerous elegies (see the correspondence columns of the *Musical Times*, January–May 1973)

English musical growth was particularly confusing during this short era because its renaissance in the late 19th century had become a turbulent adolescence, culminating in the fruitful years 1912–13, with the Balfour Gardiner concerts as a kind of coming-out party and Diaghilev's London ballet and opera season of 1914 as a sudden and passionate liaison. It was a period, perhaps more than any other, of susceptibility to wide-ranging influences: with so much Romantic experience to catch up on, composers were attempting, after their digestion of Brahms and Wagner, to absorb the nationalist styles of Tchaikovsky, his fellow Russians, Dvořák, Grieg, Verdi and Smetana, all of whom had been heard in London from the 1880s, and for the first time to imbibe the French spirit of the period between Gounod and Debussy. Minor composers such as Glazunov, Arensky and Moszkowski sometimes made a greater impact than the major ones. The ever-controversial Strauss was given a fair hearing, though Reger and Mahler seem to have been known merely as names to execrate. It was also an era of remarkable receptivity to poetry, and settings began to appear of the Pre-Raphaelites, Swinburne, Stevenson, de la Mare, Hardy, Housman, Dowson, lesser-known 16th- and 17th-century verse, and foreign or exotic texts such as translations from the Chinese (the earliest set to music being those of Herbert Giles). Developments were further moulded by the rediscovery of folksong, of the past (Sir Richard Terry began his influential liturgical performances of renaissance polyphony in Westminster Cathedral in 1901), and of the amateur and his environment, as witnessed in the competitive festival movement; by the ascendancy of the fashionable resorts (the Bournemouth Municipal Orchestra gave symphony concerts from 1895, emulated by the Duke of Devonshire's private orchestra at Eastbourne and by similar bodies in Brighton, Harrogate, Bath and Torquay); and by English musical nationalism, focussed in the Society of British Composers (founded 1905) and the activities of the Musical League of 1908–9 and 1912.

It was not, however, an age which distinguished readily between the shallow and the profound: sensation was often more highly prized than sensibility. After the war a number of composers who had ridden high on the Edwardian tide were to find themselves and their ideals stranded, clinging pathetically to superficial idioms which had faded in the space of a few short years. Four of these composers will be examined briefly, more on account of the bulk of their output than because of their contribution to English song, which in each case was of very doubtful value. They are Scott, Bantock, Holbrooke and Boughton.

Cyril Scott was a vivid Edwardian. Intense but effortless and prolific in all he attempted, from free love to yoga, he devoted himself increasingly to writing books on occultism after the first world war, and lived long enough to pulish two autobiographies, in 1924 and 1969. He was socially accomplished and had impressive charm and sincerity; accounts of him by his contemporaries show that, however little they may have understood his interests, they took him seriously. His acquaintances included Arnold Bennett, Henry James, George Moore, George Bernard Shaw, H. G. Wells, Debussy, Fauré, Alma Mahler, Milhaud, Ravel, Strauss and Stravinsky. Stefan George, whom he met at Frankfurt in 1896, particularly influenced him, being 'the first to awaken in me a love of poetry, which in turn had at one time a considerable influence on my music and acted for me as an inspiration' (C. Scott, 1969: 76). A set of immature George songs from 1899, *Sänge eines Fahrenden Spielmanns* (*Songs of a Wandering Minstrel*), survives in manuscript, showing a surprisingly strong affinity with the naïve folk background of the German *Lied* and none at all with English song. It was George who introduced Scott to the poetry of Ernest Dowson, 'the poet', as Scott said in a letter of 1959, 'that inspired me most at the start of my career' (Magraw: 289), the poet whose world-weary decadence represented just one of Scott's self-styled 'soul-states'; he made 21 song settings of Dowson's verse between 1900 and 1915. The friendship with George came to an end at George's suggestion, after the poet had confessed himself in love with Scott, who, being heterosexual, could not reciprocate. After Dowson Scott's literary concerns were varied, but he did set to music as solo songs 15 poems by Rosamund Marriott Watson (C. Scott, 1924: 74–9), wife of the novelist H. B. Marriott Watson, admitting that, while he greatly admired her better verse, 'Rosamund often permitted herself to drift into poetic platitudes in order to reap a few guineas from the editors of magazines' (*ibid*.: 75). He himself was not above a mercenary interest; he contracted with Elkin in the early years of the century for the un-limited supply of songs and piano pieces, and made Rosamund Watson write an extra stanza for his popular 'Blackbird's song' so as to furnish the approved three.

Scott's problem was the gulf between his aesthetic aims and his creative execu-tion. Around 1899, he wrote, 'My ideal was to invent a species of pre-Raphaelite music, to consist mostly of common chords placed in such a way as to savour of very primitive church music, thereby, as I thought, reminding its listeners of old pictures. I even wrote a Symphony and a pretentious Magnificat along those lines . . . ' (*ibid*.: 25). In the early George songs he did sustain an adolescent emotional sincerity by these methods, sensitively matching George's extremely simple verse (Ex. 1, from 'Prelude'), but such minimalist candour was incapable of serving Scott's creative and aesthetic ambitions, and he never explored the power of common chords to evoke strange realms of experience as Vaughan Williams and Holst did later.

Many of Scott's involvements and aspirations now seem glib and facile. His biographer's account of his turning to poetry is a case in point, and could be applied to other English composers of the period:

> . . . whenever tired of writing music he has turned to poetry, which interests and delights him not a whit less than music. He regards it as another form of music, and hazards the opinion that the poetry of a musician must always have a distinc-tive flavour about it . . . It was at about the age of twenty-one that Cyril Scott began writing verse (Hull,: 1918: 19).

Half a dozen volumes of his verse were published before and during the first world

Ex. 1

war (he set 11 of his own poems as solo songs, Goossens set one, and Norman Peterkin set one other, 'Since loneliness is long'), as well as translations of Baudelaire's *Les fleurs du mal* (1909) and of a selection from George's works (1910). Translating Baudelaire must have heightened Scott's awarenes of the value accorded by symbolist poetic aesthetics to individual words and phrases prized more for their sensuous properties than for sense; in the music of what he pretentiously termed his 'non-tonal' period (beginning with the Violin Sonata of 1907 and at its height in the Piano Quintet) the 'Pre-Raphaelite' chains of common chords developed, predictably, into a pseudo-symbolist style 'derived from regarding each chord as though it were in a separate key' (*ibid*.: 128). This amounted to a continuous indigestible string of higher-power harmonies, 7ths, 9ths and upwards. At the same time he saw fit, under the influence of modern metrical experiments in verse (to which he himself contributed), to abandon regular metre: the clotted harmonies occur in mixtures of $\frac{5}{8}$, $\frac{7}{8}$ and $\frac{3}{8}$ bars, making music devoid of direction or rise and fall in tension. Scott's technique was not even original, for his friend and fellow student Percy Grainger had pioneered it in 1901 in his extraordinary *Hill Song no. 1* for 23 wind instruments.

Not surprisingly, Scott's 'serious' works had no staying power; they may have been approved of in theory as the legitimate avant-garde, and for a while he was termed, most misleadingly, 'the English Debussy' (E. Evans, 1923: 208; C. Scott, 1924, 101–3), but the British public had no desire to hear them more than once. One looks in vain for an independent and non-commercial contemporary statement of belief in him as a major composer or seminal influence. Only Eugene Goossens, as late as 1951 (:299), was prepared to defend his large-scale works, though it is not apparent that he performed them. Scott's bland willingness to parcel his output into 'trifles' and 'serious works' was less a recognition of the growing rift between 'popular' and 'classical' musical cultures than a misguided attempt at self-advertisement; in fact the songs differ more in scale than in style from his chamber and orchestral works.

Even the songs were not at all easy to promote, despite Elkin's backing. In his biography Hull admits that 'each year a larger number of vocalists are recognising the merit of the Scott songs, but it has taken the courage and enterprise of a few more enlightened artists to bring this tardily about. Especially have we to thank Miss Grainger-Kerr, Miss Jean Waterston and Miss Beryl Freeman for actually forcing the English public to accept Cyril Scott' (:178). There were singers who never did perform his music, including Gervase Elwes, despite his friendship with Scott (C. Scott, 1969: 90).

After 1920 Scott gradually composed less. His output of published songs sank from five or ten a year to one or two, with hardly anything after 1928. Increasingly he turned to writing prose, surely his real 'serious works'. At the age of 25 he had come into contact with occultism and oriental mysticism, and he published upwards of 24 books and pamphlets on subjects of which his occult knowledge gave him a unique if unconventional awareness. A handful of these works is still in print; his music is not.

As for the songs, they vary from 'Trafalgar', 'The little foreigner' and 'Don't come in sir, please!', which really belong in the music hall, and 'The ballad singer', which would make an excellent operetta or musical theatre number, to the solo scena with orchestra 'Rima's call to the birds' (W. H. Hudson), a late work written for the Australian soprano Gertrude Johnson and performed at Grainger's suggestion in the 1929 Festival of British Music at Harrogate. In this the original orchestration and the use of figurations and of wordless vocalising to conjure up the magic of Rima's call produce an impressive effect, somewhere between Debussy and the Vaughan Williams of *The Lark Ascending*. In the 'Idyll' for voice and flute the voice part has a similar mixture of words and vocalisation, and in both parts the virtuoso writing is in a melodic style implying advanced harmony. Elsewhere, however, Scott too often relies on simplistic piano formulae, particularly the strings of parallel chords already mentioned (see especially 'Mist' and 'Night wind'), and the over-use of dominant 9ths ('Water-lilies') and compound-4th harmonies ('Arise, my love', 'A March requiem', 'She's but a lassie yet', 'Sundown' and the arabesque accompanimental figures of 'In the silver moonbeams', which is an arrangement of the traditional *Au clair de la lune* tune). The piano formulae lapse into ostinati suggestive of narcotic laziness in 'Villanelle' (Ex. 2) and in the more progressive context of 'The watchman', where two chords (Ex. 3) are repeated, in the first instance for 26 bars, under a somewhat free-ranging and unrelated melody. These ostinati seldom create impressive effects, and tend to accompany *cantabile* voice parts which have been superimposed like instrumental obbligati with little care for the word-setting, as in 'Lady June'. Occasionally this use of the voice as the richest possible vehicle of melody and harmony (in contrast to, for example, Debussy's recitative-like songs, which Scott disliked) yields effective results, as in 'Lullaby' – but here the words are extremely simple. Elsewhere, particularly in 'To-

Ex. 2

Ex. 3

morrow', 'The garden of memory', 'Our Lady of Violets' and 'Villanelle of firelight', very indifferent poetry is given drab word-setting, dampening the total effect. Sometimes he makes a successful stylistic departure, as in 'The ballad of fair Helen', where he reaches towards Bax, but in general he writes merely a lyric recognisably rooted in the ballad tradition of unadventurous strophic form, with just enough harmonic invention to save it from banality. 'April love' is of this kind, as is 'From afar', where the formula reveals a slight affinity with Fauré, but without Fauré's breadth of modulation or contrapuntal motivation; added notes are paraded without restraint.

In most of Scott's work the price paid for being a 'harmonic' composer at this culturally diffuse period is that, probably without realising it, he detaches himself from the rapidly self-refining aesthetic sensibility of 'serious' song and shows himself, at least in his earlier works, more in step with 'popular' developments. The equal note values of his voice parts in many of the Dowson settings, undoubtedly a valid response to the conversational intimacy of the poet's love-verses, betray a musical conception which would be most at home in cabaret, and they need to be sung with a concomitant rubato and confidingness (Ex. 4, from 'Autumnal'). In 'Retrospect', which on its own terms, though not on those of the recital song of this period, is an extremely well articulated piece of writing, Scott shows a strong affinity with popular song-writers such as Kern or Ivor Novello; it might sound highly effective sung by, say, Frank Sinatra (Ex. 5). It is worth noting that there the harmonic colouring amounts to no more than an improvisatory infusion of higher-power chords which sideslip semitonally from or back to a traditional cadential structure firmly rooted in C major (see the passage at 'All the old anger setting us apart' in Ex. 5). Many of Scott's songs are in C major, so his harmonic epithets often reveal themselves as empirical explorations of the black notes of the keyboard, and, as with Ireland, the parallel with jazz procedures is notable.

Ex. 4

Ex. 5

Ex. 5 (cont.)

In his later songs Scott lost this emotional frankness, and through its vain attempt to develop a greater resource of non-directional harmonic colouring his idiom could by 1932 be described, in Sorabji's words, as one 'which underneath its trumpery finery of ninths, elevenths, added sixths, joss-sticks, papier-Asie Orientalism and pinchbeck Brummagem-Benares nick-nackery, oozes with glutinous commonplace' (:63).

Sorabji's invective might also be applied to the less successful works of Sir Granville Bantock. Although their styles are easily distinguishable, Scott and Bantock were similarly motivated by eccentric and exotic aesthetic impulses, which soon seemed quaint after the war. They were also friends. Goossens gives this colourful account of them on holiday at Harlech in 1918:

> Their chief interests, at that time, were herbalism and Yogi [sic] . . . Walking among the sand-dunes one morning, I came upon the two men, one heavy and bearded, the other slim and ascetic, sitting cross-legged, Oriental-wise, in the hollow of a dune – and in a state of nature. The first was seemingly endeavouring to tie knots in the muscles of his abdomen, and the second was trying to swallow a length of solid flexible rubber tubing . . . (:138).

Bantock was born in London. His father, a doctor, forced him into chemical engineering, but Granville soon began to devote all available time to the study of Wagner and Liszt, on whose styles he modelled his own (which differed in this respect from the more Gallic lightness of Scott). In July 1889 he saw *Parsifal* and *Tristan* at Bayreuth; his passion for Liszt, fanned by Liszt's last visit to London in 1886, was nurtured by his composition teacher Frederick Corder at the RAM (which his father finally allowed him to enter in 1888), and found expression in his *Satan Monologues*, successfully submitted for the Macfarren (composition) Scholarship in 1889. The RAM at this period breathed an air of freedom that the RCM lacked, but its undisciplined methods of study aggravated problems of prolixity in the music of the one notably successful composer it produced, Arnold Bax, and nurtured the chaotic impotence of its most notorious failure, Joseph Holbrooke. On Bantock the effects were colourful. Under its auspices he studied the organ, piano, clarinet, violin, viola, horn, tuba and timpani, but not the classics; Boult's story (:57) of his enthusiastically discovering the Schubert Quintet in late middle age is symptomatic, as Boult points out, of an ill-balanced musical background and disposition. He left the RAM with a versatile technique of orchestration, like Bax, but, like Holbrooke, without a livelihood. With innate re-sourcefulness, however, he founded in 1893 *The New Quarterly Musical Review*, which flourished for three years. His article in it on Confucianism and music was the first manifestation of his lifelong love of the orient, initially gratified by a world tour with the George Edwardes revue *The Gaiety Girl* (September 1894 – December 1895) from which he brought back a monkey, eventually donated to the London Zoo, and an imagination full of exotic yearnings. Throughout his life he was prey to periodic obsessions, and in this respect he had, like Grainger, the constitution, endearing naïvety, and unrestrainable enthusiasms of a child. At various times he worked through Scottish, Hebridean, Celtic, Napoleonic and Imperial Roman phases, some of which found expression in his music.

His passion for the orient and its philosophies, however, as his daughter Myrrha stresses in her biography, was an altogether more serious involvement, 'the result of two things: his deep-rooted romantic approach to life, combined with a great curiosity in the field of literature, which soon led him to discover the sages of the East' (:33). In 1896–8, during their engagement, his fiancée, Helen(a) von Schweitzer, a poetess with whom he shared this affinity, wrote the texts for his 36 *Songs of the East* (in six cycles, on Arabia, Japan, Egypt, Persia, India and China). Many of Bantock's 300 song settings were to texts by Helen (see the list of his songs). Together they developed a life-style that was curious yet symptomatic of their diverse period. The illustrations in their daughter's biography show houses impossibly cluttered with Greek statues, Chinese Buddhas, gongs, monstrous ornaments and grotesque pieces of furniture. Not surprisingly, the Bantocks made an odd impression on fashionable Edgbaston, which Myrrha Bantock is at pains to rectify:

> I soon discovered that the Bantocks were considered odd because we did not conform to the accepted pattern . . . The Pre-Raphaelite movement, and the sycophants who followed in the wake of that new approach to art, produced in England a type of pseudo-bohemianism which was much practised. It has become a way of life for many who have neither the ability nor the sincerity of the real artist. My parents, G. B. in particular, were driven by the force of their inspiration . . . Any odd behaviour was always the genuine outcome of their devotion towards creative work . . . The fact that both Helena and Granville came from conventional homes themselves proved the sincerity which prompted their actions (:84).

Did Granville Bantock possess 'the ability [and] the sincerity of the real artist', or was his entire creative life one vast act of compulsive escapism, the reaction against an academic and administrative career in the Midlands? Both are true. His Romantic attachment to the East and to the past was unquestionably strong and sincere; it could combine successfully with his career because it *was* a Romantic attachment, in which the remoteness of his sources of inspiration was a vital part of the creative chemistry (as it was for Walter de la Mare). The Edwardian era was perhaps the last in which such escapism could find geographical embodiment.

Thus Bantock's music thrived between 1900 and 1914, was generally considered a healthy force, and even gave him a wide reputation as a modernist. An appreciation of the songs even of this period, however, raises considerable problems.

Bantock, like Bax, was primarily a large-scale composer. Fluency and length never troubled him, and at a time when many English composers were looking for verse small enough to fit their tiny lyrical confines (e.g. Housman's), Bantock's difficulty was to find texts big enough to carry his broad-gestured style intact. For many of his songs he has to split his idiom up, so to speak, into insubstantial parts: for the domesticity of Browning (discussed in Chapter III), comfortable Germanic warmth; for the various sets of *Songs for Children*, facile tunefulness; for religiosity in 'The festal hymn of Judith', half-modal successions of common chords. Love-lyrics prompt a period sentimentality, as in 'In a myrtle shade'; occasionally a forced originality provokes a styleless mess, from which 'By the rivers of Babylon' and 'Cradle song' suffer; sometimes he surprisingly fails to meet the challenge of poetry, especially nature poetry, that demands breadth, as in 'Carrowmore' and 'Longing'. 'I go to prove my soul' is under-composed. A frequent shortcoming is a virtuoso voice part which histrioni-cally distends the poetry, for instance in 'Love's secret'. The *Three Nocturnes* inhabit a far higher world than such banal trivialities as 'Morgan le Fay', 'Little Papoose Lake', 'My fairy lover' and 'The parting', though they are as a whole rather obscure and Bantock seems at a loss to know what to make of the verse in lines such as

> And deep embedded in the blackened shroud,
> The night-born children dangerously play with dark-eyed secrets.

Bantock's true spiritual home was the hedonism of the Near East, of ancient Greece and Persia. In the Epicurean philosophical yearnings of FitzGerald's *The Rubáiyát of Omar Khayyám* he could allow his opulence full rein, and his setting of the entire translation for chorus, soloists and orchestra in three parts (1906–9) is undeniably a *tour de force*. It became his most celebrated work. In the field of song four works can be singled out on the same grounds. One is the *Five Ghazals of Hafiz*. Another is *Ferishtah's Fancies*, settings of 12 lyrics and an epilogue by Browning's imaginary Persian poet for tenor and orchestra. The scale is very large, the texture sumptuous, and the general impression one of unrelieved sultriness, heavily dependent on Wagner, with one *Tristan*-like climax after another, but with a serious lack of overall direction. Performance today is unthinkable, though the work was once well known as sung by Frank Mullings. The same hallmarks characterise the *Pagan Chants*, also for tenor and orchestra, with words by Wilfrid Thorley. These are large-scale scenas, whose richness of decorative detail in both text and music puts them close to *Omar Khayyám*. Each is provided with an explanatory caption. No. 2, for instance, is headed

> Scene: – A woodland glade in Arcadia. A Faun pursued by wrathful Dryads whose Queen he has slain, creeps from the shelter of a thicket. He is weary with pain and fatigue, but alert for danger and ready for instant flight.

Whereupon the tenor, in the role of the Faun, tells his harrowing story and, at the end, 'disappears into the bushes'. Whether Bantock wished the performance to be acted is not clear. The caption to no. 3 begins, 'Scene:– The same'; no. 4 is odd, for its lengthy Straussian orchestral postlude seems to suggest a Faun who has lost his despondency, without anything in the text to warrant this.

The *Pagan Chants* are no more than curiosities, but the same cannot be said of *Sappho*. *Sappho* was published by Breitkopf & Härtel in 1906, a year after *Ferishtah's Fancies*. (In the same year Bantock completed Part I of *Omar Khayyám*, an indication not only of where *Sappho*'s stylistic and atmospheric affinities lie but also of the speed with which he worked.) It is an enormous cycle – surely the longest with English words, for it lasts an hour – for contralto and orchestra. The vocal score, beautifully printed on creamy paper, takes up 86 pages, each of which has a large margin occupied by the same decorative framing motive. In the coloured cover illustration incense is wafted from a brazier that stands on a tripod between two pillars of a temple portico, from which we look out into the night on the Homeric wine-dark sea. The title lettering is *art nouveau* (less an Edwardian trait than a result of continental publication), and includes the Greek, ΣΑΠΦΩ.

Sappho consists of a prelude and nine songs. The vocal range is wide, g to g″, and the orchestra full-size. The texts were selected by Helen Bantock from Henry Wharton's literal translations of Sappho's poems, first published in 1885. She skilfully linked many fragments, some of them mere short phrases, to give a sequence of highly emotional dramatic monologues. Many of the phrases are repeated excessively, but always in accordance with the nature of the music. The cycle has two shortcomings: a prelude from which most of the best parts of the subsequent songs are drawn, and which is thus in danger of seeming a premature microcosm of the work, and a mood which seldom varies from languishing Lesbian passion. Nevertheless, it succeeds, owing to Bantock's hypnotic flow. The prelude, of considerable length, is carried on effortless waves of sensuality that subsume its juxtaposed sections. When these sections recur later in the cantata – nearly always *en bloc*, note for note and at the same pitch – most of them seem fresh because they are little more than rhapsodic improvisational plays with compound chords, and in their new surroundings their effectiveness is maintained by more conventionally thematic sections flanking them to make an overall arch form. Indeed most of the songs are basically ternary. In the first three Bantock is careful not to use any material from the prelude, whereas in the later ones greater distance from the originals justifies longer recurrences.

Sensuality is present in *Sappho* from the first bar, as is the harp which portrays it; Bantock counteracts it with a strange little monodic motive, a rare example of restraint and one of the few places where anything less immediate than vehement passion is evoked (Ex. 6). Sappho's sexual feelings are carefully portrayed in the prelude; there is never any masculine aggression about them, but rather sustained, quivering yearning, borrowed intelligently from Tchaikovsky (Ex. 7), from Rachmaninov in languishing mood (Ex. 8), or, in the decorated return of the first song's main theme, from Wagner's Brangäne in her watchtower (Ex. 9). There is little story. In the first song Sappho invokes the goddess of love, in the second she remembers her past lover, Atthis, in the third a spring evening heralds the nightingale, and in the fourth she apostrophises love. The fifth song is the emotional crux. Its own central crisis is prepared by a beautiful passage of nocturnal fragrance (Ex. 10), leading to a Puccinian theme of wild passion (Ex. 11) which had appeared in the prelude and which twice builds to a searing climax:

I yearn and seek –
I know not what to do –
And I flutter like a child after her mother,
For Love masters my limbs, and shakes me,

The core of the cycle, which follows, is another section from the prelude (Ex. 12), and after this has died down the Lesbian conclusion is drawn in a reprise of the opening section:

Alas! –
I shall be ever maiden –
Neither honey nor bee for me.

Ex. 6

Ex. 7

Ex. 8

Ex. 8 (cont.)

Ex. 9

Ex. 10

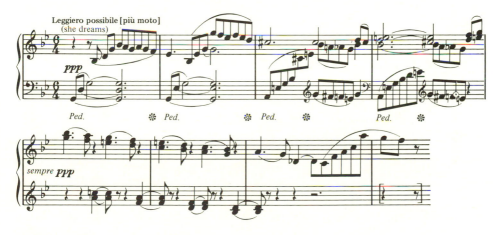

Ex. 11

Ex. 12

The crisis past, in the sixth song Sappho's lover has herself taken a (male) lover. Sappho's passion for her is unabated. The seventh song is a lament for dying Adonis (dying love?); the eighth, 'Bridal song', portrays a happy bride and groom on their wedding day; finally, in the ninth, the poet invokes the Cyprian goddess and the Muse of poetry, presumably to sublimate her passion, as her voice fades into the distance.

The charming outer sections of 'Bridal song' are not unlike Mahler's 'Von der Schönheit'. Yet clearly *Sappho* cannot compare with *Das Lied von der Erde* except in terms of date and scale, and for a song-cycle of Mahler's intensity England had to wait until Warlock wrote *The Curlew*. Yet *Sappho* is more than a monument to Edwardian opulence; its emotional content, however hyperbolic, retains life and conviction. Its lavish resources may prohibit a revival today, but musically it deserves one, which is more than can be said for most of Bantock's song output.

With Joseph Holbrooke and Rutland Boughton we reach the lunatic fringe. Such wayward and self-deceiving personalities warrant little space in this study, and neither made a positive contribution to English song, but their strange careers of mixed success and failure do point us to a few conclusions about the late-Victorian and Edwardian climate which sustained them. Both were born into the lower classes and developed lifelong grudges against society. Holbrooke's father was a music-hall pianist, and after a period at the RAM he himself took up similar employment. In such an environment his musical facility was taken for granted but never developed into idiomatic conviction. 'He professes', his biographer tells us, 'to have been able to write music at any time without waiting for a so-called "inspiration" to descend upon him, and this remarkable musical fecundity has been with him throughout his whole career' (Lowe: 4). The sad truth is that inspiration never did descend upon him. Instead, he relied on his superiority complex and, unable or unwilling to hold down a job, somehow gained the life patronage of T. E. Ellis, Lord Howard de Walden, who wrote the libretti for his operatic trilogy *The Cauldron of Annwyn* and the words for his songs 'Caswallawn' and 'An outsong'. From this secure position he pontificated about the shortcomings of modern English music and its conditions, notably in his book *Contemporary British Composers*, a work in the same inter-war class of eccentric, subjective criticism as the writings of Cecil Gray, van Dieren and Sorabji – all the products of failed or, in the cases of van Dieren and Sorabji, rejected composers.

The lesson we learn from Holbrooke is that the reversal of Stanford's problem of over-refined technique thwarted by a dearth of external stimulus was not in itself a way forward. Holbrooke's susceptibility to literature was unable to fertilise his musical style, which never developed beyond late-Romantic melodramatic 'effects' – the sole constituents of, for instance, his Byron scena for bass and orchestra, 'Marino Faliero'. It merely left a trail of red herrings, such as his String Quartet no. 3, 'The Pickwick Club', 'after' Dickens. Early on he linked his name with that of Edgar Allen Poe, in a number of orchestral and chamber works, a Dramatic Choral Symphony, and a setting of 'Annabel Lee' for male voice and orchestra. Judging from his pretentious justification of the title of his *Six Landscapes*, op. 34, in which he invokes the name and aesthetics of Whistler, he believed himself intellectually and technically equal to transmuting Poe's symbolist magic into music. But all that comes across in his melodramatic vein is a morbid temperament. This also dominates the symphonic poem *The Viking* (Longfellow) and the pathological suicide song 'The coward's exit'. Another literary connection was with Herbert Trench. The symphonic poem *Apollo and the Seaman* was written 'after' Trench's poem and at his request. The projection of lantern slides of the text at the first performance, given by Beecham in the Queen's Hall in 1908, was also Trench's idea, but the huge orchestra was just another expression of Holbrooke's megalomania. *Six Modern Songs*, op. 29, are also to texts by Trench. 'The requital' has a certain effortless attractiveness, but the others are very indifferent, and 'O dreamy, gloomy, friendly trees', to a poem later more effectively set by Gurney, is extremely dismal. As director of the Haymarket Theatre, Trench offered Holbrooke the musical directorship in 1909. He turned it down, and it passed to Norman O'Neill.

Holbrooke's final literary red herring was shared with Bantock: they were the first and probably the only English composers to set the verse of Ezra Pound to music within the period. Bantock's choral suite from *Cathay* was published in 1923; Holbrooke's four songs from op. 77 appeared in 1922–3. In these attempts one regrets Holbrooke's inability to parody the Romantic elements in his technique, which amounts to a smudged, platitudinous utilisation of the harmonies of the period. He has no controlled satire to match the poetry's epigrammatic brilliance. Perhaps he intended his obbligati, especially the clarinet, as satirical foils, but they are superfluous and unenterprising. The only gesture that rings true to Pound's experimental spirit is the fact that the clarinet parts are not printed in the scores.

Boughton's case is worse than Holbrooke's: he had more ideas than he could use but lacked not only technique but even a recognisable idiom. It is a chilling pointer to English amateurishness at the time that no one seems to have noticed these deficiencies except George Bernard Shaw, who throughout Boughton's career kept up an extraordinary cat-and-mouse game with him, execrating his music to his face and at the same time lavishing financial help on him to enable him to continue with his grandiose plans. Perhaps he simply enjoyed manipulating him. Yet when he first attended Boughton's opera festival at Glastonbury at Easter 1916 for the production of Gluck's *Iphigenia in Tauris* he was genuinely converted to Boughton's cause. The fact is that Boughton's personal magnetism overrode his technical drabness, and Shaw, who had long been calling for an English Bayreuth, could hardly reject Boughton's attempt to instigate one.

Boughton's Celtic dream-world was part of the wide Celtic renaissance which, as we shall see, fired creative imaginations as much after the first world war as before. Yet his own handling of it (prompted by his discovery of Malory in 1906), both in the specious manifesto *Music-Drama of the Future* (published with his librettist Reginald Buckley in 1911) and in *The Immortal Hour*, first produced at Glastonbury in 1914, was naïve and parochial to an extent that makes the immense inter-war popularity of *The Immortal Hour*, which ran in London from 1922, as anachronistic and acultural a phenomenon as that of *The Sound of Music* in the 1960s. Moreover, by this time Boughton's own concerns were developing radically different motives. In February 1926 he published an article in the *Worker's Weekly* explaining why he had joined the Communist Party, and a little later he acclaimed the General Strike, professing solidarity with the workers and writing them a ballet, *May Day*. Michael Hurd rightly points out that 'Of all English composers he was the only one who thought it important to declare any sort of understanding and sympathy with the events of those tragic days' (1962: 95), but his conclusion, 'That his inspiration did not quite match his sentiments in the matter is barely relevant', is inadequate, for that is exactly what *is* relevant. Bax and Ireland were right to ignore current events in their music and persist in their dark, necromantic desires, for it was for these that they had fashioned their musical techniques; how, on the other hand, can one take seriously a composer whose convictions allowed him, in his proletarian song 'The love of comrades', to alter Whitman's words so that 'I' becomes 'we', 'America' 'England', 'prairies' 'pastures' and 'democracy' 'my comrades', all set to technically crippled music as styleless and emotionless as the worst church music? From his 'Passing joys', published out of compassion by his employer Cecil Barth in 1893, to 'Lorna [Doone]'s song', written one evening in 1934 for a film at Ernest Irving's request in return for £30 (a quarter of that year's income), Boughton's record in song was one which posterity has wisely forgotten. Even his seven settings of the great socialist Edward Carpenter (who was of the Bantock circle), potentially the sort of collaboration to yield an antidote to Edwardian complacency, are musical ciphers. The expression of a social conscience in English song had to wait for Alan Bush and Auden and Britten. Hurd's life of Boughton is a valuable case-study but fails to justify a composer most of whose music does not withstand critical scrutiny.

Scott, Bantock, Holbrooke and Boughton were victims of their period in that it encouraged them to indulge in their private dreams. Although Bantock saw himself as a progressive and Boughton saw himself as a revolutionary, neither had more than an egotistic sense of what the unique interplay of tradition and innovation at this juncture of England's musical history demanded of them. They were too quick, as were Scott and Holbrooke, to dig themselves into their favourite affinities, without considering what they could create out of them. Above all, they lacked the acuity of sensibility to invest post-Wagnerian musical language with even a fraction of the potency of, say, Debussy's *Cinq poèmes de Baudelaire*. Had they been its only figures, the Edwardian musical picture would have been a gloomy and sterile one. But fortunately there were other forces at work. Vaughan Williams and Holst, for instance, possessed a far more vivid sense of their position as 'heirs and rebels'; in their letters to each other, particularly in the four Holst wrote to Vaughan Williams from Berlin in 1903 (U. Vaughan Williams and I. Holst; I. Holst, 1938, 2/1969: Appendix I), one is struck by how clearly they saw themselves as having a duty towards the revival of a national musical tradition, how young and confident they were, for all their plodding realism, how self-critical, analytical and frank, and how seriously they helped each other. There is no indication of this level of communication and awareness in the careers of Scott, Bantock, Holbrooke and Boughton.

VI

The Edwardian age (II)

George Bernard Shaw and Elgar once had a curious conversation. After a performance of Elgar's Second Symphony Shaw remarked with surprise on the advanced harmonies Elgar was using; Elgar replied that it might be true that he was becoming daring, 'but don't forget that Cyril Scott started it' (Armstrong, 1958: 13). What the conversation implied to Shaw and Elgar is not documented; what it illustrates is that Edwardian England was going on a long harmonic holiday.

Why harmonic? William Denis Browne, himself in the thick of the harmonic revolution and attempting to sum up the era as it had been represented in the 1912–13 Balfour Gardiner concerts, offered a thoughtful explanation:

> The training of a musician at this period [the late 19th century] included harmony, taught first, and counterpoint, taught second, an order of teaching which had a particular bearing on subsequent developments. A pupil learned naturally to attach more importance to the earlier study than to the second. That is, he learnt from the first to think in chords, or vertically, instead of in melodies, or horizontally; and this attitude was helped by the comparative decadence of singing and by the ubiquity of the pianoforte. Such a training would render a young musician peculiarly susceptible to the influence of a movement that was soon to make itself felt on the Continent. Debussy and others were experimenting with harmony for its own sake, and writing music which depended for its effect solely on the juxtaposition of unresolved discords. Strauss was working on somewhat similar lines in Germany, Puccini in Italy. It was not surprising that young British composers, tired of Brahms and estranged from counterpoint, should fall an easy prey to music which was both easier (when you had your models) and more exciting to produce than dry fugues and sonatas. They did indeed fall an easy prey, and some of them, like Cyril Scott, have not yet struggled out of the toils. Others, however, have just escaped, and some of these we have lately been hearing (:63–4).

Browne saw the cultivation of counterpoint and of the art of singing as the two ways out of the harmonic trap prepared by the 'ubiquity of the pianoforte' and commended Grainger as a composer who exhibited strength when writing contrapuntally. Grainger himself, however, later wrote that it was harmony that accounted for the emotional power of his and his Frankfurt colleagues' music:

> Perhaps it might be true to say we were all of us PRERAFAELITE composers . . . And what musical medium could provide the agonized emotionality needed? Certainly not the 'architectural' side of music and not the truly English qualities of grandeur, hopefulness and glory so thrilling in Elgar, Walton, Vaughan Williams and other British composers. I think the answer is 'the CHORD'. The

106

chord has the heartrending power we musical prerafaelites needed. Based on
Bach, Wagner, Skriabine, Grieg and Cesar Franck Cyril [Scott], Balfour [Gar-
diner] and I became chord-masters indeed (quoted in Armstrong, 1962: 18).

But Browne's analysis of the harmonic disease, which continues for several
pages, is shrewd though simplified (it was written for a non-specialist periodical);
certainly it was pianistic textures that dominated a good deal of Edwardian
ephemera as well as songs in which the composer gave small consideration to the
voice part, as in many of the examples discussed in the previous chapter. Nevertheless, as we shall see, harmony continued to be the most distinctive ingredient in
English song throughout the inter-war period, and had Browne survived the first
world war he would have seen English music mature while his analysis of its deficiencies was ignored. This is partly because he left Delius out of the reckoning.

Delius was the harmonic composer *par excellence*. His appreciation of the
human voice and of effective ways of setting poetry to music was extremely
limited, and since English was only one of the five languages he set to music (the
others were German, French, Norwegian and Danish) his position as an English
song composer is peripheral. Yet such was his magic and his inimitable control
over dangerously one-dimensional harmonic resources that his apparently illogi-
cal juxtapositions of poignant chords, creating a unique style which has never
been adequately analysed, affected British composers as did no other single influence. Warlock, Moeran, Orr and possibly Bax owe more to him stylistically
than to anyone else (see Palmer, 1976: 150–62, 165–81); and they commanded,
along with many lesser imitators now forgotten, a substantial portion of the song
market between the wars.

The influence of Delius in England is easy to trace after about 1910–11. At this
time we find Warlock, still a schoolboy at Eton, feverishly imbibing whatever
Delius scores he could find (Tomlinson, 1976b: 10–13). Two years later, according to Warlock himself, 'a new world of sound' was revealed to the young
Moeran's imagination too, by a performance of Delius's Piano Concerto in one of
the Balfour Gardiner concerts (Heseltine, 1924: 172; cf. Palmer, 1976: 166 –
both accounts could be correct if they refer to separate occasions, but this seems
unlikely). Prior to this, however, no clear account exists. The St James's Hall
concert of Delius's works in 1899 caused considerable interest but was an isolated
venture; Warlock (Heseltine, 1923, 2/1952: 62) claims that no work by Delius was
heard in London from this date until the performance of his Piano Concerto at
a Promenade concert in 1907, though Beecham (1959: 134) states that Ada Cross-
ley was helping his songs to circulate by singing them in England in 1905.
Grainger discovered Delius through *Appalachia* in 1905 or 1906 (Palmer, 1976:
87), but there is a tantalising lack of evidence as to when the other composers of
the 'Frankfurt group' – Balfour Gardiner, Norman O'Neill, Roger Quilter and
Cyril Scott – first made contact with Delius's music; it certainly cannot have been
while they were together at Frankfurt around 1895. Quilter knew 'almost nothing'
of Delius's music until about 1908 (Hold, 1978: 45) and first became fully aware of
its beauties very much later, seemingly after the war (Heseltine, 1923, 2/1952:
155–6). Thus it may well be that the group's harmonic traits, which probably
emanated from Scott and Grainger, were independent of Delius's until the consolidating period of the Musical League and the Balfour Gardiner concerts, by

which time all the Frankfurt composers except Scott had become fairly close personal friends of Delius. Armstrong (1958: 13) even suggests that the stylistic line of influence may have run in the opposite direction, from the Frankfurt group to Delius, but this seems unlikely, given that the essentials of Delius's mature style were fixed by about 1901.

Whatever its source, the increasingly pronounced novel harmonic dialect in songs by O'Neill from 1895 and Quilter from 1900 was noticed and found attractive. O'Neill grew up in cultured surroundings in Kensington. His father, a successful Academy painter, counted Parry, Kegan Paul, Walter Crane and J. W. Mackail among his local acquaintances. O'Neill, with another near neighbour, Somervell, as his teacher, was temperamentally suited to fashioning a song style from the lyrical suavity of Parry on the one hand and, on the other, the cosmopolitan elegance of the more tasteful ballad composers, especially those with a combination of uninhibited emotionalism and feminine grace, such as Liza Lehmann and Maude Valérie White. A new poise was emerging in drawing-room elegance, neat and fastidious in its gestures, sentimental but tasteful and recognisably French in flavour. All this is present in O'Neill's music. His early song 'Parted' rides on a gently pulsating, syncopated accompaniment that helps to launch the characteristic vocal shapes and word-setting of three subordinate 'sprung' syllables moving effortlessly on to a stressed one. This trait anticipates Quilter, much more so in the opening phrase of 'A lover's day', which must be a later song (Ex. 1); both composers were surely indebted for the three-note upbeat

Ex. 1

pattern to the popular music of their time, where it occurs in a variety of instrumental and vocal duple-time contexts. In 'Parted' O'Neill's word-setting still
seems a little clumsy, especially in view of Quilter's subsequent refinement of its
typical patterns, though the echo of a phrase from Parry's 'When we two parted'
reminds us that they are found in him also – indeed Parry has a strong con-
stitutional link, seldom given credit, with Quilter and O'Neill. Unlike Parry,
however, Quilter and O'Neill put no restraint on sentimental indulgence, but in
'Parted' this is still kept to a timid minimum, with the result that the crepuscular
heartache of the lyric is expressed only occasionally, as in the piano postlude
(Ex. 2) (a similar use of the flat 7th becomes tiresomely inevitable in Quilter).

Ex. 2

In later songs O'Neill throws inhibitions to the winds, becoming one of the first
true 'light' music composers. In fact he made theatre music his career, and in his
long period as musical director of the Haymarket Theatre, for which his successful incidental compositions included the music for Maeterlinck's *The Blue Bird*
and Barrie's *Mary Rose*, he sustained and elevated the genre with excellent taste,
as Quilter was to do with his particular type of solo song. O'Neill's later songs are
numerous, and include two large-scale ballads for voice and orchestra, 'Death on
the hills', a study in Wagnerian mood-painting of which a critic wrote that 'Mr
O'Neill seems bent, like the Fat Boy in *Pickwick*, on "making your flesh creep,"
and succeeds only too effectually' (D. Hudson, 1945: 33), and 'La belle dame
sans merci', whose first performance Francis Toye reviewed enthusiastically in
Vanity Fair (*ibid.*: 56).

Not surprisingly, in view of his theatrical experience, O'Neill's settings of four
incidental Shakespeare lyrics for voice and small orchestra are most effective –
'Tell me where is fancy bred' all 7ths and sentimentality and 'It was a lover' very
high-spirited. 'Jewels', 'When May walks by' and 'A lover's day' are strongly
Quilterian. Perhaps his best song is the unpublished setting of Belloc's 'The
night', which outdoes Cyril Scott in its continuous juxtapositions of added-note
chords, but, instead of riding roughshod over the poetry, wraps it up slowly and
intimately in its harmonic bedclothes. In the second and third stanzas there is a
b'–a' tolling phrase, first heard at the mention of 'the far lament of them / That
chaunt the dead day's requiem', which is repeated 18 times in the piano and once

in the voice, plus once in retrograde (at the point marked '*espress.*'), but is never harmonised the same way twice (Ex. 3). Here we see music not only depicting something physical, the tolling of a bell, but, as Debussy desired, suggesting 'the mysterious correspondences between Nature and Imagination'. From the first notes of the song sleep has been felt as a delicious sensation; here it takes hold of the consciousness, enveloping it and easing it hither and thither, every moment the same yet different as it wanders between two worlds.

Ex. 3

There is naturally a certain ambivalence about being a 'light' song composer or, in the case of Quilter, one of calculated elegance. Good taste is vital, for two reasons. It is needed to ensure that the stereotyped musical formulae which the style normally and, with Quilter, certainly involves are applied to poetry which is on the same level, neither lower, like the doggerel set to music by Scott, nor higher, as in the case of O'Neill's 'When music sounds', a setting which retains something of de la Mare's sense of awe but comes dangerously near to debasing the poem in sentimentality. The second function of good taste is to produce the maximum of aural titillation with the minimum of technical resource. Quilter seldom errs in either respect, but the knowledge that his songs cost him an agonised effort of composition totally at variance with the artless effect of the results puts this second attribute in a new light, suggesting that the style represents a level of creative experience above which he aspired in vain, and, as we shall see, tinging his achievement with tragedy.

Quilter's earliest surviving songs, to texts by himself, were published under the pseudonym Ronald Quinton in 1897. They are interesting but very unsatisfactory, and it is not surprising that when Quilter looked at them in 1916 he wrote on the front of his copies 'on no account to be reprinted in any form or under my name'. His op. 1, the *Songs of the Sea* mentioned in Chapter I, are not outstanding in any way, and appear uncommitted and diffident in the light of the maturity he attained surprisingly soon afterwards, but they contain sufficient unexpected features to prepare one for the alluring effect he was soon to have on English song, particularly on the approach of composers such as Warlock and Ireland who learnt to carry their style lightly. The words and their enunciation are perfectly matched to the music; again Quilter wrote them himself. They could hardly make their effects through simpler means. The first song, which was omitted on republication in 1911, is the weakest, especially in its words. The second opens with a perfectly evoked seagull's cry underpinned by a yearning sigh; the elements, incorporated as one motive throughout the song, are closely akin to Delius, though Quilter had surely not heard any Delius at this date and *Sea Drift* was yet to be written. A significant trait appearing throughout these songs, and one which links Quilter with Fauré, whom he admired (particularly because of the strength of his bass lines), is the freedom with which modal scale degrees, particularly flat 7ths and sharp 4ths, are introduced. Cadences such as that at the end of the first stanza of 'The sea-bird' (Ex. 4) and non-modulatory flat 7ths (Ex. 5, from 'The sea-bird', and Ex. 6, from 'Moonlight') were novel to England, though they had been current in France at least since Bizet.

Ex. 4

Ex. 5

Ex. 6

Quilter's op. 2 was a set of German songs to words by Bodenstedt. The first edition is inscribed 'In memory of Frankfurt days', reminding us that his training was German and that his urbane and shapely word-setting, like Parry's of the Bodenstedt Shakespeare sonnet translations, was not confined to or developed only for the English language. (Many years later Schott prepared successful German translations of a number of Quilter's songs and they became quite well known on the continent (Raphael, 1974–7).) The only partly formed style is still fresh, and rather attractively reticent. There is a sincere timidity of gesture, particularly effective in 'Ich fühle deinen Odem', where the composer seems to be capturing the first, awed love-intimacy of youth.

Op. 3 is a set of three songs to various poets. In 'Love's philosophy' (the first of the set but not the first to be published) all the virtues of Quilter's style suddenly spring into mature life. There is a controlling sense of good taste that perfectly matches the studied, genteel elegance of Shelley's love poem, in which the imagery persuades rather than excites. Delius's setting of 1891 resembles Quilter's in its constant semiquaver motion, but is more excitable and apt to overstrain the emotional impulses of the images. At the conclusion

> What are all these kissings worth,
>   If thou kiss not me?

Delius repeats the last line too often, with a chromatic winding-down of impetus, but Quilter rightly builds up a broad-gestured climax to which all the preceding lines have been pointing. From the point at which the second stanza's music departs from that of the first there is a rich harmonic accumulation of appoggiaturas (Ex. 7, *x*), and this, with the motoric piano accompaniment, links Quilter strongly with the young Fauré: both harness something of Wagner's harmonic abandon to their own lighter ends. The cadence, however, with its dominant 13th on the word 'kiss' (Ex. 7), is pure Quilter and thoroughly English. The vital lesson Quilter learnt from Fauré, apart from the characteristic use of oscillating, unresolved intermediate dominants (Ex. 8), was a new control over texture. The semiquaver motorics are woven into a harmonic web of great resource but remarkably simple means; Brahmsian heaviness has gone (there are few octaves), and the accompaniment, unlike Delius's, is easy for the pianist, though it never sounds facile. The rippling textural continuity can perhaps be traced back to Bach: Quilter's figuration has the same mixture of arpeggio chord-

Ex. 7

Ex. 8

delineation, momentary two-part counterpoint picked out in crotchets and quavers (in this case against the voice) and free melodic patternwork as a Bach allemande (Ex. 9). (Parry was perhaps the link between Bach and Quilter, although if the similarity between 'Love's philosophy' and Parry's 'My heart is like a singing bird' is more than coincidence it must have been the younger composer who influenced the older.) 'Love's philosophy' can hardly be called progressive for its time, yet its careful reconsideration of harmonic and textural functions along French lines makes it something new in English song.

In the same opus, however, Quilter falls into his particular trap of cloying sentimentality. His sentimental idiom is perhaps seen to best advantage in the well-

Ex. 9

No sis-ter flower would be for-giv'n If it dis-dained its bro-ther.

Ped.   ✻   *Ped.*   ✻

Ex. 10

Moderato quasi andantino; tempo rubato

espress.

mf

known setting of Waller's 'Go, lovely rose', where it is apt for the poem's conceit, but here in 'Now sleeps the crimson petal' it already feels stale. The song begins with a *cantilena* motive in the piano part (Ex. 10) of the kind which so often in Quilter becomes a platitude introducing a song that has little to say, and it ends by being dragged down in Tennyson's

> So fold thyself, my dearest, thou, and slip
> Into my bosom and be lost in me.

– which sounds either sexually suggestive or fulsomely mawkish. Quilter, of course, adopts the latter tone, to the detriment of his song. This disparate opus is completed with one of his comparatively rare miscalculations: a setting of Henley's 'Fill a glass with golden wine' which (in contrast to Butterworth's setting of the same text – see Chapter VII) confuses the poet of 'England, my England' with his morbid *alter ego*, which dominates this poem; the harmony is hearty in the manner of Quilter's 'Non nobis, Domine' and his patriotic second world war commission, 'A song of Freedom'.

Op. 5, *Four Child Songs*, offers little. There was a considerable market for child songs at this period; they included many settings from Stevenson's *A Child's Garden of Verses* (by Gurney, Ireland, Liza Lehmann, Somervell and Stanford as well as Quilter), but most of them, even Somervell's educational collections, show a confusion between songs *for* children and music and poetry *about* children. Often the former are used merely as pretexts for simplistic or sentimental fatuity in the late-Victorian manner. Even when, at a later date, settings from de la Mare's *Peacock Pie* provide something of more permanent value, we are given less a child's art than the childlike fantasies always present in the adult. Quilter's 'A good child', at which any discerning child would laugh, is of an unpalatable smugness, and in the last song of the set the music does not comment with sufficiently caustic irony on the self-satisfied child who cannot imagine foreign children not wishing they were English like himself.

In some of the simpler Elizabethan and Jacobean lyrics Quilter found a self-conscious emotional confectionery that suited his musical style, and it is in the *Three Shakespeare Songs* of 1905 that his mature traits first appear consistently. Some of these can become annoying mannerisms, for example, in 'O mistress mine', a string of secondary 7ths disposed as a dual line of consecutive 4ths (in the piano's introduction, Ex. 11), close-harmony chords over a pedal bass (Ex. 12), an artfully distorted sequence (Ex. 13), a clichéd cadence for the first

Ex. 11

Ex. 12

Ex. 13

stanza (compare the last vocal cadence of 'Love's philosophy'), and a repetition of the opening line (prompted by a compulsive need to tie up the conceit) which spoils the second stanza, though it also exhibits another engaging if smug formula, the cadential leading note sinking via the 6th degree of the scale to the 5th (Ex. 14). Other stylistic traits are more spontaneous inventions of the moment: the 'phrygian' dominant modulation to point the line 'I am slain by a fair cruel maid' in 'Come away, death', immediately taken up by the piano in a manner suggesting Borodin (Ex. 15), and the 'pace-variation', as Howells termed it in relation to Gurney's technique (M. Scott, 1938a), which helps to spin out the short, irregular lines 'O prepare it' and 'Did share it' into a context of two balanced four-bar phrases, though with the result of undue emphasis of the word 'one' (Ex. 16). Here, characteristically, the piano helps to effect the stretching with an inner *cantilena* under the word 'yew'.

Ex. 14

Ex. 15

Quilter's nearest literary equivalent was Robert Herrick, a natural miniaturist with a genius for making sentimentality palatable by confining it to short, close-cropped verse and clothing it in exquisite poetic conceits. Intimacy is his hallmark, particularly in his celebrated apostrophes of flowers, and this accords comfortably with Quilter's small-scale harmonic unction. Given these correspondences, Quilter's op. 8, *To Julia*, is something of a disappointment. It suffers chiefly from his ill-advised attempt to link six of Herrick's Julia poems into a cycle and bind them together with a fatuous prelude and interlude which are all too reminiscent of the links in Liza Lehmann's *In a Persian Garden*. He uses one,

Ex. 16

and only one, recurrent pentatonic motive of descending alternate minor 3rds and major 2nds, which keeps appearing with a sentimental sigh in various songs where new material or at least another motto would provide preferable variety. Its prime justification is in the exquisite fifth song, whose text consists of one statement, 'Dew sat on Julia's hair', amplified by two subsequent similes. Quilter's setting helps to keep the 'spangled' dew before our eyes with wondering concentration by recurrent use of the motto, now in his favourite parallel 4ths (Ex. 17); in this naked guise it breathes a freshness more consistently found in the harmonic vocabulary of slightly later composers such as Ireland and Moeran. Perhaps the best song in the cycle is 'The night piece', where the resources, whittled away with finesse, are enhanced by piquant touches such as the delicately

Ex. 17

etched series of mediant modulations (Ex. 18); the weakest is the finale, 'Cherry ripe', which relies too heavily on a cycle of 5ths for its recurrent '"Cherry ripe, ripe," I cry' refrain, with rather nondescript modulatory wanderings in between. It is gratifying to find Quilter breaking from his stereotype ending in the epilogue of 'To daisies', when the logic of the downward chromatic two-note cells (Ex. 19, *y*) counteracts the upward cells of the main motive (Ex. 19, *x*), but distressing to see the uncharacteristically specious word-setting, subordinated to the visual layout of the poem, in the opening of the same song.

Ex. 18

Ex. 19

Already in the *Seven Elizabethan Lyrics*, op. 12, archaic poetry is beginning to clog Quilter's style. The harmony is becoming less piquant, the texture thicker and the rate of harmonic motion too uniform. The first song, 'Weep you no more', is undistinguished, despite an attempt to let air into the accompaniment with lute-like *style brisé* touches. The second, 'My life's delight', is harmonised unhappily like a hymn tune with an air of self-satisfaction, and in the third, 'Damask roses', the slightly quizzical conceit of the poem is bogged down by the music, sticking fast in the opening harmonic mire of C major and only managing to drag itself as far as E flat for the second half, where it again clogs just when musical enhancement is needed for the punch-line 'Whether the roses be your lips, or your lips the roses'. 'The faithless shepherdess' provides variety, but the blustering roulades and their French rhythms (Ex. 20) set up a rate of motion which, far from establishing the '*capriccioso*' mood demanded by the tempo indication, overpowers the poem – a manner used more appropriately in 'Blow, blow thou winter wind' in op. 6. In 'Brown is my love' Quilter, like Gurney after him, is unable to add anything to the contemplative little poem except discursive harmonies which tend to obscure it; in 'Fair house of joy' we have a fine example of what he learnt from the elasticity of Elizabethan vocal phrases (Ex. 21), but again the harmony is too heavy and diatonically cloying.

Ex. 20

Ex. 21

However, in the penultimate song, 'By a fountainside', Quilter treats the text with an emotional intensity he does not achieve elsewhere in his Elizabethan settings. The song, whose words are Echo's lament for Narcissus from Ben Jonson's *Cynthia's Revels*, does not force its music upon the text; music is part of the poem's imagery:

> List to the heavy part the music bears,
> Woe weeps out her division when she sings.

Quilter makes it audible behind and between the poet's short elegiac phrases, by means of appoggiaturas, suspensions and thematic echoes in the 'alto' part of the accompaniment (Ex. 22). The song is free of his habitual mannerisms, and shows the firm control over every note in the texture which he was beginning to lose in *To Julia* and most of the other songs in op. 12. The 'slow fount' of the poem supplies the perfect texture for him in such passages as the third line (the first of the two quoted above), where the fountain, represented in the d″ flat–a′ flat of

Ex. 22

Ex. 23

Ex. 24

the piano part, impinges on the consciousness fractionally before the words draw attention to it, then emphasises the downward drag of the 'heavy part' by imitation (Ex. 23). The airy, lute-like elements found in the accompaniment of 'Weep you no more' are here developed exquisitely (Ex. 24).

This comparatively intense treatment of 'By a fountainside' is in line with the tired, decadent mood of Quilter's own youth in the nineties. *Weltschmerz* elicits his deepest spiritual identity, and in his previous set of songs, the *Four Songs of Sorrow*, op. 10 (entitled *Voices of Sorrow* in the autograph), the settings of Ernest Dowson seem much more heartfelt and less selfconscious than those by Scott. The strengths and weaknesses of Dowson's poetry are also felt in Quilter's settings. In the first, 'A coronal', the suspicion that the poet rather enjoys his defeatist concept of love as doomed to death is endorsed by the music, which lacks harmonic determination, being content with tonic pedals, in the manner of many Victorian composers (Ex. 25), and dominants above which little threads of part-writing fit snugly together (Ex. 26). In 'Passing dreams' poet and composer are roused from this lethargy to moments of more vibrant feeling: a 9th chord at the word 'desire', a sense of morbid religiosity followed by a harmonic stab of apprehension at 'after / We pass the gate', and a brief flowering of the music, which 'then closes' with an effetive sideslip of unfulfilment, at the lines

> They are not long, the days of wine and roses:
> > Out of a misty dream
> Our path emerges for a while, then closes
> > Within a dream.

In the third song, 'A land of silence', there is a fine example of the essence of Quilter's textural art, a musical path which 'emerges for a while, then closes / Within a dream' – the inner part (Ex. 27, *x*), presumably fashioned to express 'our delight / Hid out of sight'. Although the line is beautifully contoured, it is hinted at rather than defined, and is the product of a pianistic composer: its subtlety would be spoilt by the linear clarity of orchestral or chamber ensemble part-writing (conversely, the presence of similarly 'glimpsed' lines in the orchestral music of Delius is one reason why it is so difficult to perform). In the

Ex. 25

Ex. 26

Ex. 27

final song, 'In spring', the stamp is put on Dowson's pessimistic melancholy by a higher degree of thematic motivation than one usually finds in Quilter, namely the dying, falling four-note phrase which permeates much of the song from the introduction onwards, and tolls like a funeral knell in the gloomy refrain; somehow its futility is intensified when it tries to invert against itself at the second iteration of 'the flowers of the soul', only to land on the f′ sharp which has to fall back again (Ex. 28).

In Quilter's subsequent output there is a marked loss of freshness as he retreads idiomatic paths. This is perhaps understandable in one whose response to poetry

Ex. 28

was immediate but who had to toil to give it musical expression. The tendency to set archaic texts even when he has nothing to add to them, already seen in the *Seven Elizabethan Lyrics*, becomes more pronounced in his later work, where there is a definite division between songs in which he is deliberately expanding old techniques or trying new ones and those in which he is not. He seems to have been the prisoner of his own mannerisms in this respect. Mark Raphael tells how, being delighted by the unaccustomed freshness of the flatward modulation near the end of 'Autumn evening', at the line 'The breath of early evening chills' (Raphael, 1953-4: 20), he asked Quilter why he did not do that sort of thing more often; Quilter merely shrugged his shoulders (Raphael, 1974–7). 'Autumn evening', entirely neglected, is one of Quilter's most beautiful songs; the reverence for the image of a man musing upon autumn at his beloved's graveside keeps the expression carefully subdued in both text and music; the two are well matched, unassuming and unsentimental.

Most of the later songs in which Quilter exploits new shades of sensibility can be seen as responses to a particular poet or a particular medium. An illustration of the latter is his setting of Shelley's 'I arise from dreams of thee', a festival commission (Harrogate, 1929) with orchestral accompaniment, circumstances to which Quilter was unaccustomed, although several of his earlier and one or two of his later songs were also arranged with orchestral accompaniment (see the list of his songs). In this song Quilter develops his idiom along lines similar to Cyril Scott's, revelling particularly in higher-power dominant chords related by semitones and 3rds, but his experience in less expansive textures has given him a firmer control than Scott's over the ebb and flow of harmonic sensation – though a rise and fall in tension is still lacking, as dynamic modulations tend to take its place. Unlike Scott, he is genuinely close to the sensual symbolism of Debussy, particularly that of *L'après-midi d'un faune*, in the proliferation of arabesque detail in the accompaniment, inspired by orchestral opportunities for depicting Shelley's sounds of the night (while being also, characteristically, perfectly pianistic) – low-breathing winds, 'wandering airs', 'Champak odours' and 'the nightingale's complaint', mingled impressionistically, after a quasi-erotic climax, in the orchestral epilogue (Ex. 29). Shelley's languishing eroticism also found a ready response in Quilter; similar to 'I arise', but more precious and sentimental, is the later 'Music and moonlight', where in the airy texture, suggested by 'the guitar . . . tinkling', he has regained something of the lightness of 'Love's philosophy'. But he rises to a stronger, more virile mood altogether in the impetuous 'Arab love song' in op. 25. Here, in the pointed bass lines and unprepared 7th chords, Fauré's influence is strong; the unusually fast word-setting rides well against the sure-footed harmonic underpinning and produces a powerful sense of speed appropriate to the lover's Arab steed, 'whose hooves outspeed the tempest's flight'. The harmonic language is in itself no different from that of his less invigorating songs, and there are almost as many minor 9th chords as in Bantock, but by speeding up the pace and thinning out the texture to one of single-note points and lines and disjointed arpeggios he successfully breaks away from clotted complacency. Yet it returns in the next song in op. 25, a maudlin setting of Shelley's 'Music, when soft voices die'.

The poetry of William Blake, like that of Shelley, produced in Quilter some

Ex. 29

indifferent and some good results. Of his four settings, the first, 'The jocund dance', from op. 18, has a coy smugness which causes the poetry to irritate – some of the pert breeziness of the previous song, Keats's 'The Devon maid', seems to have rubbed off on it. Blake makes a more substantial showing in the songs that followed op. 18, the *Three Songs of William Blake*, op. 20. The first, 'Dream valley', is an unpretentious setting that quietly succeeds because verse and music achieve the same compact expression that characterises the Dowson songs. The second, 'The wild flower's song', begins with the uninspired mannerism of a tonic pedal underneath a supertonic chord (also found in 'The jocund dance'), but a sudden touch redeems it (Ex. 30); this simple juxtaposition of the chords of D major and D minor with added 7th immediately gives the song depth, but in Quilter one looks in vain for the systematic exploitation of such harmonic side-slips. The third song, 'Daybreak', is larger and richer than the previous two, a stylistic precursor of 'I arise from dreams of thee'.

A factor which divides Quilter sharply from the younger generation of success-ful song composers who reached their first maturity during or after the first world war is the total absence from his output of settings of contemporary pastoral, mythical or mystical poetry of the Celtic or 'Georgian' variety, apart from the setting of a simple love poem of a somewhat folky cast by James Stephens, 'In the bud of the morning O', and the *Three Pastoral Songs*, op. 22, to

Ex. 30

words by Joseph Campbell. Quilter was by nature an indoor or 'garden' composer (Hold, 1978) – one of his later songs is called 'The walled-in garden' – and
he must have had difficulty with poetry such as Campbell's, which demanded a
fresh, open-air style. Nevertheless, in the two outer songs of op. 22, at least, he
achieves a rustic effect. In 'I will go with my father a-ploughing' this is due less to
the obvious impressions of monodic shepherds' pipes and drone basses than to
the exhilarating series of rising harmonies, which generate excitement not only by
the B flat – G flat modulation but, within this, by the series of French ii^7-V^7 oscillations (Ex. 31). It is a charming setting, if effete compared with Gurney's. The
third song, 'I wish and I wish', a lively jig, is unusually modal for Quilter, and

Ex. 31

keeps its freshness by means of frequent chains of 4ths. The second, 'Cherry valley', has a more lush, enclosed atmosphere and a richness of detail befitting its subject. Passages of sultry harmonies in the manner of 'Daybreak' and 'I arise from dreams of thee' are mingled with more delicate touches, images of the cherry-blossom petals, in the manner of the opening of Delius's *Brigg Fair* (Ex. 32). The least satisfactory aspect of these three songs is their piano trio ac-

Ex. 32

companiment, of which the violin and cello parts are superfluous, merely doubling lines present in the piano part; they take us back into pump rooms with potted palms and background chamber ensembles.

Quilter can all too easily dominate the English song repertoire of his period by the size and accessibility of his output, by its simple warmth, and, primarily, by his easy and rewarding manner of writing for the voice. Yet his approach to the setting of poetry is at times so close to self-parody that his continued popularity needs tempering. Of the few critics to have written on Quilter, only Scott Goddard seems to have appreciated this. His article in *The Chesterian*, written as long ago as 1925, when a third of Quilter's songs were still to be composed, begins like a Shavian attack:

> Roger Quilter is the last reputable upholder of the best traditions of the English drawing-room song. In his songs there can be found all that happy philosophy of life which soothes and never disturbs. Mingled with this sensation of uninterrupted security there is a comfortable sadness that lulls the hearers into a state of decorously maudlin susceptibility not far from tears, giving them an ever deepening feeling of thankfulness for the walk of life in which their lot has been so kindly cast. All these profound emotions are expressed with a brilliance and tunefulness which would deprive any words but the most banal of their meaning. It is indeed fortunate, though probably not fortuitous, that such a relatively large amount of the words that Roger Quilter has set are slight almost to the verge of nonentity . . .
> There is another type of poem that Quilter has a fondness for attacking. It is that sort which, with the passage of years, has acquired an almost Biblical significance, accepted even as the Gospels are accepted, unapproachably posed. Shakespeare's 'Under the Greenwood Tree' and 'Blow, blow thou winter wind' are such. Here the words are so well known that they have become covered with a patina of insignificance, their meaning is so clear that they have lost all meaning. Anyone can set such a poem, any sort of a good tune will suit it, so long as the setting be jolly or sad in a general way. Delicacy of phrasing would be almost

an impertinence, as though the composer were attempting to reveal a line that everyone knew, and had realised the entire meaning of, long since. And so there come the Quilter settings of the Shakespeare lyrics, not so much unlovingly as unimaginatively done, with the general jollity of life stressed beyond belief and the unavoidable happy ending led up to and prepared by a half-disclosed, half-disguised modulation of dominant chords. With treatment such as this the words attain to senselessness and nothing is wanting in the music but delicacy of suggestion – *rien que la nuance* . . . Quilter's muse is first and foremost a direct and forceful expression of sensations that are neither complex nor concealed. His, is, above all, a confidential style, as though an arm were linked in ours and a conversation set going on lines and subjects that we are already fully familiar with; the weather, 'Blow, blow thou winter wind,' and the mention of ingratitude and forgetting of friendship, both done in the same hearty tone; or women and wine . . . In these situations Quilter is at his ease. Elegantly he paints the words each in a skilfully chosen colour, constructing a kaleidoscope of harmonies, seen through which, life becomes all prettiness, even in its sadness. It is quite false in sentiment but how charming! Can we wonder at the popularity of it all?

Goddard goes on to supply useful information about the conditions in which Quilter's songs flourished:

Roger Quilter is the foremost living English example of the singer's composer . . . It is an indisputable truth that he possesses, in as strong a degree as any song-writer, the knowledge of the disposition of the human voice and the ability so to fashion his works that the most is obtained from that instrument with the greatest facility. He is a master of his craft. One of the lasting memories of concert-going during the first quarter of the twentieth century, for a large number of people, will be the exquisite interpretation of his songs, the composer at the piano, by Gervase Elwes. It is a sad thing, but probably a true statement of the case, that the disaster which robbed music of one of her most illustrious artists, aimed, with the same gesture, a blow at the circulation of Quilter's songs. After Elwes no one has come forward who so adequately can deal with the medley of sentimentality and robustness that is the Quilter song. Just as Quilter knew how far to go with Rochester, Shakespeare, or whatever poet he chose, so as not to overemphasise what might offend, so Elwes knew to a nicety how far to go with Quilter. It was the interpretation of one gentleman by another, and, as such, unforgettably the real right thing, having a ring in it of truthfulness to type that does not obtain now with singers of the Quilter song.

In fact Elwes's definitive interpretations were to be replaced by those of the high baritone Mark Raphael, who became a close friend of Quilter from 1923, when the composer heard him sing some of the Shakespeare songs in a Wigmore Hall recital; a set of 78 r.p.m. recordings of 17 of the songs made by Raphael and Quilter is a valuable legacy of the partnership, and shows how sensitive a pianist Quilter was. Goddard then gives a gloss on Quilter's technique:

Quilter knows better than any of his compeers the exact weight of a spread chord in the treble and of a held octave in the bass. He is the magician of the chord of the ninth. No one is more certain of touch in the matter of disguised common chords where a sixth and a fifth delicately contest for the supremacy. He alone can successfully interlace chords of the 'four–two' so that the consecutive fifths titillate the ear without offending the proprieties.

Yet all this, even his serious and carefully considered conclusion, is curiously equivocal. After recommending the first and last Dowson settings above some of his more popular songs, he sums up:

Placed beside the masters of song-writers of modern times such as Fauré and Stanford, Quilter seems to have missed opportunities that his ready instinct might so well have guided him to utilise. He has preferred to proceed along the paths of facile interpretation of texts which are often either trite or smug. Influenced by the ballad composers of his youth, not untouched by the pertness of Sullivan, he yet towers above those of his kind. If in the company of Ravel and Pizzetti he is not to be noticed, in that of Teresa del Riego, Wilfred Sanderson and Graham Peel he shines with a greater brilliance than any of them.

The modern reader raises an eyebrow at the coupling of Fauré and Stanford, and notes that Teresa del Riego, Wilfred Sanderson and Graham Peel have long faded from the repertoire, but then so has Pizzetti. Ultimately one accepts Goddard's mixture of praise and condemnation as a fair estimation of Quilter's songs.

Yet Goddard's article says nothing about Quilter's aims and personal impulses, as though for Quilter song-writing was a craft which need not involve profound personal commitment. This is far from the truth. Quilter was the first of a number of English composers who attempted to sustain and fulfil a creative life almost entirely through song composition. Only Wolf and Duparc among European composers matched their single-minded application. Of the others, Butterworth and Denis Browne were to die in the first world war, and Gurney, creatively speaking, not long after; Warlock barely survived the 1920s. Alone among those who staked everything on song, Quilter survived into old age, into the 1950s. This survival was of questionable artistic value in view of the limitations which every new song made clearer; in view of his personality, outlined below, it could be thought almost as tragic as the destruction of the other four.

Quilter's songs, despite their best-selling popularity, were not written for financial gain. Although at one period (before gramophone records reduced sheet music sales, as Quilter lamented) he could have lived off his income as a song composer, he had no need to, for, unlike Bantock, Boughton, Holbrooke and Scott, he was born into an aristocratic and affluent family with a seat at Bawdsey Manor, Suffolk. He was one of six sons, and was almost disowned for becoming a creative artist by his Philistine family, who took little interest in his career. On one occasion his father, given a review of one of his concerts to read, ignored it with the same tight-lipped scorn as Delius's father had shown for the review of his St James's Hall concert of 1899. But Quilter venerated his mother, and she, a dominating, neurotic woman, reciprocated the affection with unstable vehemence.

Widely read, Quilter possessed the effortless artistic taste of the born aristocrat where his parents had possessed only Philistinism. After he had freed himself from his family his acquaintances included Henry James and John Singer Sargent and the Wagner and Burne-Jones families. His possessions, including literary treasures and major impressionist paintings, were priceless, and his wealth considerable. Nor were his musical tastes as circumscribed as his style might suggest. His fondness for 'light' 19th-century composers was supplemented by an attraction to Debussy, de Falla, Gershwin, Ravel, Sibelius, and even Stravinsky.

Why, then, did so little of these enlightened and abundant surroundings find expression in his music, and why was his musical expression, with the exception of his *Children's Overture*, the first orchestral work ever broadcast by a BBC ensemble (Briggs, I: 262), successful only in the tiny creations of song form? Unfortunately his physical constitution was frail. He could not drink or withstand intense social life. An ulcerous condition developed in his late thirties and was never properly cured. To give of himself in the occasional composition lesson, or to compose a short song, exhausted him completely. He felt from his student days that he had mastered the basic techniques of composition only with the greatest difficulty. The effort of sustained abstract invention was quite impossible; even a piano sonata theme devised for his teacher Iwan Knorr in Frankfurt ended up in a song, 'Take, O take those lips away'.

Quilter was also painfully conscious of his wealth. He was a founder-member of the Musicians' Benevolent Fund, and according to Mark Raphael 'was happiest when he made contact with people less fortunate than himself materially and could help them':

> With people of his own class he felt really at home only when they loved the arts . . . When in company and . . . somewhat worried, he stammered. I rarely saw him frown, though . . . I realised that the very act of living was an effort . . . He composed at the piano, slowly and laboriously. I remember arriving at his house for a rehearsal much too soon. I could hear him working at a phrase over and over again. He often said that he was finding it more and more difficult to compose (Raphael, 1977).

To Quilter his greatest disability was being a homosexual. Although he enjoyed at least one lasting relationship, it was probably specific frustrations that induced the periods of illness which in their turn sometimes elicited songs, as with the Dowson settings of 1907 (Raphael, 1953-4: 20; 1974-7). During and after the second world war, when he wrote a number of undistinguished songs, from which a worthwhile one such as 'Drooping wings' only occasionally shines out, his mental stability gave way. Pressures of blackmail and deception, added to a hypersensitive constitution shaken by personal loss, made of his last years a story which, if it is ever fully told, will appear tragic. Quilter's is one of the saddest examples of the fate of the homosexual in England before the relaxation of the law. Too young to be touched by more than the rotten, impotent vestiges of the sexual freedom of the aesthetic movement, he was too old to find in poetry such as Housman's, which attracted a younger generation, positive expression for his sexuality. He turned from it to cultivate a veneer of perfumed innocence and effeminate romance, as a Victorian might sniff a nosegay so as to shut out the unpleasant smells of reality. If the artificiality of Quilter's nosegay irritates us, we should remember what it protected.

As a postscript the two remaining members of the Frankfurt group, Percy Grainger and Henry Balfour Gardiner, deserve brief mention. They were the closest in personal friendship to Delius, with whom this chapter began. Grainger came closest of all five to matching Delius's harmonic power and emotional vibrancy: one has only to hear his arrangement of the shanty 'Shallow Brown' or the final stanza of 'Willow willow' to experience the intensity of which chromatic harmony is capable, though in this case it resides not in the extremity of the inflections themselves, which are quite simple, but rather in their imaginative placing and rhetoric. Quilter, to whom 'Willow willow' was dedicated, never matched this, except perhaps in the remarkable fourth stanza of 'Barbara Allen', one of his own arrangements. Both Grainger and Gardiner discovered strong affinities in literature, with Kipling and Masefield respectively, but neither was drawn toward the *Lied* tradition and both tended to offset a solo voice, when they used one, against a chorus; there are, however, a number of early Grainger settings, mostly of Kipling, for voice and piano alone, though even some of these are most sensibly identified as unison songs. Their settings generally have an outdoor, extrovert atmosphere, even when sad, and in this respect contrast diametrically with Quilter's.

With the possible exception of the early Kipling settings, Grainger's solo songs (as opposed to his folksong arrangements) can hardly be said to form a discrete category within his output; Gardiner's songs, however, do require separate consideration. Of these, his unpublished ones are as interesting as those printed. In his earliest attempt, 'The banks of calm Bendemeer', his warm-hearted sincerity, later to be felt again in 'The stranger's song', shines through all the juvenile facility with a graceful, effortless tune. 'D'un vanneur de blé' (a text which Berkeley later set in a fine early song) is similarly warm in its flexible lyricism, but the *Three Songs* of 1897 are pedestrian and ponderous. 'Full fathom five' seems to have given Gardiner an agony of self-doubt, for he wrote on the manuscript 'Knorr saw this Sept 3rd 98: I cannot write a song yet; I have no sense of detail and build every slight composition on a disproportionately large scheme', though in fact the song is not large-schemed, just heavy. Composition never came easily to Gardiner; this should heighten our appreciation of the two expansive settings of 'Dream-tryst' for baritone and orchestra (the second with a larger orchestra), and makes his destruction of his other orchestral songs, the *Two Love Songs from 'The Song of Solomon'*, 'When the lad for longing sighs' and the orchestral verson of 'The recruit', particularly sad. 'The stranger's song', one of the earliest settings of Hardy, is his best song. A simple three-stanza strophic setting in duple-time C major, it has a fine, warm tune which suits the feeling of 'simple shepherds all'. Grainger's comments are entertaining, and characteristically tell us much about Grainger as well as Gardiner:

> Balfour had such an ample exuberant nature, and I think it is no accident that HE ALWAYS MADE HIS MARK (captured his audience, convinced his fellow-musicians) when he dealt with large sounds – News from Whydah, April, Overture to a Comedy, Shepherd Fennel's Dance. I always argued with Balfour that the piano was no instrument thru which to present a nature so lordly and manly as his – whether in the form of piano solo or voice accompanied by piano. 'THE STRANGERS SONG' is one of the most glorious songs in the world; but its singing middlevoices must be played by SINGING instruments (such as strings, or horns, or saxophones) and not misrepresented by the short brittle tone of the piano (1950–1).

Gardiner's Housman setting 'The recruit', predictably full-blooded and martial, wittily incorporates into the piano epilogue, in the subdominant, a fragment of 'See the conquering hero comes' from Handel's *Judas Maccabaeus*, referred to in the poem. 'Roadways' cunningly avoids a strophic form, and 'The wanderer's evensong' is full of lush Delius-like nuances, though in their succession they somehow lack Delius's own evocative magic. It remains true to say that Gardiner is more effective in extrovert songs, of which 'Winter' and the 'Golden Vanity' arrangement are further examples. Nevertheless, 'On Chelsea Embankment', also harmonically indulgent, is well written and intense, and 'Rybbesdale' and 'The quiet garden' show a sensitive rhythmic flexibility (the $\frac{5}{4}/\frac{7}{4}/\frac{3}{4}/\frac{6}{4}/\frac{3}{4}$ (etc.) alternations in 'Rybbesdale' may perhaps be attributed to Grainger's precedent). But although he was one of the first to set Housman and Hardy to music, his style was sometimes too hearty and sometimes too sentimental for the sensibilities of later audiences. Understanding this, he gave up composition.

> . . . when a thing became unpleasant to Balfour Gardiner he took immediate steps to avoid it. After the war, in a manner just as decisive, he turned his back on music which had been the love of his life. When he came back from the 1914 war, he felt that there was no place for the kind of music that he liked and was able to write. He believed, and once told me, that music should be an intoxication – something that carried one wholly out of this world. He did not share or understand the guilt-laden mood of austerity in which the post-war generation as a whole seemed to find itself; and in these circumstances he preferred to withdraw from the scene, and devote his life to country pursuits (Armstrong, 1958: 9).

To Grainger he gave the simple explanation, 'My muse left me' (Grainger, 1951).

Gardiner's most important contribution to the Edwardian age was his extremely generous patronage of new English music. Like Quilter, he was rich; furthermore, he was exuberant and open-hearted about using his wealth to further the cause of British music, though, again like Quilter, he also helped in more private ways, as when he purchased Delius's house to enable the composer to continue living at Grez-sur-Loing. Gardiner complained, like others in the period, 'that the craze of concert-givers for novelties is a bar to progress. The desire to announce that something is to be "given for the first time" prevents many good works from being heard again (Anon., 1912: 502), and he set about remedying this in the series of eight concerts he organised and funded, conducting many of the items himself, in 1912 and 1913 in the Queen's Hall with the New Symphony Orchestra and the London Choral Society. Charles Kennedy Scott, whose Oriana Madrigal Society performed the small choral works in the concerts, paid a remarkable tribute to Gardiner in a letter to Hubert Foss, of which the final paragraph runs:

> The days of these concerts were satisfying, happy days. Balfour had a small town house in Kensington, off Edwardes Square – Norman O'Neill lived opposite. There his friends gathered; there Percy Grainger would play his own compositions, or Bax, with his unrivalled power of score-reading, the compositions of other members of the circle when their own skill was insufficient; there plans were discussed, programmes settled with eager anticipation. The moving spirit was, of course, Balfour Gardiner; no accredited institution could have supplied the stimulus that he have (Heseltine, 1923, 2/1952: 158–9).

And we have this testimony from Grainger:

> As I look over those Balfour Gardiner concerts of 1912–13 I realize how they changed the whole face of English music. Of course, the concerts did not alter the value of the music itself. But it altered the way the composers thought about themselves and the way the musical public thought about English music (1950–1).

Song was not a prominent ingredient, for the series consisted primarily of orchestral concerts, but a number of works for voice and orchestra were performed, including Cyril Scott's 'The ballad of fair Helen' and O'Neill's 'La belle dame sans merci' (both sung by Frederic Austin, for whom they were written), and Holst's 'The mystic trumpeter' (sung by Cicely Gleeson-White).

Yet notwithstanding the tributes quoted above, Bax (1943: 93) claims that Gardiner felt his concerts to have been a failure, and that after the 1913 series he gave up, disillusioned. He had certainly had difficulty managing the orchestral players, but it seems that otherwise the seeds of his disillusionment were in himself. The Edwardian age was drawing to an end; although Gardiner's impresario rôle was to a certain extent taken over by F. B. Ellis, English music such as Gardiner and his friends had been writing had to cease sporting extrovertly in its own aura of inherited cosmopolitanism and begin measuring itself critically against the modern continental repertoire. The works of Bantock, Gardiner, Holbrooke, Quilter and Scott were no answer to Strauss and the Russian Ballet. Fortunately a conscientious and far-reaching sense of independence had already been developed, in other parts of the field, before English music was suddenly left to look after itself in a blighted world when war broke out in August 1914.

VII

The first world war: its effect and its victims

The sudden wholesale embargo on cultural events and entertainment which followed the declaration of war in 1939, while it was soon recognised as a ridiculous and frustrating panic measure, was at least based on the experience of how drastically universal hostilities could affect the national way of life. In 1914, however, world war was a novel concept and although spirits had been steadily sinking at the prospect of it throughout the early summer, when it materialised on 4 August reactions were indecisive. Parry had gone sailing – and was turned back by a Navy launch for entering a minefield. 'We had been avoiding strange-looking buoys for some time' (C.L. Graves, 1926, II: 67). The Henry Wood Promenade season got somewhat diffidently under way in August, after Strauss's *Don Juan* and a Wagner night had been cancelled in deference to precipitate hostility towards German music written after 1870. In the same month the first performance of Boughton's *The Immortal Hour* took place at Glastonbury. Warlock was given the excuse he needed to leave Oxford, 'this pool of hopeless depression and stagnation' (Tomlinson, 1974: 41), after one year's study at Christ Church, and spent the summer exploring the English countryside on foot and by pedal- and motor-cycle. Moeran also took up motor-cycling, but in the less leisurely capacity of a despatch-rider, having enlisted in August; later in the war he was seriously wounded in France and Bax thought that particles of shell lodged near the brain may have contributed to his later instability of character (1951: 125). Warlock's friend and fellow undergraduate, the poet Robert Nichols, claiming to have had in September 1914 'a far sharper imaginative notion of what modern war was like than most of my contemporaries, did not expect to survive' (Gray, 1934: 81), but generally there was an optimistic assurance that the Prussians would be cooped up in Berlin by December. Cyril Scott's father and friends were in the minority in being initially depressed at the prospect of an early victory for Germany – though from his psychic information sources Scott himself learnt that the Allies would finally pull through (C. Scott, 1924: 223). Butterworth, folk-dancing at Stratford when the war broke out, wrote to a friend that 'There will be plenty of time to think about volunteering after the first enthusiasms have cooled down' (1918: 16), but within a month he had enlisted, along with his fellow musicians F. B. Ellis, R. O. Morris and Geoffrey Toye, in the Duke of Cornwall's Light Infantry. Still in barracks with a group of northern miners in November, he noted in his journal on the 29th that 'the working people of Durham County . . . are willing to stand almost anything, if only they are to be allowed to get out and finish off the war' (*ibid.*: 46).

Soon, however, it became clear that there was no question of the war quickly being 'finished off' by either side. Rupert Brooke was the first young English artist of promise to die in the war, though of a fever and not in action, on board the *Grantully Castle* off Gallipoli on 24 April 1915. England received the news with shock and patriotic hysteria, fanned by the quotation of Brooke's sonnet 'If I should die' by Dean Inge in his Easter sermon at St Paul's Cathedral only a few days previously. An account of Brooke's burial in the olive grove at Gallipoli was sent back to England by his close friend the composer William Denis Browne, commissioned on the same ship. Whilst on board, Brooke had drafted a poem about dysentery, 'The dance', for Browne to set to music (Hassall: 317), but Browne himself died in the fierce battle at Gallipoli on 4 June, and the friend-ship remained outside the annals of scurrilous song. Another composer, Frederick Kelly, whom Brooke and Browne had not known previously, was on the *Grantully Castle*. He survived Gallipoli, gaining the Distinguished Service Cross, and composed an orchestral Elegy for Brooke, but was killed at Beaucourt-sur-Ancre in France on 13 November 1916. Meanwhile Butterworth's death, in the battle of the Somme at Pozières on 5 August 1916, before he could hear of his Military Cross for action the previous month, caused a fresh wave of sentiment and sentimentality. A fourth English composer's death, which by contrast went almost unnoticed, was that of Ernest Farrar in France on 18 September 1918. His memory was to inspire the most impressive piece of English first world war music, the Piano Sonata by his friend Frank Bridge, as well as the touching song 'In memoriam' with words and music by two of his pupils, H.P. Dixon and Harry Gill (McVeagh, 1975–81). Finally one should mention Jerrard Wilkinson, a close friend of Butterworth who also died in the Somme offensive (see Rankin) and who wrote a few songs, including one, 'Suzette' (Elizabeth Piercy) (*1916*) worth reviving for its Edwardian charm. In addition there were other composers who died in action whom it is not possible to enumerate here.

Apart from Bridge's sonata and his later *Oration* there was little English music of lasting value prompted overtly by the war. Bax, in a BBC radio broadcast of 1949, was uncertain whether the more caustic, expressionistic techniques and colours used for the first time in his first two symphonies were stimulated by his response to the war. The mood of terror in Holst's 'Mars' from *The Planets* was conceived before the war. And although, according to Vaughan Williams in a letter to his second wife, his *Pastoral Symphony* is the impression of a desolate, war-torn French landscape rather than of cows looking over gates (U. Vaughan Williams, 1964: 121), in general the English musical reaction to the war was to forget it as quickly as possible. Bliss for one could not forget it, and to exorcise his nightmares, as late as 1930, he wrote the choral symphony *Morning Heroes*, incorporating settings of war verse by Whitman, Wilfred Owen and Robert Nichols, as well as Li Po and Homer; but by this time England was closer to the next war than to the last, and Vaughan Williams's *Dona Nobis Pacem* of 1936, which, like *Morning Heroes*, sets to music 'The city arming' from Whitman's *Drum Taps*, is an urgent plea for peace in the face of a rapidly rearming Europe. From Holst to Britten's *War Requiem* of 1962 the line of war music is one of large-scale works demanding a greater or lesser degree of experimental technique to match the subject. Until Britten began to reconstitute the elements of expression in song composition in the 1930s there was a manifest assumption that technical advance was out of place in song and a tacit agreement to leave war verse, like the new poetry of Eliot and Pound, untouched. John Ireland (who did not serve in the war) wrote *Two Songs: The Cost (Songs of a Great War)* with texts by Eric Thirkell Cooper in November 1916 and *Two Songs* to Brooke poems ('If I should die' and 'Blow out, you bugles') in 1917–18, and Bridge set 'Blow out, you bugles' for tenor and orchestra in May 1918. But the idealistic patriotism of the old era, expressed by Brooke and Grenfell, was being rendered ironic and irrelevant in the bitter realities of the Somme and Passchendaele, and the poetry of the agony and the pity, the verse of Wilfred Owen, Isaac Rosenberg and Charles Sorley, remained unsung. 'The experience of the War was emphatically one which could not be conveyed in debilitated nineteenth-century poetic conventions' (Enright: 162), and English song, throughout its Romantic Indian summer right up to the second world war, was relying largely on 19th-century musical conventions of form, style and expression, however freshly it presented them. Even Gurney, both poet and composer, kept his two arts carefully separate. His poetry, exploring rough, untraditional modes of expression influenced by Gerard Manley Hopkins, was written in the trenches and is often about the trenches. Apart from 'By a bierside', 'In Flanders', 'Severn meadows', 'On Wenlock Edge' and 'Even such is time', his songs, polished gems of Romantic intimacy, were largely composed in rural seclusion in England, and with a few non-topical exceptions they avoid references to war. Of the most notable poet to survive, Siegfried Sassoon, there is only a handful of settings within the period, including one by Gurney ('Everyone sang') and seven by Cyril Rootham, the latter not of war poems.

The war, then, had little direct effect on the course of English song, though it may have lent it greater prominence, there being fewer opportunities for the performance of large-scale works during wartime. The inter-war fruition of the English sensibility was not so much an escapist reaction to the horrors of war as the continuation and maturing of lines of development begun in the pre-war era. 'It was as if their [war] experiences had deepened in them a love of eternal and natural things rather than impelled them to express their disillusionment with mankind' (Kennedy, 1964: 150). This reaction was not peculiar to composers; some war poets, notably Robert Graves and Edmund Blunden, returned to more peaceable themes. Writing of September 1918, Graves tells how 'to forget about the war, I was writing *Country Sentiment*, a book of romantic poems and ballads' (1929, 2/1957: 228) – though 20 years later, when Gerald Finzi was helping to publish 'Nine of the clock', one of Gurney's three settings from the collection, Graves was so ashamed of his early verse that he insisted on appearing under a pseudonym (letter from Finzi to Robin Milford, 1940). Perhaps the clearest indication that the war poetry of Owen and Rosenberg was only one side of the coin was that the *Georgian Poetry* venture survived the war, as we shall see.

Not surprisingly, the war did produce a number of curiosities and museum pieces in the form of songs. Charles Wood's two patriotic songs have already been mentioned. *King Albert's Book*, a memorial to the gallant but unsuccessful stand of Belgium against the Germans, appeared under the auspices of the *Daily Telegraph*, *Daily Sketch*, *Glasgow Herald* and Hodder & Stoughton at Christmas

1914. In addition to a number of short literary tributes and some vivid illustrations by well-known artists, the following musical contributions were elicited, most of them written for the occasion:

Johan Backer-Lunde	She comes not when noon is on the roses (Herbert Trench)
Cowen	Hail!: A hymn to Belgium (Galsworthy)
Debussy	Berceuse héroïque
Elgar	Carillon: Chantons, Belges, chantons!, op.75 (d'Émile Cammaerts)
German	Hymn (Homage to Belgium, 1914)
P. E. Lange-Müller	Lamentation
Liza Lehmann	By the lake (Ethel Clifford) ('to be sung by Madame Clara Butt')
Mackenzie	One who never turned his back (Browning, from *Asolando*)
Mascagni	Sunt lacrymae rerum!
Messager	Pour la patrie (Hugo)
Ethel Smyth	The march of the women
Stanford	But lo! There breaks a yet more glorious day (Bishop Walsham How)

Elgar, for the first time since *Sea Pictures*, came into his own as a song composer. 'Land of hope and glory', adapted from the trio section of *Pomp and Circumstance March no. 1* (1901) to feature in the *Coronation Ode*, op. 44, of 1902, was the typical embodiment of contemporary jingoism – which, however, was not as widespread or important an attribute of the Edwardians' musical leanings as is commonly believed, Elgar having been its one significant exponent. He had written 'A soldier's song' (first published in 1890 in the *Magazine of Music*) as early as 1884; it is grim stuff, contending with such expressions as 'Hear the whiz of the shot as it flies'. 'Land of hope and glory', however, was soon universally acclaimed for the fine tune it was, and during the war it began to enjoy the status of an unofficial national anthem which it has retained ever since. 'In fact Elgar was not happy with the words of 1902 and at the beginning of the war had a new and more suitable set made by Benson . . . but no one wanted to sing these lines in preference to those they knew' (P. M. Young, 1955: 172–3). Elgar's 'Carillon', op. 75, the recitation with orchestra in *King Albert's Book*, is musically no more than a curiosity, but as such it proved tremendously popular:

> It was first performed at Queen's Hall on 7 December 1914, recited by the poet's wife, Tita Brand, who was the daughter of the first *Gerontius* Angel, Marie Brema. Early in 1915 Elgar took the L.S.O. on a provincial tour performing *Carillon* in every town, with Constance Collier and sometimes Cammaerts himself as reciter. The work caught the mood of the moment. The patriotic fervour of the words, matched by fiery and where necessary gentle music, excited audiences to white-heat and, according to Dunhill, 'created a sensation in the concert-hall the like of which London can never have witnessed either before or since'. Henry Ainley and Réjane were among those who declaimed it. So, at private gatherings, were Schuster and Lalla Vandervelde, daughter of Edward Speyer and wife of a Belgian minister. It was at one of these private performances that Alice was reminded that England still had some way to go before it could call itself musical (Kennedy, 1968: 224).

Porte also vouched for its renown:

> The fame of *Carillon* soon spread all over England and eventually to America, where it was received with tremendous acclamation. Elgar wished it to be used

in order to help the Belgian relief work, and it is said that it earned large sums of money for this cause. Early in 1919, during the Armistice period, the piece was produced in Belgium itself and the effect on the audiences was reputed to be memorable. Practical proofs of success were the heavy orders received by the publishers in London for Belgian towns (:164).

It was recorded by Henry Ainley in 1915 and survived to make a reappearance in the second world war, republished in 1942 as a recitation, with piano, of a Binyon poem 'Over all this home-land of our fathers'. (Another Elgar exhumation of the second world war was 'Song of liberty', set to *Pomp and Circumstance March no. 4* with words by A. P. Herbert which, in the trio section, fit the tune excruciatingly badly; this is far worse than anything from the 1914–18 period, and indeed far less tasteful than Elgar's own use of material from the same march for the song 'The King's way', commemorating the opening of the street of that name in London in 1910.) Elgar went on to compose two further accompaniments for the recitation of poems by Cammaerts: *Une voix dans le désert* with orchestra, op. 77, which incorporates a song 'Quand nos bourgeons se rouvriront', and 'Le drapeau belge', op. 79. *The Fringes of the Feet*, four songs for baritone to poems by Kipling, was another war effort, to which a fifth song, 'Inside the bar' (Gilbert Parker), was added to be sung by all four baritones, three of whom had 'assisted' the principal singer, Charles Mott, in the previous songs, apparently with a *mise en scène* (*The Times*, 12 June 1917, following the first performance). The verse, which is perky, topical and partly satirical in its comments on naval wartime endeavour, hardly suits Elgar's muse, which seems not to rise to the level of liveliness required by the words. But the cycle proved successful, touring the provinces with Elgar as conductor, until, on its return to the Coliseum, Kipling objected to the way his verse was being used and the run was halted. Elgar made his customary complaint that somehow he was always prevented from being a commercial success (Kennedy, 1968: 226–7). No other composer prominently exploited imperialism in the vein of Kipling; Grainger's Kipling settings present a much wider view of the poet. Elgar's only other monodic war song was 'Fight for right', a setting of verses by William Morris which Elgar dedicated to the movement of that name in 1916. The same venture was responsible for Parry's 'Jerusalem':

> An undated letter from Dr. Bridges, belonging to an earlier stage of the War, makes it clear that it was he who suggested that Parry should write 'suitable, simple music to Blake's stanzas – music that an audience could take up and join in'. He wanted it for a meeting of the 'Fight for Right' movement in the Queen's Hall, and suggested that, if Parry could not do it himself, he should delegate the task to George Butterworth – who was unhappily killed in the year 1916 (C. L. Graves, 1926, II: 92).

The thought of Butterworth writing 'Jerusalem' instead of Parry is not a felicitous one. Its first performance, given by a choir of 300, was conducted by Walford Davies at a 'Fight for Right' meeting in the Queen's Hall on 28 March 1916. It was subsequently heard on 13 March 1918 at an Albert Hall concert (for which Parry organised the music) marking the final stage of the 'Votes for Women' campaign, and this movement virtually claimed it for its own (*ibid.*: 92–3). 'Jerusalem', more than any other English song except 'Land of hope and glory' since 'Rule, Britannia', has become part of the national heritage, but whereas 'Land of hope and glory' is, for all its inspired melodiousness, a four-square tune with maudlin words fitted to it, 'Jerusalem' is a model of subtle phrasing, finely sculpted declamation and melody free of clichés – principles which Parry pioneered and which have distinguished English solo song in its finest periods. For such a refined tune to have become so popular is surely unique. Its success must have brightened what little was left of Parry's old age. The question of whether 'Jerusalem' was conceived primarily as a solo song, however, seems unanswerable.

Parry and Stanford both wrote hymns for aviators. '*May* 13 [1915]. – . . . Clara Butt's Concert at Albert Hall at 8.30. My "Aviator's song" quite out of place', Parry noted in his diary (*ibid.*: 74). Stanford, wasting no time after the commencement of hostilities, also wrote 'The king's highway' in August 1914 for the Prince of Wales's National Relief Fund, with an *ad lib.* two-part chorus. Later he published 'A carol of bells' (the only patriotic war song sung by Gervase Elwes (Elwes: 251)), and his 'There is no land like England', to patriotic words from Tennyson's *The Foresters*, was published in Volume I of *The Motherland Songbook* in 1919. O'Neill dedicated his 'Eagles of England' to the Royal Air Force. Such hybrids merit merely documentary attention, for they had neither the popular attributes of 'Keep the home fires burning' nor the serious aesthetic purpose of their composers' non-occasional songs, even when they appear to have been conceived as solo songs rather than as unison songs for massed voices. Bantock's 'The march' sets a bad poem about the thousands of the slain marching past (a cubist picture of them doing so appears on the front cover) and compensates for poor musical material by spattering the voice part with marks of encouragement such as '*con angoscia*', '*con voce sommessa*' and '*con elevazione*'. Martin Shaw responded immediately the war broke out to the patriotic doggerel printed in the newspapers:

> The feelings inspired by the beginning of the war stirred me afresh to composition, which I had almost abandoned. I wrote six 'Songs of War' – mostly settings of verses from *The Times*. John Ireland liked these and thought one of them – 'Venizel' – my best song. Stephen Gwynn sent me a stirring poem of his – 'Clare's Brigade' – and I put music to this; but I am afraid it quickly became out of date. Percy Dearmer persuaded the Oxford University Press to publish these, and so to make, I believe, their first essay in music publishing (:120–1).

However, this account of 'Clare's Brigade' (a unison marching song for the Irish Division) and *Six Songs of War* raises false expectations as to their merits. Of the latter (*1914*), the first, with a text taken from the *Westminster Gazette*, is about a torpedo boat. The second refers to Nelson, Drake and other bygone heroes, while the third concerns the holding of a fort, and the fourth urges Erin to stay united and strong, a plea which fell on deaf ears. The fifth, an impression of 'chimes of Flemish loyalty', sets a text by D. Bonnaud, 'the famous Parisian "Chansonnier" now on active service at the front' in a translation 'by the "Times" special correspondent at the front'. The words of the sixth, a nostalgic reminiscence of a French locale, are by 'Captain W. A. Short, an officer in command of a battery at the front'. Such topicality spelt inevitable obsolescence, and although the *Six Songs of War* were evidently of sufficient popularity to merit republication in 1916, they have long been forgotten. So has Edmonstoune Duncan's solo setting of Woodrow Wilson's closing words in his speech to the United States Congress, 3 April 1917 (Antcliffe: 221). More worthy of remembrance is Frederick Keel's gentle setting (*1921*) of William Morris's poem 'In prison', composed in 1915 in the Ruhleben (Berlin) prisoner-of-war camp in which, along with Edgar Bainton and Benjamin Dale, he was interned.

> . . . we all know that a dead poet lives in many a live stockbroker. Many of these people, before they fade into the light of common day, have had an intuitive glimpse which neither age, nor experience, nor knowledge can ever give them, and which, if they but knew it, in their self-satisfied middle age, had been their finest hour. One sometimes wishes one could collect all the beautiful single songs which have been written by young people in this early uprush of feeling. Songs, which even if published get quickly overlaid when no work follows to substantiate the personality. Sometimes death may take the place of this fading into the light of common day, before enough has been written to show the true worth of a composer.

Gerald Finzi, voicing a perception central to the understanding of much English song of the period, proceeded in this RCM lecture (1955, II: 6–7) to refer specifically to two composers of whose work he had intimate experience, Ivor Gurney and Ernest Farrar. Gurney cast himself as one of 'war's embers': he had at least moments of glowing creativity before cooling to a cinder. With Farrar, however, as with Kelly, Browne and Butterworth, it is essential to make a distinction, lacking in Finzi's eulogy on the lyrical impulse which was abundant in all four of them, between promise and achievement. All four were in fact slow developers, and their songs testify more to the painful process of self-discovery than to youthful brilliance. Butterworth's brilliance was largely posthumous, in that he became the perfect model of his own poignant subject-matter, 'The lads that will die in their glory and never be old'. Henry Hadow, writing to Butterworth's father in June 1917, fell prey to a hackneyed view of him, placing the customary false emphasis on his thwarted promise:

> We little realized how short the time was to be.
>   He will rank, with Brooke and Julian Grenfell, among the real poets who, in this war, have given their lives for their country . . . Yet the music will live – 'great in what it achieved, greater still in what it promised' – and will remind future generations that England gave her best to the sacrifice (Butterworth, 1903–22: 16).

It was this emotional colouring which Edward Dent wished to avoid in his rôle as executor for his former student Denis Browne, who has remained far less known and sung as a result. But Browne undoubtedly possessed the greater potential, intellectually and technically. With Butterworth it is difficult to see where he might have turned from the polished yet limited perfection of *A Shropshire Lad*, even if his exposure to Vaughan Williams's *London Symphony* was leading him slowly towards the more advanced stylistic territory glimpsed in his incomplete Orchestral Fantasy.

Farrar was the weakest of the four. Though he responded to the moods of the times, writing choral settings of Whitman, Housman, Henley and both Rossettis, as well as a number of instrumental works of pastoral and Celtic inspiration, his musical personality never showed signs of becoming much more than parochial. His songs, with the exception of 'Brittany', have not remained in the repertoire. Finzi, who studied with him in Harrogate in 1914–16, used Farrar's setting of 'Silent noon', which he found stood up to Vaughan Williams's celebrated version (we shall also encounter a third setting, by C. W. Orr), in his RCM lecture as an illustration of a published song which became 'quickly overlaid'. In fact one can see both why it was 'overlaid' and why Finzi wished to uncover it: it is a deeply felt essay in melodic and harmonic sensuality, yet curiously unbalanced, like some of Finzi's own songs, in its sectional and tonal structure (it begins in C but closes in D flat), with an unmistakable sense of anticlimax at the end (Ex. 1). 'Brittany' sets to music a text by E. V. Lucas, known for his travel books and anthologies of wayfaring poetry that included much the same sort of material as 'Brittany' itself, bridging the gap between Stevenson and the Georgians. The setting is attractive but superficial, and foreshadows the songs of Michael Head – popular because most of the singer's effects are built in by the composer, pretty without the liability of being genuinely arresting. Elsewhere

Ex. 1

Farrar does not have a great deal to offer. 'O mistress mine' and his two last songs, 'Diaphenia' and 'The lover's appeal', bring grace but not compulsiveness to their respective poems, while in the *Two Pastorals* the musical tone is not unlike Quilter's, if lacking his polish and suffering from the texts by Norman Gale. As a whole the *Vagabond Songs* are probably his best.

Frederick Kelly is a more tantalising figure. Like Grainger an Australian who studied for a time at Frankfurt and developed into a professional pianist, he first pursued an undergraduate career at Balliol College, Oxford, where his close and lasting association with Tovey began. Tovey, whose private life was seldom happy, seems to have strained the friendship through his emotional attachment to Kelly's sister, and the two men probably also suffered from mutual artistic jealousy (Grierson: 112–17). Tovey possessed an intellect more analytical than creative: the style of his two sets of six songs – though he may have composed more (see Grierson: 150) – is far too academic to be effective, except perhaps in 'I wandered lonely as a cloud' from the second set. Kelly veered the other way, and in his eight published songs he shows a fertile delight in technical invention. In the *Two Songs*, op. 1, this is coupled with a well-controlled sense of craftsmanship in a manner no less accomplished than that of the early Frank Bridge. We have here and Edwardian style perfectly preserved, unravaged by any forebodings of linguistic crisis.

On 22 July 1901 Kelly wrote to Balfour Gardiner from Sydney, Australia, 'I have set one of Shakespeare's sonnets "Shall I compare thee to a summer's day" etc. but it is fearfully influenced by your friend Grainger's "Away in the land of the Japanee"' (Gardiner: 1901–61). (The Grainger work in question is 'At twilight', for tenor and unaccompanied mixed chorus, not published until 1913.) The setting of the celebrated sonnet is a courageous one. Kelly's imagination is fired by the poem, but in somewhat unexpected ways. Each of the poem's iambic pentameters is set to a four-bar phrase, so the accommodation of five strong syllables per line involves more than one accent in some bars; Kelly achieves this by a flexible use of triple time which, although it tends to give an unbecoming lilt to the text, does produce some subtly Brahmsian stretching and contracting of the phrases beyond their four-bar boundaries, helped by touches of cross-accent. The treatment of the opening line, the searching for a comparison, is particularly happy: the intermediate dominant of the relative minor leads in as if with a gradual concentrating of the mind (Ex. 2). In respecting the tight integration and continuity of the sonnet form, however, Kelly is compelled to develop a musical continuity which, being wholly lyrical in execution, feels too one-dimensional, and smothers the structural poise of the sestet with its climactic expansion; he tries to compensate by interweaving a purely musical motivic structure at the climax (Ex. 3, *x*), based on a three-note rising scale which has been growing upwards from the line 'Nor lose possession' and indeed was present in the first line as well as inverted in the introduction. The problem is a common one: the music attains its breadth of conception only through its response to the quality of the poem, yet the poem loses its own structural identity in the process. Only at certain points do the two fuse, as in the highly charged repetition of the final line, especially at the yearning, Tchaikovskian augmented 6th on the word 'life'.

Although throughout the song the piano writing is idiomatically resourceful, in

Ex. 2

Ex. 3

the fine winding-down from the climax on the last page the gestures seem orchestral. This may also be said of 'Aghadoe', the second song, written in 1903 and not
dissimilar in its effect to Elgar's 'The pipes of Pan', which had been published in
1900. Here the Irish ballad by John Todhunter, with its relentless cantering narrative, is given vocal intensity by the imprecatory repetitions, four or five times in
each of the seven stanzas, of the word 'Aghadoe', turning cadentially around
tonics or dominants except in the fourth stanza, where the emotional pitch is
heightened when the vocal axis of c' is underpinned by a 6–4 chord in A flat
major, thus becoming a mediant. In this exercise in Poe's 'supernal beauty',
where verbal tone and effect are far more important than meaning, it is nevertheless the inventive compendium of figures in the accompaniment, perhaps influenced by the finale of Grieg's op. 7 Piano Sonata, that fills out the strophic
variation to an aesthetic whole, and it is this that suggests orchestral colouring.
The chromatic curves remind one of Bax, yet, despite their frequent proliferation, every note tells; Kelly attains to Stanford's ideal of economy in the setting of

ballad poetry more arrestingly than Stanford himself, and also foreshadows Finzi (see, for instance, 'For Life I had never cared greatly'). The song is a technical *tour de force*.

But in Kelly's later set of six songs, op. 6, dedicated to Gervase Elwes, his technique becomes his own enemy. The piano accompaniments gain complexity at the cost of concentration, the proliferation becomes diffuse, and there is little really memorable writing. Part of the trouble is that with his broadening horizons Kelly is in danger of losing touch with his stylistic background; here he departs from English models in a mêlée of vaguely cosmopolitan Tchaikovskian effects. Perhaps the training at Frankfurt under Knorr (himself a friend of Tchaikovsky), coming after the rigour of Oxford and of Tovey's companionable mind, was detrimental. He certainly endeavoured to keep himself tightly harnessed to Tovey during this period: in addition to writing a set of waltzes for piano duet on a reciprocal postal basis between 1905 and 1911, the two men sent each other canonic puzzles on postcards. Possibly also his setting of Wordsworth's 'I wandered lonely as a cloud' ('The daffodils') (1910) was a conscious response to Tovey's earlier one. Yet Tovey's is the more integrated setting, and none of Kelly's op. 6 songs shows the earlier discipline or sustained inspiration. The choice of poetry does not help; Wordsworth's daffodils are beyond him. He treats the first two lines as miserable and melancholy and introduces them on the piano by a long chain of downward chromatic chords which outdoes Tchaikovsky's *Pathétique* Symphony; his subsequent endeavour to generate a contagious dance-rhythm and sustain it in the piano part is rather feeble. The two Logan Pearsall Smith poems are too close to the vernal doggerel of countless poetasters to be a wise choice: in 'March' Kelly spurns the suggestion of almost unwilling surprise at the signs of spring which, especially in the last line ('Sudden the blackbird sings'), constitutes the poem's originality, and makes the observation inappropriately graphic in an accompaniment which goes from the florid to the positively Wagnerian in outpourings of birdsong in the postlude. The Li Po translation comes across as a rather banal experiment in oriental sensibility: Kelly was no Mahler. In Shelley's violent poem 'When the lamp is shattered' he starts strongly (Ex. 4) but he is unable to span the repetitions of this opening motive with satisfactory material, and the motive's strenuousness sounds empty. The least flawed of the six songs is the other, smaller-scale Shelley setting, 'Music, when soft voices die'. Even here the modulations seem unnecessary and undirectional, but the much simpler texture, with its fragmentary countermelodic lines in the accompaniment, is well handled.

Ex. 4

Could Kelly have survived a creative crisis such as Bridge underwent? Without such a crisis could he have regained the concentration shown in his op. 1, or was he already in op. 6 becoming one of Finzi's 'dead poets'? The speculation is futile, though it must be said that for all their insecurities and banalities the op. 6 songs are too fecund and original to be dismissed as outright failures.

Butterworth was less gifted with natural fluency, but set out to achieve certain modest, though radical, aims with a crystalline integrity almost unparalleled in song composition. He left little compositional dross. According to Boult and others there were plenty of songs which he destroyed before going off to war, and two settings of Robert Bridges, 'Crown winter with green' and 'Haste on, my joys!', now lost, were described after his death by his father as 'slight in character, and evidently early in date' (1918: 109). A setting of Stevenson's 'I will make you brooches', published posthumously in 1920, is disappointing, being much hampered by a persistently mixolydian modality which only once, in a manner highly reminiscent of Vaughan Williams's setting of the poem in *Songs of Travel* (presumably earlier), lets the sun come out with a modulation to the dominant, rare for Butterworth, at the words 'bright blows the broom'. Otherwise his settings of poetry are restricted to a carefully chosen handful of lyrics, all partaking of the qualities germane to his purposes.

His single Shelley setting, for instance, is of a poem which swings to and fro on a slender pendulum of lovesick diffidence:

> I fear thy kisses, gentle maiden,
>   Thou needest not fear mine;
> My spirit is too deeply laden
>   Ever to burden thine.
>
> I fear thy mien, thy tones, thy motion,
>   Thou needest not fear mine;
> Innocent is the heart's devotion
>   With which I worship thine.

W. E. Henley, a rallying figure for the 'counter-decadence' of the nineties and all too famous for 'Invictus' and 'England, my England', may seem a strange partner for the quietly introspective Butterworth, but his collection *Echoes*, containing particularly concise lyrics which were frequently drawn upon by other composers, has moments of a similarly wistful mood. Love, 'a spirit that comes and goes', is however also tinged with a darker *fin-de-siècle* fatalism:

> Fill a glass with golden wine,
>   And the while your lips are wet
> Set their perfume unto mine,
>   And forget,
> Every kiss we take and give
> Leaves us less of life to live.

For Butterworth the war, with its unpredictable fusion of relationships, seems to have provided the final sublimation of desire in action. He belonged to an Edwardian generation of artists who, living under the shadow of Oscar Wilde's trauma of the previous decade and in a reactionary climate, could no longer adopt the flamboyant life-style of the aesthetes or give way to melodramatic despair; their understating and underplaying of emotion led rather to an introverted narcissism of which they found an exact expression in Housman:

> Oh fair enough are sky and plain,
>   But I know fairer far:
> Those are as beautiful again
>   That in the water are;
>
> The pools and rivers wash so clean
>   The trees and clouds and air,
> The like on earth was never seen,
>   And oh that I were there.
>
> These are the thoughts I often think
>   As I stand gazing down
> In act upon the cressy brink
>   To strip and dive and drown;
>
> But in the golden-sanded brooks
>   And azure meres I spy
> A silly lad that longs and looks
>   And wishes he were I.

Here the mood, supported by its lyrical expression, is one of diffident inaction which, although allowing for the occasional lash of intensity – 'To strip and dive and drown' – remains unfulfilled and ambivalent: the lad is only 'in act', and the word 'drown' is not to be taken literally, except on a shadowy, deeper level of meaning.

It is important to be aware of the visual dimensions of these poems set by Butterworth in order to appreciate what he was trying to do in music. Wilde's 'Requiescat', which he set in 1911, has the tiniest of stanzas:

> Tread lightly, she is near
>   Under the snow,
> Speak gently, she can hear
>   The daisies grow.
>
> All her bright golden hair
>   Tarnished with rust,
> She that was young and fair
>   Fallen to dust.

These enable the imagery of death and frigidity – 'snow', 'rust' and 'dust' – to be implanted in the mind at the end of a line with the slightest of monosyllabic strokes. Housman similarly, by ending 'Loveliest of trees' with the word 'snow', touches his picture with a lightness which is to be taken as a metaphor for blossom but at the same time holds ironic implications of literalness: all too soon it will be winter again:

> And since to look at things in bloom
> Fifty springs are little room,
> About the woodlands I will go
> To see the cherry hung with snow.

Butterworth's self-appointed task was to find a musical style to bring out this delicate balance of lyrical ease and suggestive force. Folksong was to provide the lyrical ease, without the conventional paraphernalia of keyboard introduction, figuration, modulatory procedure and climax demanded by the hitherto accepted framework of the Romantic song or ballad stanza. This substitution of a modal model for a tonal one was typical of the time; Butterworth led the way in seizing its implications. The accompaniment could no longer be expected to conduct a more or less pre-formulated harmonic argument, for modal harmony, perhaps a contradiction in terms, was notoriously difficult to make sound organic. On the other hand, its independent (non-dominant, non-cadential) placing of triads could express to good effect the reticence we have noted in the poetry Butterworth chose to set, and this could also be built upon to provide an overlay of more sophisticated harmonic densities, which in the most complex songs results in a fabric of impressionism reminiscent of Debussy. Economy is always the most positive consideration, however, and in his *Eleven Folksongs from Sussex*, mostly arranged (according to Michael Dawney) between 1906 and 1909, we see exemplary settings of pre-existent tunes which may be considered as studies for the original songs that followed. Rather than surveying Butterworth's output chronologically, the following discussion endeavours to show how, within it, varying levels of invention and nuance grow from this simple basis.

'When I was one-and-twenty', from the *Shropshire Lad* settings, represents the simplest stage: a traditional tune is harnessed to the words, and only the regretful last line, 'And oh, 'tis true, 'tis true[, 'tis true]', elicits original vocal composition, in the shape of a simple extension of the folk tune's final phrase. The accompaniment is no more than a sometimes discontinuous series of common chords, with plenty of 'weak' first and second inversions which avoid over-colouring the tune. In fact the music hardly makes any difference to the flow of the verse. Nowhere else does Butterworth use a genuine folk tune, but he adopts much the same procedure in 'Think no more, lad' and the dorian 'With rue my heart is laden'. 'When the lad for longing sighs' is a similar instance, this time in the aeolian mode; the triads give way in the second stanza to a line of 3rds (later developed as 6ths), and these turn into a primary expressive device in some of the more ambitious song settings. At the very end, the triadic vocabulary fleetingly takes on a new linguistic significance: an expected plagal cadence onto E is interrupted by a 6–4 chord on G, which descends to its first inversion on E, which is then left sounding on its own: the cadence is not resolved. The purpose is clearly for the music to mirror the quiet irony of the poem's last line and give it time to sink in.

Two further examples illustrate Butterworth's approach to Housman's ironic or pregnant endings. In 'The lads in their hundreds' a flowing melody is accompanied by harmony which is not modal but which nevertheless avoids semantic development by being limited to a handful of chord-positions, none of which has an overall compass of more than an octave and a 5th; only at the end, after the poem's final line, 'The lads that will die in their glory and never be old', does it delicately expand outwards to a compass of an octave and a 7th, and even here the thrill of grandeur in the text is kept open-ended and reflective, rather than conclusive and platitudinous, by a final cadence that deliberately mixes plagal and perfect (Ex. 5). In 'Is my team ploughing' the mode is dorian throughout, with no foreign notes, but the harmony is only triadic for the living man's replies. For the ghost's nostalgic but increasingly searching questions the accompaniment is more expressive – an example of how the force of Butterworth's style relies on the superimposing of coloured harmonies, borrowed from various composers of the late-Romantic tradition, upon a transparent base. In this case the harmony is

Ex. 5

Ex. 6

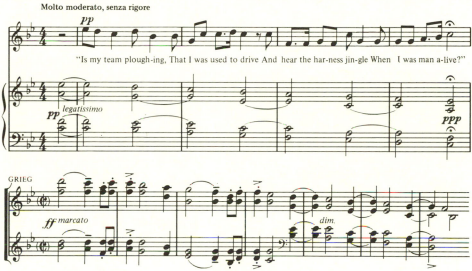

lifted wholesale from Grieg (Ex. 6, from the String Quartet; the same passage also appears in the Piano Concerto). The aesthetic success of the song, which is considerable, consists in matching the controlled shock of the poem's last line with a closing musical gesture that combines the inconclusiveness of modal harmony with the poignancy of a chord derived from the middle of the sequence: we are left with an unresolved added 6th above the mode's final (Ex. 7).

When dealing with poetry other than Housman's, Butterworth's references to folk music are more fragmentary. The setting of Wilde's 'Requiescat' appears under-composed as a result: he seems to provide nothing in their place. There is a variety of expressive device, such as the sinking to A flat at the word 'Tarnished', the parallel-4th harmony just afterwards, the breath-holding reflective silences brought into relief by stellar arpeggios at 'Peace, Peace', the tremor of feeling as the upward octave dominant at 'dust' breaks into parallel 3rds, and its thickening into epitaph-like parallel 3rds in the epilogue. But these nuances are glimpsed more as possibilities than as fulfilments. In 'I fear thy kisses' the signs of emotion are even more subdued, showing through with a heavy heart in the harmonies at 'laden' and 'maiden' but not conveying the continuity of thought, which is

Ex. 7

Ex. 8

Ex. 9

obtained by a delicate, extremely spare structure of two phrases (Ex. 8), of which the second opens the voice part. At the end of the first stanza the first motive is heard with an inversion of itself to form an added-7th double arpeggio, and the second, gaining momentum, turns into semiquavers; together they give the second stanza a wispy continuum of semiquaver arpeggios, yet the harmonic gestures are often unconvincing, as at the words 'heart's devotion' and at the indecisive return to B flat major/minor thereafter. At the end Butterworth tries another added-6th effect, all logically worked out in terms of parallel voice-leading, but without the genius of 'Is my team ploughing' (Ex. 9). One cannot but admire Butterworth's refusal to take any element of tonal rhetoric for granted in these two songs, yet the result is somehow stylistically too disembodied.

This sort of writing proves fertile elsewhere, however. In 'Oh fair enough are sky and plain', cited above, an aeolian G minor is the basis of the two elements, a 'sighing' pair of chords which together include all the notes of the mode (Ex. 10), and another sighing gesture (Ex. 11), the voice's opening phrase (as in 'I fear thy kisses'). Although a premium is misguidedly placed on a series of rather impotent

Ex. 10   Ex. 11

6–3 chords in the first and last stanzas (the third and fourth stanzas of 'Requiescat' suffer likewise), in the middle the structural mosaic coheres into a moving
setting of the words. Ex. 11, extended into a line fleshed out at one point with
3rds, endows the reflected images of 'trees and clouds and air' in the piano part
with limpid attraction which intensifies to frustrated longing as its triadic core is
repeated a tone higher, the previous pedal d rising to e at the phrase 'The like on
earth', whereupon the pair of chords (Ex. 10) invitingly reappears as a beautifully
spaced, resolving dominant major 9th as the enticing thought of plunging into the
water is developed; but the sinister implications of the act take the first chord
back, via a distorted resolution under the word 'dive', to its original specification, on G, now *sff*, at the word 'drown'. Further reflective play is made with the
spacing and the progression in the piano epilogue.

The structural and expressive elements outlined above are seen at their best in
Butterworth's celebrated setting of 'Loveliest of trees'. His control over the
expressive motives allows him on the one hand to pare the texture down to a
radical minimum in the song and on the other to build the motives up later in the
same year (1911) into an orchestral rhapsody, *A Shropshire Lad*, where they
expand organically without in any way dwarfing the song in retrospect. In
'Loveliest of trees' he again takes a three-note descending scale, which launches
the voice part, as his basic motive (Ex. 12). It is by extension a tetrachord (see the

Ex. 12

piano part under the words 'along the bough', after which the original version is
inverted in the voice), but a twist is interpolated here at the beginning, making the
interval of a 3rd. This twist expands, through its statement at the words 'Wearing
white', into the triumphal 'Eastertide' motive, where it is thickened into vaguely
ecclesiastical block chords before returning to its original form, but now omi-
nously shorn of its inward turn after the 3rd as the sense of departing time, persisting with the 3rd (g' sharp to e') throughout the second stanza, begins to sink in.

The 3rd here also takes on a vertical dimension whose exploitation as disembodied chains of parallel 3rds, so characteristic of Butterworth, is at its most telling in the sweetness of the piano epilogue; it is dwelt on even further in the haunting opening of the Rhapsody. But the most inspired motivic touch is the very first
phrase, where the tetrachord and its twist interlock to give a sense not only of
intense wonderment at the beauty of the cherry blossom – a wonderment which
sinks powerfully into the consciousness as the downward 3rds expand, via a 4th
and then a 5th, into a rich, deep chord – but perhaps also a graphic hint that the
blossom is already fluttering off the tree to the ground (Ex. 12).

The Henley cycle, *Love Blows as the Wind Blows*, for voice and string quartet,
lies somewhat off-centre in respect to this perfection of expression, although it
was composed in 1911–12, during the same period as the Housman songs, or
slightly later. It is seldom performed. In working with larger forces Butterworth
is in danger of abnegating his technical virtues of spareness and limpidity; the
string quartet, which, Howes finds, 'contrary to expectation, hardly ever makes a
good accompaniment for the solo voice' (1966: 310), hampers him and
occasionally gives rise to mawkish harmonies. Yet this cycle is not musically
barren, and in its later (1914) version for small orchestra it affords a view of the
composer's broadening sensibilities. Henley's poetry is responsible for its
strengths as well as its weaknesses. Its Victorian atmosphere leads Butterworth to
turn away from folksong and rely much more on borrowings and graftings from
mainstream European composers: Wagner, Tchaikovsky, Debussy, Fauré and
Elgar. There is also a *Leitmotiv* (Ex. 13), stated at the opening of the first song

Ex. 13

Molto moderato, senza rigore

(on the horn in the orchestral version). This song lacks poetic binding force:
Henley's end-of-the-year mood, in an amorphous, ambling metre, hardly goes
beyond clichés:

> In the year that's coming on, rich in joy and sorrow,
> We shall light our lamp, and wait life's mysterious morrow.

This calls up a fabric of undistinctive four-part harmony and counterpoint alternating with more arresting static periods reminiscent of Duparc, yet the necessary
tonal control is lacking. A fine modulatory upsurge at 'We shall weave it stronger
yet' is followed by a clumsy, cramping whole-tone transition to express the sense
of 'ere the circle closes', and the attempt to match the waiting for the 'mysterious
morrow' at the end of the song with alternating *Waldweben* (see below, p. 164)
on a B major added 6th and G major dominant 7th does not quite convince – it
just sounds as though the song ends in the wrong key. The second poem is in two
similar eight-line stanzas: three lines express life's formality and order, the fourth
states, by contrast, the motto 'Love blows as the wind blows' (Butterworth sets
his *Leitmotiv* to this), and the last four, starting from the repeated 'blows!',

work up a little whirlwind of love's waywardness culminating in the last line, 'Love blows into the heart'. Except for the whirlwind, which is broken by his harmonically graphic but obstructive depiction of 'A spirit that comes and goes', Butterworth faithfully attempts to mirror this structure, but in so doing fails to establish a musical autonomy, a problem which is bound to arise in setting such a poem.

From this point on we have in effect two different song-cycles. In the orchestral version, on the final word 'heart', the *Waldweben* of the end of the first song, together with their restlessly shifting bass line, reappear in the clarinets and gradually point the music towards a modal G minor, where it settles down for the last song, a moving poem of consolation for lost love. The transition is delicate (Ex. 14) and helps to justify in retrospect the similar ending of the first song. In

Ex. 14

the original version, however, the second song, with a further, subdued statement of the *Leitmotiv* in the accompanimental epilogue in the key of A, moves to C sharp minor for a third song, 'Fill a glass with golden wine', a gloomy meditation on the imminence of death. This would have worked well with orchestra; there are some fine touches, such as the abrupt, hollow transition from C sharp major to minor with a subdominant 9th before the words 'nearer death'. The final serene modal picardy cadence in C sharp minor clinches the associations of death, and then, after a '*piccola pausa*', the fourth song begins in G minor. The cathartic effect is no weaker than in the orchestral version, but the implications are quite different: it is as though love is lost suddenly through death whereas in the later version it fades gradually through changeability. Were there personal reasons for the change? In either case the sweetness of consolation through memory is powerfully felt in the last song. Here the G minor quaver ostinato (see Ex. 14) gives touching expression to the assurance of the immortality of memory, and succeeds where the first song failed in providing a structural anchor for the flights into distant keys at the points of heightened happiness, for one of which,

> And old, immortal words
> Sang in my breast like birds

the *Leitmotiv* returns, as it does at the end of the piece, in the peaceful instrumental epilogue.

The serenity that Henley attains in this fine poem is matched in the music, which relies on an impressionistic continuity of mood-painting far removed from the folksong ideal. Only one of the Housman settings contains something similar, and that is the odd man out of the set, not included in the planning stages of the cycle and possibly written later, 'On the idle hill of summer'. This, surely Butterworth's finest song, is technically his most resourceful, yet paradoxically his recourse to the language of Wagner and Debussy to create its mood of sensuous subjectivity places him back in the late-Romantic tradition, from which he had been standing aloof (Ex. 15). Here for the first time he seems to

Ex. 15

have come fully to grips with his post-Wagnerian environment, and shows a startling intensity in immersing himself in it; folksong suddenly seems immature and irrelevant. Might this achievement have marked the adoption of a less precious stance? Ironically, the only thing it was to mark clearly was the premonition of his own end:

> East and west on fields forgotten
>   Bleach the bones of comrades slain,
> Lovely lads and dead and rotten;
>   None that go return again.

William Denis Browne has been left until last because he was the most promising of the four. In Butterworth free creativity had been continually cramped by diffidence, partly an unwillingness to defy his father, who was General Manager of the North Eastern Railway and strongly opposed his son's adopting a musical profession. Antagonism between the two gradually subsided as Butterworth's genius became recognised, but there is no evidence to suggest that he would ever have thrown himself into a composer's career with the energy and sense of fulfilment that military activity and folksong collecting brought to him. With Browne, however, there were no such negative factors. He was set for a brilliant career, as the following biographical account (Taylor, 1973) indicates.

Born at Leamington in 1888, he was awarded open scholarships both in mathematics at Harrow and in classics at Rugby, accepting the latter in 1903. There he made friends with Rupert Brooke, who was a year his senior. In 1907 he entered Clare College, Cambridge, with a major scholarship in classics, and became extremely involved in acting and music. He formed a circle of friends which included Edward Dent, Armstrong Gibbs, Vaughan Williams and the singers Steuart Wilson and Clive Carey. Dent acknowledged him to be 'by far the cleverest' of this circle (1924: 42). From 1910 he devoted all his time to music, becoming organ scholar at Clare, gaining a distinction in Part II of the MusB degree, and transcribing lute music for Dent. After a holiday in Germany in 1912, part of which was spent at Busoni's home, he took up a music teaching post at Repton, but moved to London in November 1912 as organist of Guy's Hospital. His close friendship with Brooke – whose intellectual superior Howells (who knew them both) considered him to have been (1974) – drew him into the artistic circle of Edward Marsh, and his musical activities included composition teaching at Morley College, giving the first London performance of Berg's Piano Sonata, and writing reviews for *The Blue Review* (*Rhythm*), *The Times* and *The New Statesman* on a variety of musical subjects including Scriabin.

The wide range of his intellectual involvement and his unfettered, sunny creative disposition (which was also characteristic of Brooke) are reflected in his music. Some church music, some orchestral dances and a suite, a piano piece, a choral setting of Tennyson's *The Kraken*, an incomplete ballet and nine songs survive. Given this scant output we may question whether the urge to compose would have flourished (the orchestral movements are mostly arrangements of each other), but we need not doubt the fertility of technique, as a chronological survey of Browne's songs will show.

Two early Tennyson songs, 'Move eastward' and 'The snowdrop', apparently published by Stainer & Bell in 1910, are lost. The former, performed by Carrie Tubb with another Browne song (one of them with organ accompaniment) at a 'Tribute to the Fallen' on 30 October 1919, was described as weak by *The Times* the next day. The two Yeats settings, Browne's earliest dated songs, are negligible – clumsy and unmemorable in a manner that owes nothing to English traditions of song composition and gains no strength from elsewhere. The undated 'Isle of lost dreams' is more attractive but is a curious response to Fiona Macleod's Celtic sadness, sounding in places remarkably like a hymn tune. 'Parting' also has the squareness of a hymn, and the subdominant cadence at the end of its second line could have been written by S. S. Wesley. The dismal poetry is set in an appalling translation, which one hopes was not by Browne himself, and whose worst moments will prevent its being sung, but Hugh Taylor is surely too harsh in saying that 'The whole style reminds one of Hatton's *The wreck of the Hesperus*' (1973: 35). Had the self-pitying tune been made to sound more definitely ironic and the over-composed piano accompaniment (a common fault of Browne's) with its funereal throbs been more strongly characterised, in orchestral images, the result could have been a viable study in Mahlerian lugubriousness.

Browne's four latest songs are his best. The least profound of them is the lilting $\frac{6}{8}$ setting of Henry Constable's 'Diaphenia', with slightly seductive inner chromatic lines and oompah accompaniment which link it more to the vaudeville than to the *Lied* tradition. It is charming in its artlessness, but its three-bar phrasing is carefully crafted. In his two other 17th-century settings he tackles more challenging texts. 'Epitaph on Salathiel Pavy' sets a lovely poem by Ben Jonson about a famous boy chorister-actor who died at the age of 13. In many of their songs both Moeran – whose 'Rosaline' has points of similarity with 'Diaphenia' and the 'Epitaph' – and Warlock were to share Browne's concern with creating an easy-going 'affection' in which a flowing tune gives equal measure to each syllable and allows the poem's metre to speak without obvious rhetoric. It is up to the singer to apply the rhetoric with careful sub-phrasing and rubato, which the text's sophisticated syntax necessitates. Since each long and short line-pair in the text makes up a (usually unpunctuated) Alexandrine, the syllabic pacing results in long, almost plainsong-like $\frac{10}{4}$ bars with an anacrusis and a feminine rhyme spilling over at each end. The accompaniment is modal in a way quite different from Butterworth's and much more reminiscent of Elizabethan composers: Browne's lute-song transcriptions have borne fruit. In the third stanza archaism is enhanced with wisps of pastiche plainsong counterpointed note for note against the vocal line. The introduction and linking passages, constructed in an invertible counterpoint of ascending triads and a chromatic descending line, reflect Vaughan Williams's earlier 'Tears, idle tears' and are reflected in Finzi's similarly elegiac 'Come away, death'.

Each song was by now proving more interesting than the last. In February 1913, two months after writing the 'Epitaph', Browne composed what has become his best-known song, a Lovelace setting, 'To Gratiana dancing and singing', written for Steuart Wilson. Denis Arundell described it in the *Cambridge Review* (1926) as 'one of the few great songs written by a recent British composer: it will live after all the Warlocks and Vaughan Williams' (H. Taylor, 1973: 37). Herbert Howells (1974) named it as one of the dozen or so tunes that had been present in his mind all his life (the melody, however, was taken by Browne from an anonymous 'Allmayne' in Elizabeth Rogers' Virginal Book, used in the Milton tercentenary performance of *Comus* in which he acted at Cambridge in 1908. The characteristically full piano chords now sound rich instead of thick, and the constant hand-crossing, still a rather unnecessary mannerism in 'Diaphenia', adds to the exhilaration, as does the diatonic boldness resulting from an experiment in 10ths, possibly influenced by Busoni (Ex. 16), which is at its most effective in the second, descending half of the tune, where the suspensions begin. But the strength of the song lies chiefly in its dramatisation of the poet's experience. The independence of the voice part from the accompaniment, which, with the 'Allmayne' melody, represents the dance consort, replete with lutes, citterns and pandoras, emphasises the poet's rôle as a detached though passionate observer: the musical

Ex. 16

Ex. 17

Ex. 18

impression is that he describes Gratiana's performance from an awed distance in the crowded ballroom, his graphic experience relayed in graphic diction (Ex. 17). In the second stanza, '*pp lontano*', it is as though he has left the room to reflect on the scene, or is recounting it later with the dance music still in his head; only then does his, and others', hopeless admiration, which left the floor 'paved with broken hearts', sink in on him and us (Ex. 18).

However, Browne's last song, a setting of de la Mare's 'Arabia', written a year and a half later, is his most advanced. It first appeared in print in December 1919 in *The Monthly Chapbook*, an arty periodical issued by Harold Monro's Poetry Bookshop; this particular issue (see the jacket of the present book for a reproduction of its cover design) was devoted to four English songs and a 'note' on the marriage of music and verse by Dent, the other songs being 'Nod' (de la Mare) by Armstrong Gibbs, 'At the turn of the burn' (G. Townsend Warner) by Malcolm Davidson, and 'Melmillo' (de la Mare) by Clive Carey. Browne had anticipated the atmosphere of 'Arabia' in his setting of Francis Thompson's opiate reverie 'Dream-tryst' (1909), a radical study in hypersensibility which has remained unpublished; most of its original attributes – delicate filigree-work arpeggios, tonalities defined by single chord-complexes, frail, semi-*parlando* melody, and evocative pentatonics in both melody and harmony – bear richer fruit in 'Arabia', though 'Dream-tryst' is in places more experimental. 'Arabia' is as close to the spirit of late Debussy as any Englishman came. But it is less well known than 'Gratiana' because it is not altogether convincing. Its strange power of evocation, present from the weird opening bars with their eerie fade-out (borrowed from Schumann's *Papillons*, op. 2), is at once too fragile and too disturbing to be communicable (Ex. 19). the choral setting of the poem, in *Songs of Enchantment*, by Armstrong Gibbs, Browne's acquaintance from Cambridge days, is more approachable and more immediate in its harmonic imagery. Browne's is more fragmentary: tempi remain unstable, tonalities evaporate or cling to one or two chords, melodic lines do not connect. But Browne's setting is also more tinglingly narcotic, more truly 'crazed with the spell'. Here, as in 'Dream-tryst', he is haunted by chords consisting of a triad with a superimposed bare 5th a degree apart (Ex. 20). There is every reason to suppose that, had he lived, he would have built upon the exquisite sensibility of 'Arabia'; but he died, and English song continued in less exotic channels.

Ex. 19

Ex. 20

II

THE LYRICAL IMPULSE BETWEEN THE WARS

VIII

Introduction: the uses of technique – style and personal symbolism in John Ireland

It is possible to adopt a very gloomy view of England between the wars. Acting out the charade of a long weekend (R. Graves and A. Hodge), many aped New York and Paris by succumbing to the modernity of flappers, bobbed hair, jazz, angular furniture and eurhythmics, while many others gradually became entrenched in a vague English pastoralism tinged with nostalgia, characterised by the Black Country novels of Francis Brett Young and comfortable fireside speeches of Stanley Baldwin (Cannadine, 1977), mock-Tudor semi-detached houses, morris dancing, hiking and charabanc outings to Stratford upon Avon. Some were out of joint with the prevailing environment; in music Balfour Gardiner comes to mind as one who, through some psychological process not entirely clear, or maybe simply through honesty, could no longer compose and instead took to forestry for the rest of his life. His less well known fellow composers Norman O'Neill and Frederic Austin shared his disillusionment, as an account by Austin of a Mediterranean holiday the three of them took in 1931 makes clear: 'It was . . . to be a last golden aftermath of the happy years in which we, with other kindred creative spirits, had lived and worked, before the first world war had touched everything we had known with its disintegrating finger' (D. Hudson: 117). This period was also the starting-point of another disillusionment – radical, political, and altogether more productive: the cutting voices of Auden and his contemporaries, which came to include Britten's, were beginning to be heard. But for most people, the 'weekend' approach to music was adequate. 'The time for social and political commitment to intertwine with mass entertainment had not yet arrived . . . No dance or jazz bands accompanied the Jarrow marchers' (Whitcomb: 172). Nor did any English composers. Instead they witticised in the Café Royal or Pagani's restaurant, or hiked and roistered through the Sussex downs, according to urban or rural disposition.

There was more to the picture, of course. Although composition was still looked upon as a leisured pursuit until 1939, it was free to take its stance anywhere between mindless gregariousness and highly personal, visionary aspiration. Vaughan Williams's music covers the whole range, from the rollicking good humour of folksong arrangements for brass band to the ecstatic spirituality of 'The new ghost'. So do the songs of Peter Warlock. At the most personal end of the spectrum all but a nominal link with the pseudo-cultural concerns of leisured society was broken. The composer was alone, sometimes frighteningly alone. It is with a strong belief in the deep worth of personal vision as expressed by poet and

159

responded to by composer that the next chapters explore various aspects of song in England between the wars.

These aspects show no clear break with 19th-century Romanticism, and can be seen rather as its culmination. Gurney's style was rurtured by Stanford and Parry, Housman and Hardy settings date back to the turn of the century, the poetry of the 'Georgians' grew directly out of 19th-century styles, and the Celtic revival was a universal Romantic phenomenon. In fact, neither 1900 nor 1914 nor any date before 1939 can be taken to mark the end of Romanticism in English music. The first world war, as we have already seen, held the door open for composers to step through to a final phase in which the expression of Romantic states of mind was achieved through the images of nature and identification with national traditions of folksong and poetry.

What then distinguished lyricism in song after 1918 from its earlier manifestations? The subject-matter was little altered, but there was a new confidence in technique. For the first time perhaps since Purcell, the English composer possessed a technique which was not a major stumbling-block to him. He was conscious of framing his chosen poetry in music of excellent workmanship; gone were the old problems of word-setting, and gone were all but the last picked bones of the ballad. Admittedly some entirely discounted modern music. Gurney, for one, 'examined its spiky technique, harsh sounds, and dry themes. His disappointment was complete. "It's Napooh", he said, in the lingo of the British Expeditionary Force, and felt his time was too short to bother more with it' (M. Scott, 1938b: 6). But on the whole, the odd harmonic or rhythmic pungency no longer needed to cause traumas to composer or listener, for by 1921 Goossens was filling London concert halls with his *Rite of Spring* performances, even though Schönberg's name was still taboo (Goossens: 161–2).

A delight in the craft of expression similarly dominated poetry. On the one hand there was the urbane technical wizardry of Edith Sitwell, on the other J. C. Squire's successful new literary monthly, the *London Mercury*, which replaced *Georgian Poetry* in the 1920s as the focus for eclectic, lyrical and basically conservative poetry. Squire's first editorial, in 1919, set the stage 'for the more ephemeral literature of the Twenties; it was not to deal with the pressing questions of the day, but with the eternal problems of "art"', and it provided an outlet for poets like Masefield and Bridges, 'the best living "exponents of verse" (a phrase which conveys the contemporary view of poetry as a fine art rather than as an embodiment of thought)' (R. Graves and A. Hodge: 50–1). The *Mercury* paralleled the predisposition of OUP's new music department, set up by Hubert Foss, which from 1924 issued large numbers of songs by Howells, Moeran, Vaughan Williams, Warlock and others.

The resourcefulness of technique in English song between the wars was made possible by a number of composers whose output began well before the war years. They had learnt to find their voice through setting poetry to music, and built up a reserve of style for others to draw on. This applies particularly to Quilter, Vaughan Williams and Ireland. However, Quilter had nothing new to say after the war, and Vaughan Williams, like Bax and Bridge, paid less attention to song in the twenties and thirties while he conquered and reshaped the larger instrumental and choral genres. Of the composers well established before the first world war, only Ireland concentrated on song after it. As we shall see, it was a concentration of peculiarly personal intensity.

> . . . there is for every man some one scene, some one adventure, some one picture,
> that is the image of his secret life, for wisdom first speaks in images . . . this one
> image, if he would but brood over it his life long, would lead his soul, disen-
> tangled from unmeaning circumstance and the ebb and flow of the world, into
> that far household, where the undying gods await all whose souls have become
> simple as flame, whose bodies have become quiet as an agate lamp (W. B. Yeats,
> 1900a: 140–1).

John Ireland was born in the same year as his acquaintance Frank Bridge,
but unlike him left no early songs. It would have been interesting to see what texts
had attracted Ireland as a student, and how he dealt with them, but whatever he
wrote for himself or for Stanford must have been destroyed. He published very
few songs before his maturity, which dates from *Marigold* of 1913. He was now 34,
and had established the technique which served him without radical change for
the rest of his creative life – which in song, though not in other genres, ceased
rather abruptly in the thirties. This chapter investigates facets of that technique,
and the personal uses to which it was put, concerning which Ireland was unusually
selfconscious and single-minded: he rarely wrote anything that does not strike
one as having an intense, highly organised personal bearing, even though one
often encounters problems in defining it. Most of his song output represents a
considerable canon of consistent self-expression, and as such it is a model of
English inter-war lyricism.

Several of his songs lie somewhat outside that canon, however. The 11 duets,
like the unison songs, were presumably written for music festivals and schools,
and some of them are technically admirable. More to our purpose, the earliest
surviving solo songs, the *Songs of a Wayfarer*, remind us by their title and their
date of *Songs of Travel* and the Edwardian *Wanderlust*. Ireland never identified
with this as fully as the older Vaughan Williams did, nor succumbed to its
residual tendency towards pastoral superficiality like Michael Head; so it is unfortunate that several of his most popular and approachable songs belong to its
world rather than to that of his more personal vision. The prime example is 'Sea
fever', described by Henry Colles as 'a song in which I venture to think that the
composer has only half caught the mood. Possibly he has seized too quickly at a
single aspect of it' (1928: 14). Masefield himself disapproved of the setting because its '*lento*' tempo indication belied the restless sense of urgency, redolent of
Robert Louis Stevenson, with which he had imbued the poetic rhythm; he thought
that Gordon Cleather was the only singer who could restore that impression in
performance (Longmire, 1969: 80–1). Ireland himself, according to Kenneth
Wright, 'affected to hate being known as the composer of *Sea Fever*' (*ibid.*: 50),
but told Gerald Moore that he considered it his best song (G. Moore, 1953: 108).
It is not, but it has certainly been his most popular since its early days, as Kenneth
Wright recalled:

> . . . he owed a debt to Betty Chester who sang it hundreds of times in 'The Co-
> Optimists'. The days of radio's paramount influence in promoting 'pops' had
> yet to come. Even then (c. 1924) *Sea Fever* had become so popular, that 'lis-
> teners-in' voted it the most popular of all British songs; a rather ironical fact,

for several London publishers had turned it down before it finally got into the hands of Willy Strecker of Schotts, who published it with the firm of Augener in 1915 (Longmire, 1969: 50).

Technically its emotional effect is achieved in a rather disingenuous way: an apparently forthright and honest 'wayfaring' modality is accompanied by thick, cushioning chord progressions and harmonic slides to which Ireland was all too prone (in this respect resembling Delius), and which remained a recurrent weakness of his music ('The East Riding' is a similar song). The most original touch occurs in the last verse, where the comforting cycle of 5ths in the second half of each stanza, a trick probably learnt from Stanford's 'Drake's drum', entails a chromatic alteration from B natural to B flat for its first chord, suggesting an intensified pang of yearning; it is balanced by the flattened supertonic alteration in the penultimate chord of the song. Of his other two Masefield settings, 'The bells of San Marie' consists of much the same sort of thing, while 'Vagabond', an exercise in the vernacular, is frankly embarrassing when set to music. Ireland is unable to assume a convincing rustic guise. However, he is more successful in his two pre-war boisterous songs. In both 'Hope the Hornblower' and 'When lights go rolling round the sky' there is a hearty flexing of technical muscles. The style of the former sounds fresh and promising at a number of points, such as the Fauré-like harmonic oscillations at 'Follow me, hearts', the subdominant pedal under tonic harmony at 'The sun's on meadow', and the mediant cadential preparation at 'we ride'. In the latter there are numerous instances of similar effect, notably the rollicking modulation to the subdominant in the middle, and a taste of rejuvenated Sullivan in the piano introduction. Both songs owe something to 'Devon, O Devon' and 'The Old *Superb*' from Stanford's *Songs of the Sea*. Yet this mask of good humour was to be more fittingly worn by Warlock, and although it recurs in the mature Ireland, as in 'Great things', 'Weathers', 'The journey', 'I have twelve oxen', and the various Elizabethan settings, particularly 'The merry month of May', it is not essential. He could put his technical equipment to more serious uses without any kind of mask.

His capacity for serious expression is already apparent in *Songs of a Wayfarer*, except in the stiffly diatonic last song, 'I will walk on the earth', which spoils the cycle. At this stage there is still something adolescent about it; in two of the songs it speaks through a poetic framework giving an overall effect of rather bashful diffidence. In 'English May', the first of Ireland's closely felt Rossetti settings, the poet is saying that if only this were *not* an English (i.e. grey, disappointing) May – which leaves the pastoral composer in something of an interpretative quandary. Ireland does not fully solve it; his tonal procedure sounds stunted rather than poised. In 'I was not sorrowful' (which Dowson entitled 'Spleen' – but it is not the same poem as in *Marigold* and it is not from Verlaine) he is faced with the problem of expressing tiredness and oblivion, indifference rather than pain. Perhaps he succeeds, at least more than Delius does in his setting from *Songs of Sunset* (*1911*): the constant rhythmic figure of four semiquavers and a quaver in $\frac{6}{8}$, suggestive of the rain on the window panes, sometimes varied to become constant semiquavers, is a very apt embodiment of the mood.

In this early cycle it is not as yet clear, however, what he is hoping to accomplish in song. There are no obvious poetic preferences (except the obscure James

Blake), and no one overriding style. These began to crystallise in *Marigold*. But before considering that cycle, it will be helpful to refer to one of Ireland's later songs, an obviously appealing setting in which his mature stylistic traits stand out very clearly. The poem, 'Santa Chiara (Palm Sunday: Naples)', is by Arthur Symons. The basic musical framework of the song is unimpressive: a rather self-consciously ritualistic piano introduction and epilogue define the occasion, and the vocal line is underpinned by a mixture of cycles of 5ths and chromatic slides treated similarly to those in 'Sea fever', even with a similar chromatic alteration of the cycle near the end – a B natural under the word 'palm'. But in the middle the self-absorbed mood is relieved for a while:

> The sea is blue from here to Sorrento
> And the sea-wind comes to me,
> And I see the white clouds lift from Sorrento
> And the dark sail lean upon the sea.

The eyes are lifted to something outside the self, in static – or ecstatic – contemplation. Musically this is done by modal figuration, a sophistication of Vaughan Williams's early treatment of the same device, built on static chords shifting largely in mediant and submediant jumps, except at the end when the cycle of 5ths begins to be reinstated. The influence is clearly French, and Ireland's fondness for Debussy and, particularly, Ravel is evident when the piano's left-hand melody begins to parallel the voice part in octaves (Ex. 1). Ireland has created a kind of musical symbolism, along the lines of the poetic symbolism of Poe, Mallarmé and Baudelaire. Certain musical procedures, particularly those involving

Ex. 1

coruscations over static or oscillating triadic harmonies, shifting by non-dominant means, are explored and savoured because of their power of suggestion and evocation. Technically the trick is an old one, dating back to Wagner's *Wald-weben*, and we have already met it in other composers, but it is more central to Ireland's art than to his predecessors'. As a symbol it nearly always represents nature, but it is not simply an image (though clearly there is a musical metaphor, that of undulating waves, in Ex. 1). Its significance is more subjective, for it connects the external world with the internal realm of the self: it shows the timeless beauty of nature captured by the individual in a timeless moment.

Ireland once asked, 'How can the critics even begin to understand my music, if they have never read Machen?' (Longmire, 1969: 20) The writings of Arthur Machen, with which Ireland first became acquainted through his *House of Souls* in 1906, are now little read, but their power over a young mind at the turn of the century is easily appreciated. Machen was one of the first English authors to base his art almost entirely on symbolism and the power of suggestion. (He gave a famous proof of this power when he invented the vision of the angelic Bowmen of Mons for the *Evening News* in 1914; thousands of soldiers promptly claimed to have seen them.) His material, often reminiscent of Poe, was chiefly the underworld of fauns, satyrs and all manner of Celtic occultisms, but although these were of great significance to Ireland as well as to Machen the literary achievement was possible without them, as can be seen in one of his best novels, *The Hill of Dreams*, published in 1907. Here he is concerned only with the sensations which his hero, a hypersensitive young writer, is capable of experiencing. The more the hero cultivates these, the fewer external reference-points are necessary to provoke them in him. With many echoes of Pater and the aestheticism of the 1870s and 1880s, the narrative becomes in places a symbolist manifesto:

> The fancy that sensations are symbols and not realities hovered in his mind, and led him to speculate as to whether they could not actually be transmuted one into another . . .
> He could imagine a man who was able to live in one sense while he pleased; to whom, for example, every impression of touch, taste, hearing, or seeing should be translated into odour; who at the desired kiss should be ravished with the scent of dark violets, to whom music should be the perfume of a rose-garden at dawn (:116–17).

We are in the era of Scriabin, Bantock, Bliss and others, and their attempts to fuse the sensations of colour and smell with music. And when, by virtue of the ability to transfer sensations from the objects that produced them to those he wishes to conjure up, the hero imagines himself to be living in Roman times, the author comments:

> Here lay hidden the secret of the sensuous art of literature; it was the secret of suggestion, the art of causing delicious sensation by the use of words. In a way, therefore, literature was independent of thought; the mere English listener, if he had an ear attuned, could recognise the beauty of a splendid Latin phrase (:126–7).

The key point here is the complete subjectivity of the approach. To Ireland this meant that 'the secret of the sensuous art' lay in submitting himself to the imagery in his texts and expressing in music, not the images themselves, but the states of mind and feeling that they inspired. Thus when he set a pastoral poem to music he was expressing not the beauty of nature but the personal ecstasy of which the beauty of nature, part cause, is the corollary or symbol. And he normally chose a poem in which this personal correlative was explicit. A fine example is the rarely sung 'Earth's call: silvan rhapsody', in which Harold Monro's sonnet is fashioned, with a remarkable expansion, into a song on the scale of a scena. The procession of vivid images of nature is explored only as a series of symbolic waymarks to the sensuous progress of two souls exploring one another; the opening lines of the sonnet prepare us for this:

> The fresh air moves like water round a boat.
> The white clouds wander. Let us wander too.

And by the closing lines the images, having been worked through as, in a sense, foreplay, are left behind in a world of sound; only one symbol is left:

> I can't hear anything to-day, can you,
> But, far and near: 'Cuckoo! Cuckoo! Cuckoo?'

The cuckoo (present in the music) is 'earth's call', the voice of nature, but, at the same time, the final symbol of sexual love, after an accomplished act of fulfilment which has been expressed in the long preceding piano passage. Thus Ireland's shimmering coruscations, the pleasurable sensations of tone (Ex. 2)

Ex. 2

developed to the utmost throughout the song, represent an ecstasy, a timeless moment of symbolic fusion between the outwardness of nature and the inwardness of love.

This sort of writing is one of four or five personal symbols which recur in Ireland's music, and most explicitly in the songs. Nowhere is the symbolism of ecstasy so positively achieved as in 'Earth's call'; elsewhere his concerns range far more towards the darker end of the emotional spectrum, through passion to pain, sorrow and despair. Admittedly passion can be bright, as we shall see, and sorrow can be beautifully limpid, as in his perfect setting of Brooke, 'Spring sorrow'.

Here for once the technical paraphernalia of symbolism is dispensed with altogether and the poem speaks straight through a musical frame simpler than that of 'Linden Lea' and imbued with no more artifice than a wistfully archaic cadence structure (Ex. 3; see Searle: 52–3) and a telling flattened 7th at the point of highest tension (Ex. 4). But in most of the songs Ireland develops his musical symbolism, and it is the dark side of nature – and of his nature – that predominates.

Ex. 3

My — heart all Win - ter   lay so numb, The   earth so dead and frore,

Ex. 4

And the   haw-thorn hedge— puts forth its buds

We can see how he used music, and song in particular, to express that darkness, but we know little about its factual basis. He tells us in the songs that it is manifested through unhappy love, but it is difficult to be more specific, for Ireland, like Elgar, was forever cryptic where his own innermost feelings and commitments were at stake. We are still hampered by lack of information concerning his earlier years; we know only that an unhappy childhood, of which he himself was loth to speak, cast shadows throughout his life. Possibly the death of his mother shortly after he entered the RCM continued to affect him deeply. It is difficult otherwise to account for the fact that for 'personal reasons' he did not seek to publish one of his finest songs, 'What art thou thinking of?', in which a mother with good humour shares her young child's fantasy of heaven until suddenly, when the quavers cease, she realises (or is it Ireland, the son, who realises?) that more serious depths have been touched:

> 'Oh I would be glad to go there, mother,
>   To go and live there now;
> And I would pray for thy coming, mother;
>   My mother, wouldst not thou?'

The period to which most of the songs belong is little discussed in the later personal reminiscences of John Longmire (1969) or those of the other friends drawn upon by Muriel Searle in her more recent biography (1979). Longmire rather tantalisingly leaves more questions than answers. He tells us of Ireland's precipitate and disastrous marriage to a pupil in 1927, annulled on grounds of non-consummation. He also mentions Ireland's fervent friendship with another pupil, Helen Perkin, 30 years his junior, which he wrote into the last movement of his Piano Concerto, but which soon subsided into permanent estrangement when she married someone else. But neither Longmire nor Searle mentions the paederastic side of Ireland's nature (see Ireland, 1936–62), yet if we ignore it we cannot fully understand the songs, which must surely be seen as a personal testament.

Marigold set the pattern for what was to come. It is headed *An Impression*, but of what or whom, and why the title 'Marigold', we are not told. The cycle is clearly concerned with sublimating an intense experience. Love is all light and poise, all springtime imagery, in the first song, 'Youth's spring-tribute', a sensitive setting of Rossetti's Sonnet XIV from *The House of Life*, not unlike 'Silent noon', only less passionate in its imagery. The musical symbolism starts delicately, with a cooler variant of Ireland's 'ecstasy' procedure, here oscillating calmly on imperfect cadence units whose added notes do not conceal their origin as Debussy-like chains of parallel triads poised, with their false relations, away from tonal argument (Ex. 5). Later in the sonnet this procedure takes on a more throbbing pulse, from 'So shut your eyes upturn'd, and feel my kiss / Creep . . .', until it finally breaks softly into another of Ireland's primary symbols, that of the heat of passion (Ex. 6). For this he has recourse to Strauss rather than Debussy or Ravel, for it is based on the sensuous curves of chromatic appoggiaturas, counter-

Ex. 5

Ex. 6

thrusting in pairs. Had he learnt this symbol from *Der Rosenkavalier*? Longmire thinks so (1976: iii). Even in this generally bright song, however, there are shadows: at the curiously offhand line, 'On these debateable borders of the year', and in those that follow with their images of blackthorn blossom and snow, the diffidence found in *Songs of a Wayfarer* is again present. It gives rise to cold, chromatic waverings up and down in octaves which can be classified as a third archetypal symbol, that of non-possession, denial, frustration. Here the feeling is neutral; elsewhere it can be bleak, or, as in the rising passage in the second song, 'Penumbra', at the line ''Mid many eyes a single look', warmly nostalgic – a mood which often flows over into maudlin sentimentality, as in the rather pointless song 'If there were dreams to sell'. All is not well with love in these premonitory images of 'Youth's spring-tribute', and in the second song we find a mood of frustration, which Rossetti expresses in an unusual manner, tossing back and forth a sequential series of negative statements ('I did not look upon her eyes') and parentheses, sublimated in the music to something like stoicism through a fourth symbol, in its quasi-liturgical modality redolent of fortitude or submission (Ex. 7). In the third song, the 'spleen' is vented with a lack of tonal stability and little whole-tone nuances which can be seen as a contradiction, or distortion, of the chromatic passion in the first song (Ex. 8). There is a sense of dislocation and numbness here whose expression is sufficiently characteristic of Ireland's music to be classed as a further recurrent symbol. Yet something in this depressing sequence of songs is larger than the individual stages depicted:

> Dear, so thou only move thine head,
> Shall all mine old despairs awake!

Ex. 7

Ex. 8

Ex. 9

Ex. 10

At this point in 'Spleen' a motive that has run through all three songs reappears (Ex. 9), whittled down from its more wistful earlier form in 'Youth's spring-tribute' (Ex. 10) to become painfully spare; like Ex. 5 it is based on the descending 4th. This thematic insert emphasises the continuing pain of the whole experience, particularly when it comes at the end of the second song:

> So shall the tongues of the sea's foam
> (Though many voices therewith come
> From drown'd hope's home to cry to me,)
> Bewail one hour the more, when sea
> And wind are one with memory.

Yet even here the verse has a sweetness of cadence at the word 'memory' which Ireland grasps by ending the song with a subdued version of his ecstasy symbol, as if to say that the permanence of memory is not regrettable or wholly painful; in the last song, at the last lines

> I am so tired . . .
> Of everything alas! save thee.

he even affirms that the freshness of happy love is retained, by a pure reference to the cycle's opening motive.

It was a long time before Ireland wrote another song set of comparable scope. 'A song from o'er the hill', dating from the same year as *Marigold*, is virtually a travesty of a Victorian ballad, and thereafter he composed few songs until the end of the war, being busy with major works for piano, the Second Piano Trio, and the Second Violin Sonata. The songs provoked by the war itself, in which he did not serve, have faded somewhat. 'A garrison churchyard' is sentimental, and the two published Thirkell Cooper settings tread an uncomfortable line between pathos and bathos; only the second, 'The cost', which briefly touches on first world war realism ('I only know he sighed a bit – / I felt him catch his breath'), deploys even a modicum of the technical resource of *Marigold*. How personally the cry of 'Give me back my friend' in this song is to be taken is suggested by a letter Ireland wrote to a research student in the year before he died, in which he stated that this, like his two other unpublished songs, 'What art thou thinking of?' and 'If we must part', had been held back for 'personal reasons' (Magraw: 329). The setting of Brooke's 'The soldier' ('If I should die') suffers from its attempt to fit a sonnet into a two-stanza strophic form, and 'Blow out, you bugles' has a rather unsatisfactory hymn-tune flavour with parallel triads and marching bass lines, far from the expansive character of Bridge's setting. But the first of Ireland's Housman settings, 'The heart's desire', composed at the same time, strikes home with admirable, unproblematical freshness: the 'ecstatic' harmonic mood is cleanly controlled here, and the song points towards the stylistic firmness of 'Earth's call', 'Spring sorrow' and 'The bells of San Marie' of the following year. The nursery rhyme sequence, *Mother and Child*, also of this productive year 1918, represents an interesting attempt to simplify his musical language in accordance with the simple texts. On the whole it is fruitful, and some of the songs, especially the earlier ones, are delightful; sentimentality, however, not always avoided in Ireland's music, takes over in the last two songs of the set, with their Victorian attitudinising about death. Here he writes for the adult viewing the child, not for the child itself.

There is a renewed sense of personal involvement in the two Mary Coleridge settings. 'The sacred flame' develops a fine sense of alternate intimacy and spaciousness by its contracting and expanding chords and chord sequences. Then with the three Symons songs Ireland plunges back into the expression of some state of crisis:

> . . . I dream of the days forgotten, of love the dream,
> The desire of her eyes unappeased, and the peace of her brows.

The poetic image for 'the desire . . . unappeased' is a gnawing rat; the musical one is Ireland's third symbol, the salient chromatics representing the pain of non-possession (Ex. 11), later pared down, without their softening harmonies, to the bleak gesture, recurrent in Ireland's music, of two chromatic lines in contrary motion (Ex. 12). In the last of the three songs, 'Rest', one of his most tender, the

Ex. 11

Ex. 12

Ex. 13

Ex. 14

mood is one of quiet resignation, but the peace of the external world is invoked only to show that there can be no corresponding rest in the heart. Passion, though resigned, still lies there, and from the deceptive tranquillity of the accompanimental figure (Ex. 13) it gradually emerges, first at the thought of 'Summer murmuring / Some sweet, slumberous thing', in the form of Ireland's symbol for passion, the lush fabric of multiple chromatic appoggiaturas, here moulded into a monophonic gesture of sliding triads (Ex. 14). The first song, 'The adoration', is powerful because it suggests already at the outset a subsumation of the pain of the composer's experience into a frame of almost frightening self-control, frightening because bitter in content yet devoid of his characteristically self-indulgent pity. The meaning of the poem is not easy to grasp, but it seems that in turning away from lost or dead love the protagonist is trying to turn towards religious adoration instead: this apparently is Ireland's interpretation, for the pilgrim's steady tread in the opening ostinato is represented by a figure like the passion motive but with the chromatic appoggiaturas, in other words the passion itself, replaced by more ritualistic diatonic ones. At the same time, the repetition of this figure gives an overall effect more like the 'ecstasy' symbol, but with the ecstasy subdued into religious contemplation. Momentarily at the thought of 'weary lands far hence / That I have journeyed through' – presumably the exhausting emotional territory of frustrated love – the appoggiaturas of passion reappear, but they are stilled again. The conclusion is bitter; it is too late to find solace in religious devotion:

> I cannot take your gold
> And frankincense and myrrh;
> My heart was growing cold
> While you were following her:
> Take back your gold and myrrh.

Yet the mood of contemplation continues; it is as though, oblivious now to all passion, the soul trudges on into the night.

Perhaps surprisingly, a brief period of joy was to follow in the songs. In January and February 1920 Ireland wrote two of his happiest and possibly his best songs, settings of Huxley's 'The trellis' and Sidney's 'My true love hath my heart'. Here for the last time he sees love as productive and fulfilled. In 'The trellis' Huxley's rapt verse, not unlike D. G. Rossetti's in vocabulary and nature imagery, is surrounded with the quiet, wondering aura of the 'ecstasy' symbol (Ex. 15) which, after 'And we lie rosily bow'r'd', flames into a forthright state-

Ex. 15

ment of the 'passion' symbol. Here the three downward steps before the chromatic appoggiaturas, again reminiscent of Strauss, themselves constitute another recurrent motive (Ex. 16), one which reappears, slightly altered, to form the backbone and flavour the harmony of 'My true love hath my heart', expressing the poem's assurance of requited passion.

By the time Ireland composed *The Land of Lost Content* in 1920–1, however, experience had again developed to bitter crisis. Some of the Housman poems chosen display a grimmer fortitude than anything approached so far. After the beautiful celebration of transience in 'The Lent lily' it becomes clear that all

Ex. 16

happiness is in the past. The somewhat fulsome symbolic chromatics of 'Ladslove', a song typical of Ireland in his less palatable moods, represent an unappeasable yearning, which collapses with a sigh on a downward 5th over a supertonic chord towards the end of each stanza (at the words 'perish' and 'jonquil'). This formula had been used to similar effect earlier, in 'The cost', and it is echoed in many other places, perhaps most persistently in 'When I am dead, my dearest': the downward 5th, particularly as part of a cycle in the bass, often as we saw in 'Sea fever' with chromatic sidesteps, is used time and again as an important harmonic anchor in Ireland's style as well as being prominent melodically. In the third song, 'Goal and wicket', an element new to Ireland's songs appears: irony, almost always present in Housman's poetry. Musically the effect is that, having worked through the intensity of his feelings, he almost maliciously detaches himself from them with the help of two new symbolic procedures. One is the replacement of his old mainstay, cycle-of-5ths harmony with melodic chromatics (passing notes or appoggiaturas), by a further development of the chromatic sidestepping found in the cycles of 5ths: now whole chords bear only a dislocated chromatic relation to one another (Ex. 17), and with these the bass sets up

Ex. 17

a sort of parody of a sequence. This style can be effectively disturbing, as when after the first line of the poem the preparation of a cycle-of-5ths cadence (g sharp – c sharp – F sharp) towards a tonic B major chord with major 7th leads instead to a chord (at 'Here stood I') whose bottom half (root and 5th) and grace note are shifted up a semitone. The other new procedure is a rhythmic energy hitherto unexplored in his songs, though already part of his instrumental style. It consists of what can be called 'French rhythms' – simple and tidy quantitative divisions of a metrical pulse, employed with a variety that often obscures or contradicts the underlying triple or duple time. Such rhythms, dating back to the measured speech-rhythms of Lully and even the 16th-century chanson, are found throughout the music of Bizet, Fauré and Ravel. Ex. 18 is complemented by the sarcastic ostinato left behind in the bass at the end of the song. In the fourth song, 'The vain desire' (suffixed in the autograph manuscript 'Dies Irae: January 8 1921') the nostalgic, fruitless chromatics return together with a softened use of chromatic dislocation of cadential cycles of 5ths which looks back to earlier

Ex. 18

Ex. 19

usages (Ex. 19). But in the fifth, 'The encounter', irony is again prevalent. Above a tritonal bass ostinato, a new and alarming musical language is spoken, which coolly parodies the passionate appoggiaturas of the previous symbolic usage (Ex. 20); there are also more French rhythms (see the piano part, bars 9–10 in the score). This ironic detachment does not have the last word, however: in the final song, 'Epilogue', greater importance is still placed on passion that yet lives in the memory:

> I shall have lived a little while
>   Before I die for ever.

– in accordance with which, after the words 'Happy is the lover', the 'passion' symbol reappears in its fullest form with the three downward steps.

The last of these personally laden bursts of song, and the strongest, indicates a crisis around the years 1926–7. 'When I am dead, my dearest', although dating from July 1924, had been inscribed 'To A.G.M.: Cerne Abbas, June 1925'. The important *Three Songs* are suffixed 'for February 22, 1926', while the autograph of *We'll to the Woods No More* is headed 'to Arthur: in memory of the darkest days' and suffixed with an inscription fiercely scratched out and replaced by 'for

Ex. 20

A.G.M.: February 22 1927'. Other dedications referring to the same date for the years 1922, 1925, 1929 and 1944 appear in the piano music, the earliest being 'Pro Amicitia, Feb. 22, 1922.' A.G.M. was Arthur Miller, who had been one of Ireland's choristers at St Luke's, Chelsea, and 22 February was presumably his birthday (Searle: 62). Their relationship was evidently of the deepest significance for Ireland.

Hardy's obsessive remembrance of a fair woman finds a strong response in Ireland's *Five Poems by Thomas Hardy*. (The other Hardy set is less intense and less personal, though musically more approachable and altogether one of Ireland's most attractive cycles.) By now the pattern of symbolic references will be familiar. But here for the first time the symbols lose something of their evocative power for the composer, as he feels his way into poetry of an uncoloured truthfulness for which their impressionism is perhaps no longer entirely adequate. As a result the music becomes strangely inarticulate in places, in a way that is not so noticeable anywhere else in Ireland's output. The pained chromatics grit their teeth with a new acerbity (see the opening of no. 2), and even the 'passion' symbol has changed shape considerably (Ex. 21, from no. 2). In 'The tragedy of that moment', apart from an uncomfortable reminiscence of the style of 'Sea fever' at the words 'deeper than the sea', a new darkness prevails, in the murky

Ex. 21

Ex. 22

textures and especially in the recurrent chord (Ex. 22). The former style is really only felt in the passage in no. 3 at the words 'It was that strange freshness you carried into a soul', and in the epitaphic tenderness, similar to the mood of nostalgic acceptance which *Marigold* and *The Land of Lost Content* both finally attain, of the melting passage at the lines 'They may say: "Why a woman such honour?"' in the last song. Except in the first of the Symons songs, Ireland has not yet learnt to go beyond this nostalgia.

In the *Three Songs*, however, it appears at first that he has. The message of the first two songs is that where love has failed, the deepness of friendship is ultimately far more valuable. There is a slightly satirical tone in Emily Brontë's poem (the first song) with its imagery of the 'wild rose-briar' for love and 'holly-tree' for friendship; this is conveyed from the start in the music, with its French rhythms, jogging bass, and semitonal clash on the first chord. In the second song, however, Ireland settles down to warm, almost sentimental seriousness in his celebration of friendship in misfortune,

> A flame that slander cannot move,
> But burns in darkness doubly bright.

How personal is this expression? Could he possibly have written the anonymous words himself? So passionate is he about this depth of friendship that, at the word 'burns', the old chromatic appoggiatura triads flare up for one bar. Yet as soon as we hear the opening of the third song, 'The one Hope', even this vision of comfort is rudely destroyed (Ex. 23). Much of the language of this song, including the opening with its accented tritonal compound 4th, uncannily resembles

Ex. 23

that of Bridge's Piano Sonata. Both are unusually stark. The 'unforgotten pain' is stronger here than anywhere previously, and at first the vision of 'vain desire' (did Ireland consciously lift this phrase from the poem to be the title for the fourth song of *The Land of Lost Content*?) and 'vain regret' going 'hand in hand to death' seems terminal. What, however, is 'the one Hope'? In Rossetti's poem it is not entirely clear: the 'sunk stream' of peace, or 'the gift of grace unknown', or 'Hope's one name' itself, a self-sufficing invocation. With Ireland, however, it takes more precise forms; they are familiar. The 'flowering amulet' to be culled is clearly the hope of regaining lost love, for at that point in the text a direct quotation of the opening of 'The trellis' appears in the accompaniment, followed by a '*pp espr. e dolciss.*' statement of the 'passion' symbol, in its definitive form with the downward steps. Is this a testament of faith, or simply a yearning that still needs expression? However Ireland meant it, he did not use it again in his published songs. In the second Housman cycle, *We'll to the Woods No More*, he seems consciously to be withdrawing from the sad concerns of love and regret, and it is surely significant that the two texts set are taken from Housman's *Last Poems*. But there are still a number of backward glances: the opening of the cycle is suggestive of 'The adoration', the opening of the piano epilogue is not unlike 'The rat', and at an eerie passage in the first song (Ex. 24) we are taken back to

Ex. 24

the benumbed opening of 'Spleen' (Ex. 8). The lasting impression, however, is created by the third and final piece, which is for piano alone and is headed by two lines from 'Hawthorn time', a poem which Ireland had set, not outstandingly, as a song eight years earlier:

> Spring will not wait the loiterer's time
>   Who keeps so long away;

There is a double suggestion at work here. The predominant one is of life moving onward without him, a sense of objective regeneration which his subjectivity cannot hold back. This is couched in a fertile structural continuity full of his characteristic French rhythms. It is a statement of affirmation and acceptance. Yet at the same time the quotation implies that spring is quickly gone, and there is an ever-present pain in the music which he cannot banish, suggesting that he is aware of having missed his chance. A cryptic little passage, which concludes the piano epilogue, had first appeared at the terminal words 'no more' in the first song (Ex. 25), and both pieces end with a glum minor triad with added minor 6th. But whatever the degree of personal despair we are to read into and over the

Ex. 25

affirmation of the natural order, Ireland was writing his sorrows into his songs almost for the last time. One more setting each of Symons, Rossetti and Dowson followed (the latter, the unpalatably self-pitying 'If we must part', was not published in his lifetime); after that, what he wrote was part of a different picture.

IX

The music of Ivor Gurney

I would not rest till work came from my hand
And then as the thing grew, till fame came,
(But only in honour) . . . and then, O, how the grand
Divination of ages grew to faith's flame.
Great were our fathers and beautiful in all name,
Happy their days, lovely in considered grain each word,
Their days were kindness, growth, happiness, mindless.

I would not rest until my Country were
Thronged with the Halls of Music; and until clear
Hospitality for love were e'er possible . . .
And any for honour might come, or prayer, to certain
Fondness and long nights' talking till all's known.

Madness my enemy, cunning extreme my friend,
Prayer my safeguard. (Ashes my reward at end.)
Secrecy fervid my honour, soldier-courage my aid.
(Promise and evil threatening my soul ever-afraid.)
Now, with the work long done, the the witchcraft I bend
And crouch – that knows nothing good, Hell uncaring
Hell undismayed (Kavanagh: 212).

. . . there is no doubt that, according to the rules of the world, Gurney was a more than difficult person. He seems to have expected life entirely on his own terms. No-one was more unteachable or more difficult to befriend or to help, and even the best of his friends seem to have found his irresponsibility and arrogance, his unawareness of anything outside himself, to be more than they could accept for long. He was as near as anyone could be to the fictional idea of genius. But in this there was not the least trace of self-consciousness. The truth is that his mind was enflamed from his earliest days. That excitement, 'Rarely, rarely comest thou, Spirit of Delight' was with him at all times (Finzi, 1954).

He, Stanford, told me that, of all the pupils who came under him at the College, the one who most fulfilled the accepted idea of genius was Ivor Gurney (Greene, 1938: 2).

'A good man, sir, quite all right. Quite a good man, sir, but he's a musician, and doesn't seem able to get himself clean' (Gurney, quoting his own regimental sergeant-major's description of him, 1917).

The story of Ivor Gurney is affecting, compelling, and tragic. In considering Elgar, Parry, Quilter, Butterworth and Ireland, an attempt has been made to show that a sympathetic reading of a composer's songs can give rise to a certain amount of biographical or psychological interpretation which in turn can enhance one's understanding of the music. With Gurney, given his 1700 poems and countless let-

179

ters, the extra-musical factor is so extensive that recent critical interest has focussed on his life and poetry rather than his music. Since the publication of Michael Hurd's excellent biography in 1978 little further need currently be said in this respect; there is, however, pressing need for an appraisal of his songs, which are still relatively little known and sung and even less understood. Gurney himself considered his composer's gift to be higher than his poet's – 'one learnt that the brighter visions brought music; the fainter verse, or mere pleasurable emotion,' he said of his own experience in the war (1922: 319) – and he constantly viewed its expression and development as the sole object of his life: 'Your remarks on Pain and Death are very good and true,' he wrote to Marion Scott from the trenches in 1917, 'but: If this does not mean I can do great work for English music, then it is waste to me. I should years and years ago have done with living but for that thought – of making Musical History for England, and out of Gloster stuff' (1913–22). That his hopes of musical greatness were delusory in their fervour was perhaps a large part of his tragedy, but this need not hinder an evaluation of the songs' originality, a quality which in the context of the period under review should appear considerable.

Some account is necessary of the state of Gurney's collected output of songs (listed below, pp. 456–62). As far as we can tell, he wrote about 300 – fewer than Bantock and Fritz Hart, but far more than other English composers of the period. He did not group many of them into cycles, and this makes it difficult to discuss them comprehensively and methodically. A few were published during his active lifetime and early asylum years, between 1920 and 1927, but most remained in manuscript, to be patiently and slowly collected by his heroic friend and mentor at the RCM, Marion Scott. It seems likely that Gurney, who depended heavily on Marion Scott and never resented her concern for him, handed over most of his manuscripts to her shortly after their composition; there is certainly a precedent for this in the poems and few songs he composed whilst serving with the British Expeditionary Force in France. She, however, did little with the songs, though it is possible that she was responsible for some at least of the 1920–7 publications; when the young Gerald Finzi, who never knew Gurney personally, first approached her in 1925 with a view to making a collection of them, he had to begin by sorting and dating them (G. Finzi, 1937–53; Hurd, 1978: 185–6). A number of manuscripts were gathered in from Gurney's friends, and one or two items, including the Rupert Brooke songs sent by Gurney to Edward Marsh, probably in 1922 (Hurd, 1978: 143), and discovered by Christopher Hassall in 1959, joined the collection, now in Gloucester City Library, only after Finzi's death in 1956. It is possible that further items will appear.

Grouping the songs for purposes of evaluation is difficult. Four main stylistic periods can be identified: Gloucester, from 1904 to 1911; the RCM, from May 1911 to 1914; army training in England, service in France and hospital in Britain, from 1915 to October 1918; and freedom in Gloucestershire, High Wycombe and London, with further study at the RCM, followed by confinement in mental hospitals, from October 1918 to December 1937. The striking fact is that only about 20, 15 and 18 songs belong to the first three periods respectively; all the rest were written between 1918 and 1926, with two particularly intense bursts of creativity in 1920 and 1925 but nothing at all in 1923. From the following years, until his death in 1937, we have no songs. His last creative period represents his stylistic maturity, yet even before its inception he had already shown signs of mental disturbance (Hurd, 1978: 120–34; Trethowan), and it is vital to an understanding of Gurney's style to appreciate that traces of imbalance and decay are present in nearly all his songs from this period. Finzi, when he first came across 'Sleep', written in 1914, sensed a fatal intensity in Gurney even at that date; he later described it as 'an incandescence . . . that tells of something burning too brightly to last, such as you see in the filament of an electric bulb before it burns out' (1955, II: 7; J. Finzi, 1974). Gurney's manifest insanity of September 1922 is only indirectly a turning-point in his composing career, in that as structures his songs become gradually less compelling after this date. The basic style remains, however. A further obstacle to separating artistic development from artistic decay in the post-war period is mentioned by Marion Scott in her preface to the first OUP volume of songs (1938a):

> Gurney . . . had a habit, each time he re-copied a song, of making alterations or permutations, some small, some rather considerable, in the music. These were not all revisions. Quite often they occurred because, when he wrote out a song again from memory, his mind had meantime changed the details unconsciously. Hardly any two autograph copies of his songs are identical. Nor can it be said the later versions are better than the first, or *vice versa*, for his songs furnish examples of both.

In particular, his datings on the manuscripts of a number of songs that he rewrote or recopied in 1925 suggest that he had lost or destroyed earlier versions.

Gerald Finzi and his co-editor Howard Ferguson were faced with the question of how much of this large output from 1918 to 1926 was publishable. To compile the first four volumes of ten songs each, published by OUP in 1938 (the first two), 1952, and (edited by Ferguson alone after Finzi's death) 1959, they sorted through the entire corpus during several weeks in late 1936 and/or early 1937, Ferguson sight-reading the accompaniments and Finzi playing the voice parts an octave higher on the piano, with Finzi's wife, Joy, taking notes (Ferguson, 1974). Afterwards Finzi wrote to Marion Scott:

> The sorting has been even more difficult than I expected, chiefly because there is comparatively little that one can really be sure is bad. Even the late 1925 asylum songs, though they get more and more involved (and at the same time more disintegrated, if you know what I mean) have a curious coherence about them somewhere, which makes it difficult to know if they are really over the border. I think the eventual difficulty in 'editing' the later Gurney may be great: a neat mind could smooth away the queernesses – like Rimsky-Korsakov with Mussorgsky – yet time and familiarity will probably show something not so mistaken, after all, about the queer and odd things. However, there are some obviously incoherent things and a good many others of which one can say that it would be better for them not to be published.
>   For the remainder, my crude and arbitrary method of grouping into ✔ ✔ for good; ✔ good or adequate; (✔x when I don't quite know my own mind); x bad; must seem ridiculous – like a Baedeker guide! (1937–53; Hurd, 1978: 184–5)

Conversely, 'queerness' is present in nearly all the published songs; there are very few unflawed by passages in which the train of thought weakens and the sense of direction falters. The selection for publication, though wise, could only be based on an empirical offsetting of the level of inspiration in a song's basic material against its structural weaknesses. It must further be pointed out that Finzi gave a single or a double tick to about 100 songs, considerably more than were published.

It is not easy to present an analysis of Gurney's musical achievement with such a broad body of material. That of C. W. Moore (1966) is largely statistical: he discusses Gurney's favourite tonalities, F major (35 songs), D flat major (30), E major (26) and D minor (25), and then describes the 'typical' Gurney song:

> . . . the song would be in the key of F major with a melodically flattened seventh degree, range from d to e', and would have a tessitura around b. Its poem would consist of two stanzas of four lines, each of which would contain four iambic feet.
>
> A two-measure introduction would contain motivic elements which would act as a unifying device for the accompaniment and anticipate the first melodic phrase. A basically chordal accompaniment maintains the song's fundamentally duple meter, while the melodic line has a generous quantity of triplets, creating two-against-three with the accompaniment. No doubling of the voice line would occur in the accompaniment. There would be complete agreement in both climax and accentuation between the text and its musical setting, and melisma would appear on important words of the text and would be used either for emotional emphasis or for word painting. Also, at the high point of each stanza, there would be an upward modulation to the Neapolitan or a third relation. A four-measure postlude overlaps the final vocal phrase and recalls material from both accompaniment and melodic lines before cadencing from a dominant seventh chord to the tonic (:166–7).

It is preferable in the present context to take a small number of Gurney's songs, both published and unpublished, and examine them individually in detail in order to arrive at some understanding of his style. First a survey must be made of the pre-1918 songs.

Apart from three insignificant items of juvenilia, Gurney's first songs date from 1907. 'Passing by', a setting of the poem 'There is a lady sweet and kind' here attributed to Herrick, is technically competent, surprisingly so for a 17-year-old, but exhibits its command of chromatic harmony with the sentimentality not of the Elizabethan lover but of the Victorian organist (Ex. 1). Nevertheless, it also has a foretaste of Gurney's characteristic use of independent voice and accompaniment at the words 'so pleased my mind', and a somewhat Haydnesque wit (which, perhaps regrettably, disappeared in his mature compositions, though it remained amply present in his letters and poems) in the postponements of a perfect cadence at the end of the stanza, depicting the lover's pointless infatuation and lengthened in the last stanza to 'And still I love her . . . and still I love her . . . and still I love her . . . still I love her till I die' – even if the manner of composition here suggests the organ student trying to hold off the end of an improvisation until the liturgically apt moment. Gurney responds to his text, but has not yet found his mood and tone of voice. The same is true of most of his early songs. His first Housman setting, 'On your midnight pallet lying', also dates from 1907; it is not very arresting, being much indebted to Stanford's 'Drake's drum'. For the Stevenson settings he may have taken *Songs of Travel* as his starting-point, inasmuch as 'Song and singer' ('Bright is the ring of words') is decidedly reminiscent of Vaughan Williams's 'Whither must I wander'. Of his Henley settings, 'Dearest, when I am dead' is his most fulsomely Edwardian

Ex. 1

song, an overblown affair of no originality, while his Heine setting 'I would my songs were roses', typical of its period, is similarly maudlin though technically accomplished, with a persuasive tonal arch indicative of the future. The best of the pre-RCM songs is 'When June is come'. There is a naïve facetiousness in the word-setting, not inappropriate to the poem, and a captured freshness of style informing, for instance, the dominant modulation, unusual for Gurney, in the second line and the subdominant sideslip at the end of the stanza (Ex. 2). This sideslipping and his method of generating a repeated melodic unit out of the piano introduction and in turn generating the melody's continuation out of that unit (Ex. 2, *x*) are premonitory of his later style, for almost all his mature songs adopt the same processes (as described by Moore, above), even if they are disguised; but that style itself is still nowhere to be seen.

While Gurney was in army training in June 1915, waiting for his battalion to be sent to France, he considered his decision to join up and looked back over his composer's achievement thus far: 'Anyway, there's the Elizabethan songs, Edward, the Twa Corbies, the Sea, and Kennst du das Land – two of which seem to be lost and one a sketch' (1913–22). Most of the songs from the four preceding years were eventually published, but of those that were not the two he mentions here, 'Dreams of the sea' (W. H. Davies) and 'Kennst du das Land' (Goethe), both of which do survive, are the most striking. One of the others, 'Star of the morrow gray', which exists only in a copyist's hand but relates stylistically to the five Elizabethan settings, is less arresting but interesting for its uncharacteristically closed formal scheme of ABABA + coda, in which the three-line A section is itself constructed as an *aba* unit. 'Dreams of the sea' begins with another closed

Ex. 2

formal unit, a musical entity which starts and finishes in B minor, with an under-lying accompanying figure of gloomy triplets almost identical to that used later in 'The scribe', for the first stanza; this time, however, the stanza has four lines, and the melodic pattern is *abac*, in which a sudden modulation to E flat major for the beginning of *c* creates a tension which is released back into B minor only just in time for the end of the stanza (Ex. 3). The problem is that there are four stanzas. In the second at the same point Gurney attempts to repeat the tonal surprise and extend it into an arch to carry the third stanza; however, this involves a shift from E flat major to E flat minor, a darkening of colour very characteristic of his later

Ex. 3

style, where it nearly always marks the point at which tonal concentration flags. A creaking sideslip down to C sharp minor weakens the continuity further, and since the triplet figure is now lost for a while, by the middle of the third stanza it is as though Gurney has forgotten that he is depicting the sea; he reverts to the initial tonality and rhythm, with difficulty, only for the final stanza. Here, however, he does achieve some compensating unity by making the last line's modulation lead this time to C sharp minor, thus recollecting the middle of the third stanza after the E flat section.

A similarly inarticulate modulatory device occurs in 'Kennst du das Land', where at the climax of the first stanza a consecutive pair of $V^7d–ib$ progressions

Ex. 4

(Ex. 4, *x*) are rather precipitously cast in the minor mode. The bass line, thus descending (with an octave break) from c down to d in whole tones, is logical enough, but necessitates a sinking enharmonic change which belies the rhetoric of the voice part and provides a quite inappropriate harmonic heaviness for 'steht?', the final word of the question posed in the poem's first line. As so often in his later songs, Gurney has attempted to carry the poem on a far-flung harmonic span but has not quite reached the other side safely. This incidentally may be the song he referred to as a sketch, for he has rewritten the end of the second stanza, and the manuscript incorporates some further pencil amendments, perhaps by

Stanford, who with his fondness for the German *Lied* probably suggested the setting in the first place. One of these amendments seems to advocate allowing an extra half-bar on the word 'steht?', with an appoggiatura; this, however, would function too late to redeem the harmonic argument.

The tonal arch is carried rather more securely in 'The twa corbies', written at about the same time. This time there are five four-line stanzas – one more than in 'Dreams of the sea'. The first two and the last have basically identical music, in A minor. The sudden and distant modulation comes after the second, and jolts the music into D flat. Its significance is not that the jolt is required by the verse at this point, for it is not, but that, functioning structurally like a vastly expanded secondary dominant, it gathers attention for the telling moment of eventual arrival back in the tonic, and builds up a tension parallel to that of the ballad narrative. As in 'Dreams of the sea' the new key, the sharp mediant, shifts to its tonic minor, C sharp, at the beginning of the fourth stanza, and through a melodic line which wells up passionately in both piano and voice it unexpectedly flares out into A minor on the last word of the stanza, 'bare', as though the stark reality of the knight's corpse has suddenly thrust itself on the awareness (Ex. 5).

Although probably shaped instinctively rather than consciously, Gurney's tonal plans are in his later songs often ambitious to the point of incoherence. In such instances it is distressing to see the initial motivic inspiration so soon bogged down in a harmonic mire. Yet, strangely, the danger so obviously present in 'Dreams of the sea' and other early songs is much less evident in the chief songs

Ex. 5

of this period, the five 'Elizas' (as he sometimes called these settings of Elizabethan texts). Hurd devotes some space to praising them (1978: 38–9), and Gurney, in a letter of July 1912 to his poet friend F. W. Harvey, showed himself rightly proud of them:

> It's going, Willy. It's going. Gradually the cloud passes and Beauty is a present thing, not merely an abstraction poets feign to honour.
>
> Willy, Willy, I have done 5 of the most delightful and beautiful songs you ever cast your beaming eyes upon. They are all Elizabethan – the words – and blister my kidneys, bisurate my magnesia if the music is not as English, as joyful, as tender as any lyric of all that noble host. Technique all right, and as to word setting – models. 'Orpheus', 'Tears', 'Under the Greenwood Tree', 'Sleep', and 'Spring'. How did such an undigested clod as I make them? That, Willy, I cannot say. But there they are – Five Songs for Mezzo Soprano – 2 flutes, 2 clarinets, a harp and 2 bassoons, by Ivor Gurney, A.R.C.O. (*ibid.*: 37).

The key to their freshness is the vivid response to Elizabethan poetry, producing a spontaneity of texture and structure allied to the use of woodwind and harp as accompaniment rather than piano. 'Orpheus', 'Under the greenwood tree' and 'Spring' in particular are a good deal looser than the other songs considered so far. In the case of 'Under the greenwood tree', the weakest of the five, this looseness and its attendant tonal anarchy render the song generally unsuccessful, though when Finzi scored it for strings it seems to have given him some textural and rhythmic ideas for the third movement of *Dies Natalis*. 'Orpheus', however, and especially 'Spring', are delightful. In 'Orpheus' the tonal disintegration comes at a point appropriate to the text:

> In sweet music is such art,
> Killing care and grief of heart
>   Fall asleep, or hearing, die.

whereas in 'Spring', the only one of the set for which the instrumental scoring survives, the brilliant instrumentation rests, formally and tonally, on a ternary substructure of classical convention, the outer sections moving to and from the dominant and the central one exploring more distant keys in an episodic rather than rhetorical manner. In many ways this song is untypical of Gurney, particularly in its perky, square-cut melodies and in the extended use of an augmented triad at two points. 'Tears' has far more indications of his postwar, 'Georgian' style; for example the seamless, contemplative setting of both stanzas and the penchant for weak V^7d–ib cadences in distant keys at crucial moments – in this case the same one twice, in an irrelevant D minor, to usher in the second half of each stanza regardless of the tonal placing of the preceding interlude in C major the first time and C sharp major the second. The miracle of the set is 'Sleep', Gurney's best-known song. Its constant semiquaver accompaniment looks forward to the postwar songs, and any structural obscurity is subsumed by the sense of ecstatic delirium of the whole, expressed as much in the subtle and beautiful waves of the voice part, which rises from d″ flat through crests of e″ flat, f″ and g″ flat, to a″ flat in the second stanza, and in its independence from the harmonic rhythm, as in the ambiguity of that rhythm and the richness of the chords. The tonal ambiguity is important, of course – the song ends not in B flat minor but in D flat major – and, to one commentator at least, the effect is disturbing:

'Insomnia' might well have been the title for it. Here, the care and the long annoy are overpowering – inescapable. Here, 'O let my joys have some abiding' becomes a burning hunger, a passionate cry. It is entreaty, but agonized because vain (G. Moore, 1953: 96).

Also important, and increasingly so in Gurney's later songs, is a certain ambiguity of chord positioning. In Ex. 6, at x and y, the 5th of the chord and the middle note of a compound 5th are taken as bass notes for the purposes of connecting these two points with each other by the intervening bass step movement; yet there is also, implicitly, a delayed chromatic voice-leading between the E flat at x and E double flat at y, and it is E double flat which stands in a cadential relationship to the final chord, D flat major, not B double flat (A natural) as leading note to the rightful tonic B flat minor. However, right at the end (Ex. 6, z), a new B_1 double flat is stated, *below* the bass E double flat, and left unresolved, except perhaps by upward transposition to the solo a' flat in the next bar. Gurney probably learnt the sonority of z from the organists' 'acoustic bass' trick; it suggests to the ear another E_1 double flat an octave below the one that is played, which would resolve to the lowest D_1 flat in the final chord.

The fact that Gurney was trained as an organist should not be overlooked in an analysis of his musical style. Many of his more lyrical songs, even 'Sleep', owe their accompanimental continuity, with all its weaknesses, not to a predilection for consistent pattern-making like that of, say, Fauré, but to a dreamy mind capable of improvising at the piano what it had learnt at the organ. He treated the

Ex. 6

written notes with licence when accompanying himself at the piano (Howells, 1974), and Marion Scott further testifies that 'he . . . used both pedals together . . . very freely. The piano accompaniments, as played by him, were often a lovely wash of sound forming the background to the voice. The effect cannot well be written out – it was too spontaneous' (1952). The implications of his organist's background are twofold. First, his style not only closely parallels that of Herbert Howells's organ Psalm Preludes and Rhapsodies of the same period, but in certain mannerisms shares with Parry's chorale preludes (apart from Elgar's Sonata the only English Romantic organ music of much consequence at that time) a common origin in Bach, whom both Parry and Gurney revered with a passionate if idiosyncratic understanding. The use of pseudo-motoric semiquavers, for instance, particularly tied over the beat, is already unsatisfactorily present in the second stanza of 'Dreams of the sea', and in his last songs it often clogs the texture beyond repair. Second, he naturally found composition almost impossible while serving in France, where he very seldom had access to a keyboard, but on the few occasions when he did manage to write songs circumstances forced him to fashion them as concatenations of discrete, economical but evocative musical gestures rather than lyric arches with background wash. This blunt use of musical expression, tending towards an orchestral rather than a keyboard conception, paralleled his experimentation with language in his poems, but was generally abandoned after the war except in isolated songs such as the setting of de la Mare's 'The ghost'.

The first song of this type, and the most impractical, is 'By a bierside'. This was only recently published for the first time, and it receives generous consideration in Hurd's biography (1978: 77–84, 79). Gurney sent it to Marion Scott in a letter postmarked 18 August 1916. The immediacy of its inspiration is quite obvious when the final line, 'It is most grand to die', is considered with Gurney's laconic comment in his letter, 'events yesterday evening gave one full opportunity to reflect on one's chance of doing this grand thing'. Yet he was also thinking in more classical terms, as we see from a letter of September 1916:

> You please me in saying that it gives you the impression of looking down at a bier. In my mind I saw a picture of some poet-priest pronouncing an oration over the dead and lovely body of some young Greek hero . . . At last I begin to fulfil some part of my desire – to see and tell the ultimate truth of things, and especially of the primal things' (1913–22).

A month earlier he had made it clear that 'the accompaniment is really orchestral, but the piano will get all that's wanted very well'; he further pointed out, 'Once I could not write away from the piano; that was written in the front line' (*ibid.*). Inevitably, though, despite Gurney's pride, the song appears disjointed. Marion Scott must have said this, for in the September letter he replied:

> About binding the song more closely, that may be so too; but I cannot alter it out here. I need to play things over and think – for the present – about alterations; and then leave it, and return. Anyway it is good enough. The repetition of that figure, in the orchestral version would insist bar after bar on a different thread of the counterpoint, or at a different octave as [Ex. 7a] then [Ex. 7b] then at an octave higher and so forth, with trumpets especially at the loudest with accented notes. The piano version can be made significant enough (*ibid.*).

Ex. 7

And, presumably after further critical comment, he returned to the passage in a letter a month later; 'the four Es' were eventually altered to three g's and an e″ in the fair copy (but see also his letter of October 1916 to Howells, quoted in Thornton: 112):

> I am not sure you are not right about the figure being repeated after 'Death opens unknown doors'. It may mean a couple of extra bars . . . The four Es must stand, even if the lady should need four trumpets to back her up. She is supposed to make a row like a brass band there. This only is admissible beside the repeated notes, and it is from an unwilling writer [Ex. 8]. Compree? (1913–22).

Ex. 8

Despite the song's loose *arioso* construction, it contains moments of a more intense, unconventional beauty than Gurney had hitherto attained, except perhaps in 'Sleep'. Some of them – at 'Death drifts the brain with dust', 'Death makes the lovely soul . . .' and 'Death opens unknown doors' – are decidedly Elgarian, and it is not surprising, with death continually present, that *The Dream of Gerontius* was one of the English works that Gurney carried in his head as an inspiration, along with Vaughan Williams's *Sea Symphony* and Howells's Piano Concerto, as his letters testify (see Thornton *passim*).

'In Flanders', the second of his 'trench' songs, a setting of a poem of home-sickness for Gloucestershire by his friend F. W. Harvey, is less grandiose and more cohesive, though evidently Gurney, forwarding it to Marion Scott in January 1917, was worried that she might criticise it as she had 'By a bierside' for diffuseness:

> This valuable fragment dates anywhere between April 1916 and now. Or is it September or August 1915? Goodness knows. However, here it is, cast up with the flotsam and jetsam in more or less permanent form, with – woe is me – another orchestral accompaniment, dammit.
>
> Well, it drew me out of lethargy for a space, and was no more trouble than an ordinary fatigue. Surely, it reflects the words? But on the other hand, ought there to be a figure to bind it together? And (my usual thought) is it Oldfashioned? And though undoubtedly music in places, is it Immature? Or will its freshness carry it off? Is it fresh? (1913–22)

Three weeks later he returned to the question:

It would seem that 'Flanders' *ought* to have some binding figure, and yet – I think it is all right there. But what of the change from D to D minor, B flat minor, C minor in about three bars? Ask Herbert [Howells] please . . . (*ibid.*)

The modulatory passage in question (published a semitone lower) is in fact surprisingly expressive, its irregular shifts of key and register mirroring the lines

> The giant clouds go royally
> By jagged Malvern with a train
> Of shadows.

As for the 'binding figure', the melodic line which Gurney spins to express the curves of the hills against the skyline (Ex. 9) is quite adequate as a recurrent

Ex. 9

theme. More to the point, it is peculiarly apt as an image of the contour of the Gloucestershire hills and their spirit of freedom, and as such holds the key to much of Gurney's melodic inspiration as a Georgian rural composer. Gurney himself was confident about this origin and scope of his creative expression, as a letter to Marion Scott in March 1917 shows:

> As for 'In Flanders' – of course he would do it well, bless him. I'm glad he went to Robinswood Hill; the view there is absolutely magnificent. Do you know, standing off from my song, I can now see that the very spirit of my county is quick in the song. Gloster itself shines and speaks in it. It is as if, on the long night work, some kind spirit of home visited me, when I think of it. And the end of the song is exactly like the 'high blue blade' fading away to distant Bredon just above Evesham . . . Surely it is impossible that God will not let me say all this out in music? (*ibid.*)

Gurney assigned to Howells the orchestration of 'By a bierside' and 'In Flanders', which were performed (by a baritone, though Gurney had intended the former for contralto) at the RCM, and the first two sentences above suggest that Howells had made a trip to Robinswood Hill, near Gloucester, in connection with the task, perhaps to gain inspiration; after all, Chosen Hill is also close by, and the previous year he had dedicated his Piano Quartet 'to the Hill at Chosen and Ivor Gurney who knows it'. But Gurney's nostalgic preoccupation with Gloucestershire leads him into a curious ministerpretation of his friend's poem. In the following lines, Harvey's antithesis between the 'low' imprisoning circle of the flat Flanders horizon and the freedom of the 'high' heart yearning for the Gloucestershire hills is clear:

> Where the land is low
> Like a huge imprisoning O
> I hear a heart that's sound and high,
> I hear the heart within me cry:

– yet Gurney sets the first two of these lines to the warmest music in the song, evidently taking them to refer to the beautiful Severn plain in which he was nurtured.

Both 'In Flanders' and 'By a bierside' owe their inspiration to powerful visual images. So does 'Severn meadows', written shortly after 'In Flanders' and on much the same subject; it is a rare instance of Gurney's setting his own words to music, though as it happened not very memorably. In two songs written slightly later, however, the verse more abstract. With his setting of Ralegh's poem about his own imminent death, 'Even such is time', he has taken to heart the concern about a 'binding figure', and employs an archetypal 'fate' motive of three repeated notes and a downward 5th, sometimes inverted, to express first death and then, in the finely judged instrumental postlude (again surely orchestral in conception), resurrection. The best of these contemplative, non-strophic, *arioso* wartime songs is the last, 'The folly of being comforted', composed in hospital in Britain in the automn of 1917. It is an intimate meditation about love – despairing, lost love – rare for Gurney, and dates from the time of his futile attachment to Nurse Drummond (Hurd, 1978: 118–19). Although it is unquestionably one of his greatest songs it is rarely performed for, like 'By a bierside', it demands from the singer great maturity and sustained control of a kind required otherwise in this period only by Germanic composers, notably Strauss and Mahler. This is especially true of the devastating ending. In this song, more frequent access to a piano has increased Gurney's power of harmonic integration, but an orchestral conception still seems at the forefront of his mind, and there is an inspired freedom of counterpoint and dissonance between voice and accompaniment, sometimes recalling Schumann, at points such as 'O she had not . . .', 'wild summer', and the word 'of', as well as the long and intense F sharp appoggiatura, in the final phrases (Ex. 10); this was probably not learnt at the piano, since it was already beginning to flower in the songs written in the trenches. The song's greatest achievement, however, is in the further development of the idea of a 'binding figure', the ability to build a musical structure which parallels the psychological argument of Yeats's sonnet. A friend has tried to console the poet for his lost love: time will destroy her beauty and lessen the pain. But after the first

Ex. 10

six lines the poet's heart replies that age will only make her more noble and beautiful and thus there is no comfort in time's passing. Although Gurney's musical reaction to these ponderings occasionally suggests a Wagnerian monologue, his fundamental technique is of Brahms's 'developing variation', as Schönberg described it. The initial motive grows, and alters as specific parts and aspects of it grow (Ex. 11). Then, as the hope of the first part of the poem fails, the motive (Ex. 11, *x*) withers, most expressively (Ex. 12), before growing again (this time in the voice first, at the phrase 'But, heart, there is no comfort') with a fiercer determination; it reaches a climax after the word 'clearly', as despair is realised, and sinks again with a series of after-shocks (Ex. 13). Another misinterpretation must be mentioned, however: the lines that follow,

> O she had not these ways,
> When all the wild summer was in her gaze.

Ex. 11

Ex. 12

Ex. 13

really belong within this climax; Gurney's placing of them after it, with his wonderfully rich setting of the words 'wild summer' (Ex. 10), suggests nostalgia for the past, which is not the point of the poem at all.

'Once I get back,' Gurney had written prophetically from France in February 1917, 'for a while I will simply reek songs; mere exudations . . .' (1913–22). The transition from Gurney the sporadic composer of non-strophic, sometimes sparse dramatic or reflective monologues such as we have been considering to Gurney the continual spinner of lyrical, strophic or at least continuous melodies with a full and largely continuous accompaniment must have been a conscious one. To a certain extent it represented the picking up of threads dropped before the war, yet the lyrical outburst might not have taken such a consistent and, ultimately, repetitive shape had 'Georgian' poetry not emerged as a definite pastoral movement in English verse in the intervening years. We shall return to this movement and its expression in music in the next chapter; here it should be mentioned that a great many of Gurney's songs are settings of poets who appeared in the Georgian anthologies, and that the majority of those composed after or shortly before his release from hospital in 1918 deal with the self and nature and are above all overwhelmingly lyrical. There are specific and varied types of song, of course, some of which do not conform with this generalisation: ballads, taking after 'Edward' and 'The twa corbies' (e.g. 'The lowlands of Holland', 'The bonny Earl of Murray'); a quick $\frac{3}{4}$ drinking song ('Hawk and Buckle'); $\frac{6}{8}$ Irish reels ('The fiddler of Dooney') and their slow counterparts, $\frac{6}{8}$ lullabies ('The cloths of heaven', 'Cradle song', 'Nocturne' and 'The birds', all musical variants of one another and charming in style); nocturnal fantasies (All night under the moon' and 'Lights out', both repeating the idea of 'Sleep', but less successfully); and an intensely beautiful simple love-song, 'Down by the salley gardens'. One or two songs look back to the wartime style. But on the whole there is an ambulatory self-repetitiveness about Gurney's lyrical norm which finally destroys itself in his asylum songs. This account of Gurney's music concludes with a study of three Georgian settings from the 1918–22 output, of which they represent a cross-section. The first two, of Brooke's 'All suddenly the wind comes soft' (Gurney entitles it 'Heart's pain') and Belloc's 'Most holy Night', have a sufficient number of representative features for Moore's description of the typical Gurney song to seem a necessity and not an arbitrary exercise in statistical analysis. The Belloc setting is undoubtedly a more successful song than the Brooke, which has hitherto remained unpublished, but both have weaknesses as well as moments of great beauty. In the third, Bridges' 'Thou didst delight my eyes', the mannerisms are much less cloying; this is one of Gurney's very finest songs. The complete musical texts of 'Heart's pain' and 'Most holy Night' are given as Exx. 14 and 16.

'Heart's pain' is one of the songs that suggest that there was a fundamental melodic pattern living in Gurney's mind and that it was called up again and again by contact with nature. His contact with nature normally took the form of countryside rambles, and we know from his notebooks and from personal reminiscences (M. Scott, 1938c: 6–7; Raphael, 1974–7) that he sometimes composed on these occasions. The flow of accompanimental semiquavers from the very beginning (he rarely makes them generate gradually) reproduces the strolling background out of which his thoughts arose. The accompaniment's tread is perhaps not so specific here as in, say, 'Walking song' or 'Black Stitchel' or 'The fields are full', but it has the same origin and purpose. The melody grows out of it, again not as obviously as in some songs (see Ex. 2, and 'The Latmian shepherd', 'You are my sky' and 'Ha'nacker Mill' in OUP's Volume I), but convincingly none the less: the basic c″ sharp – b′ cell appears twice in the first two bars of the melody at prominent points, arising from the three statements of it in the piano introduction underneath the treble f″ sharp – e″ (two prolongations of the latter occur in the voice part, one at the lower octave – see Ex. 14, *x* and *y*), and both the introduction and first line of melody end with e′ – f′ sharp – b′, over similar harmony though with different metric placement. Thus the accompaniment begins by suggesting the environment and the voice part the composer extracting thoughts from it; and the poem itself is an account of this process. The poet not only constructs a series of images out of his observation of nature, for instance likening the emergence of buds in spring to the reawakening of sorrow in the heart, but makes it clear that spring is the *cause* of the reawakened sorrow; thus 'cry' in the final stanza implies a kind of emotional pun, its sense modulating between the burgeoning bird-sound and the 'pain' that it induces in the poet and that he hears reflected in it. The point of the poem is to stress the agency of nature in man's realisation of his emotions; this is a particularly Georgian corner of Romanticism.

Gurney's continual use of a melodic prototype is perhaps his way of expressing that agency. The openings of a number of songs are given in Ex. 15: some of them are in the major, some the minor, and the minor ones nearly always sound modal because of a flat 7th and/or sharp 6th. He works with two-bar and four-bar phrases, as in the melody of 'Most holy Night' (Ex. 16, which should be set

Ex. 14 (cont.)

Ex. 14 (cont.)

beside those of Ex. 15), allowing for a figuratively appropriate crotchet's lengthening on 'sleep' and consequent re-barring. 'Most holy Night' also shows the
traditional roots of Gurney's melody in its (tonally) binary expectations of a
dominant cadence at 'sleep', a subsidiary subdominant relative minor cadence at
'close', and a return to the tonic at the end of the melody. The fact that the first
half modulates not to the dominant but to G minor, the mediant, is indicative of
an almost obsessive avoidance characteristic of Gurney's style and period, and is
an ancillary aspect of folksong influence. 'When on a summer morn', which does
go to the dominant, is unusual. Folksong, and more specifically perhaps dance
tunes such as those in the Petrie Collection, are probably at the root of the rhythmic mannerism seen in 'Heart's pain' and elsewhere again and again (e.g.
Ex. 15): the melody starts in quavers, duplet or triplet, or dotted distortions of
them, but settles down with the help of four (or more) semiquavers, most often at
the end of the second bar. As can be seen from 'Most holy Night', where the four
semiquavers are pervasive but differently placed, the figure may involve slurring
syllables of the text; an instance such as 'I will go with my father a-ploughing',
where until we see the other appearances of this melodic archetype it seems
almost inconceivable that the contour and rhythms were not a purely spontaneous reaction to this particular text, is a stroke of genius.

The least poetic stimulus could draw forth Gurney's melodic thread; he himself
wrote, in a letter of November 1916, 'It is not always necessary to read a poem

Ex. 15

through to start setting it', and continued, with reference to his 'By a bierside', 'I had only the first two lines in my mind, or perhaps three, when I began to write, and did not finish till my idea was complete. I did not trouble about balance or anything else much; it came, and after five years or so, I will write sonatas in the same way' (1913–22). But this was a sad mixture of perception and delusion. True, his songs nearly always do complete their ideas, and the endings are often exquisite, but the lack of balance or propulsion experienced midway is often a severe weakness. Gurney never really solved the problem of a substitute for the classical binary tonal balance, with its dominant modulation. If he keeps a basically strophic limitation to the melody, as he does in 'Heart's pain', he nevertheless often refuses to round it off tonally. In 'Heart's pain', the roughly ABA distribution of melodic material for the three stanzas would have been clear enough had the last note of the first stanza, on the word 'pain', been a b′ in E major, but already in the third line he has set off on his tonal wanderings, and the 6–4 chord on 'buds' is singularly ill-placed. It comes too soon in the song to convey either release of tension or a strong pointer to a new area of tonal dominance (two uses

Strauss, for example, frequently makes of the chord); and it is unable to hold the D major chord in a kinetic state until its significance, as a subdominant of A major, which is in any case odd, becomes apparent at the end of the stanza. He tries again to articulate a modulation with a 6-4, this time to C major, and there is another, very typical, to C minor at 'numb'; but by this time all sense of direction has been lost. The tonal problems of the middle stanza are only eased with the enharmonic change at its end, as E major comes into sight once more. The attempt is, of course, to express the numbness of winter in the music, but it seems that what is needed for the central section in a relatively expansive song like this (in comparison with, say, Ireland's setting, which is much simpler) is the faculty to calculate and create a contrasting musical texture rather than pursue a disintegrating continuation of the initial idea.

When the clarity of the initial idea does return, for the final stanza, the song immediately picks up again, and Gurney shows particular strength in his devices for intensification: the triplet quaver variant at the point of return to the opening bar's music (Ex. 14, *a*); the use of melodic turns (Ex. 14, *a*, *b*, *c*); the lingering on the top f″ sharp at the words 'earth has woken' (cf. 'wind comes soft' in the first stanza) and its heterophonic paraphrase in the top part of the accompaniment, which also forms the first, elliptical use of chromatic passing notes (c″ sharp – c″ natural and finally b′); the telescoping of the D major 6-4 chord into the first phrase, and the fleetingly chromatic approach to it – all these details help to redeem the song from lack of concentration. Again, however, the danger of rhapsodic incoherence arises, as Gurney attempts to explore yet more keys in the course of the final stanza, and between the second and third lines finds himself perched on a dubious subdominant of C major. There is a purpose in this, which can be felt retrospectively, for the song's masterstroke is the dissolution of texture, four and three bars from the end, into a widely spaced dominant with flattened 5th, minor 9th, and 13th, of which the former two notes (F natural and c″ natural) are the most poignant elements, beautifully expressive of the poet's yearning, and can both be traced back to the C major subdominant mentioned above; indeed, the c″ natural is present in every intervening bar. But Gurney has a dual function for the F, which he modifies to an f′ sharp under the word 'hedge' in the penultimate line; its neighbour g′ is similarly modified to g sharp just before the last line of the poem, and it forms an expressive appoggiatura to the f sharp (piano, left hand, eight bars from the end) which is then repeated above the song's final word, 'pain', as an obvious and touching reminiscence, a step higher, of the song's opening. Embedded in this reminiscence is one of Gurney's characteristic changing-note patterns (c″ b′ d″ c″), in semiquavers, whose d″ natural, resolving up to d″ and d‴ sharp in the next bar, adds to the Neapolitan poignancy of the simultaneous reinstated F natural resolving down to E. The point of all this is that by the end Gurney has ingeniously explored the expressive possibilities of naturalising, within E major, all four sharps of his key signature, and the white-note passage halfway through the stanza is a preparation for this.

'Most holy Night' (Ex. 16) is far stronger. Here Gurney avoids the problems of through-composition by setting the poem not strophically but as a bar form (AAB). This obviates the need for external modulation, but is made possible only by omitting the second of Belloc's four stanzas: Gurney is not concerned with the 'lament' of the 'dead day's requiem'. His setting is conceived as a sensuous, perhaps even erotic, fantasy, as is made clear by the *Liebestod*-inspired melodic changing note in the build-up to the broad climax in the final stanza, and by the exploratory inventiveness of some of the accompanimental figuration which, having originated in the organ loft, here finds itself at home in a more voluptuous conceptual environment. The four significant interpretations of this poem in our period are remarkably different: O'Neill's, discussed in Part I, is the most impressionistic, with its play on tolling bells in the second stanza; Gurney's is the most sensuous; Rubbra's (1925) maintains the idea of a lullaby, taken from the second stanza, throughout, with a cradle-rocking figure; and Warlock's (1927), in response to the Roman Catholic background of Belloc's apostrophe, is an intoned prayer, complete with ritual bells and their reverberation at the end of each invocation. Each seizes on one idea in the poem; all four are vivid, unified and successful.

The melody of Gurney's 'Most holy Night', as has already been stated, is basically a regular eight-bar structure in two-bar groups; this is marked in Ex. 16. The lengthening of the phrases, observable in the first stanza, is increased in the second: there is now a whole bar extra after 'croon', as well as an extra half-bar after 'blest'. This latter puts the beginning of the final two-bar phrase, 'In my brief rest', not on the first beat, where, despite the barring, the corresponding 'Give me repose' is felt as being placed in the first stanza, but on a three-note anacrusis of quaver triplets (Ex. 16, *c*1). Hence the a' flat ('brief') is now the first beat of the bar, as it is when the phrase returns at the end of the final stanza. A further anacrucial lengthening occurs at the beginning of the final stanza (Ex. 16, *c*2). This gives the impression that the B section of the bar form is taking off with an entirely new pattern, but although this is true of the melody the two-bar metric framework with quaver anacrusis is still fundamental, as can be seen in Ex. 16's bracketed phrases. The passage marked *c*3 is simply an extra bar stemming from a striking augmentation of the melodic changing note on 'from'. The third of the stanza's two-bar phrases is stated by the piano. It occurs after the traditional midway tonal pivot, here heightened by the fact that the preceding dominant 7th on 'resting place', produced by e'' flat becoming e'' natural, sounds gauche until it shows itself to be a secondary dominant by resolving at this point onto a (subdominant-function) triad of F minor: the piano takes over the e'' natural left hanging by the voice and treats it as a (dissonant) leading note to f''. The voice answers with a fourth two-bar phrase and, finally, appropriately making the B of the bar longer than the A, a fifth phrase, equivalent to the fourth of the other two stanzas.

Harmonically there are far fewer problems than in 'Heart's pain'. The substitution of mediant for dominant halfway through the first stanza is repeated in the second, but here the additional extra beat after 'croon' allows at least some hint of dominant before the turn to F minor. A typical tonal excursion seems to be beginning, at the start of the third stanza, with A flat minor (whose c'' flat is introduced strikingly in the previous bar), but here it is not only unproblematic because unconnected with strophic demands, but also surprisingly concise: the chromatic voice-leading into which it develops (d'' flat – d'' natural – e'' flat – e'' natural – f''/g'' – a'' flat – a'' natural – b'' flat, rising, followed by c' – c' flat – b

Ex. 16

Ex. 16 (cont.)

Ex. 16 (cont.)

flat – a natural – a flat – g, falling, in the six bars from 'Hide day-dawn', Ex. 16, *h*) never really loses sight of the tonic. Perhaps the most remarkable harmonic aspect is the stretching out of a single subdominant/supertonic entity at the end of the final stanza, beginning on the a' flat with F bass on 'holy', for $4\frac{3}{4}$ bars before the final perfect cadence. The voice, dropping to a g' against this, gives the impression of having fallen asleep.

A most inventive style of accompanimental figuration holds this chord in its long suspense. A melodic line (Ex. 16, *e*) has already begun which consists of 13 different three- or four-note patterns occupying 15 crotchet beats; in other words, only two of them are repeated. Initially the second and third sound like 'developing variation', but as the invention becomes freer it is clear that Gurney's prototype is more baroque, no doubt another instance, like the *style-brisé* final cadence (Ex. 16, *z*), of his organist's susceptibility to Bach. Like Bach's, his feeling for line is unorthodox but precisely calculated. The bass line marked *g*, for instance, six bars before the end of the song, delays the descent of the scale to F by a melodic turn which is angularly but nicely counterpointed against the top part. The most extended melodic line is that which accompanies the second stanza, asserting a more continuous counterpoint to the voice part than in the first stanza, often with wilful independence. It begins with a deeply expressive, rather Elgarian inner motive at the close of the first stanza (Ex. 16, *a*1); this is imitated, with intervallic enlargement, a 5th higher (*a*2), and then, over one of Gurney's 'acoustic bass' tonics (*b*), the long line (*d*) begins, making frequent motivic reference to the three initial notes of *a*, particularly at a sort of fulcrum (under 'By my bedside', boxed in Ex. 16) where the line's upward progress is rather curiously halted for a while. It reaches its zenith on b″ flat at the halfway point of the stanza, then continues in a series of lesser but expressive peaks, finally coming to rest under the first word of the final stanza. The motive *a* is noticeably reasserted at the end of the second stanza (under 'brief rest'), and again in the penultimate bar of the passage.

The effect of wayward intricacy in 'Most holy Night' represents Gurney's style at its most rhapsodic, and it is easy to appreciate how the proliferation of line, here under control if difficult to balance with the voice part in performance, could lose cohesion in his asylum songs. 'Most holy Night' works when a singer with sufficient powers of *bel canto* projection can bring out the underlying simplicity of harmonic shape in the melody. In this respect Gurney's songs require the same refined technique as Strauss's; there are few singers who can sustain either. Yet a number of his songs present opportunities for *bel canto* singing without such difficulties, and this chapter concludes with a brief mention of perhaps the finest of these, the setting of Bridges' 'Thou didst delight my eyes'. It is still difficult for the voice to achieve sufficient depth and intensity to carry the rather lush opening to each of the three stanzas *ahead* of the offbeat accompaniment, but apart from this syncopation the piano part contains little that does not work with the voice rather than against it: melodic proliferation is restricted largely to the very beautiful meditations at the end of each stanza. But Gurney's greatest achievement in this song is his rare containment of his typical modulatory wanderings within a clear and balanced structural framework. Here the melodic plan is strophic – not without a considerable amount of fluent variation, metrically necessary because Gurney sets the six-line trimetric stanzas (with much *enjambement*) in $\frac{4}{4}$ in a way that suggests only five, or perhaps even only four, melodic phrases. But, characteristically, the harmonic destiny of each stanza is different. The first stays in the tonic, D flat. The second loses its way after a stretched modulation to D major and collapses, with one or two diminished triads, at the inconclusive and frustrated lines

> And short my joy; but yet,
> O song, do not forget.

This collapse moves from b″ flat in the piano part, down through a″ natural (+ a′), a′ flat, and g′ natural to g′ flat, where the voice part momentarily coincides on the last word of the stanza. This g′ flat resolves (in the bass, as G flat), as a dominant 7th of the home tonic, D flat, which would be an unsatisfactory way of arriving home if, as is often the case with Gurney, there were no further tonal excursion to balance it. But in this song there is. The third stanza proceeds similarly, but when it gets to the D major dominant further harmonic progression is held up as the poet's mind gropes for the appropriate image for his memory of love; then, almost triumphantly, the bass and treble both slip outwards semi-tonally to a D flat major 6–4 as the abiding image is coined:

> A sail, that for a day
> Has cheered the castaway.

This climax and its image are very heavily loaded with emotion, the mixture of fulfilment at having been 'cheered', if only fleetingly, and tragedy at lasting self-loss being beautifully expressed in Gurney's setting of the final word, 'castaway', not on the tonic as a conclusion to the preceding downward scale but on the somewhat interrogatory dominant. The song is perhaps valedictory to Gurney's life, cheered so briefly by his creative vision, cast away as it eventually was.

X

Georgian poetry and Georgian music

The intensely personal exploration of style and symbol in the songs of Gurney and Ireland should not blind us to the shared concerns of their period. Indeed, Gurney himself requires further consideration in the wider contexts of this chapter. It has already been suggested that the inter-war ambience was primarily one of lyrical retreat; two of the identifiable forms which that retreat took will be examined here. Put simply, they are a retreat to the country and a retreat to the fantasy world of childhood. The first characterises the Georgian poets in general, the second the most distinguished of their number, Walter de la Mare.

Some account of the history and scope of Georgian poetry must be given before its relation to music can be judged. Its prime mover was Edward Marsh, an indefatigable patron of the arts who worked as Winston Churchill's private secretary on and off for a quarter of a century from 1905. He used his post in the Civil Service as a passport to artistic resourcefulness, much as others used their wealth. Christopher Hassall's biography recounts how the Georgian venture was born on 19 September 1912 at Marsh's house, where Rupert Brooke often stayed overnight when in London:

> Brooke was sitting on his bed half undressed, and the conversation turned to the public's lack of interest in modern poetry. No one seemed to realize that there was a poetic renaissance. *The Everlasting Mercy*, published the year before, had reached thousands of readers (in fact Masefield was the most widely read poet at that time), but there were at least a dozen other writers of comparable merit whose work was undeservedly neglected. Brooke suggested that he might try playing a practical joke on the public which would at least draw its attention to poetry. He would write a book himself under twelve pseudonyms and issue it as an anthology selected from the poems of a dozen promising writers. Marsh's view was that there was no need to go to all that trouble when there must be twelve representative flesh-and-blood poets with material ready to hand. They began to count. As well as Masefield and Brooke himself there were of course Gibson, Davies, de la Mare, and Bottomley. They included A. E. Housman and Ezra Pound, and Brooke added his Cambridge friend Elroy Flecker, who had shown some promise. Marsh came out with the idea that Brooke should compile his anthology from the work of these writers, but he declined. It needed someone older and of more authority – but what could it be called? They believed that Victorianism in literature was gone for good and that a new era had begun. Marsh pointed out that the natural thing was to name eras after reigning sovereigns, the new reign was itself as new and hopeful as the renaissance in poetry, which train of thought led him to come out with what he afterwards described as 'my proud ambiguous adjective – *Georgian*'. But Brooke didn't like it. He thought it

sounded too staid for a volume designed as the herald of a revolutionary dawn. He imagined that the book might provide a useful field for experiment, but Marsh argued that experiments were best confined to the poet's rough notebook; such an anthology must present only fully evolved and finished work if it was to win over an apathetic public (189–90).

'Georgian' was indeed an 'ambiguous adjective'. In 1912 George V had only recently become king, and it suggested a sudden plethora of talent (Swinnerton: 283), but all too soon it became associated exclusively with the 'georgic' rural tradition of verse, as the poetry in the anthologies appeared more and more to exhibit 'a combination of false rusticity and simplicity, glibness of feeling and a studied lucidity of style that was merely modish' (Hassall: 683) – a criticism directly applicable to many of the song settings of the 1920s. Nevertheless, the term stuck, and in addition to the poetry there appeared (though not under Marsh's aegis) five volumes of *Georgian Stories* in the 1920s, and in 1942 a volume of *Georgian Essays* whose authors included Belloc, Buchan, Chesterton, Churchill, Conrad, Galsworthy, Gosse, Huxley, A. A. Milne, Quiller-Couch, Santayana and Virginia Woolf.

Marsh produced five poetry anthologies, in each case drawing his selection from the publications of the previous two or three years. The first two were well received; the third suffered from its notable disregard for the rising tide of war poetry (partly due to Marsh's editorial policy of representing only living poets or dead poets who had been been previously represented while still alive – which also excluded Edward Thomas from the series); the fourth, and least incisive, was compared unfavourably to the Sitwells' annual anthology *Wheels* (Murry, 1919) which, with Eliot's later *Criterion*, emphasised the distance between *Georgian Poetry* and modernism; the fifth was the last, though a sixth was contemplated. The following is a list of poets newly represented in each of the anthologies.

Georgian Poetry 1911–1912	*Georgian Poetry 1913–1915*	*Georgian Poetry 1918–1919*
Lascelles Abercrombie	Ralph Hodgson	Francis Brett Young
Gordon Bottomley	Francis Ledwidge	Thomas Moult
Rupert Brooke		J. D. C. Pellow
G. K. Chesterton	*Georgian Poetry 1916–1917*	Edward Shanks
W. H. Davies	W. J. Turner	Fredegond Shove
Walter de la Mare	J. C. Squire	
John Drinkwater	Siegfried Sassoon	*Georgian Poetry 1920–1922*
James Elroy Flecker	Isaac Rosenberg	Martin Armstrong
W. W. Gibson	Robert Nichols	Edmund Blunden
D. H. Lawrence	Robert Graves	Richard Hughes
John Masefield	John Freeman	William Kerr
Harold Monro	Maurice Baring	Frank Prewett
T. Sturge Moore	Herbert Asquith	Peter Quennell
Ronald Ross		Victoria Sackville-West
Edmund Beale Sargant		
James Stephens		
R. C. Trevelyan		

By 1940 solo song settings had been made of texts by most of these poets, the exceptions being Ross, Sargant, Trevelyan, Rosenberg, Moult, Pellow, Armstrong, Hughes, Quennell and Sackville-West. It cannot be ascertained that the anthologies themselves were widely used by composers, for in fact surprisingly few of the poems in them were set to music, possibly because Marsh tended to avoid obviously popular poems by his contributors, whereas composers did not. The point is that *Georgian Poetry* paralleled rather than influenced Georgian music.

De la Mare settings, of which there are more than of any other contemporary poet, even Housman or Yeats (see Gooch and Thatcher, 1976), are in a category of their own, and will be discussed separately. Of the others, the most often set were Brooke, W. H. Davies, W. W. Gibson, Edward Shanks and James Stephens. Graves, Lawrence and Sassoon are more highly regarded now; but most of their verse would have been too great a challenge for the song composers of the time.

Nearly half of the known song settings of these poets that come within our period are by five composers: Herbert Howells, Benjamin Burrows, Michael Head, Cecil Armstrong Gibbs, whose 38 de la Mare settings form the largest single group, and Ivor Gurney. Gurney made settings of 17 of the 40 poets represented in the anthologies, and moreover set 17 of the poems printed in the anthologies themselves – nearly half the number of such settings that can be traced. However, there is no evidence that he drew specifically on *Georgian Poetry*: his knowledge of many of these poets was probably not limited to anthologies. The number of Georgian settings by Gurney amounts to about half his output if one includes in the category poets of the same period and flavour but for one reason or another not represented in Marsh's anthologies – Belloc, Bridges, Hardy, F. W. Harvey, Housman and Edward Thomas.

Gurney is the Georgian composer *par excellence*. Although he seems never to have used the term of himself, others did. Both Vaughan Williams and Howells included references to the Georgians in their tributes to Gurney in the *Music and Letters* symposium, Vaughan Williams saying that 'These writers had just rediscovered England and the language that fitted the shy beauty of their own country' (1938: 12) and Howells remarking that 'Before the "Georgians" got together in 1912 he [Gurney] had already found out their settable verse. His very finest songs are not only settings of their poems, but they form the subtlest existing musical commentary upon them . . . Gurney's melodic speech is a "kindly" human utterance – as gentle as the outline of the Malverns' (1938: 14–15). To strengthen these comparisons, and bearing in mind that Gurney was a writer as well as a composer, it will be helpful to trace some of his attitudes towards Georgian modes of thought and expression in his correspondence.

First, as he wrote in July 1916, he was concerned less with universality of poetic expression than with the spirit of place: 'We may have no great poets, but poetry so saturated with the very spirit of England has not been written before. When I try to call up a certain Autumn Evening at Minsterworth years ago, and now worlds away, it is our younger poets who give me help' (1913–22). One can point to periods in the artistic history of many countries in which not only an apprehension of national flavour has been important but the lure of a particular locality has given rise to some sort of creative colony with a common source of inspiration. This is difficult to assess sociologically or aesthetically, but it is clearly a Romantic phenomenon of which perhaps the most outstanding examples are the English Lake poets and the American Transcendentalists of Concord, Massachusetts. In the period of the Georgians, one might instance the poets who settled at Boar's Hill near Oxford (Blunden, Bridges, Graves, Masefield and Nichols), or, more to our point, those who just before the first world war were all living within a few miles of each other in Gloucestershire (Hassall: 262): Abercrombie, Robert Frost, W. W. Gibson, Edward Thomas, and Gurney and his poet friends, F. W. Harvey and Jack Haines – these three voicing in their works a very similar expression of delight in Gloucestershire. Poetry perhaps needs this identification with a locality more than music, but it is remarkable, and an intimation of the correspondence between poetic and musical expression in the period, how many English composers also belonged to the same lower Severn landscape: Elgar and Parry, Gurney and Howells, Holst, C. W. Orr and Finzi. Anyone who has stood in the Severn valley at the close of a brilliant day in midwinter and seen the simultaneous setting of the sun over the Malverns and rising of the moon over Bredon Hill directly opposite cannot doubt the intensity and sincerity of belief of those who have found this region as fit a subject for the artistic portrayal of beauty as any human face or body.

This consideration has already arisen in the discussion of 'In Flanders' in the previous chapter (pp. 190-2); it is worth adding that Gurney and the Georgian poets were not alone in focussing their fervour for the English countryside upon the West Midlands at this time. Even allowing for the precedent furnished by Housman in writing of 'those blue remembered hills' west of Bromsgrove, the similarity in mode of expression between the two passages quoted below and Gurney's comments on 'In Flanders' is remarkable, and suggests that a singularly specific image of the English landscape corresponded to people's dreams in the inter-war period:

> . . . from my own garden . . . I see the hills known to all of you, beginning in the north-east, the Clents; and beyond, in Warwickshire, Edgehill, where the English squire passed with horse and hounds between the two armies; Bredon, the beginning of the Cotswolds, like a cameo against the sky, and the wonderful straight blue line of the Malverns, little shapes of Ankerdine and Berrow Hill, and, perhaps most beautiful and graceful, his two neighbours, Woodbury and Abberley; and Clee Hills, opening up another beautiful and romantic world and presenting a circle of beauty which I defy any part of England to match.

> . . . one of the widest and fairest [prospects] in all England: the dreamy, green expanse of the Severn Plain; the level line of the Cotswolds – pale blue as the chalk hill butterfly; Bredon (beloved hill!), a half-strung bow; Malvern, peaked and fantastic like scenery on a stage; Abberley, with its tower; two waves of Clee; and, beyond it all, a tangle of unnamed hills.

The first passage is from a speech by Stanley Baldwin, the second from unpublished papers by Francis Brett Young (both Cannadine: 105-6, 108).

The image of a line of hills has also been used to illuminate the spirit of Howells's melodic lines, at their most radiant in the early chamber works and *Hymnus Paradisi*; Howells himself in the early 1920s referred to Vaughan Williams's *Pastoral Symphony* in the same terms: 'None of the themes in this Symphony have exciting lines . . . they will not draw faces or produce crude pictures of craggy heights. But they will often give you a shape akin to such an outline as the Malvern Hills present when viewed from afar' (Howells, 1922: 127; Palmer, 1978: 37). It has even been suggested that the 'secret' underlying idea in

Elgar's *Enigma Variations* is that the contours of the main theme follow the outline of the Malvern Hills (alas, they do not).

Such considerations unfortunately present no firm handle for criticism. Howells's music can become formless when it confuses the aesthetic demands of melodic contour with those of a line of hills viewed broadside on; moreover it is questionable how fruitful the mere celebration of passive beauty is for the artist – a central Georgian problem. The Georgian generation reversed the aesthetes' dictum that nature imitates art, as can be felt in the following passage from one of Gurney's letters, written in December 1916:

> What the artist needs is not so much technique, as a greater appreciation of beauty so generally overlooked. Why should not the violet be considered as the chief work of God visible to us? And yet it is the bunch and the coloured vase that must make up most people's mental idea of that lovely thought of innocence. The Artist must learn to feel the beauty of all things and the sense of instant communion with God that such perception will bring. 'To feel Eternity in an hour.' Blake knew that to attain to this height not greater dexterity, but greater humility and beauty of thought were needed. And the composer must judge his work by this standard – that his work be born of sincere and deep emotion sufficiently controlled by the intellect to be coherent and clear. And if this thought be deep and worthy, who shall say it will not shape its proper expression? (1913–22)

We read this as an unwitting piece of self-criticism, in the awareness that in his songs, as we have seen, Gurney's own 'sincere and deep emotion' is not always 'sufficiently controlled by the intellect to be coherent and clear'. Yet the problem is not necessarily defective technique, though it sometimes is in the case of Gurney and Finzi and nearly always of Vaughan Williams. Indeed, much of the music of Howells and Gibbs and even Head, with its polished excellence of style and care of construction, fits neatly into the inter-war picture of pride in an achieved professionalism. The limiting factor is the tendency towards conventional subject matter. To quote Gurney again, writing in June 1917:

> There are not many things that make worthy art. They are, Nature, Home Life (with which is mixed up Firelight in Winter, joy of companionship etc.). The intangible Hope (which means all music can hope to express). Thoughts on Death and Fate. And there are no more. It is right, as RLS wrote, for a young man consciously and of purpose to regard his attempts as Art only, but this is a half stage, and should soon end, if the young man has anything to say (*ibid*.).

Gurney's elevation of 'Nature, Home Life' and 'Firelight in Winter' can read almost as a parody of the Georgian frame of mind:

> Some day I also must live in a little greystone Cotswold house, with one largish room for the music room; with a garden to flame in summer against the cool greys and greens of house and trees and hedges, and there invite my friends to tell me of the great world and what goes on there between the mansions and the slums. O for a garden to dig in, and music and books in a house of one's own, set in a little valley from whose ridges one may see Malverns and the Welsh Hills, the plain of Severn and Severn Sea; to know oneself free there from the drill-sergeant and the pack, and to order one's life years ahead – plans, doubtless to be broken, but sweet secure plans taking no account of fear or even Prudence but only Joy. One could grow whole and happy there, the mind would lose its sickness and grow strong; it is not possible that health should wait long from such steady and gently beautiful ways of life. The winters hardships should steel one, the spring bring Joy, Summer should perfect this Joy, and Autumn bring increase

> and mellowness to all things, set the seal of age and ease on things not before
> secure. I grow happy writing of it . . . (*ibid.*).

With the troops in France in May 1917 this dreaming was understandable, but
when he attempted to enact it after the war without the slightest inkling of how to
organise his life the results were tragic. Howells was more of a realist: after a
three-year period of febrile creativity in Gloucestershire following a breakdown
of health early in 1917, the desire to support a wife and raise a family took him in
1920 back to London, where he lived for the rest of his life, diligently pursuing a
career of teaching, festival adjudicating and 'commercial' composition for
school, church and festival. His Georgian sensibility, evident in the chamber
works and some of the early songs, was virtually extinguished in 1920, which
made its later rekindlings as in 'The goat paths' of 1928, examined below, all the
more fresh and vivid.

Most of the Georgian poets had experienced nature very closely, at first hand;
witness Masefield's seafaring and W. H. Davies's 'supertramping'. At one
extreme, however, their attempts at minute observation of nature could seem
contrived, as Gurney's criticism of Ledwidge in a letter to Marion Scott of
January 1917 suggests (though Gurney is here in effect only counteracting one
minute observation with another, and there is something slightly absurd about
the whole dialectic, as Gurney may well have appreciated): '. . . having seen the
Observers appreciation of Ledwidge's description of the robins note as being like
tiny cymbals, I looked for a robin, found one, heard it – and dont agree,
altogether. He must have thought a lot to have written that description – it being
too out of the way to be spontaneously observed' (*ibid.*). At the other, they were
a prey to complacency, as Hugh Ottaway has pointed out:

> . . . they are content with their 'lost content', and that is fatal. Howells, no doubt,
> has written his share of this minor pastoral and elegiac music, but in the main his
> sense of anguish and of aspiration have raised him well above it. And implicit in
> his vision of the beautiful is a keen awareness of its transience and vulnerability.
> There is nothing complacent in that (1967: 899).

There was nothing complacent in Gurney, either, as writer or composer. But
while agreeing with Ottaway's appreciation of Howells, one can identify an equivalent to Georgian poetic complacency in certain aspects of the music of the
period. As far back as Elgar there is a consistent desire in many English
composers to substitute modal or pseudo-modal procedures for traditional
dominant-based tonality. This need not be linked to the use of folksong; simple
stylistic traits such as replacing the fifth degree of the scale, melodically, with the
sixth, as in the opening motive of the slow movement of Howells's Piano
Quartet, can inform an abstract idiom. Elgar, for instance, is continually sub-
stituting a mediant chord for a dominant or a submediant for a tonic, to avoid
perfect cadences; a harmonic analysis of 'Praise to the Holiest in the height' from
The Dream of Gerontius would exemplify many such procedures. In his late
works this bespeaks melancholy introversion rather than complacency, but the
adoption of similar modes of expression by a number of younger composers
acted as a curb on their originality. To take an early example, Dunhill's 'The
cloths of heaven' from his cycle *The Wind Among the Reeds* tries to make a
virtue out of wateriness. Perhaps it succeeds; others do not. Finzi in particular

was prevented from finding his true voice with confidence for a long time by the sterile, colourless simplicity of his early songs in the cycle *By Footpath and Stile* and in some of *A Young Man's Exhortation*. The music of Michael Head, a more abiding but slightly different case of Georgian complacency, is discussed in Chapter XIV. It is perhaps interesting to speculate whether, had English song been endowed with a figure equivalent to Edward Marsh as anthologist and impresario, sufficient critical attention would have been drawn to it in the early 1920s for its characteristic limitations to be rooted out before perpetuating themselves in figures such as Head.

Space precludes a comprehensive survey of settings of Georgian poets. What follows is, rather, a brief examination of some of the typical patterns of thought and expression in the poetry and their musical treatment in eight settings by six composers, Finzi, Gibbs, Gurney, Howells, Vaughan Williams and Warlock. One such treatment, of Brooke's 'All suddenly the wind comes soft', has already been discussed (above, pp. 196–201), where the poet's linking of the processes of nature with his emotions was noted. The observations which follow are of the same kind, and mark out something approaching a progressive scale from complete, objective passivity towards nature to total absorption in the self and the feelings. Music can be called in to articulate various points along this scale, and criticisms are offered with a view to forming a general estimate of Georgian song.

> Slowly, silently, now the moon
> Walks the night in her silver shoon;
> This way, and that, she peers, and sees
> Silver fruit upon silver trees;
> One by one the casements catch
> Her beams beneath the silvery thatch;
> Couched in his kennel, like a log,
> With paws of silver sleeps the dog;
> From their shadowy cote the white breasts peep
> Of doves in a silver-feathered sleep;
> A harvest mouse goes scampering by,
> With silver claws, and silver eye;
> And moveless fish in the water gleam,
> By silver reeds in a silver stream.

There are 23 settings of this poem, 'Silver', from de la Mare's *Peacock Pie*, listed in Gooch and Thatcher (1976), though only those by Armstrong Gibbs (1920), Britten (1928) and Berkeley (1946) are at all well known.

Gibbs seems to understand the poem's rhythm and atmosphere so completely as to come as near as is possible to what one might desire as a 'definitive' setting of the text. The poem is a transfixing counterpoint of movement and stillness. Normally active creatures are quite still – the kennelled dog 'like a log', the sleeping doves, and the 'moveless fish'; moreover the dog and doves are framed in archways, frozen, as it were, halfway in or out (the dog's paws lie outside the kennel, the rest of him inside), and the fish are suspended against the implied movement of the stream. Only the moon, normally passive, moves, 'slowly', in her 'shoon', peering 'this way and that'. The paradox is enhanced by the feminine gender given to the active moon as opposed to masculine for the passive dog.

Gibbs's setting expresses these contrasts perfectly in musical terms. Chords normally suggestive of strong harmonic movement are kept poised without resolution (with particularly frequent use of the C major triad in its 6–4 position), and the depiction of the moon's slow pacing is restricted to one stationary note, an offbeat E pedal. An additional element, the inner motive e′ – f′ sharp – g′ – e′, is added at the moment it becomes clear that the moon not only walks but 'peers', and the sense of the scene's delicately grasped transience is conveyed by the avoidance of comfortable metric patterns in the ostinato: from the beginning it suggests two 3-bar units, then one of 4 bars, two of 5 bars, one of 6 (2 + 2 + an altered 2), followed by complete disruption and, as the pattern is re-established, a 5-bar phrase (a further lengthening of the opening's 3- and 4-bar units), 1 bar, and three final chords of 1 bar each. Yet all is not as passive as it might seem; the personification of the moon in the poem, though conventional, is a projection of the self onto the inanimate; the observer's gaze must also be moving to follow that of the moon. This is well brought out in Gibbs's setting: as the gaze is lowered from the (upstairs?) casements and thatch to the dog at ground level, so is the music, from an E tonality down to C – then up again to A major as the gaze travels up to the dovecote. But the real point of the poem is that the moon, hence the observer, is felt as an intruder into nature's realm of sleep and night. The rhythm of the poem's first line indicates furtiveness, as does the word 'peer', and the sense of looking into bedroom windows is emphasised by the word 'catch' – as though caught in the act. The dog may pounce if it wakes up, and the sudden scampering of the mouse, with the predatory connotations of 'silver claws' and 'silver eye', almost humorously underlines this. Gibbs's setting does the same. His offbeat E pedal is heard as one hears one's own heart beating, and as the stillness is suddenly broken with the '*poco agitato*' recitative at 'A harvest mouse goes scampering by' the observer is brought to our attention by the sudden *parlando* use of the voice, and his heart misses a beat in the accompaniment. There is in fact a good deal of tension in the poem, as there is also in the music, where it is not only harmonic tension, but is achieved by these various reflections of the poem's implications.

By comparison, Vaughan Williams's setting of his niece Fredegond Shove's 'Motion and stillness' (1922) as the first of his *Four Poems* appears vague and ineffective.

> The seashells lie as cold as death
>   Under the sea,
> The clouds move in a wasted wreath
>   Eternally;
> The cows sleep on the tranquil slopes
>   Above the bay;
> The ships like evanescent hopes
>   Vanish away.

The dreary mood of the poem is clear enough, perhaps too clear, from the first line; so is that of the setting, with its glum 4ths and 5ths. What is less well defined is the viewpoint. As with 'Silver', there is a moving human gaze in the poem, upwards from the seabed to the clouds, down again to the cows and finally outwards to the ships on the horizon. However, not only does Vaughan Williams fail to depict this (his accompaniment moves downwards for the clouds, though admittedly the voice part lies higher), but he does not clarify the ambiguity of the lines about the cows: are they mentioned as a very solid image to contrast with the evanescence of human hopes and distance of the ships, or do they 'sleep', are they 'tranquil', in the same framework of death as pervades the other images? Vaughan Williams raises the tessitura and tonality to an A major triad at the start of these lines, yet, with typically vague bitonality, allows the triads to sink again in the piano's left hand while the right hand works towards its melodically climactic e″ before the final lines; this lack of overall direction and control, to which nothing definitive is added in the last two lines, leaves merely a cipher at the centre of the song. The protagonist's viewpoint is undefined.

At first the lack of an active viewpoint may seem to limit Francis Ledwidge's poem, 'Desire in spring':

> I love the cradle songs the mothers sing
> In lonely places when the twilight drops,
> The slow endearing melodies that bring
> Sleep to the weeping lids; and, when she stops,
> I love the roadside birds upon the tops
> Of dusty hedges in a world of Spring.
>
> And when the sunny rain drips from the edge
> Of midday wind, and meadows lean one way,
> And a long whisper passes thro' the sedge,
> Beside the broken water let me stay,
> While these old airs upon my memory play,
> And silent changes colour up the hedge.

Here is a classic example of Georgian observation of nature, fresh and vivid and accurate but to what extent creative if it creates no context and is merely a catalogue of 'my favourite things'? Lord Dunsany's introduction to Ledwidge's *Songs of the Fields* (1916) makes no great claims for him as a poet: 'Of pure poetry there are two kinds, that which mirrors the beauty of the world in which our bodies are, and that which builds the more mysterious kingdoms where geography ends and fairyland begins . . . Mr Ledwidge gives us the first kind' (:9). And it is not necessarily easy to mirror further in music those things of nature which Ledwidge mirrors in his verse. Gurney finds it difficult. His scene-painting in music is severely limited and not very effective: a twittering e″ inverted pedal for the 'roadside birds', a chromatic slow descent at 'midday wind' and another, richly harmonised over a static melody note, for 'silent changes', and a broadening to $\frac{4}{4}$ for 'long whisper' are about all he manages, and Ledwidge's descriptive language tends to feel awkward in the lyrical clothing of Gurney's spun melody. One can guess, given Gurney's own admission about 'By a bierside' (above, p. 200), that the first few lines of the poem, about 'the cradle songs the mothers sing' and 'The slow endearing melodies that bring / Sleep to the weeping lids', were what fired his setting. Yet perhaps he is right not to focus on the pictorial. As in Brooke's 'All suddenly', there is an element of personal yearning in the poem; in Ledwidge it is understated, present only in the title, the image of the mothers, the 'lonely places', and the 'weeping lids', and then left unexpressed except in the idea of staying by the 'broken water' while the 'old airs' play upon the memory. One feels that the word 'memory' belongs nearer the end of the poem, that the last two lines and their rhymes have been deliberately transposed; Gurney as it were transposes them back again, reinstating the lyrical material of the opening, with its slightly wistful right-hand *cantilena*, flat 7ths and favourite four-semiquaver figure, in a way which strengthens these emotional implications of the poem.

In Edward Shanks's poem 'The fields are full', from *The Queen of China* (1919), the interplay is not between the observer and the observed but between the observed and its simile:

> The fields are full of summer still
> And breathe again upon the air
> From brown dry side of hedge and hill
> More sweetness than the sense can bear.
>
> So some old couple who in youth
> With love were filled and overfull,
> And loved with strength and loved with truth,
> In heavy age are beautiful.

The stanzas complement each other in a way which would invite a strophic setting; yet, characteristically in a Georgian poem, the vibrant physical sense of the beauty of nature remains uppermost: 'More sweetness than the sense can bear' is a powerfully evocative line, after which the jolt into the simile of the old couple comes as rather blunt and anticlimactic. Music, however, can provide unity of mood through a balance or symmetry of expression lacking in the poem. Warlock's setting, 'Late summer' (1921), achieves this in terms of his most overtly Delius-like chromatic style, self-indulgently but effectively employed. His musical material is abstract enough to be appropriate equally to the description and the simile; he distinguishes the latter by a modulation to the mediant, where he begins by treating the second stanza as a strophic repeat (with metric variations) of the first, but uses only subsidiary motivic material (♪͡𝅘𝅥 ♩) in the accompaniment. He then underlines a subtle point in the poem: that the cadence of the final word, 'beautiful', not only calls to mind the languid sensuousness of the first stanza, but has transmuted it into something firmer, through the key words '(over-) full', 'strength', 'truth' and 'heavy (age)'. Warlock reintroduces the accompaniment's chief motive (¾ ♪ ♪ ♩. (𝄾)) under each of these words, places his melodic climax on the word 'strength', and slips gradually back into the tonic E major by emphasising flattened voice-leading notes under the key words (e′ natural and f′ sharp under 'strength', B natural under 'truth', a natural under 'beautiful'). The structure of a poem can of course also be enhanced by the musical unity of a postlude, which here recapitulates the song's opening, with small but striking differences.

Gurney's setting of the same poem, not one of his best, is less controlled and slightly disturbing. He sets up one of his archetypal 'walking' figurations for the first stanza, giving a stronger conviction of his physical presence in the landscape than Warlock does, and blithely begins the second stanza strophically. Typically, though, he gets sidetracked at the ecstatic thought of being 'overfull' with love, with remote and swooning modulations. Then he pulls up short, as though suddenly realising that the youthful passion cannot last: the semiquaver figuration ceases, and the wrench back to E major, striving upwards with no help from the piano on the words 'strength' and 'truth' but falling back down at 'heavy age', is slow and laborious. Only the final word 'beautiful', at which the accompanimental figuration tentatively and disjointedly creeps back in, seems to offer definite consolation. Which dominates, the object or its simile? Perhaps only Gibbs, in the other extant setting of this poem, keeps the simile subservient to the pictured landscape, by adopting at the start of the second stanza a new and clearly parenthetic texture of high, wispy pairs of triplet quavers, which negate the $\frac{3}{4}$ time signature and are in a shifting enharmonic relationship to the overall tonality, with mostly 6–3 chord positions. This gives way to the gently respiring, atmospheric parallel-triad figure of the first stanza only for the final line.

For a wholly convincing, and explicit, relationship between landscape and human figure we can turn finally to songs by Howells and Finzi. Howells, though he valued his personal acquaintance with many of the Georgian poets (Howells, 1974), actually made few noteworthy settings of them, apart from some of his de la Mare songs. There are five completed Gibson settings, four from *Whin* (1918) and one, 'Girl's song', from *Friends* (1916). In these Gibson's manner is that of a vagabond folk poet, and Howells's response, to combine folky tunes with accompaniments of economical and often abrasively transparent device, suits him less well than it suited his teacher Stanford or his successor Britten, though the effect can be exciting, for example in the devilish dance of 'Old Skinflint', which accelerates continuously. However, in his setting of James Stephens's 'The goat paths' from his song-cycle *In Green Ways* (the title of the volume of poems containing 'The goat paths') he created one of the most moving embodiments of the Georgian frame of mind. Despite being in some musical respects a copy of Vaughan Williams's setting of Shove's 'The new ghost', it uses the pastoral clichés with consummate, intricate artistry. Stephens's poem is in eight stanzas whose clipped, close-cropped lines suggest the goats moving to and fro on their little paths and picking at this and that:

> And the goats
> Day after day,
> Stray
> In
> Sunny
> Quietness;
> Cropping here,
> And cropping there
> As they pause,
> And turn,
> And pass –
> Now a bit
> Of heather spray,
> Now a mouthful
> Of the grass.

The poetic rhythm, generated by the frequent repetition of words and by rhymed assonance ('Day after day, / Stray' and 'Spray', and in a later stanza 'Stray / Away'), is inevitably lost in the flow of the musical setting. Indeed, Howells was surprised, on hearing Stephens read the poem aloud, how fast was that rhythm, 'unbelievably like a dynamo, utterly unlike the leisurely pastoral idyll I'd conceived it as' (Palmer, 1978: 16). Nor does he mirror with melodic repetitions Stephens's frequent (separated) repetition of whole verbal phrases. It is his confident freedom, similar to Vaughan Williams's, in translating the poem into musical terms, that elevates the setting.

The poem's transition from nature description to personal involvement is smoothly achieved: the paths follow the hill in the first stanza; the goats follow the paths in the second; in the third they penetrate 'the deeper Sunniness; / In the place / Where nothing stirs'; in the fourth the poet enters the scene; he puts himself in the place of the goats in the fifth, dreaming of shunning contact with the outside world (as had the goats on his approach) in the sixth and of awaiting and finding some kind of nirvana in the last two stanzas:

> I would think
> Until I found
> Something
> I can never find;
> – Something
> Lying
> On the ground,
> In the bottom
> Of my mind.

Howells does not find it necessary to duplicate this transition in the music. Rather he is concerned to weld the quietness of nature and quietness of the mind into one musical pattern. The opening four bars demonstrate this sufficiently (Ex. 1). The melodic theme is of an obviously pastoral nature, both rhythmically, in the interplay of duplet and triplet crotchets (later on, semiquavers are added to the pastoral rhythmic fount (Ex. 2)), and modally, if the d′ natural is heard as a flat 7th to a tonic e′. Its three-part imitative counterpoint suggests the intertwining paths or the movements of the goats upon them. But harmonically already in this

Ex. 1

Ex. 2

opening an intensely meditative, spiritual atmosphere is set up by the counter-point. The implied parallel triads in bar 1 (brought out by the '*col Ped.*' direction), the augmented triad at the beginning of bar 2, and above all the upward mediant shift in bar 3 (d′ to f′ natural roots are implied, involving an f′ sharp – f′ natural false relation, a favourite juxtaposition in both Howells and Vaughan Williams) create a remote harmonic experience far from the world of dominant relations. Howells brings his song to a climax in the sixth stanza, for here the poet's dream of retreating to the 'deeper / Quietude' is determined and here, accordingly, the 'other-worldly' mediant, and now also tritonal, triadic shifts with their false relations are most fully developed, in two directions at once (Ex. 3). Here there is also, in the piano's left hand, a diminution of the opening

Ex. 3

theme (this diminution first appeared in a more precise form at the start of the fifth stanza – see Fig. 6 in the score). But perhaps the most striking aspect of the whole song is Howells's willingness to let the poem speak for itself, a stance rarely exploited by his English contemporaries except Holst and Vaughan Williams. There are several passages in which the accompaniment is motionless or totally silent; the ending, with the piano's single e′ fading into silence like the 'something' slipping from the poet's mind, is an inspired calculation.

Finally let us consider a much later song which none the less strongly outlines the Georgian frame of mind: Finzi's setting (1956) in *Oh Fair to See* of Blunden's poem 'Harvest'. As in Shanks's 'The fields are full' the poet is viewing a harvest scene, this time, however, overtly in the first person singular:

So there's my year, the twelvemonth duly told
Since last I climbed this brow and gloated round
Upon the lands heaped with their wheaten gold,
And now again they spread with wealth imbrowned –
    And thriftless I meanwhile,
What honey combs have I to take, what sheaves to pile?

I see some shrivelled fruits upon my tree,
And gladly would self-kindness feign them sweet;
The bloom smelled heavenly, can these stragglers be
The fruit of that bright birth? and this wry wheat,
    Can this be from those spires
Which I, or fancy, saw leap to the spring sun's fires?

Unlike Shanks, the poet here looks for a simile within himself. There he finds only a negative one: the creative harvest has not matured but withered. The greater part of the poem after the first stanza is taken up with this reflection, which is thus a reversal of the process implied in the previous examples: here an image of the self is not projected onto observed nature, but an image from nature (an unfulfilled harvest) is projected onto the self. Since the self-absorption is so undisguised, and suits Finzi's introverted temperament, in his setting he makes little reference to the concrete images of nature; like so much of his vocal music, the song is largely an internal, semi-*arioso* monologue articulating its thoughts with his stock rhetorical and expressive devices (some of which are discussed in Chapter XIII); these tend to illuminate the mood of a strong word rather than its visual appearance or its movement (e.g. false relations at '*wry* wheat', '*poison* berries', on the adjectives, not the nouns). Finzi is not a graphic composer, except on well-handled occasions such as 'I peer, I count' (the vocal line strains its downward gaze in a pair of 7ths), 'the weeds run high' (the accompaniment rises above the voice), and 'those spires / Which I, or fancy, saw leap to the spring sun's fires' (the vocal line grows upwards like wheat in a series of thrusting leaps, and glitters in the sunlight of a burst of semiquavers). There is, however, an artful twist at the end of the poem: since creativity has been fruitless, so is introspection; the poet returns to the real harvest at hand, and sets off down the hill to enjoy it. Nature provides and demands no creative repayment: 'Earth accuses none that goes among her stooks.' She is indifferent to man, the pathetic fallacy is rejected. Only at this solution does Finzi's setting break out for any length of time into uninhibited movement, using a favourite jaunty quaver bass presaged earlier, at the lines 'the bloom smelled heavenly, can these stragglers be / The fruit of that bright birth?' Yet for Finzi, using this poem in what he knew was the premature evening of his life as a mouthpiece for his perpetual anxiety that there would never be enough time to complete his desired output of compositions, it is a *schwer gefasster Entschluss*. The movement dies down again, and the song ends with the same subdued and blankly questioning motto that both began it and articulated the question after the end of the first stanza (Ex. 4). The joy of nature

Ex. 4

[Andante espressivo]

does not have the last note; Finzi appears to reject the escapism, even if in doing so he accepts only death in his final *tierce de Picardie*.

Walter de la Mare's first volume of poetry, *Songs of Childhood*, was published in 1902. Nearly 20 more volumes appeared during his long lifetime (1873–1956), including *The Listeners and Other Poems* (1912), *Motley and Other Poems*

(1918), *Flora: A Book of Drawings* (1919) and *The Veil and Other Poems* (1921). Musical settings have been drawn from all these, and Armstrong Gibbs also set a song from the novel *Henry Brocken* (1904) and wrote a score for the play *Crossings* (1919), but above all it was *Peacock Pie: A Book of Rhymes* (1913) that appealed to composers – children's verse, like much of what was set from the other volumes. Composers were not particularly quick to discover this poetry: there seems to be no setting earlier than Browne's 'Arabia' of 1914, published, with two other de la Mare settings, in *The Monthly Chapbook* for December 1919. Gibbs's earliest settings were made in 1917, and by 1920 he had written a fair number. Gurney's were composed between 1918 and 1922. Howells produced a spate of *Peacock Pie* settings in August 1919, sketching as many as four in a day. The corpus broadened in the 1920s with Bliss's *Three Romantic Songs* and solo settings or groups by Arthur Benjamin, Benjamin Burrows, Walter Clement, Walford Davies, Victor Hely-Hutchinson, Frederick Keel and Norman Peterkin. Whilst still a student Britten made many settings, including three two-part songs published in 1932 and a group of solo songs of 1928–31 published in 1969 as *Tit for Tat*. More recent solo settings have included three by William Wordsworth (late 1930s), Berkeley's *Five Songs* (1946), *Songs of the Half-Light* for high voice and guitar (1964) and three more songs, *Another Spring* (1977), and Howells's *A Garland for de la Mare* (1969, though incorporating much earlier sketches). Gibbs continued to set de la Mare's words throughout the 1920s and 1930s, often for massed voices, and outlived the poet to write a *Threnody for Walter de la Mare* for strings and string quartet in July 1956. He also wrote an instrumental suite called *Peacock Pie*.

De la Mare appreciated musical settings of his work. Howells testified, 'I always enjoyed talking music to de la Mare; he was one of the few poets I've known who really *understood* music – one always felt he was on one's wavelength, that for instance his concept of "rhythm" was identical with one's own' (Palmer, 1978: 16), and the poet seems to have accepted the supremacy of two of the finest settings, Howells's 'King David' and Gibbs's 'Silver', in that of each, according to Howells on separate occasions (Howells, 1974; Palmer, 1978: 16), he 'said he didn't want anyone else to set it'.

Both Howells and de la Mare recognised the unique quality of Gibbs's settings. Howells, writing to him in 1951, said 'You've never yet failed in *any* setting you've done of beloved Jack de la Mare's poems', and, two months later, specifying a number of his songs which included 'Silver' and 'A song of shadows', 'These move me every time I hear them: and always will. And because they are so *complete*, there are no reservations of any kind in one's love of them.' And in 1955: 'I've always felt that you share with CVS[tanford] a capacity to say so much in such [a] direct, uncomplicated manner' (Gibbs, 1918–60). De la Mare himself corresponded as a friend with Gibbs over the years, stating in March 1933: 'Every now and again, too, I have had copies of your new settings sent me, and you must have thought me particularly graceless for not writing to tell you what a joy it is to think that you still find some of the old rhymes inviting' (*ibid.*). He mused further:

> In connection with a mass of notes, most of which no doubt will prove utterly useless, on the question of verbal craftsmanship, I have again and again speculated on the precise process involved in the setting of a song – what *in* the words,

> I mean, usually gives the initial impulse and so on? This varies, I suppose, with different composers, and is often excessively difficult to recall . . . What would you say *is* the usual nucleus? – Verbal sound – rhythm – idea – etc.? (*Ibid.*)

One wonders how Gibbs replied; we must remain content with his brief comments on 'Setting de la Mare to music' in the *Journal of the National Book League* (1956).

Armstrong Gibbs was born in Great Baddow, Essex, in 1889, and spent nearly all his life in nearby Danbury. He belonged to the sizeable group of English composers of his generation for whom composition lay somewhere between a bread-winning occupation and a leisured pursuit: he enjoyed a private income from the family toothpaste business, but it was not large enough to save him from having to teach at the RCM (from 1921) and adjudicate at endless music festivals. No doubt the festival work became addictive, and in this respect his career closely paralleled that of Howells. Both wrote – and Gibbs's output was enormous – unison, two-part and other choral songs for the school and festival markets whose virtues are only those of *Gebrauchsmusik*; Howells's music, because of this, had little to say between 1920 and 1935, and that of Gibbs, despite Howells's appreciation quoted above, was not distinctive enough always to keep its head above mediocrity, in whose depths plenty of his vocal and choral settings, including some of de la Mare, could drown unlamented.

The circumstances of his early collaboration with the poet, however, were fresher. Gibbs had attended preparatory school at The Wick, Hove, and after passing through Winchester and then Cambridge, where his acquaintances included Edward Dent, Vaughan Williams, Steuart Wilson and Charles Wood, and where in 1913 he and some friends successfully and lucratively faked an exhibition of post-impressionist paintings, he returned to The Wick as a teacher in 1915. Teaching allowed him little time for composition, but he did complete his first batch of de la Mare settings – originally cast as partsongs for the school choir, according to Gibbs himself (1958: 66). The composition and publication history of these early settings is unclear; most of them went through various regroupings and arrangements. 'Five eyes' and 'A song of shadows' were both rejected by a publisher at first, but 'Nod' appeared in *The Monthly Chapbook* (December 1919), and through the bludgeoning persuasion of Sir Hugh Allen, Director of the RCM (where Gibbs was studying under Vaughan Williams), Stainer & Bell issued an album of five de la Mare settings in 1920. Winthrop Rogers, Curwen and Stainer & Bell then took ten songs (including 'Nod' and 'Five eyes'), publishing them 1921–2, and thenceforward whatever Gibbs offered was accepted. However, the most catalytic event, personal contact with de la Mare, had already occurred. Gibbs wanted a children's play, for which he could provide music, for The Wick School headmaster's retirement in July 1919. Late in 1918 he decided to write to de la Mare, merely on the strength of friends they had in common, and within two months de la Mare had supplied the text of *Crossings*. Gibbs then found that 'His inspiration stimulated mine, and the music began to flow with that ease and rapidity that only a wholly congenial task can bring about' (*ibid*.: 58). Rehearsals made the boys of the school very enthusiastic; Edward Dent offered to stage-manage the production, bringing his friend J.B. Trend down from Cambridge to help him, and enlisted Adrian Boult as conductor.

Gibbs played the piano in the band, which otherwise consisted of a flute, three violins, viola and cello. De la Mare stayed at the school for the final fortnight of rehearsals, and the play was produced on 21 June 1919. Rarely can so many significant personages have worked together in such an unpretentious environment. Boult, referring to the event 60 years later in a letter to the present author, recalled that 'we all enjoyed the play, the music, the acting, and every-thing to do with it, immensely'. The suite of incidental music was later performed at a Queen's Hall Promenade concert, and the music was included in the privately printed text of the play in 1921. The four solo songs were published separately by Curwen in 1924. In December 1950 BBC Radio broadcast an abridged version of the play with Gibbs's music.

The *Crossings* songs represent Gibbs at his most attractive. They are within a child's vocal capacity, simple and tuneful, unsubtle yet haunting, and possess the qualities of de la Mare's verse as expressed by T. S. Eliot:

> The whispered incantation which allows
> Free passage to the phantoms of the mind
>
> . . . by those deceptive cadences
> Wherewith the common measure is refined;
> By conscious art practised with natural ease;
>
> By the delicate, invisible web you wove –
> The inexplicable mystery of sound (Bett: 107).

Gibbs's technique here is not impressionistic (whereas it is in his choral setting of 'Arabia' from *Songs of Enchantment* (1925), though not as selfconsciously as Browne's in his setting – see above, pp. 155–6), nor does it resort to cosmetic modal devices: everything is clear, ingenuous, and entertaining. Yet 'the common measure' is indeed 'refined . . . by those deceptive cadences'. At the end of 'Araby', for instance, a world of yearning is encountered in merely two chords, between the F minor of 'a boat drift back' and the *tierce de Picardie* resolution under the last word (Ex. 5): the elliptical harmonic progression, avoiding a dominant bass, lends the cadence a Fauré-like enchantment. Again, in 'Ann's cradle song', the transition from tonic minor (verse) to tonic major (refrain) manages to avoid the banal with its frank sequence of 7th chords in the manner of

Ex. 5

Quilter and its chromatic appoggiatura chords before the dominant 7th (Ex. 6). In all the songs one finds a childlike simplicity of technique which accepts devices of musical colouring without hackneying them – in the 'Candlestick-maker's song', for instance, the compound 4ths, the flat 7th returning to the dominant at the line 'Rests for thee a paradise' (Ex. 7), and the final major transformation of that same cadence (Ex. 8). The effect is to make us yearn for such simplicity of acceptance ourselves, to cross over into the world of children. This is surely the signficiance of the title of the play, which concerns a family of children. Left

Ex. 6

Ex. 7

Ex. 8

alone in a strange, empty country house, they play at being adults, whilst the only adults who naturally befriend them, the tradespeople and a beggar, are those who are not enmeshed in society's formalities and can share in their unfettered imaginations. De la Mare 'liked tiny music' (Brain: 28) and gets it from Gibbs; yet underneath the neatness and containment and the fairy delicacy there is often a more ghostlike shadow. De la Mare's ghosts (and there is one in *Crossings*), Eliot's 'sad intangible who grieve and yearn' (Bett: 107), seem to represent the idea of secret self-knowledge, like the revelations of private destiny in J. M. Barrie's *Dear Brutus* of 1920: such knowledge entails the recognition of loss and separation, of the unattainable. Gibbs's setting of 'The stranger' puts this recognition, of the figure Dream holding in one hand 'the fruit that makes men wise' and of the loss of that wisdom at daybreak, into rather stronger, more heavily laden chromatic language than he uses in *Crossings*; another setting, of 'The exile', expresses it all in unaccompanied monody punctuated only by short, spread, modal chord progressions, as though the singer is some solitary Greek harper. And as Barrie's Peter Pan is isolated from the Darling family by his inability to grow up, so Sallie, the romantic elder daughter in *Crossings*, is isolated from the perfunctory world of adults through her attachment to the Candlestick-maker, the 'queer half human creature' who 'is Dream, Romance, the other World' (Gibbs, 1918–60), as de la Mare explained to Gibbs on sending him the *Crossings* scenario in December 1918.

Gibbs's talent was a minor one, and his de la Mare settings are most memorable for their tunefulness, their professional tidiness of technique, and their performability. On the whole those that employ a rich Romantic or chromatic texture to articulate warmth of feeling or colouring, such as 'Dream song', 'Lullaby', and 'Music unheard', are more effective than those plainer settings, such as 'Nod' and 'Five eyes', where the influence of Vaughan Williams is not always beneficial. His success in setting both de la Mare's and others' poetry is unpredictable: sometimes he lapses into sentimentality (e.g. when writing for children in 'Juliet Anne'); sometimes he avoids it, as in 'The tiger-lily', a moving song whose attenuated tonality and textural restraint elevate the words above their latent religiosity. Some of the de la Mare settings are disappointing, such as 'The mountains', which reads like a sketch for 'Silver', and 'Love in the almond bough'; others, like the *Crossings* songs, 'Dream song' and 'The bells', deserve to be better known.

There are two aspects of de la Mare's poetry which do not come across in Gibbs's music. One is a feeling for narrative. Although he seldom overtly employed ballad forms and devices, de la Mare possessed a genius for telling stories in verse. This was primarily a function of his entering into the world of children, but some of his most striking uses of narrative in poems for children were disturbingly adult. 'King David', from *Peacock Pie*, has nothing to do with children, and its restrained use of narrative conventions (e.g. archaisms of syntax, 'no cause . . . had he', or of phrasing, 'in no wise heeded') lends it a large-scale grandeur quite beyond the expectations of its metric dimensions: we share in the mysterious moods of a great king. This is wonderfully emphasised in Howells's setting, the work which, the composer said, 'I'm prouder to have written . . . than almost anything else of mine' (Palmer, 1978: 16); it is a very big piece. Howells knew exactly how to realise the pregnant passages in the narrative mode: the beginning of the third stanza, 'He rose', uses silence, gesture and the adoption of a new tone of voice (i.e. the modulation to E major) as evocatively as any accomplished narrator. It is this same use of silence that produces the emotional power of de la Mare's poem 'The ghost', one of several similar narratives making curt, blunt use of question-and-answer dialogue in *Motley and Other Poems*. The one- and three-word sentences in the final two stanzas hold all the 'chaos of vacancy' and the 'vast sorrow':

> Silence. Still faint on the porch
>   Brake the flames of the stars.
> In gloom groped a hope-wearied hand
>   Over keys, bolts, and bars.
>
> A face peered. All the grey night
>   In chaos of vacancy shone;
> Nought but vast sorrow was there –
>   The sweet cheat gone.

Gurney's unpublished setting paces the poem masterfully. The knocking continues for some while before the 'hope-wearied' protagonist dares to ask, in a low c sharp monotone, 'Who knocks?'; the dialogue of short, cancelling phrases between the man and the ghost is compressed to show that it is all really an interior monologue, the man dashing his own yearnings as they arise; then full emotional play is given to the subsiding of the moment's hope (see Ex. 9).

Ex. 9

Finzi thought that this song was 'not quite complete'. Surely it is complete. It is doubtful whether Gurney would have wanted or been able to add anything to the eloquence of his silences in this reticent yet powerful setting.

An equally impressive, though far more violent, setting of the previous poem in *Motley*, 'Mistress Fell', was made in 1928 by Benjamin Burrows. Burrows, an obscure freelance music theory tutor who led an unadventurous life in Leicester (Daubney, 1979), produced 93 songs in two years (1927–8). These *Liederjahre* were inspired largely by an infatuation with Jane Vowles, a young singer he was teaching. Unlike most of his English contemporaries, Burrows was not a natural melodist, and appeared at his best in relatively large-scale, dramatic settings, where he could rely on conveying a weighty accumulation of emotion through the poem without having to encapsulate the song's essence in a single lyric shape. Hence the effectiveness of 'Mistress Fell', which Burrows printed privately on his own Bodnant Press musical typewriter in the early 1950s. A stranger is questioning a woman in a graveyard: he gently asks her three questions about her dead lover, each more penetrating than the one before, but all to variants of the same subdued musical theme. The three questions give the poem a mythical atmosphere, but there is also something daemonic and at the same time classical about it, which Burrows's setting brings out. We can tell from the wild forward movement of the music, though not, surely, from the poem (except perhaps from the line 'Thus have they told me'), that Mistress Fell is mad with grief. At the stranger's first question she shrieks her reply, starting on a g'', as though startled in the act of talking to her lover's grave. As he draws her story out of her, her replies become longer and rise higher, through f'' sharp, g'' and a'' (Ex. 10) to a final melismatic b'' flat on the word 'all' as she confirms her love:

> 'Not tears I give; but all that he
> Clasped in his arms, sweet charity;
> All that he loved – to him I bring
> For a close whispering.'

The other element in the poetry of de la Mare which Gibbs does not draw out is the strong suggestion of the sinister, often identifiable as death. For instance, is Mistress Fell about to expire in those last lines quoted above, and if so, is it through grief or by her own hand? W. H. Auden wrote appreciatively of de la Mare's 'sense of the powers of evil' and 'his conviction that what our senses perceive of the world about us is not all there is to know' (:21), and in this second understanding lies the key to the first: it is easy to miss the unsettling undertones if one dwells on his surface effects. This is most true of *Peacock Pie*, where very frightening visions can be read into some of the poems. For example, the suspicion that Mrs Gill is lying dead in her cottage in 'The mocking fairy' may make the fairy a dancing angel (or demon) of death. The blindness of creatures to human beings in 'All but blind' may suggest human blindness not to a benevolent God but to some huge threatening ogre, as in 'Tit for tat'. The range of poetry in *Peacock Pie* is wide enough for different personalities and different generations to have found quite different affinities in it, and this has been true of its illustrators as well as its composers. Heath Robinson's drawings for the 1916 edition include some very sinister ones, such as those for 'The old house' and 'Tit for tat', but also a number of wan, naked youths of the Beardsley type that hardly

suggest a world of children's innocence. Lovat Fraser's drawings (1924) are far more solid and mundane, whereas Jocelyn Crowe's pastel cameos for the 1936 edition reflect the tiny neatness of the poems, and the line drawings of Emett (1941) their delicate emotional effect. Of the musical settings Gibbs's are the least imaginative. His *Five Children's Songs* are limited technically to a certain nursery fastidiousness, redolent of fussy nannies, though with some Gallic charm (Ex. 11); only here and there do less confined vistas open up, as in the use of the

Ex. 11

same rocking theme (c' – a' – d") in both 'Old Shellover' and the following song, 'Hide and seek' (denoting 'out of the dream of Wake / Into the dream of Sleep'?), and the inconclusive chords (an augmented triad and a dominant 13th respectively) which end these songs. In 'John Mouldy' (not from *Peacock Pie*), a strongly contrasting companion-piece to 'Silver' in his op. 30, he is forced to find musical expression for the blatant poetry of eerie decay; however, it is not very transfixing (Ex. 12). More interesting is the way this offbeat ostinato recurs in a song written a year later, 'The mad prince', a setting of the penultimate poem in *Peacock Pie* whose riddles betray, as in 'Mistress Fell', the mad grief of love lost in death, and suggest that the whole book, whose title is taken from this poem, may be songs for a mad prince. Gibbs's ostinato comes in after this stanza:

> Who said, 'Peacock Pie'?
>   The old King to the sparrow:
> Who said, 'Crops are ripe'?
>   Rust to the harrow:
> Who said, 'Where sleeps she now?
>   Where rests she now her head,
> Bathed in eve's loveliness'? –
>   That's what I said.

Ex. 12

Certainly the ideas of children, ghosts, death, decay (e.g. 'Rust to the harrow'), love and madness are constantly interrelated in de la Mare's pregnant verse.

Howells's published set of six songs from *Peacock Pie* shows much more awareness of this openness of interpretation, with the effect that only two ('Mrs MacQueen' and 'Full moon') settle into the Georgian comfort of stylistic assurance; in the others the use, particularly, of unresolved dissonance and ostinato (Palmer, 1978: 40) seems to question the meaning of the poems, just as the dunce in one of them questions the meaning of his alienation, with a sparse and cryptic musical idiom which can only be described as experimental, and which was probably influenced by Bartók. They give the impression of sketches, but vivid sketches, and it is a shame that Howells discarded some of his other *Peacock Pie* settings.

Perhaps no composer has consistently solved the problem of a tone of voice for de la Mare's poetry. It rarely lends itself either to uninhibited emotionalism or to self-effacing simplicity. His images have often challenged a young composer's technical assurance, but a glance at the early settings by two composers from the generation after his, Britten and Berkeley, show what a hit-or-miss affair their attraction to him was. Neither Berkeley in the *Five Songs* of 1946 written for Bernac and Poulenc, nor – surprisingly – Britten in the adolescent settings that have been published as *Tit for Tat* attempts to enter the phantasmal world of a child's imagination; on the contrary, Berkeley's 'Poor Henry' is objective, laconic, and really not very amusing. Perhaps, paradoxically, they were too

Ex. 13

young. Both fail to capture the magic of 'Silver'. Both show an unexpectedly warm response to romance and nostalgia, Berkeley in 'Mistletoe' and Britten in 'A song of enchantment' and 'Autumn', though his 'Vigil' is a curiously choked way of trying to express romantic loss and is not very convincing. Both are at their best in the dark-toned world of ghostly horsemen, soldiers and punitive ogres. The first of these images gives Berkeley rhythmic scope, the second an opportunity for neoclassical play on triads, 4ths and confronting 2nds (Ex. 13, from 'The horseman'), and the third, in 'Tit for tat', furnishes Britten with a violently epigrammatic outlet for his moral conscience. The latter, however, is a concern sufficiently removed from the lyric moods of inter-war England to belong more properly to the final stages of this study.

XI

Housman and the composers: documentation and evaluation

> The fate which Housman's poems deserve, of course, is to be set to music by English composers and sung by English singers, and it has already overtaken them. He will live as long as the B. B. C. (Connolly: 40).

A. E. Housman's volume of 63 short poems, *A Shropshire Lad*, was first published in February 1896 by Kegan Paul, at the author's own expense. Initially it did not attract much attention. The first edition ran to only 500 copies, of which 150 were sent to the USA, where the work quickly became popular, its fame spreading at first more rapidly than in England; many American musical setttings of the poems were subsequently made (see Gooch and Thatcher, 1976: 365–97). A second edition of 500 copies was brought out in September 1898 by Grant Richards, who remained Housman's publisher for the rest of the poet's life. A third edition of 1000 copies was printed in February 1900, and a fourth edition of 2000 in January 1903. Thus the popularity of *A Shropshire Lad* in England was by no means immediate, and it was only in the nine or ten years preceding the first world war that the poems became really well known. It was at about this time that composers began to write to Housman and Grant Richards asking for permission to set the poems to music. Housman's attitude was, on the face of it, benevolent: 'In response to such requests he almost always gave, or told me to give, permission. A Mr Ettrick must have been one of the first to write in this connexion. Like most of the others he offered a fee. Permission was given; a fee was refused' (Richards: 54). It has not been possible to trace Mr Ettrick, to whose letter Housman replied in June 1903, or his settings, or any other settings before Sir Arthur Somervell's cycle *A Shropshire Lad*, which was published in 1904 and received a performance, probably its first, on 3 February 1905 in the Aeolian Hall, sung by Harry Plunket Greene. The *Musical Times*, hardly noted for comprehensive reviews at this period, supplied little detail, and that with its customary diffidence, but indicated an enthusiastic reception:

> The Cycle comprises a series of songs which would seem to relate memorable incidents in the career of a lad who starts life in a village and ultimately becomes a soldier. We are inclined to think the music is amongst the best Dr Somervell has written; at any rate the work so pleased that Mr Plunket Greene announces that he will repeat the Cycle on March 9 in the same hall (XLVI, 1905: 188).

Somervell was a well-known and respected composer, Plunket Greene a prominent recitalist and the Aeolian Hall a flourishing concert venue, so it is likely that it was acquaintance with this cycle that led other composers to make settings of Housman. Five of the *Songs of Travel* were also in the programme, so perhaps

Vaughan Williams was present. It is difficult to tell, however, how many of the later Housman composers were aware of Somervell's cycle; C. W. Orr for one admitted to the present author in 1974 that he did not know it.

A setting of 'When I was one-and-twenty' by Stephen Adams also appeared in 1904. 1905 saw the publication of Dalhousie Young's royalty-ballad setting of 'Bredon Hill'. Balfour Gardiner's 'The recruit' and 'When I was one-and-twenty', the latter an attractive setting with wistful chromatic touches, appeared in 1906 and 1908 respectively; the former and his setting (now lost) of 'When the lad for longing sighs' were performed with orchestra in the Queen's Hall in 1906. It is not clear whether or not these composers or their publishers bothered to obtain permission from Housman or Richards to use the words, either as underlay in a score (to which Housman assented) or as a printed text on a concert programme (which he consistently refused – see below); Richards only mentions composers over whom there was some dispute or noteworthy comment, and the absence of a statement on the printed copy, as in the case of Graham Peel's 'In summertime on Bredon', is no sure indication that permission had not been sought. It is also unclear whether Housman objected to composers' forming cycles out of poems by himself and other authors in the same way in which he objected to his verse being included in literary anthologies. Not that many composers have done this; some exceptions are H. K. Andrews, Bax, Balfour Gardiner, Robin Holloway, Elisabeth Lutyens and George Whitaker.

Around 1908 two important composers started work on *Shropshire Lad* settings. One was Ivor Gurney, whose 'Loveliest of trees' and 'Is my team ploughing' date from this year, although they were not published until 1926 (in the Housman cycle *The Western Playland*), having been revised in 1918, 1920 and 1921. Gurney had also made a setting of 'On your midnight pallet lying' in November 1907 (see above, p. 182). His acqaintance with *A Shropshire Lad* may well have stemmed only from 1907, for it was in this year that he gave his friend Canon Cheesman a copy of the latest edition. Whether any of his settings reached performance at this time is not known. He obviously intended to perform them, since he wrote a letter to Housman which provoked this response in May 1908 to Grant Richards:

> Mr. I. B. Gurney (who resides in Gloucester Cathedral along with St Peter and Almighty God) must not print the words of my poems in full on concert-programmes (a course which I am sure his fellow-lodgers would disapprove of); but he is quite welcome to set them to music, and to have them sung, and to print their titles on programmes when they are sung (Richards: 81).

Something of the 18-year-old composer's youthful naïvety must have come through in his letter to call forth Housman's curt humour in this way; presumably his writing paper was headed 'Gloucester Cathedral', for he was an unofficial assistant organist there at the time. The other composer was Vaughan Williams. Following his period of study with Ravel in Paris (January–March 1908), he wrote *On Wenlock Edge*, a cycle of six of Housman's poems for tenor, string quartet and piano. The third song in the cycle, 'Is my team ploughing', was performed in what must have been its original version, for voice and piano, on 26 January 1909 in a concert sponsored by Gervase Elwes and James Friskin. *The Times* described the song as 'a miniature tragedy of the utmost force and originality' (Kennedy, 1964: 91). Whether the remaining songs were also complete at this stage is not known. The first performance of the whole cycle was ten months later, on 15 November 1909 in the Aeolian Hall. This time the concert was promoted by Elwes and Vaughan Williams and the programme contained songs by Brahms and others, Vaughan Williams's String Quartet in G minor, and *On Wenlock Edge*, in which the Schwiller Quartet was joined by Frederick Kiddle, the accompanist. Some of the songs were not in fact sung, because Elwes was suffering from laryngitis and had to curtail the programme, but *On Wenlock Edge* was performed complete, causing Vaughan Williams to comment to Elwes's wife, 'If Gervase can sing like that when he has laryngitis, I hope he may always have it!' (Elwes: 196; Kennedy, 1964: 92) On this occasion the *Musical Times* mentioned the concert but not the song-cycle.

This event marked the beginning of a series of chilly references to Vaughan Williams in Housman's letters to Richards. A few days before the concert Vaughan Williams had called on Housman

> and made representations and entreaties, so that I said he might print the verses he wanted on his programme. I mention this lest his action should come to your ears and cause you to set the police after him (Richards: 90).

It is quite likely, of course, that he had already printed the words and asked for permission as an afterthought. A further mention of the incident in a letter to Richards of June 1917 would seem to suggest this:

> Vaughan Williams did have an interview with me six years or more ago, and induced me by appeals ad misericordiam to let him print words on the programme of a concert for which he had already made arrangements; but the permission applied to that concert only. I knew what the results would be, and told him so (*ibid.*: 157-8).

Vaughan Williams also fell foul of the poet over an aesthetic consideration, as a further letter to Richards shows:

> I am told that composers in some cases have mutilated my poems, – that Vaughan Williams cut two verses out of *Is my team ploughing* (I wonder how he would like me to cut two bars out of his music), and that a lady whose name I forget has set one verse of *The New Mistress*, omitting the others. So I am afraid I must ask you, when giving consent to composers, to exact the condition that these pranks are not to be played (*ibid.*: 181).

The lady in question was Christabel Marillier, whose setting, 'A farewell', which makes things worse by repeating the last line of the first stanza, was published in 1920. Housman wrote this letter in December 1920; six and a half years later he had not forgotten the episode:

> As to Is my team ploughing Mr Orr must be warned not to omit part of the poem, as I am told Vaughan Williams did . . . (*ibid.*: 221).

Vaughan Williams, when asked if he minded this letter being printed, replied:

> You may print anything you like. If the biographer consents I think I ought to be allowed my say, which is that the composer has a perfect right artistically to set any portion of a poem he chooses provided he does not actually alter the sense . . . I also feel that a poet should be grateful to any one who fails to perpetuate such lines as:

> The goal stands up, the keeper
> Stands up to keep the goal.   (*ibid.*)

In March 1917 Gervase Elwes made a recording of *On Wenlock Edge*. This may be what Richards is referring to below, though 'song' in the singular could indicate Graham Peel's 'In summertime on Bredon', which was also recorded by Elwes: 'On November 6 [1916] one of the many composers wants to make a gramophone record of a song and the firm of music publishers writes for permission: [Housman replies] "They can make their record if they like: all I want is not to have to write letters"' (:154). The Elwes *On Wenlock Edge* recording was very fine, and helped enormously to foster the cycle's popularity. In 1923 Housman profited from it financially – 'Boosey have suddenly enriched me with £6 for gramophone rights, Vaughan Williams I think . . .' (*ibid.*) – but not spiritually, for when his friend Percy Withers played him four of the songs from this recording he showed alarming signs of mental agitation (Withers, 1936: 701 and 1940: 82–3; W. White: 208–9).

To return to 1909, the year of completion of *On Wenlock Edge*: no other settings dating from this time are documented, though it seems likely that there was a fair number, now apparently lost, including the one mentioned below:

> . . . on August 17 [1909], one more applicant has to be given permission to publish settings of the *Shropshire Lad*, but this time he 'must be told that this permission conveys no exclusive rights of any kind'. Somebody must have been warning Housman of the possibility that one or other of the composers to whom the poet so readily granted permission might be under the impression that he was the only one so favoured. Such an impression would, of course, have been entirely erroneous – and anyhow the composers who had by then set the poems to music must have amounted to scores! (Richards: 87)

The following also testifies to lost settings: in connection with Graham Peel's 'In summertime on Bredon', one of six *Shropshire Lad* settings by him published in 1910–11, Housman stated in July 1912 that 'he probably altered the title because Bredon Hill has been set to music by so many composers and he wanted to differentiate, which I think is harmless' (*ibid.*: 111). Yet Peel's 'Bredon Hill' is only the fourth or fifth of those traceable, a number hardly warranting the 'so many'. Another letter from Housman to Richards, dated 11 November 1909, suggests that Frank Lambert's setting of 'The street sounds to the soldiers' tread' (*1914*) may date from that year: ' "The terms" on which Mr Lambert may print my words with his music are that he should spell my name right' (*ibid.*: 90). Butterworth's settings were certainly begun at this time, and occupied him until 1911; another letter of Housman's, written in November 1911, indicates an intended public performance of the songs in November or December 1911 (though six of them, the *Six Songs from 'A Shropshire Lad'*, had already received their first performance earlier in the year, at the Aeolian Hall on 20 June): 'The composer Butterworth is said to say that he has your express permission to print my words on concert programmes' (*ibid.*: 105). (Butterworth then admitted that his memory was at fault.)

No Housman settings were published in England during the early war years. After Hugh Priestley-Smith's *From the West Country*, a rather uninspired cycle dated 'Birmingham, March 1913', nothing appeared until John Ireland published 'The heart's desire', a haunting setting of the last three stanzas of 'March', in 1917, 'Hawthorn time' (''Tis time, I think, by Wenlock town') in 1919, and the cycle *The Land of Lost Content* in 1921. This last takes its title from the first line of the second stanza of 'Into my heart an air that kills', a poem which Ireland wished to print at the head of the cycle, although he did not set it to music. But he was thwarted by Housman in a letter of March 1921: '[Allow Mr Ireland] to set to music all the poems he wishes, but he must not print No. 50 as a motto; nor No. 40, which is what he means' (*ibid.*: 185). Evidently one or more of Ireland's settings, undoubtedly the earlier, had been recorded, for 18 days later Housman wrote again: 'I do not want revenue from gramophone and mechanical rights, and Mr Ireland is welcome to as much of it as his publisher will let him have. I hope it may be sufficient to console him for not being allowed to print the poem he wants' (*ibid.*).

The 1920s saw a general boom in song publication in England, and the Housman industry was at its most productive at this time. After a number of insignificant settings by Janet Hamilton, Henry Ley, Willie Manson and Christabel Marillier and a chromatically overwrought version of 'When I was one-and-twenty' by Bax, all published between 1918 and 1921, came a veritable cavalcade of Shropshire Lads, beginning with Gurney's *Ludlow and Teme* and compositions by Muriel Herbert, Marillier, C. W. Orr, D. M. Stewart and Stanley Wilson, all appearing in 1923. Bliss, one of whose earliest songs had been an unpublished setting of ''Tis time, I think, by Wenlock town' (*ca* 1914), published a setting of 'When I was one-and-twenty', in a style most uncharacteristic of him, in America in 1924. Armstrong Gibbs's 'When I was one-and-twenty' and the cycle *Ludlow Town* by Moeran, whose earliest Housman settings of 1916 were with one exception unpublished, appeared in 1924, and in 1925 there were works by Hubert Foss, Hilda Milvain, Kendall Taylor, and Orr again. Settings by Dyson, Edwin Rose, Moeran (two songs, one revised from 1916), Gurney (*The Western Playland*) and Bax (a lovely setting of 'In the morning') followed in 1926, and four more Orr songs in 1927. The flood receded abruptly in 1928 with songs by Rebecca Clarke, Marillier and Dom Thomas Symons, and Ireland's second cycle, *We'll To The Woods No More*. Benjamin Burrows composed 13 Housman songs in 1927, but only two of them were published, by Augener in 1928. Finzi was also occupied with Housman song sketches during the decade, none of which he completed. No wonder Constant Lambert protested, a few years later, that 'since the Shropshire Lad himself published his last poems some ten years ago it may without impertinence be suggested that it is high time his musical followers published their last songs' (1934: 284).

At first sight it seems remarkable that the *Last Poems* of Housman, published in 1922, to which Lambert refers, were not seized upon by composers as they were by members of the literary world, including Grant Richards, who without any signs of encouragement from Housman had been eagerly awaiting a sequel to *A Shropshire Lad* for some years. Of the works mentioned above, only a handful were settings of *Last Poems*, D. M. Stewart's *Four Songs* being the earliest and Ireland's *We'll To the Woods No More* the most important. Perhaps composers who read the *Sunday Times* were frightened off by Ernest Newman, who with characteristic precocity defined the difficulties before anyone had had time to compose any settings. His point was that *Last Poems* did not possess the obvious musical qualities inherent in *A Shropshire Lad*, which by contrast – though he greatly exaggerated the contrast – displayed 'concision and intensity in one, the utmost simplicity of language, freedom both from involution of structure and from simile, and a general build that was virtually that of musical form' (1922: 7). Quite what he meant by the last remark is open to conjecture. Altogether he was no more happy with the Housman corpus than Lambert, though he did not mean to discourage further attempts: 'The predestined composer of "A Shropshire Lad" is not visible anywhere on the present British musical horizon. Perhaps he has not yet been born' (*ibid*.). However, time has surely shown that there could be no single musical Messiah where Housman was concerned. One wishes that Newman had given *Last Poems* a chance to work their way into composers' rather slow creative faculties before commenting; it would have been interesting to hear what he thought of the later 1920s settings. Nevertheless, the best Housman settings remain the earlier ones: Butterworth's, Vaughan Williams's *On Wenlock Edge* and Ireland's *The Land of Lost Content*.

To date Charles Wilfred Orr has been the most prolific setter of Housman, but despite this and despite his possibly conscious endeavour to fulfil Newman's demands by 'doing for Mr Housman what Wolf did for Mörike, for Goethe, for Eichendorff, and others' (Newman, 1918: 393), one cannot consider him as the saviour for whom Newman was looking (his music is discussed below, Chapter XIV). Of his 35 songs, 24 are to poems by Housman, all of them except two, 'Soldier from the wars returning' and 'In valleys green and still', from *A Shropshire Lad*. They appeared in print sporadically between 1923 and 1954. On 6 October 1930 we find him writing to Richards with a request

> . . . that he should be allowed to have prepared a good German translation of certain poems from *A Shropshire Lad*, musical settings of which he had been given permission to publish, in order that he might be enabled to arrange for publication by a German or Austrian firm, since 'at the moment there is such a slump in the English music-publishing business' (Richards: 254).

This last was an observation which Warlock too had made the previous year. The request was refused by Housman, and the songs, with others composed up to 1932, were eventually published in English as a cycle of seven by J. & W. Chester in 1934. Orr's comment about the publishing situation is reflected in the sharp decline in Housman settings printed after 1928. No solo settings were published in 1929 and 1931, and only two, Michael Head's 'Ludlow town' and Harold Thomas's 'We'll to the woods no more', in 1930. A few, mostly insignificant, appeared throughout the 1930s, by minor composers such as Robert Ainsworth, David Branson, Redgrave Cripps, Alan de Beer, Alan Gray, Humphrey Procter-Gregg, George Whitaker and C. Woolley. To these must be added Moeran's sensitive setting of 'Loveliest of trees', published in 1932, and Orr's penultimate contribution, *Three Songs from 'A Shropshire Lad'* and 'The Isle of Portland', which Chester brought out in 1940. Not surprisingly, there are few other wartime settings, and those published after the war (See Gooch and Thatcher, 1976: 365–97) add little to the general corpus, with the exception of Orr's 'In valleys green and still' and Vaughan Williams's *Along the Field*. The latter was composed as a cycle of nine Housman songs, five of them from *Last Poems*, for voice and violin: seven were sung by Joan Elwes on 24 October 1927 in the Grotrian Hall, London. One of the nine, 'The soldier', was subsequently destroyed, and it is not known of which poem this was a setting. The other eight were revised and published in 1954. Finally Berkeley's unpublished *Five Songs* of 1940 should be mentioned. These are striking settings of poems, two of them posthumous, in which the homosexual overtones, acknowledged only after Housman's death, are prominent.

Two composers are conspicuously absent from the above survey. One of them is Warlock, who, despite the affinity he might have been expected to have with the suicidal element in Housman, disliked the poetry, referring to it as 'all that business about clay' (Copley, 1979: 172), and made only two settings (in 1913) from *A Shropshire Lad*, now lost; the other is Howells. Howells related that on one occasion, dining at Trinity College, Cambridge, he was seated next to Housman. At this date he had made about a dozen unpublished Housman settings. On learning that Howells was a composer, the poet expressed the hope that he was not going to set any of his verses to music, and proceeded to execrate the settings of Butterworth and Vaughan Williams. Just before Howells was released for the dessert, Housman said, quite without provocation, 'Young man, do you believe in suicide?' Thankful that he had not published his settings, Howells went home and burnt them (1974; for a slightly different account see Palmer, 1978: 16).

Why was Housman so frequently set to music? That the musical response was all part and parcel of his general popularity is not strictly true, as can be seen from the relative paucity of settings following the publication of *Last Poems*. Composers do not set poems to music merely because the poet in question is currently respectable or fashionable, and indeed often the poets they set are unfashionable – though a poet's popularity is bound to make his verse more easily accessible. One suspects that in this instance it was partly acquaintance with Housman settings by their fellows that induced composers to produce their own Shropshire Lads.

But Housman was attractive to composers chiefly on account of two qualities in his verse. The first of these was pastoralism mixed with a strong flavour of fatalistic, *fin-de-siècle* gloom, both carrying overtones of repressed homosexuality. Some of the composers, including Butterworth and Ireland, can be seen in retrospect to have identified, the latter sometimes to the point of self-pity, with the homosexual element. The identification may have been only subconscious, for the homosexuality, as has already been mentioned, was not publicly alluded to until after Housman's death in 1936, with the publication of the more explicit *More Poems* (1936) and *Additional Poems* (1937 and 1939).

The second cause of attraction to composers was Housman's universally recognised 'musical' quality. Before we examine what literary critics have understood by this musicality, and how it may in some cases have misled composers, it should be pointed out that not all the poems possess it. An Edwardian melodist skimming *A Shropshire Lad* would be puzzled by the very first poem, '1887'. At first it seems a simple panegyric on Queen Victoria and her loyal soldiers on the occasion of her Jubilee. But as he read on he would realise that as such it does not ring true.

> It dawns in Asia, tombstones show
>   And Shropshire names are read;
> And the Nile spills his overflow
>   Beside the Severn's dead.

This is too terse for a glorification of noble death. The growing impression of undercurrents of irony, resigned and disenchanted if not bitter and cynical, is confirmed by the final stanza:

> Oh, God will save her, fear you not:
>   Be you the men you've been,
> Get you the sons your fathers got,
>   And God will save the Queen.

(Housman once denied that this poem has anything more to it than its surface meaning, but this may just have been a characteristically defensive response to too close questioning about the nature of his art (Weber, 1946: 104–5).) The position of '1887' at the beginning of *A Shropshire Lad* is crucial, in that it establishes the happy prosperity of the Queen's 50th reigning year as a background to the preoccupation with the inevitability of death which gradually grows on the reader's awareness. It has never been set to music. And of the last poem in the book, 'I hoed and trenched and weeded', equally important in its place as a poignant epilogue summing up Housman's poetic legacy, there seems to have been only one, unpublished, setting. In not framing their cycles with these poems composers have lost a major constituent of *A Shropshire Lad*'s sense of span and unity; there has been no attempt to match this scope in music. Newman, in the article quoted above, noticed this:

> Had we a Wolf among us, it would not have been a mere poem or two here and there from the collection that he would have set . . . he would have set virtually the whole of the sixty-three poems, doing for Mr Housman what Wolf did for Mörike, for Goethe, for Eichendorff, and others (1918: 393).

A composer was bound to shake his head over '1887', wondering how the subtlety of its oscillating and conflicting nuances could be reflected in music. The difficulty lies in the fact that in a way Housman has already set it to music for us, as he has most of his poems. Literary critics appreciate this; prone as they are to using musical terminology, they have strongly emphasised the musical element in the poetry. Indeed, the very first reviewer of *A Shropshire Lad* drew attention to it in *The Times* of 27 March 1896:

> . . . the essentials of thought and music . . . are there in no niggard measure . . . his gift of melodious expression is genuine (Richards: 6).

Three weeks later Hubert Bland took a similar line in *The New Age*, in a review which Housman himself once said pleased him more than any other:

> This direct expression of elemental emotions, of heart-thoughts, if we may be permitted the phrase, is the dominant note of all Mr Housman's works, as it was of Heine's alone among modern singers (*ibid.*: 10).

More recently, Cleanth Brooks said of 'Bredon Hill':

> He made at least five attempts to get the phrasing right . . . I think that you can
> 'hear' the shift in tone as I read this last stanza . . . The note of exasperation – the
> irritated outburst against the noise of the bells – is a powerful, if indirect way, of
> voicing the speaker's sense of loss (Ricks: 73).

Christopher Ricks makes Housman's musicality the chief point of his essay 'The
nature of Housman's poetry':

> To me his poems are remarkable for the ways in which rhythm and style temper
> or mitigate or criticise what in bald paraphrase the poem would be saying. [Con-
> cerning *More Poems*, VI] . . . The poem says a dour glum cramping thing, but
> how does it say it? With gaiety and wit that are, if you like, utterly inappropriate.
> Instead of the 'steady' tramp of military fortitude, there is the exquisite interlac-
> ing of a dance . . . It was . . . this power that drew Housman, the power of music
> radically to change what is said (:106–14).

Had Ricks's essay appeared 70 years earlier it might have served to warn composers of the difficulties of trying to superimpose anything on the balance of
opposing forces perfected in the poetry:

> His sense of decorum, in fact, is a larger one than that which oppresses a lot of
> contemporary verse, where we find that the rhythm and movement simply say
> again in their own medium what the diction too is saying. A violent expressiveness
> can become as tedious as a thrice-told tale . . . (:109–10).

So a musical setting of Housman seems bound to tell the tale at least twice, by
emphasising one aspect of the poem: either the flow of the rhythm at the expense
of the hard sentiment of the words, which often have a Heine-like sting in the tail,
or the basic meaning at the expense of the sense of smooth, continuous movement. It was precisely the 'violent expressiveness' to which Newman objected in
On Wenlock Edge:

> Dr Vaughan Williams's setting flies in the very face of all that is most delicate,
> most artistic, most human in the poem. What is the use of the poet softening the
> final blow as he does if Dr Vaughan Williams is to deal it afresh at the dead man
> with a sledge-hammer? What is the use of the friend saying 'Never ask me whose'
> in a *pianissimo* when he has just hurled the 'I cheer a dead man's sweetheart'
> at the ghost's head with a noise and an agitation that would let the most stupid
> ghost that ever returned to earth into the secret . . . (1918: 397).

Shortly before, on the same page, he accused Vaugham Williams of being melodramatic. Vaughan Williams's settings may sometimes be inappropriate, but
there is a strong element of melodrama in Housman's poetry, which springs at
least in part from its affinity with the Border ballads, and led Henry Ainley to
recite 'Bredon Hill' as a monologue (Hamilton: 62).

However, the essence of Housman's perfection, according to Ricks, is 'a counterpointed stress' (:111), which is easily covered or destroyed when the poem is
'doubled' with music. This is one of the most basic problems of musical settings
of any poetry at any period, but it is particularly acute within the Romantic
sincerity of the *Lied* tradition. In short, how do you convey poetic irony in a
song? (see Stein, *passim*; also Appendix II)

The task would perhaps be easier if the counterpoint were in two parts only.
But in some of Housman's best poems there are so many strands working in different directions that the result can be compared to a serial construction, an

impression borne out by Richard Wilbur's analysis of 'Epitaph on an army of mercenaries' (Ricks: 85–105). This poem too has hardly ever been set to music.

Housman's counterpoint is most effective on the printed page. Reading his poems silently, one can fix one's mind now on one shade of meaning, now on another, or on two or more at once, without losing the balance, but one cannot do this when hearing them read aloud: then the apparent simplicity dominates, and one suffers the same pitfalls as the composer. Did Housman himself ever try reciting them? We do not know, although his famous account of how poetry worked on him emotionally would suggest that it entered his heart through the brain and not through the ears and lips: 'Experience has taught me, when I am shaving of a morning, to keep watch over my thoughts, because, if a line of poetry strays into my memory, my skin bristles so that the razor ceases to act' (:47). But just how concerned he was about the difficulties of a rhetorical performance, either spoken or sung, it is impossible to determine. He does not seem to have been at all musical, or at least was not conversant with classical music – a point discussed at length by William White (1943) and the poet's sister (K. E. Symons, 1944) – and it is therefore unwise to read anything more than a general dislike of composers' claiming his poems for their own into his adverse comments on their settings.

Even in the poems whose lyric simplicity would seem to pose no problems there can be snags. The second poem of *A Shropshire Lad*, 'Loveliest of trees', has a first stanza which has warmed the heart of many composers:

> Loveliest of trees, the cherry now
> Is hung with bloom along the bough,
> And stands about the woodland ride
> Wearing white for Eastertide.

Here is something comfortably similar to 'Im wunderschönen Monat Mai' which opens Schumann's Heine cycle, *Dichterliebe*. (Heine, of course, was one of the influences Housman acknowledged, as we have seen, above, p. 11.) It opens Somervell's *Shropshire Lad* cycle in a flood of intimate, Schumannesque inspiration, as it opens Butterworth's (in the published version at least), and it comprises the sole contribution to the Housman corpus of many other composers: there are at least 35 settings (Gooch and Thatcher, 1976: 377–80). But in one version after another one feels that the composer has been carried away by the allure of the first stanza to the extent of not considering how he or she is going to cope with the remaining two:

> Now, of my threescore years and ten,
> Twenty will not come again,
> And take from seventy springs a score,
> It only leaves me fifty more.
>
> And since to look at things in bloom
> Fifty springs are little room,
> About the woodlands I will go
> To see the cherry hung with snow.

There is no doubting the poignancy of the scene and the intensity of the poet's response. But at the same time there is a touch of good-humoured characterisation in the rather slow arithmetic of the Shropshire Lad, the hero of the anthology who here makes his appearance for the first time. How does one set this arithmetic to music? The English composer, having plunged headlong into the first verse with pastoral ecstasy, must somehow keep going and hope to emerge sententious in the last line, and of seven settings studied none, with the possible exception of Butterworth's, is convincing in the middle stanza.

This is to say not that it is impossible to set Housman to music satisfactorily, but that many of the composers have been led astray by the very musical qualities of Housman's verse and its settability: the simple, flowing metre with little *enjambement*, the infallible scansion and rhyme, and the largely monosyllabic vocabulary, which ease the path so completely for the composer that they can ultimately prove more of a hindrance than a help, because they were never intended as a gift to composers but as a swift and smooth vehicle for Housman's own apophthegms. Nevertheless, there are a number of poems with which one can obtain perfectly good musical results provided one mirrors the lyrical ambience, the metrical poise, faithfully and lets the superimposed nuances speak for themselves straight from the text. Such a poem is 'The Lent lily':

'Tis spring; come out to ramble
  The hilly brakes around,
For under thorn and bramble
  About the hollow ground
  The primroses are found.

And there's the windflower chilly,
  With all the winds at play,
And there's the Lenten lily
  That has not long to stay
  And dies on Easter day.

And since till girls go maying
  You find the primrose still,
And find the windflower playing
  With every wind at will,
  But not the daffodil,

Bring baskets now, and sally
  Upon the spring's array,
And bear from hill and valley
  The daffodil away
  That dies on Easter day.

The vital point here is that the feeling of the transience of beauty is not dealt as a blow or an anticlimax or a sting in the tail but is integrated into the whole structure, both metric and grammatical. Metric, in that the five-line pattern of each stanza causes the first four lines to lose their customary feeling of entity and finality and to be drawn towards the last (treatment and results are similar in 'Bredon Hill'); grammatical, in that the whole poem is in effect one sentence (the full stops are followed by 'and' and 'and since'), in which the acceptance of transience and the decision to try to capture its beauty, destroying it in the process, are seen as the logical culmination of the argument.

Thus for a setting of the poem to persuade, the lyrical unity must be reflected in the music. Ireland's achieves this perfectly. The feeling of fragility is there from the start in the gently oscillating, closely spaced chords. The harmony does not develop at all; it just reflects the gently ebbing and flowing intensity of emotion by undulating up and down in a series of 3rds. There are no cadences, and hardly any common chords. Ireland has captured the poignant feeling of transience without solidifying it. The only way in which he has not quite done justice to Housman's implications is in misjudging the speed of movement of the poem. It is a little too relaxed, so that phrases such as ''Tis spring; come out to ramble', 'the winds at play' and 'Bring baskets now, and sally / Upon the spring's array' strain at the leash.

Gurney's setting in *Ludlow and Teme* compares very unfavourably with this. He plunges into the first, second and fourth stanzas with an exhilarating vernal romp, only to reach an overwrought climax and collapse conspicuously each time he comes across the daffodil. He also makes the mistake of separating some of the verbal phrases by lengthy instrumental interludes. The overall effect is of losing the sense of transience without ever having captured it.

It is unlikely that Housman can ever gain much by being set to music; sometimes he can lose much. On the other hand, there are at least two outstanding instances of his having unwittingly, or rather unwillingly, performed a great service for English music. In the case of Butterworth, Housman's rôle was that of a catalyst, in that he emerged largely unchanged and unscathed in Butterworth's settings, at the same time acting as the liberating agent which helped the composer to develop a personal idiom. For instance, Butterworth's *Suite for String Quartette*, which is his only entirely abstract instrumental work and was probably written before the *Shropshire Lad* songs, has an idiom which is colourless and innocuous, often rhythmically cluttered, a residue of Parry, Stanford, Elgar and folksong, whereas in the *Shropshire Lad* songs the poetry has stimulated him to add touches of colour and more intimate sentiment. Of this there are many memorable examples in addition to those discussed in chapter VII: the whole of 'Loveliest of trees', so rich in ideas that it provided the material for his orchestral *Shropshire Lad* Rhapsody; the unresolved minor added 6th chord at the end of 'Is my team ploughing'; the sudden modulation from A major to G minor before the grief-stricken fifth stanza of 'Bredon Hill', followed by chords representing both keys in tortuous alternation; and the major added 6ths in 'On the idle hill of summer', beautifully evocative of summer drowsiness. The other happy outcome of Butterworth's sensitivity towards Housman's poetry was that it forced him to keep his musical language pared down to the bare essentials. Morton Zabel's description of Housman's poetry, that 'his lyrics speak from the threshold of silence itself' (Ricks: 124), is equally applicable to Butterworth's music. He was one of the few English composers to command such simplicity at the time, as a glance at the styles of most of his contemporaries described in Part I of this book will show. It is difficult to see what his compositional style could have led on to, but the lack of potential development need not detract from his achievement, which within its tiny orbit was considerable (see above, pp. 144–52).

Housman's other major contribution to the development of English music was to provide Vaughan Williams with a text on which to build *On Wenlock Edge*. Housman once said that composers 'regard the author merely as a peg to hang things on', to which A. V. Butcher added the comment 'Omit the word "merely", and every musician will agree wholeheartedly (1948: 338). But in 1918 musicians certainly had not agreed wholeheartedly over *On Wenlock Edge*. Edwin Evans wrote a glowing appreciation in the June issue of the *Musical Times* (1918: 247–9) which included the statement that Vaughan Williams was faithful to the spirit and meaning of Housman's poetry. Unfortunately it also included some not very kind comments on Ernest Newman's supposed attitude towards English music. Newman retorted in the September issue with a much longer, belligerent article (1918: 393–8), which has already been quoted. He pointed out the severely limited extent to which Vaughan Williams can be said to present the true Housman in his settings, but he remained deliberately blind to what for Vaughan Williams was the crucial issue, namely that the composer took only what he wanted from the poems, emotional material which evoked a powerful response in, to use the poet's own words, 'the blood that warms an English yeoman'. Newman showed no interest in the fact that Housman's poems stimulated an original style in Vaughan Williams (which Whitman's in the contemporary *Sea Symphony* did not), not to mention medium – piano, string quartet and voice, a combination later explored by Gurney – that was still fairly novel in English composition, though it had been used earlier by Chausson and Fauré. In 'Bredon Hill', above all, we have an impressionistic picture of the poem's background, startling in its imaginative boldness and emotional directness, nearer to Ravel's *La vallée des cloches* than to any contemporary English tone-painting, and far in advance of Vaughan Williams's other completed works, looking forward to the *London Symphony* of 1914.

Many impressionistic pictures occupy very large canvases. The fact that *On Wenlock Edge* is emotionally large-scale and, at times, outspoken has not always been given due emphasis, but neither has the fact that Housman's poetry is too. Despite the look of his verse on the page, Housman was no miniaturist: he had no concern with small ideas or small feelings. How large some of his concerns were an analysis of 'Bredon Hill' would show. The subject-matter encompasses nature, geographical and temporal distance, sex, marriage, difference and antagonism between the sexes (the bells 'ring to call' *her*, suggesting a chauvinistic agnosticism in the lad and a detaining of the lass against her will or at least her conscience), divine punishment, death, human self-righteousness and sinfulness (the 'good people' in the final stanza is doubly ironic), and human frailty (reading the last line to suggest either that the lad's atheism dissolves in the face of bereavement or that he will follow her by committing suicide), and running through the whole is the image of bells (other musical images in Housman are military, e.g. distant drums and bugles). Such issues are not conveyed by small music, hence Vaughan Williams's 'Bredon Hill' is finer than Butterworth's and Somervell's, in which the music is not large enough for the poem's drama. Butterworth himself had to broaden his style and scale to do justice to a poem of very similar model, 'On the idle hill of summer'. In fact some of the best interpretations of Housman occur when the verbal text itself is not present, and only the archetypal drama and its images remain: Butterworth's Rhapsody speaks for itself, as do many of John Ireland's pieces, perhaps most intensely the slow movement of his Piano Sonata. The murmur of nature, the bells, the distant drums, the yearning love are there; it is a Housman study in all but name.

Apart from Gurney, whose attempts to set Housman were on the whole not very successful, only one composer approached Housman expansively: Benjamin Burrows, notably in 'Bredon Hill' and 'The soldiers' ('In valleys green and still'). 'The soldiers' incorporates a courageous attempt to make the irresistible appeal of martial music manifest, but the figure used for the portrayal, with its ragtime syncopations (Ex. 1), falls between impressionism and popular pastiche, to the

Ex. 1

embarrassment of both. Ives might have managed it with more flair. Burrows, whose talent was dramatic rather than lyric (see above, pp. 228–9), produced his best Housman song in 'The oracles', a poem in *Last Poems* set by no one else and having nothing to do with the Shropshire Lad. Thoughts of death are instead given a classical setting. It is surprising that Housman did not use his classical knowledge more frequently in his poetry. Here he compares the self, seeking from the heart knowledge of the certainty of death, to a Spartan consulting the Dodona priestess in the face of invasion; in either case resistance, by suicide or by combat, is useless. The mixture of drama and melodrama suits Burrows well. A throbbing tonic pedal in C sharp minor underpins most of the song, over which is

Ex. 2

Ex. 2 (cont)

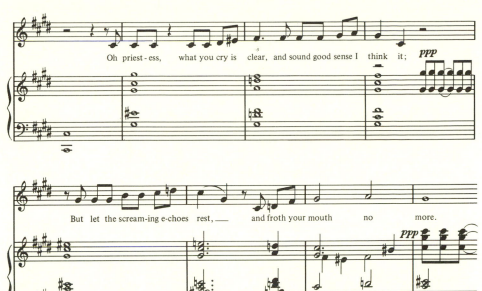

built up a long, restless piano introduction, whose repeated triplet quaver chords are variously used to suggest both the gentle tolling of the oracular cauldrons and the martial music of an approaching army, and whose double-dotted rhythms convey both the urgency of the consultation and, again, the army. Interwoven with this graphic writing is an effective *arioso* vocal style, not unlike Finzi's (see Ex. 2, part of the second and third stanzas of the poem); it is particularly arresting at the beginning of the second stanza, where the accented word 'my' in 'I took my question' turns the song inwards upon the self with an impatient jolt (Ex. 3). Altogether Burrows builds up a somewhat hyperbolic, petulant fantasy of melodramatic self-hatred and self-pity, which perhaps comes nearer to the truth of Housman's character than many a wistful, neatly contained setting from *A Shropshire Lad*. (For further discussion of the musical interpretation of Housman's poetry, see below, Appendices II and III.)

Ex. 3

XII

The Celtic twilight

> . . . what lies at the root of all Celtic mysticism and wonder is the sense of a great loss. To the Celt, and those . . . possessed of the Celtic spirit, the material universe appears as symbol of a lost kingdom; and art is an incantation which can restore to a certain extent that which has been lost . . . All of [the English Romantics] in some measure reverted to the origins of music in the first ages of man when folksong was an incantation, an effort to bring back what had been lost (Palmer, 1977: 7).

The Celtic revival in literature, if it is seen as dating back to Macpherson's Ossianic poems of 1760, is almost synonymous with the origins of the Romantic movement; as a late-19th-century phenomenon, however, it gathers and focusses a number of Romantic preoccupations in such a way as to project them firmly into our own century. In this chapter some of the musical aspects of that projection will be investigated.

Ernest Renan's *The Poetry of the Celtic Races*, written after an exploration of Brittany in 1856, was published in French in 1857 and later translated into English (Renan, 1896). Matthew Arnold elaborated on Renan's ideas in articles in the *Cornhill Magazine*, advocated (unsuccessfully) a Chair of Celtic Literatures at Oxford, and produced his own book *On the Study of Celtic Literature* (1866–7). Arnold's *Tristram and Iseult* appeared in 1852; soon Wagner was writing the poem of his far more passionate and infinitely more far-reaching musical dramatisation of the story, and treatments of the legend were subsequently made by Tennyson, Swinburne and Hardy. Celtic and religious studies mingled in John Rhys's *Celtic Britain*, published by the Society for Promoting Christian Knowledge in 1882, and in his series of lectures 'The origin and growth of religion as illustrated by Celtic heathendom'. William Sharp's *Lyra Celtica*, a sizeable anthology of Celtic verse, appeared in 1896, with an enlarged edition in 1924; many of its poems were set to music. Sir James Frazer's enormously influential *The Golden Bough* of 1890–1915 was a major landmark in the development of comparative mythology and must have given added impetus to the bewildering variety of spiritual causes, such as Madame Blavatsky's theosophy (with which Yeats became involved), that were rampant at the turn of the century. The Pan-Celtic Society was founded in 1899, and issued *Celtia: A Pan-Celtic Magazine* from 1901. Many attempted to discover strains of Celtic ancestry in their blood in order to be admitted to the society (Saddlemeyer, 1965).

Certain aspects of the movement need to be isolated. One is the way in which it compounded the issue of 19th-century nationalism with the more portentous issue of race. Renan had written: 'If the excellence of races is to be appreciated by the purity of their blood and the inviolability of their national character, it must needs be admitted that none can vie in nobility with the still surviving remains of the Celtic race. Never has a human family lived more apart from the world, and been purer from all alien admixture' (:4). Obviously this was a way of thinking which could and did lead directly to Nazism. Its dangers were less apparent at the time, and several composers shared the fascination with race. Balfour Gardiner wrote to Percy Grainger on 21 December 1924, 'I am getting interested in racial questions – indeed I always have been – and I have not realized till lately what a huge literature exists on the subject. [He mentions Lothrop Stoddard's *Racial Realities in Europe*, and *The Passing of the Great Race*.] But I feel very suspicious, as one always ought to be about mere generalization' (1901–61). Grainger himself was addicted throughout his life to speculative rubbish about racial characteristics; the following, from a letter to Roger Quilter (8 October 1947), is a fair sample:

> One great point about yr Kingliness is its utter Englishness. Vaughan Williams is a very noble and benign being, but he is more or less Welsh. And Cyril [Scott] has the slightly druidical streak of the West Countryman. Elgar was noble, but he was a Colonel rather than a King. Balfour [Gardiner] is a patriarch rather than a King. He is, if anything, pre-King. But he seems, as you do, thoroughly East-British – what in Anglosaxon is called 'Angelcynne' (English-Kind). That your mother had so purely, and she was innately queenly as you are kingly (*ibid.*).

Grainger's views on artistic hegemony were eccentric in the extreme; he also extolled the qualities of blue-eyed composers, and, as is well known, tried to avoid using words with Latin roots, sometimes with hilarious results. However, his 'tone-crafter's' (composer's) 'lightning-flashes of race-lay-bare-ment', as he called them, came in response to a less idiosyncratic need, felt by many in this period, to develop an alternative to the classical tradition in art, to get away from the dominance of the Mediterranean and central Europe, to look north and west rather than south and east. That urge was at least 100 years old; why it became so strong at the end of the 19th century is difficult to say.

Politics were certainly a key factor. Although Warlock's interest in matters Celtic seems to have been aroused by the Breton composer Paul Ladmirault and he later set some carols to music in Cornish, and although Fiona Macleod wrote about Scotland in her Celtic poems, it was in Ireland that the Celtic imagination found its strongest stimulus, and Ireland, geographically the most remote of the Celtic areas, has always been politically restless, but never more so than in the period in question. A group of poetic political activists calling themselves Young Ireland flourished as early as the 1840s, and their anthology *The Spirit of the Nation* was reprinted many times in the later 19th century. In subsequent generations poetry kept aloof from politics, but by the time of Yeats the involvement was again strong, although Yeats himself, in no way a rebel, had many disagreements with the nationalists over the extent to which political purposes should dictate the concerns of poetry (Marcus: 1–34). In 1916 two poets, Padraig Pearse and Thomas MacDonagh, were shot for their part in the Easter rebellion; six years later, Southern Ireland had become independent.

However, it was identification with the spiritual, not the political Ireland, that sustained the Celtic twilight glimmer. To participate it was not necessary to live in

Ireland – Yeats spent much time in London, and Joyce was an exile. It was not even necessary to be Irish; Bax, the foremost Celtic exponent in music, had no Irish blood, but could still say that when, in 1902, he came across Yeats's narrative drama *The Wanderings of Oisin*, 'in a moment the Celt within me stood revealed' (1943: 41–2). In his autobiography he offers an explanation of 'this rather rhetorical phrase':

> In a famous passage . . . Renan . . . declared that 'The Celt has ever worn himself out in mistaking dreams for reality,' but I believe that, on the contrary, the Celt knows more clearly than the men of most races the difference between the two, and deliberately chooses to follow the dream. There is certainly a tireless hunter of dreams in my own make-up . . . I am an appreciative inhabitant of this world . . . yet a part of me is not of it . . . when I read of the warrior poet who forsook his father Fionn and the Fianna at the call of a demon leman, and wandered for three hundred years amongst enchanted islands in the dove-grey western seas beyond the ultimate shores of Ireland in quest of a content that he never found, even in the white arms of an immortal, then my dream became localized and I knew that I too must follow Usheen [= Oisin] and Niamh from Ireland into the sunset (*ibid.*: 42).

He then elaborates on the Celtic preoccupation with the unattainable (elsewhere he terms it 'nympholepsis'), using an effective objectifying technique of putting the critique into the mouth of a petulant 'cranky English student of the Celtic genius' presumably invented for the purpose:

> . . . this country is too inherently romantic . . . to take any sort of pleasure in things as they are – a healthy secret known only to those civilizations that have passed through the purging flood of the Renaissance . . . never does poet – noble or humble – extol Here-and-Now. Cathleen ní Hoolihan is for ever complaining that she could be happy if things were otherwise – if the King of Ireland's son were at home . . . You will never look upon your hills outside a mood that is a little preoccupied with beauty gone on the wind – with Deirdre's white feet in long-dried dew – with the wild geese, that fled from Ireland generations ago or are to fly back hither out of some future sky. The present is always illusion for you, even when the lark spins over your heads. You will never know the 'burly joy' of which Meredith sang in the English May . . . it's an inherent Celtic quality – nothing whatever to do with the miserable social history of the last few centuries . . . you have never been anything else than romantic. Why! did not your Michael Comyn foreshadow the whole of European neo-romanticism in his 'Lay of Tír-na-nÓg' at a time when Goethe and Wordsworth and Coleridge were mewling and puking in their nurses' arms? Celtic Renaissance indeed! How can there be a rebirth of an idea that has never died? (:43–4)

This, then, is Bax's understanding of the Celtic element in himself. It is only an element, a point perhaps understressed in the two passages quoted, and we must remember that the lure of a Celtic dream-world was most fruitfully intense when pulling against a conflicting half of the personality. Thus Bax the English composer was set against his *alter ego* Dermot O'Byrne, the pseudonym he used when living for periods in Ireland purely as an author, and his looking westward to Ireland was contrasted with his looking eastward to Bohemia and Russia; for him, both directions held strong associations based on romantic experience, as his autobiography explains, and the contrast can easily be heard in his music. Similarly Yeats the dreamer contrasted with Yeats the modern man of action, as Richard Ellmann makes clear. Ellmann also points out (:76–7) how many other

Celtic associates of Yeats felt the need for a pseudonym, amongst them Æ
(George Russell) and Fiona Macleod (William Sharp); one could add Seumas
O'Sullivan (James Starkey). Sharp's case, a most curious one, was pure schizo-
phrenia: he regarded his *alter ego* as his romantic lover. In music the Warlock/
Heseltine duality also springs to mind, much overplayed though it seems to have
been by Cecil Gray; certainly Warlock's penchant for Celtic melancholy and
yeomanly jollity represent two personality traits no easier to integrate than the
musical styles which he employed to express them.

The Celtic impulse was antithetical to the Christian tradition, though much
bound up with the twilight zone where Christian and pagan mythologies merge;
'Why are these strange souls born everywhere to-day? with hearts that Christianity, as shaped by history, cannot satisfy' Yeats had written in 'The tragic
generation' (1926: 388) of the artists of the 1890s, many of whom were Celtic in
origin or sympathies. It was also, in Yeats's view, a folk movement, attempting,
in the Irish drama in particular, 'to restore what is called a more picturesque way
of life – that is to say, a way of life in which the common man has some share in
imaginative art' (1923: 168). But there was some disingenuousness here. Yeats
was in no sense a man of the people, and although Irish literature of his period
uses the legends and landscapes of the Irish folk, it also uses the hothouse intellectual techniques of French symbolism. The same is true of music: a contour of
folk melody in a complex symphonic movement or even in a song by Bax or
Moeran does not make the movement or the song a work of folk art. Even less is
the Celtic impulse documentary. Whereas the poems of Moira O'Neill, John
Stevenson, A. P. Graves and W. M. Letts in settings by Stanford and Wood enter
into the villages and the parlours of the Irish peasantry, the next generation's
Celtic twilight concerns itself more with their visions and loves, keeping them out
of doors with nature – though there are of course exceptions, most notably the
works of Synge, whose *Riders to the Sea* gave rise to operas by Fritz Hart,
Vaughan Williams and others and a projected one by Gurney. Thus when Bax crit-
icised Stanford, Wood and Hamilton Harty, it was for not having 'penetrated to
within a thousand miles' of the 'Hidden Ireland', not of the manifest Ireland (see
above, p. 33).

One further facet of the Celtic revival, particularly as shaped by Yeats, needs to
be mentioned: the concern with symbolism. Yeats explains the power of symbols,
which he had grasped even before his contact with the French movement via
Arthur Symons, in a remarkable essay, 'Magic' (1901), where he ascribes it to the
workings of collective memory:

> I cannot now think symbols less than the greatest of all powers whether they are
> used consciously by the masters of magic, or half unconsciously by their succes-
> sors, the poet, the musician and the artist . . . Whether their power has arisen
> out of themselves, or whether it has an arbitrary origin, matters little, for they
> act, as I believe, because the great memory associates them with certain events
> and moods and persons. Whatever the passions of man have gathered about,
> becomes a symbol in the great memory, and in the hands of him who has the
> secret, it is a worker of wonders, a caller-up of angels or of devils. The symbols
> are of all kinds, for everything in heaven or earth has its association, momentous
> or trivial, in the great memory, and one never knows what forgotten events may
> have plunged it, like the toadstool and the ragweed, into the great passions (1903:
> 64–5).

Mythology may thus be a way of accounting for the power of a symbol. For instance, the wind is a symbol used repeatedly in the works discussed below. It clearly stands for human restlessness, for awareness of the futility of action and desire, hope and security, and in his *Collected Poems* Yeats explains in the notes to 'The hosting of the Sidhe' from *The Wind Among the Reeds* how in Irish folklore the wind's associations are accounted for by treating it as a sign of the passing of the Sidhe (Gaelic for 'wind'), the battle-host of Faery, the ancient gods who play havoc with human activity and desire. Their chief calls:

> Away, come away:
> Empty your heart of its mortal dream.
> The winds awaken, the leaves whirl round,
> Our cheeks are pale, our hair is unbound,
> Our breasts are heaving, our eyes are agleam,
> Our arms are waving, our lips are apart;
> And if any gaze on our rushing band,
> We come between him and the deed of his hand,
> We come between him and the hope of his heart.

Many of the poets of the Irish renaissance were set to music. We shall not be especially concerned with most of them, but it is worth noting that of the earlier poets represented in Justin McCarthy's anthology *Irish Literature* (10 volumes, Chicago, 1904) there are known musical settings of about half within our period, while of the later poets there are plenty of settings of most of the major figures, including Yeats, Æ, Seumas O'Sullivan, James Stephens and Padraic Colum, as well as of minor poets such as Joseph Campbell and Eva Gore-Booth. Fiona Macleod, Celtic though not Irish, was often drawn upon, and we shall examine some of the earlier settings of Joyce. His inclusion in a study of the Celtic twilight may at first seem odd, but it can be shown that settings of his poems, and in particular of *Chamber Music* by Moeran, further the musical expression of the Celtic spirit. The remainder of this chapter concentrates on these, on settings of various poets by Bax, and on settings of Yeats by Warlock and Hadley.

First, however, two points concerning Yeats must be made. It was the early, dreaming, melancholy Yeats that was repeatedly set to music, and there are relatively few settings of his later poetry, from *The Green Helmet* (1910) onwards, in which he moved away from such selfconsciously Celtic modes of expression. 'A coat', from *Responsibilities* (1914), indicates in his terse later style his attitude to those who latched on to his early manner:

> I made my song a coat
> Covered with embroideries
> Out of old mythologies
> From heel to throat;
> But the fools caught it,
> Wore it in the world's eyes
> As though they'd wrought it.
> Song, let them take it,
> For there's more enterprise
> In walking naked.

No doubt Yeats counted the composers who set his verse to music amongst the 'fools', and this leads to the second point: his attitude to music. Bax, who knew them, claimed that 'Both A. E. and W. B. Yeats were tone-deaf' (1952: iv); Yeats admitted as much about himself. Nothing could distinguish him more obviously from Joyce, a fine tenor who had composed art songs in his youth and had an extensive knowledge of Italian opera and its singers. Yet, with his characteristically Irish incantatory approach to the performance of poetry (which makes the recordings of him reciting his own verse unforgettable), Yeats was unable to leave music alone. Around 1900 he developed an idea of half speaking, half singing poetry to the accompaniment of a psaltery. An instrument was constructed for him by Arnold Dolmetsch and an attempt was made to teach a technique to the actress Florence Farr, the general idea being that plucking a string of the psaltery would establish a pitch for a word or group of words to be chanted. The attempt was unsuccessful, though recital tours were made. The whole idea was one of the more bizarre of the periodic attempts in history to revert to Greek ideals, and perhaps merits a footnote in an account of *Sprechstimme* (W. B. Yeats, 1903: 16–28; Hone: 190–2; Wade: 354, 362, 373–5, 404–5; A. Symons; Farr). At other times Yeats organised the composition and performance of music in connection with his plays and the poems in them, working especially with George Antheil, Walter Rummel and the painter Edmund Dulac as composers, but making severe strictures concerning the ancillary rôle which music should play. His position on the setting of words to music could be dismissed, *pace* Clinton-Baddeley (:151–64, and see above, p. ix), as irrelevant to the history of the art song – which he rejected as a form of expression – were it not that the strength of his prejudice caused him to employ a censor, herself unmusical, to examine all musical settings of his poetry pending publication. Warlock, barred from publishing his Yeats settings by the arbitrary decisions of this censor, politely pointed out the injustice of the situation in a letter to the *Musical Times* of February 1922, but turned to Yeats for his texts no more. His early setting of 'The cloths of heaven' was rewritten to words by Arthur Symons as 'The sick heart', and the opening of 'The everlasting voices' was eventually reused in 'Rest, sweet nymphs'; other Yeats settings by him, including one in the original version of *The Curlew*, were destroyed or lost (Tomlinson, 1974: 31 and 1976a). Bax presumably had similar problems with 'The fiddler of Dooney' of 1907, for he eventually published it in 1919 as 'The enchanted fiddle', having substituted similar words, probably by himself. He admitted (1949) that he found Yeats's poetry 'too good' for setting to music, but one wonders whether he might not have made more than just his one other Yeats setting (of 'To an isle in the water', now lost) had there not been a likelihood of censorship jeopardising publication.

The songs of Arnold Bax have never been much sung. Given the English suspicion of virtuosity, this is perhaps not surprising, since Bax was writing, as early as his unpublished songs of 1900, piano accompaniments and sometimes voice parts of considerable density and difficulty: 'Young Bax's stuff sounds like a bevy of little devils!' Parry remarked of a performance of his *Celtic Song-Cycle* of 1904 (Bax, 1943: 27). This is not to say, however, that the piano parts are clumsy; they are generally effective and commensurate with the broadness of thought, inasmuch as there is nearly always an orchestral conception at the heart of Bax's piano writing. The opening of the very large-scale 'From the uplands to the sea'

(1905), of which a version with two-piano accompaniment was also made, indicates the scope of a Strauss tone-poem rather than a song (Ex. 1). Strauss's influence, here and elsewhere, is not in itself deleterious; nevertheless, certain criticisms must recur in an assessment of Bax's songs. One is that his lack of sympathy for and understanding of what is grateful for the voice tended to undermine his technical professionalism. Mark Raphael (1974–7) once had to explain to him, while a singer was struggling with a particularly awkward passage in one of his songs, that certain vowels inevitably get modified on high notes; Bax did not know. Another is that his over-fondness for chromatic inflection could easily become a mannerism of applied grotesqueness. He may take a regularly constructed melody, such as that of the setting of Fiona Macleod's 'Heart o' beauty', which is again Straussian, and subject it to foliate bas-relief in the manner of a Celtic sculptor afraid of leaving a surface uncovered (Ex. 2, *x*). When this kind of invention is harmonised the accompaniment's voice-leading tends to make the piano writing turgid or obscure. The chromatically altered chords (*x*) of Ex. 3, from two further Macleod settings, 'A Celtic lullaby' and

Ex. 1

Ex. 2

Ex. 3

'The white peace', would sound effective if pointed into symbolic emphasis by orchestral colouring, e.g. stopped horns in Ex. 3(a), but that of Ex. 3(b) in particular does not seem to stand for anything as a piano accompaniment; certainly it does not illuminate the word 'plain' which it sets in the first stanza, though 'pain' in the second may indicate its origin. At other times, as in Ex. 4, which is from the extraordinary and unsatisfactory 'Magnificat (after a picture by D. G. Ros-

Ex. 4

setti)', the effect of unnecessary chromatic alteration (*x*) seems simply tasteless, particularly since here it is recurrent, the passage with its 'Linden Lea' opening at the words 'For behold' being a sort of refrain. Yet Bax's technique is not generally deficient, and occasionally he refines his voice-leading into an impressive smoothness; in 'The flute', originally written to a Norwegian text, he sets himself the challenge of depicting a 'tune . . . sad and gay' of unbearable beauty, and meets it successfully (Ex. 5). This is a powerful song, despite the somewhat uncomfortable reminiscence of 'A presage falls upon thee' from Part II of *The Dream of Gerontius* in its final section; furthermore, the translation by Edmund Gosse is good, and the elaboration of technical means used to create its effects contrasts in no way detrimentally with the much simpler construction of an analogous symbolic image in 'I heard a piper piping'. The differences are instructive. In 'The flute' the symbolism is not Celtic in mood: the flute speaks of a heaven which is for the present unattainable but is still aspired to, and does so with an alluring tonal warmth. In 'I heard a piper', however, we are told that the sound 'seemed but a part of the hills' melancholy / No piper piping there could ever be jolly', and the technical apparatus used to indicate passive acceptance of this melancholy is a bare, static modality, pentatonic for the flute and dorian for the voice.

Such acquiescent simplicity is rare in Bax, however. As a composer of Celtic music he too often faces a dilemma: to express the Celtic spirit seems to require simple purity of melody, especially when simple poetry is being sung; yet the weight of emotion which lies behind the simplicity demands, from a composer steeped in the Romantic tradition, a complex musical symbolism. This problem is prominent in his first significant Celtic work, *A Celtic Song-Cycle* (1904), which like many of his other songs of this early period sets poetry by Fiona Macleod. The homespun melody with which both the piano introduction and the voice part begin is perfectly appropriate to the opening lines ('O far away upon the hills . . .'), and includes references to common traits of Irish folk melody, such as the outlined upward major 6th (Ex. 6, *x*), the triplet (*y*), and the semi-pentatonic downward scale pattern, much loved by Moeran (*z*). But Bax cannot resist developing this melody in an organic manner. He does it well, climbing by stages to g″ sharp (there is a correlating further climax, on a″, in the song's final section) and

Ex. 5

Ex. 5 (cont.)

Ex. 6

Ex. 7

then descending to the note from which he began (Ex. 7). This is expressive of the rising of the heart 'like the wind', but it destroys the folk element and also produces some atrocious word-setting. Moreover the accompaniment, whose constant ♪♩ ♫♪ arabesques are in themselves no hindrance to the Celtic flavour, suddenly loses its comparative harmonic simplicity with a chromatic slip at the moment the emotions become involved – the moment of spying the fawn, which is evidently the symbol of a fleeting love, as the rest of the cycle makes clear. And in the refrain that follows Bax feels the need to employ all the turbulent paraphernalia of chromatic triplets to bring out the symbolic reference to 'the wind's song on the hill'. The abrupt return, after this, to a variant of the opening melody's second phrase, though expertly related to its shape in the first section, comes as an incongruous jolt. The problem reappears later in the cycle. With a typically Celtic emphasis on hopelessness, in all but the first of the five songs the fawn is lost. In the second song this produces some heavy-handed symbolism both from the poet and from the composer (Ex. 8):

> O sands of my heart what wind moans low along thy shadowy shore?
> Is that the deep sea-heart I hear with the dying sob at its core?
> Each dim lost wave that lapses is like a closing door:
> 'Tis closing doors they hear at last who soon shall hear no more,
>   Who soon shall hear no more.

The third song is impressive for the sheer Wagnerian passion which it manages to inject into Fiona Macleod's fantasy of desire, though technically it is scrappy; the frenzy is bypassed rather than resolved in the fourth song, already mentioned, the 'Celtic lullaby'. The final song, 'At the last', boldly attempts a further confrontation of simple intoning and elaborate symbolism. The text is brief:

Ex. 8

> She cometh no more:
> Time too is dead.
> The last tide is led
> To the last shore.
> Eternity!
> What is Eternity,
> But the sea coming,
> The sea going
> For evermore?

It is sung entirely on a monotone, b flat, except for the final syllable, which rises to a dominant d′. Meanwhile, the sea of eternal loss comes and goes underneath with a variety of augmented and diminished harmonic figurations. All needs to focus on the final interrogatory rise to d′, but at this point Bax unfortunately chooses to reintroduce, in the accompaniment, his initial 'death' motive, which is stylistically derivative, dissonant, and in the context altogether ungainly. It jars badly, and again suggests the need for orchestration, particularly for the bitonality (a characteristic usage) of its second chord.

Bax was only 21 when he wrote these songs, yet already his style was quite clearly one which could spread its contradictory impulses at ease only in large surroundings; none of the songs is short, let alone simple. He needed at this stage, perhaps unconsciously, a context in which he could incorporate song melody as one element or section, not as its whole span. A song that shows him working towards this is the setting (1905) of Allingham's poem 'The fairies'. Like his much later song 'Wild almond' this is in effect a symphonic scherzo. A brilliant if extravagant compendium of musical figures and gestures, including a blatant ragtime syncopation, is brought into play to illustrate the mischievous colourfulness of the 'little people'; some of them, particularly the musical description of the 'old king' (Ex. 9), cry out for orchestration. (Britten said the same of the accompaniment of 'Wild almond' when he received the manuscript from Harriet Cohen (Cohen: 281).) Then there is a sudden change of mood to domestic pathos in the poem, at 'They stole little Bridget / For seven years long', and Bax moves into a completely different 'trio' section, with a rich Elgarian tune and walking bass. He uses triplets and upward 6ths again, though the tune does not sound too obviously

Ex. 9

Irish. Finally the scherzo returns in shortened form, complete with a recapitulation of the first two stanzas and a last witty upward flourish in the piano. The later song 'Glamour' can likewise be seen as a scherzo with trio elements, and its manuscript contains orchestral indications; so can 'The enchanted fiddle', on a smaller scale.

From 1910 onwards Bax concentrated his technical powers on the construction of instrumental works, where they could find greater scope. First in sonatas, then, between the wars, in his seven magnificent symphonies, the conflicting elements of *melos* and symbol which had first sprung up in his early songs continued to confront each other, but with more ample articulation. His song output, which had consisted mainly of first a Pre-Raphaelite phase, then a Fiona Macleod phase, and then a Rückert and Dehmel phase, diminished drastically after 1911. Perhaps his finest song-cycle was *The Bard of the Dimbovitza*, with orchestra, of 1914, based not on Irish but on Rumanian peasant poetry, and very seldom performed. Here the verse often has a cutting ironic edge which suits him rather well yet is lacking in his Celtic texts. He made three song settings of Æ in 1916; one of these, 'Parting', put into the Celtic language of 'wind-blown tresses' that mood of post-coital yearning and restlessness which in its larger, social implications was so much a part of Bax's unsatisfied life. Characteristically, though, it was the larger implications that still needed expression, and accordingly the song was built into the important large-scale Symphonic Variations for piano and orchestra later in the same year (Scott-Sutherland: 53–4).

Few of his songs after the war show his technique at its fullest. One or two of them, like 'The pigeons' and 'Out and away', are stylistically experimental. Others, notably the settings of Herbert Trench, Hardy and Housman, are true successors to the pre-war songs, and indeed the intense harmonic treatment of 'In the morning', though overbearing for Housman's verse, makes it one of Bax's most revealing songs:

> In the blue and silver morning
>   On the haycock as they lay,
> Oh they looked at one another
>   And they looked away.

(The melancholy penultimate chord of this song, before its resolution to a major tonic triad, will be encountered again in this chapter.) The setting of his brother's poignant poem 'Youth' is another faultless gem of self-expression. But the arrangements of old English and French melodies are indications of a narrowing horizon. Although the French arrangements are delightful and show a new polish in his style, they are – except for the enchanting first two, from which the nightingale's song of 'Sarabande' must be singled out for its intense beauty – not very personal. Perhaps regrettably, the same must be said of his two sets of Irish songs (1921–2). Here the Irishness is more obvious than before the war, but also more superficial. Bax by this time felt himself a stranger in Ireland, as he relates in the touching final pages of *Farewell, My Youth*. 'Rann of wandering' and 'As I came over the grey, grey hills' are simply harmonisations of pseudo-Irish strophic tunes, complete with flat 7ths and, in the former, the common repeated-note ending, although 'As I came over' has a stirring brassy introduction and a contrasting third stanza. Elsewhere, as we have seen in 'I heard a piper', folk-like melodic arabesques are allowed to stand on their own without the persuasive textural commentary of the early songs; there is a surprising clarity and simplicity, for instance, in 'Cradle song' (Ex. 10) and in the keening of 'Rann of exile'. But the effect, certainly in 'Cradle song', is primarily picturesque. The two songs that stand out are from the *Five Irish Songs*. No. 1, 'The pigeons', explores a remarkable degree of dissonance to express the painful associations that the pigeons' coos have for a childless woman, 'like a child's hand at the breast' (Ex. 11), but fails to integrate it into the harmonic framework that surfaces periodically. No. 4, 'Across the door', also has a problem of formal integration,

Ex. 10

Ex. 11

for the fiddle music, depicting a barn dance, with which it begins, dissolves as the amorous couple slip out into the open air. The musical style and content of the rest of the song, at least in the accompaniment, are quite different. But the yearning of a romantic Celt for an unrecapturable moment of love necessitates this change; and this is what really matters to Bax (see below, Ex. 12).

All sounds, all colours, all forms, either because of their pre-ordained energies or because of long association, evoke indefinable and yet precise emotions, or, as I prefer to think, call down among us certain disembodied powers, whose footsteps over our hearts we call emotions; and when sound, and colour, and form are in a musical relation, a beautiful relation to one another, they become as it were one sound, one colour, one form, and evoke an emotion that is made out of their distinct evocations and yet is one emotion. The same relation exists between all portions of every work of art, whether it be an epic or a song, and the more perfect it is, and the more various and numerous the elements that have flowed into its perfection, the more powerful will be the emotion, the power, the god it calls among us (W. B. Yeats, 1906b: 243–4).

Celtic symbolism, though strongly localised, is not contained: it deals with the unfathomable seats of emotion. Bax, responding to this, latterly expressed it in works of symphonic scope. Yeats, at the close of his essay 'The autumn of the body' (1898), felt confident that 'we will not cease to write long poems, but rather . . . we will write them more and more as our new belief makes the world plastic under our hands again' (1903: 304), yet long symbolist poems were not much written, and Frank Kermode comments on the difficulty of sustaining symbolic relationships for any length in a poem: 'with the aid of music . . . a long poem might be possible, whereas if it has to resort to continuous narrative or doctrine it becomes at best a series of short poems tediously bound together by prose. But the difficulties are enormous . . .' (:132). Warlock's *The Curlew* in its final form consists of four poems by Yeats, three short ones from *The Wind Among the Reeds* and a somewhat longer one, 'The withering of the boughs', which is broken up by its refrain, from *In the Seven Woods*. The poems are linked by music into a continuous setting; this is, in effect, the long symbolic poem about which Kermode speculates. Warlock recognised that the sheer weight of emotion evoked by the melancholy symbols (the curlew, the wind, the water etc.) needed music of corresponding length and heaviness, and the result is 25 minutes of the most sublimely depressing music and poetry imaginable, 'possibly the finest piece of English music written in the present century' (C. Wilson, 2/1967: 156). *The Curlew* is an emotionally draining experience; Cecil Gray, to whom it was dedicated, could no longer listen to it after Warlock's suicide (1934: 247). The poet voices his lost love in a returning series of benumbed remembrances and images which correspond with the desolate marshy landscape in which he is wandering. It is interesting to see which identical or similar emotive words the poems that Warlock chose have in common:

'He reproves the curlew'	'The lover mourns for the loss of love'	'The withering of the boughs'	'He hears the cry of the sedge'
curlew		curlew ($\times 2$) peewit ($\times 2$)	
cry crying ($\times 2$)	weeping	cried cry	cries
water		lake foam	lake
the West			West
passion	despair	pitiful lonely	desolate
dimmed	pale dim	pale dim ($\times 2$)	

eyes	looked	blind	
long	end (×2)	unending	
	away	long	
		years	
hair	hair		
breast	heart		breast (×2)
wind		wind (×3)	wind
	hands		hands
	friend		beloved
	love		
	dreamed	dreams (×3)	sleep
		sleepy (×2)	
		asleep	
		lay	lie
		depths	deep
		wandering	wander
		wander	

We find a similar pattern of recurring ideas in Warlock's score. In neither the poems nor the music is the pattern methodical or balanced, in fact the freedom of reference is a crucial contributing factor to the work's power. Thus *The Curlew* is in no way structured with symphonic logic, and although Warlock himself referred to it in a letter of March 1924 as 'a kind of symphonic poem' (Heseltine, 1920–9), its manner of prolonging musical material is closer to that of an operatic scena; indeed, both the instrumentation and the melodic shape of the opening inescapably recall Act IV of Verdi's *Otello*. However, certain tonal relationships, mentioned below, may have significance, and certain short sections do return complete. Some of the most prominent musical elements are enumerated below.

Ex. 12

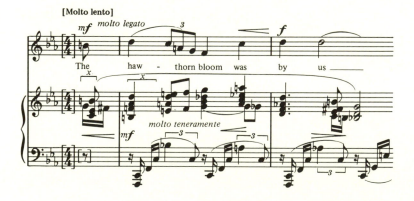

1. The work is dominated by a chord based on a minor triad with compound 3rds added above to the 13th (Ex. 13 (a)). We shall meet elements of this chord again in Moeran and Hadley, and it is perhaps present in Bax, e.g. at *x* in Ex. 12 (from 'Across the door') and in his 'In the morning' (see above, p. 261). Its two commonest forms in 'Celtic twilight' music are a minor triad plus 7th and 9th (Ex. 13 (a), *x*), and a minor triad plus 9th and 13th (Ex. 13 (a), *y*). The former is

Ex. 13

found at letter B in *The Curlew*. It is a profoundly melancholy sonority; the identical chord concludes the desolate coda of Frank Bridge's Third Quartet, written a few years after *The Curlew*, and Warlock himself used it again (written enharmonically as G flat minor) very near the end of the last piece he wrote, the solo version of 'Bethlehem Down', where it underpins the word 'music' with uncanny effect. The compound chord of Ex. 13 (a) can be 'horizontalised' into a minor scale with sharp 4th (Ex. 13 (b)), and whole sections of Warlock's score are based on it, for instance two bars at B (Ex. 14). The three-note cell of semitone plus minor 3rd (Ex. 13 (b), *z*) features prominently, for instance in the curlew's monodic song at the opening of the work, though it is also very freely varied (Ex. 15 *z*1). Ex. 15 also contains slightly larger motives that can be regarded as

Ex. 14

Ex. 15

'curlew' themes, which recur throughout the work, still largely built on the same minor scale (Ex. 16 (a), (b)). Later in the work *z* is extended to form a scale of alternating intervals (see Ex. 17, from after letter *z*). Sections are based on the minor scale of Ex. 13 in various transpositions; for instance, a foretaste of Ex. 16 (a) opens the work in E minor, then the cycle of 5ths brings us to B minor (a variant

Ex. 16

Poco più mosso
(a)

O   Cur - lew,   cry   no more   in   the   air,

(b) [Very slow]
C.A.

Ex. 17

Fl.   Vln II   Vla

Ex. 18

of Ex. 16 (b) in bar 2 of the piece), F sharp minor (Ex. 14), and C sharp minor (Ex. 16 (b) at c). In the last four bars of the work this underlying scale is in F minor, far distant from the opening dominant cycle.

2. Another prominent element is what might be termed the 'wind' theme. This is much more static, consisting of a melody in 10ths, with many false relations, over a dominant pedal. It sounds indebted to Bartók, particularly with its Magyar snap (♪.), and first appears in F sharp at A (Ex. 18). The pair of introverting minor 3rds and their continuation (Ex. 18, *a*), which have initially grown out of Ex. 13, z just before A, are much utilised later in the piece, particularly after the second song at K. They can be seen in the second violin tune at Y (Ex. 22), as well as in passages growing out of obvious statements of Ex. 18, e.g. from P in the third song right the way through to the '*trem. sul ponticello*' passage, and possibly also, expanded into major 3rds, at the earlier lines 'I long for your merry . . . words', in the vocal intervals and swaying string triplets. Ex. 18 comes a great many times. At its second appearance, at D, it picks up the 'curlew'

rhythm from the end of Ex. 16 (b), and also a lower 4th in the bass undermining its 6–4 status. This unsettling compound 4th chord later grows into a common Warlock device, the transposition of a lute's open strings (Ex. 19, the held string chord after v), and, very chillingly, a distortion of this chord is heard three times in the last song (x and afterwards) on the strings, *pp* and *con sordino*, as though the strings of a ghostly lute have been stirred by three faint breaths of wind. Although Ex. 18 appears in various harmonic guises, the parallel 10ths are for a long time inviolate, until the whole phrase begins to be used as the basis for development in the third song (around P). Later in the third song Ex. 18 is worked anew, as an eerie, trite hurdy-gurdy melody (Ex. 20). This is surely a clear example of how Yeats saw symbolism arising from collective memory: nowadays we are not exposed to mediaeval hurdy-gurdy minstrelsy, neither was Warlock, yet we know on hearing the tune that it fits with and illustrates the dream of bygone kings and queens with their singing, gold-chained swans. It is one of the most powerful passages in the work.

3. Certain other scale formations are given currency. Apart from semitonal chromatics, alternating tones and semitones (Messiaen's Mode II) are found at various points (e.g. Ex. 21). Possibly more patterns could be found.

4. The short second song is composed entirely in Warlock's 'Delius' style, which is a homophonic succession of strongly emotive 7th chords, each one often suggesting a different key, connected by chromatic voice-leading in one or more of the parts. This style is particularly associated, as here, with lilting siciliana compound rhythms, such as ♩ ♪ and ♩. ♫ .

Ex. 19

Ex. 20

Ex. 21

5. Successions of chromatic chords not in homophony but in clogged, near-atonal polyphony suggest van Dieren's influence. This is most obvious in the tortured passage at ʏ in the last song (Ex. 22).

6. Passages of parallel triads or discords occasionally appear (Ex. 23).

7. Atonal, recitative-like passages of great desolation appear in the flute and the voice. The tendency is towards chromatic introversion and dodecaphony. The early passage on the flute (Ex. 24) returns in part at ʜ and again, with a wild extension, to introduce the last poem, which is sung in one despairing arc by the voice unaccompanied; its loneliness recalls the parallel passages in Mahler's 'Der Abschied' from *Das Lied von der Erde*. The vocal line keeps turning back on itself tortuously, but nevertheless reaches a high a′ before twisting down again.

8. The instrumentation, in addition to effects of *tremolando, sul ponticello, con sordino*, harmonics and endlessly held notes in the strings, is highly charged: cor anglais and flute, surely the most melancholy of instruments, are often used here on their own or with motionless accompaniment. The symbolic effect of the writing for these instruments must not be underestimated: for most of the piece one or both of them, or a stringed instrument imitating their phraseology, is playing some asymmetrical phrase whose abundance of short upbeats (sometimes single notes, sometimes a whole group) and avoidance of progression in equal note values give the effect of the ever-present song of the lonely bird.

Ex. 22

Ex. 23

Ex. 24

Space does not permit a general discussion of other composers' settings of
Yeats. Many of them, though attractive, are not particularly illuminating or
particularly twilit; such are the many settings of 'The fiddler of Dooney' (Bax,
Browne, Dunhill, Gurney), 'Down by the salley gardens' (Ernest Bullock, Gurney,
Ireland, Martin Shaw), 'When you are old and gray' (Bridge, Bullock, Gurney)
and 'Innisfree' (Burrows, Bush, Darke, Gurney, Peel). Dunhill's cycle of four
songs from *The Wind Among the Reeds*, published in 1905 and scored for tenor
and orchestra in a revised edition of 1924, includes the earliest known Yeats
setting, 'Half close your eyelids', first published in *The Dome* in 1900 (see above,
p. 2). Although the cycle and its songs are stylistically insecure, this one, the most
interesting of the four, almost approaches the manner of Satie in its trance-like
acceptance of non-progressive harmony (Ex. 25). Warlock came across this
setting as a young man, and, as he told Colin Taylor in a letter of 1912, found it
'very beautiful' (Copley, 1979: 158).

Ex. 25

None of these Yeats settings enters as deeply into the Celtic twilight as *The
Curlew*; only 'Ephemera' by Patrick Hadley, who was half Irish, approaches it in
scope. This setting of a poem from *Crossways* is scored for high voice, flute,
oboe, clarinet, piano and strings. Composed in 1924, it was probably influenced
by *The Curlew*. It is an immature work, and Hadley may have been wise not to
publish it; many of its fingerprints, particularly traits of texture and instrumentation, appear more assured in another song of farewell, the 'Scene from *The
Woodlanders*' of 1925, and in his later works for voice and ensemble, such as
'Mariana'. Yet its sincerity gives it great beauty, and it bears interesting comparison with *The Curlew*. The main difference is that although the poem itself,
with its over-burdening language of autumn to express the waning of love, can
seem even more melancholy than the poems in *The Curlew*, Hadley gives it a
surprisingly positive thrust. It is difficult to say whether this is a miscalculation or
a deliberate interpretation based on the last section of the poem, but less difficult
to pinpoint the contributory musical factors. One is the definite sense of shape,
with a heady climax at the lines 'Before us lies eternity; our souls / Are love' sinking into peaceful resolution at the final words 'and a continual farewell'; after
this the tortuous fugal theme, which opens the piece in a clotted way suggesting van

Dieren (Ex. 26) and returns in the middle, is ingeniously and satisfyingly bathed in the F major chromatic harmonies (Ex. 27, piano reduction by Peter Tranchell) used earlier at the reference to the stars. Another factor is the chordal structure: Warlock's minor chord (Ex. 13 (a), with *y*) puts in an effective appearance, but only once, at the word 'leaves' for the emotive vignette 'she had thrust dead leaves . . . / In bosom and hair'; elsewhere it is chords based on dominant 7ths that appear most consistently, particularly those on two dominant 7ths with roots a tritone apart (Ex. 28). These chords are too assertive, too dominant, in fact, for their crepuscular text, though they are counterbalanced by the plethora of whole-tone chords in the $\frac{12}{8}$ section. A third factor is the careful contrast developed between passages which set the scene, passages spoken by the man, passages spoken by the woman, and passages of description or narration. Unlike *The Curlew*, the effect is not that of a desolate monologue. Altogether the ebb and flow of yearning puts the work closer to Delius.

The musical Celtic twilight found perhaps its most touching, and certainly its most approachable, encapsulation in Moeran's settings of Joyce and O'Sullivan. His *Seven Poems of James Joyce* were composed in 1929, to texts from *Chamber*

Ex. 26

Ex. 27

Ex. 28

Music – the collection of small, beautifully wrought and unpretentious lyric verse which appeared in 1907 and seems to represent a distillation of several centuries of a lyric tradition which Joyce, with his musical experience, was well able to appreciate. 'The poems in *Chamber Music* have all that a musician looks for in a poet's arrangement of words – syllables that can be articulated, range of expression within little compass, situation, contrast; and, above all, the charm that is in a spontaneous rendering of some stirring mood – a charm which, being akin to melody, musicians readily feel.' Thus wrote Padraic Colum (:13), who with Joyce's own comments as authority saw them as stemming from Elizabethan song. He also found them 'without a trace of Irish influence', but there is no doubt about the Celtic flavour in Moeran's settings. In extracting seven of the 36 poems without altering the order he skilfully retained Joyce's progression of moods and experiences, moving from the excitement of young love to the nostalgic retrospect after love has ended. Crucial to the balance of the cycle is an implied hiatus between the fourth and the fifth songs, where a leap is made straight from Joyce's 16th poem to the 31st, creating an impression that, between the gently seductive ending of the fourth song

> O cool and pleasant is the valley
> And there, love, will we stay.

and the sighing reminiscence of the opening of the fifth, where the past tense suddenly appears,

> O, it was out by Donnycarney
> . . . My love and I did walk together

a long time and much experience have elapsed. The weight of experience, the heaviness of the passing of love and a final acceptance of love's ending give the song-cycle its Celtic basis; indeed, the last song's text is virtually a paraphrase, in sentiment and imagery, of 'Ephemera':

> Now, O now, in this brown land
>   Where Love did so sweet music make
> We two shall wander, hand in hand,
>   Forbearing for old friendship' sake
> Nor grieve because our love was gay
> Which now is ended in this way.
>
> A rogue in red and yellow dress
>   Is knocking, knocking at the tree
> And all around our loneliness
>   The wind is whistling merrily.
> The leaves – they do not sigh at all
> When the year takes them in the fall.
>
> Now, O now, we hear no more
>   The villanelle and roundelay!
> Yet will we kiss, sweetheart, before
>   We take sad leave at close of day.
> Grieve not, sweetheart, for anything –
> The year, the year is gathering.

However, the bitter–sweet equipoise of this verse is not so quiescent in the anguished ending of Joyce's final poem, which Moeran does not set and which is a violent, despairing dream: 'My love, my love, my love, why have you left me alone?' Moeran seems to feel something of this in the second stanza of 'Now, O now', where his wind whistles far from merrily in a variant of Ex. 18 from *The Curlew*. Moeran takes many musical procedures and symbols from Warlock, with whom he had shared a cottage for three formative years shortly before composing these songs. The bitter–sweet siciliana rhythms, which Warlock himself had used in both his other surviving Yeats settings, are ubiquitous in the first and last songs. For both composers these rhythms hold archaic associations; they are expressive not just of the sadness of past ages but of a sadness *for* past ages. This fits perfectly with lines such as 'Strings in the earth and air' and 'we hear no more / The villanelle and roundelay' in the Joyce poems. The feeling of nostalgia is enhanced by Moeran's reintroducing the 'strings in the earth and air' accompanimental figure not only in the sixth song, where it is rhythmically straightened out to express the falling rain, but also right at the end of the final song, where it underlines the closing of the year's cycle (Ex. 29). The little sigh which escapes it (*x*) is found at the opening of Moeran's other Joyce setting of 1929, 'Rosefrail', and the rather glum chord onto which it finally settles in the fifth bar from the end is of course Ex. 13 (a) with the *y* component.

Moeran, like Hadley, was half Irish, and felt the affinity more and more as he grew older. Although an Irish jig can be sensed as early as 'The lads in their hundreds' from his Housman cycle of 1920, the Joyce songs are the first work in which he overtly responds to Irish folk melody, on which he drew in his music more than did Warlock, Hadley or Bax. The relation is clearest in 'O cool is the valley', particularly in the three *tenuto* repeated notes of the accompani-

Ex. 29

ment and the 4–3–1 cadence at the words 'sometime go' (parallels to both can be found in Bax's song 'Youth', on which Moeran surely modelled his 'In youth is pleasure'), and in the strong upward major 6th of the vocal opening. He further integrated the Irish folk element into the large orchestral works which followed in the 1930s and 1940s, when he was living for much of the time in Kenmare, County Kerry, where he died in 1950. Yet these works also develop the more abstract Celtic symbols; for example, the first movement of the Cello Concerto is saturated with the chords and scale of Ex. 13, and Ex. 29 fleetingly and wispily appears in the third movement of the Symphony.

The Cello Concerto is probably Moeran's most intense and best-structured communication of the Celtic spirit, and it is easy to overlook the Seumas O'Sullivan songs, written just before, in 1944. One of these, the not very arresting 'Invitation in autumn', is a large, full-blooded song in which Moeran returns to the style of his RCM teacher John Ireland, whose excessive influence on Moeran's music until about 1925 is all too evident in his early songs. But the other six constitute a set of which it is difficult not to believe that Moeran is consciously looking back, as the second world war draws to its close, over the whole English song tradition of his passing generation:

> I will go out and meet the evening hours
> And greet them one by one as friend greets friend,
> . . . And learn the things old times have left unsaid,
> And read the secrets of an age long gone,
> And out of twilight and the darkening plain
> Build up all that old quiet world again.

There are still things 'left unsaid' in the styles and affinities of his contemporaries and forbears, and by now he has grown experienced enough to say them without plagiarism; thus the touches of Stanford in the folksong-like setting of 'The poplars' and in the poetic conceit of 'The dustman' and the taste of John Ireland in the declamation of 'A cottager' can take their place. Yet Warlock's compound minor chord is there too: 'Lullaby' is full of it, and the moment when it slips from G minor down a semitone to Warlock's and Bridge's F sharp minor at the syllable 'cry-' of 'the herons are crying' is poignant in the extreme (Ex. 30). It keeps returning on the old familiar symbolic words: 'dreams', 'murmur', 'gray', 'wet', 'away'. In the final song, it points and underlines what Moeran finds hard to

Ex. 30

accept: that his world is fading; that for him there is to be no emerging from the twilight. There is no looking forward beyond death:

> O herdsman driving your slow twilight flock
> By darkening meadow and hedge and grassy rath;
> The trees stand shuddering as you pass by;
> The suddenly falling silence is your path.
>
> Over my heart too, the shadows are creeping;
> But on my heart forever they will lie;
> O happy meadows and trees and rath and hedges,
> The twilight and all its flock will pass you by.

The voice hardly stirs from its monotonous f sharp; it remembers the spontaneous upward spring of folk melody briefly in the penultimate line, and the piano peals as though in joyous birdsong; but the *Curlew* chord (Ex. 13 (a)) returns, first on E minor for the word 'twilight', then, as the human voice ceases, with its sad bird-like cry through rising 3rds on G minor, B flat minor and C sharp minor, in a harmonic crescendo of frustration and anguish, only to sink again, finally, to B minor, where its dissonant elements one by one slowly fade into a minor triad with unresolved added 6th (Ex. 31).

Ex. 31

XIII

Time and destiny: the Hardy songs of Gerald Finzi

Although the view of Thomas Hardy as an unrelievedly pessimistic author has been energetically disputed, it was that of many of his contemporaries, who found his novels morbidly gloomy, immoral and anarchical. *Tess of the d'Urbevilles* (1891) was described in the *Quarterly Review* (1892) as 'an extremely disagreeable story [told] in an extremely disagreeable manner' (Stewart: 168); it sold exceptionally well. *Jude the Obscure* (1895), arguably his masterpiece, had an even more outraged press and, according to Hardy in his 1912 postscript to the Preface, was burnt by a bishop (W. W. How, Bishop of Wakefield – 'probably in his despair at not being able to burn me'. In short, Hardy, though he disliked the hostility caused by his rôle strongly enough to give up novel-writing altogether, was, particularly in the last decade of the 19th century, a provocative voice of his time, capable of arousing a vehement response. Throughout his life he was given to strong, sweeping statements, such as 'I have been looking for God 50 years, and I think that if he had existed I should have discovered him' (F. E. Hardy, 1928: 293) and 'The more we know of the laws and nature of the Universe, the more ghastly a business one perceives it all to be' (Stewart: 35). Permeating the novels and the poetry, these views reinforced the impression he made on the 'first generation atheists', to borrow Hugh Ottaway's phrase (1972), making them respect him as a figurehead of literary Darwinism.

What drew Gerald Finzi so repeatedly to Hardy's poetry? He grew up as a second-generation agnostic, temperamentally mellower than Hardy. Hardy's rejection of Christianity was brittle, and often irritably defiant. Finzi's was more nostalgic: personally unable to accept the Christian myth, he was nevertheless capable of wishing that its truth might be regenerated for him. This was an attitude that Hardy voiced only rarely, notably in 'The oxen', a poem which Finzi set to music; at other times he suggests no very close parallel with Finzi. Finzi's musical vocabulary is simple and restricted; Hardy's use of language in the poetry has astonishing breadth. They led very different lives. Hardy was active and restless, with a powerful imaginative mind which personal unhappiness, ostensibly the outcome of his marriage to Emma, caused to shoot out dark questionings and self-contradictory philosophies. Finzi, after an unhappy childhood, steadfastly devoted himself to the achievement of unassuming personal fulfilment in composition; he married happily and composed quietly and conscientiously in rural seclusion, apparently unrebellious even when, before the age of 50, he learnt that he had a fatal illness which would allow him only a few more years of life.

275

But these differences are less profound than the similarities. Underneath Finzi's constant cheerfulness and boundless vitality lay a fundamental sense of isolation. Environmental security was valued highly in his marriage and in his subsequent family life because it had been lacking in his own upbringing; the emphasis was on home-grown produce and conservation, the latter finding its outlet in the growing and saving of endangered species of apple tree, of which he possessed about 400 different varieties in his orchard at Ashmansworth. Similarly, his need to express Wordsworth's and Traherne's sense of childhood ecstasy was a sublimation of what had been denied him in his youth, whose insecurities and shadows never lifted, as his widow, Joy Finzi, has pointed out:

> Arriving last in a family of five – an unwanted addition to a bursting upper floor nursery and not welcomed by his sister and brothers – he always felt a stranger among them . . . The change of circumstances that followed [the early death of his father], the [1914] war, and loss of Ernest Farrar, his first composition teacher who was killed at the front, sharply shadowed his sense of security in a comfortable middle class family (1973).

The approach of the second world war was an even greater strain on him, for he was particularly sensitive to outward events. On 12 March 1938, the day of Germany's entry into Austria, Joy Finzi noted in her journal, as was her custom, comments he made that day: '"You must know what I feel like – it's like watching a man done to death, only this is a civilisation and the last stand of central European culture." "The tide is receding."' Two days later she wrote: 'G has had bad sleepless night – and has been too disturbed by political events in Austria to do much work. [Quoting him:] "More persecution for the individuals who do not fit into a regime of physical force."' And again, on 5 October, she quoted: '"I can feel nothing but the suffering of humanity and the fear for the future of civilisation."' It is easy to see how, particularly at times like these, Finzi turned to Hardy for the sense of experience shared; the poetry allowed him to externalise his fundamental misgivings about life by giving them musical expression. There are a number of references to Hardy in the journal during this year. On 25 October, Joy quoted from a letter he had written her:

> 'I sat on our [prehistoric] Barrow . . . and read Wm Rutland's new little life of Hardy . . . I'd like you to read it sometime or other . . . perhaps it will give you some idea of why I have always loved him so much and from earliest days responded, not so much to an influence as to a kinship with him (I don't mean kinship with his genius, alas, but with his mental make-up). Here is a passage from the book: "The first, manifest characteristic of the man who wrote *The Dynasts* is his detestation of all useless suffering that fills the world . . ." And here's another: "it is an interesting paradox that Hardy should have placed so high a value upon intellectual reason, while his own mental life was almost entirely governed by emotion."'

Finzi recognised this last comment as being equally applicable to himself. A few months earlier Joy recorded him as saying, after reading Meredith's *Love in the Valley*, '"Feeling is greater than experience and that you must always remember. One cannot shout it out enough."'

There was one sensation that both Finzi and Hardy never ceased to feel: the inexorability of time. Finzi, a slow, fastidious composer who tended to put sketches away in drawers for years before bringing them out to complete them, was continually dogged by the sense that time was too short for all he wished to write. The feeling became acute, of course, after the diagnosis of Hodgkin's disease in 1951, when Finzi wrote in the preface to his own catalogue of works, 'at 49 I feel I have hardly begun my work – [quoting Tychborne] "My thread is cut, and yet it is not spun; / And now I live, and now my life is done"' (1941, 1951: 2–3). The war aggravated it; on 16 March 1941 Joy Finzi wrote in her journal:

> This next call up will include men of Gerald's age – to him it is now only a few weeks until 'the billows go over my head.' He said early this morning, Milton on his blindness best expressed what ceasing his work meant to him:
>
> When I consider how my light is spent
> Ere half my days, in this dark world and wide,
> And that one Talent which is death to hide,
> Lodged with me useless . . .

(Finzi had set the Milton sonnet to music in 1928.) On 1 June 1943 Joy wrote similarly: 'The passing of time at such a vital moment in his life when he was just achieving an easier technique is a constant remorse.' To offset this ever-present sensation of time slipping away from under his feet, the completion of a musical work, however slight, took on a spiritual urgency, as he wrote to William Busch in October 1938: 'I should feel really suicidal if I didn't know that a song outlasts a dynasty' (J. Finzi, 1938–56). This view of art was a necessary fixed point in a world dominated by Hardy's pessimistic acceptance of evolutionary theory; it finds its clearest expression in Finzi's preface to his own catalogue of works, which he entitled *Absalom's Place*:

> It was Thomas Hardy who wrote 'Why do I go on doing these things?' . . . some curious force compels us to preserve and project into the future the essence of our individuality, and, in doing so, to project something of our age and civilization. The artist is like the coral insect, building his reef out of the transitory world around him and making a solid structure to last long after his own fragile and uncertain life. It is one of the many proud points of his occupation that, great or small, there is, ultimately, little else but his work through which his country and civilization may be known and judged by posterity . . . Something is created out of nothing, order out of chaos; and as we succeed in shaping our intractable material into coherence and form, a relief comes to the mind (akin to the relief experienced at the remembrance of some forgotten thing) as a new accretion is added to that projection of oneself which, in metaphor, has been called 'Absalom's place' or a coral reef or a 'ceder or shrubbe' . . . As usually happens, it is likely that new ideas, new fashions and the pressing forward of new generations, will soon obliterate my small contribution. Yet I like to think that in each generation may be found a few responsive minds, and for them I should still like the work to be available. To shake hands with a good friend over the centuries is a pleasant thing, and the affection which an individual may retain after his departure is perhaps the only thing which guarantees an ultimate life to his works (1941, 1951: 1–3).

The final sentence echoes the last stanza of James Elroy Flecker's poignant 'To a poet a thousand years hence':

> I who am dead a thousand years,
> And wrote this sweet archaic song,
> Send you my words for messengers
> The way I shall not pass along.

> I care not if you bridge the seas,
> Or ride secure the cruel sky,
> Or build consummate palaces
> Of metal or of masonry.
>
> But have you wine and music still,
> And statues and a bright-eyed love,
> And foolish thoughts of good and ill,
> And prayers to them who sit above?
>
> How shall we conquer? Like a wind
> That falls at eve our fancies blow,
> And old Maeonides the blind
> Said it three thousand years ago.
>
> O friend unseen, unborn, unknown,
> Student of our sweet English tongue,
> Read out my words at night, alone:
> I was a poet, I was young.
>
> Since I can never see your face,
> And never shake you by the hand,
> I send my soul through time and space
> To greet you. You will understand.

It is hardly surprising that Finzi set this poem to music, and did so most successfully. In fact he buried a copy of his setting under the porch of his house at Ashmansworth (McVeagh, 1975–81). He also expressed the time-fixation in an image coined to explain his feeling of isolation from his brothers and sisters during his lonely childhood, when he had already found a sense of identity with poets of previous ages; it was like 'a group of telegraph wires, each being able to communicate forward and backward to eternity, but never to the closely adjoining lines on either side' (J. Finzi, 1973).

In his Hardy songs the attitude to time tends to be ambivalent. In many of the poems Finzi sets, notably in 'Life laughs onward', 'The clock of the years', 'The dance continued' and 'In five-score summers', stress is laid on the inseparability and equal reality of past, present and future. The spirit of evolution is seen conversely as the link with tradition. But when Hardy sees the present mingling with the future the expression is often rather negative, a voicing of graveyard obsessions dealing with the eventual decomposition of human bodies into their natural elements. Of the many poems on this subject, Finzi set to music 'In five-score summers', 'Transformations' and 'Voices from things growing in a churchyard'. Often there is a note of satire, a ridiculing of conventional notions of progress. It is particularly effective in 'Channel firing', a forceful expression of the sense of time as seen from the grave. Here Hardy manipulates time most subtly: he begins by doubly defying it, in fancifully assuming that man's future continues in the grave, and in paradoxically setting that extension of temporal existence in the past:

> That night your great guns, unawares,
> Shook all our coffins as we lay,
> And broke the chancel window-squares,
> We thought it was the Judgment-day
>
> And sat upright.

The central purpose of the poem is to focus on the present, as described by God:

> 'The world is as it used to be:
> All nations striving strong to make
> Red war yet redder.'

Then we are projected into the future again: Hardy doubts the integrity of God's intention to stop the progression of time, for God continues:

> 'Ha, ha. It will be warmer when
> I blow the trumpet (if indeed
> I ever do; for you are men,
> And rest eternal sorely need).'

Past and future are then neatly linked in one stanza:

> So down we lay again. 'I wonder,
> Will the world ever saner be',
> Said one, 'than when He sent us under
> In our indifferent century!'

But the concept is deliberately whimsical; Hardy shrugs off and diffuses the theme:

> 'Instead of preaching forty year,'
> My neighbour Parson Thirdly said,
> 'I wish I had stuck to pipes and beer.'

– and Finzi is too careful a follower of Hardy to enforce it against the poet's will; so we have to look elsewhere for an earnest expression of the continuity of life and time. We find it in 'In time of "the breaking of nations"':

> Only a man harrowing clods
>   In a slow silent walk
> With an old horse that stumbles and nods
>   Half asleep as they stalk.
>
> Only thin smoke without flame
>   From the heaps of couch-grass;
> Yet this will go onward the same
>   Though Dynasties pass.
>
> Yonder a maid and her wight
>   Come whispering by:
> War's annals will cloud into night
>   Ere their story die.

This, together with the poems comprising the cycle *By Footpath and Stile*, belongs with Finzi's earliest Hardy settings, which are weak and ineffective. For once he had been betrayed into responding to a poem too quickly; had he set it later in life, it might have made one of his more telling songs.

One of the limitations of Finzi's view of art is that it makes no direct demand for originality. There is no striving to grasp the new, the as yet unexpressed. As has been said of Hardy, 'As artist, he prefers an old world, whose accumulated tragedies he can count as part of his own experience' (Barton: 269). This brings us to the question of the extent to which the art of each of them is based on the incorporation of traditional elements into technique. Finzi's technique is in many ways ultra-traditional: his backwash of watery modality, which leaves the early, rather unapproachable *By Footpath and Stile* stranded in stylistic limbo, is never wholly absent, though it is less pervasive and more directional in the mature works written during and after his period of study of 16th-century counterpoint with R. O. Morris in the later 1920s. The conservatism is appropriate enough to Hardy's poetry; it keeps Finzi close to the traditional soil, and this is the background that is needed – though sometimes he makes heavy weather of it, as in 'The market-girl', of which Bax made a preferable setting, full of spontaneity and Irish lilt to fit the long-lined dactylic canter of the poem. When it is diatonic Finzi's idiom seems to derive from Parry, for whom he acknowledged an increasing admiration in later life, and, as with Parry, Bach shows through often more clearly than influences from intervening periods: unmistakably in the two 'arias' from *Dies Natalis* and *Farewell to Arms*, almost to the point of pastiche in the Grand Fantasia for piano, and less obtrusively elsewhere, for instance Ex. 1,

Ex. 1

from 'A young man's exhortation'. He wrote such contrapuntal passages all too easily, often at the price of weak harmony; here the idiom tends towards complacency, which is hardly the mood of the poem. When he really wishes to express indifference, as in 'For Life I had never cared greatly', he does so much more effectively: forgetting the clogged counterpoint he concentrates on a very subtle tune, no less beautiful for being subdued, almost offhand.

The vocal line in 'For Life I had never cared greatly' has something of the contours of a hymn tune – a considerable influence on Finzi's melodic thought, as in 'Carol' from the Five Bagatelles and its vocal equivalent, 'Ditty' in *A Young Man's Exhortation*. However much he disguises the simplicity of his vocal lines by irregularising the phrase-lengths and elasticating the rhythms to the mould of speech-stresses, one is nearly always aware of the fundamental plan of a neatly and simply phrased tune that needs no accompaniment to give it structural balance. This is apparent in Ex. 2, the voice part of the first and second stanzas of 'The sigh' (the melodic pattern is repeated, with speech-rhythm variations, for the third and fourth stanzas while the fifth has a new melodic line). The strong tradition in evidence here is less that of folksong, with its attendant modality, frequent angularity and ever-present implications of either narrative balladry or the dance – though these can be found in Finzi, notably in 'Rollicum-rorum',

Ex. 2

'Budmouth dears' and 'Two lips' – than that of the 18th century. For Finzi this means the simple, tuneful diatonicism not so much of Bach and Handel as of the minor English composers whose orchestral works he collected and edited (he possessed a remarkable library of 18th-century English music, now at the University of St Andrews); for Hardy, whose metric patterns Finzi impeccably mirrors in his melodic structures, it means the rich church music tradition of instrumental psalm and hymn playing into which he was born, both his father and his grandfather having been string players in Stinsford parish church. Certain old tunes were very dear to Hardy: he mentions the 18th-century *Mount Ephraim* in 'The choirmaster's burial' (Britten quotes it verbatim in his touching setting of the poem). In 'After reading Psalms XXXIX, XL, etc.' he creates an evocative piece of macaronic verse which, fittingly and effectively, Finzi sets to music with gentle satire in the manner of an Anglican chant.

When melodic folksong influence is apparent in Finzi, it is of that sort of folksong that is closest to the homeliness of the hymn tune. 'Linden Lea' was Vaughan Williams's response to this type of melody, and it is not surprising that Finzi in turn responds to 'Linden Lea', as did so many of his contemporaries; he borrows from its first line in 'The sigh' and 'Ditty' (see especially the beginnings of the second and fourth stanzas) and from its semi-fugal interludes in 'Rollicum-rorum' and 'Summer schemes'. This quality of homeliness, although Arthur Jacobs links it with the German *volkstümliches Lied* (:158), may suggest a peculiarly English diffidence well suited to Hardy's customary tone of indifference or equanimity in the face of nature's indifference to man, and has the effect of making Finzi's vocal lines quite unforced, natural, and often emotionally low-pitched and conversational; in short, they are the sort of thing which we might expect to make up ourselves were we to try to sing a line of Hardy's poetry, and in this they could hardly be more different from Britten's floral, decorative melodic inventions. They seem to have an inevitable rightness about them; they clinch unforgettably those striking lines of Hardy's where he uses words and phrases which are perfectly familiar to us, but which we do not expect to find in the context of lyrical poetry; the effect is that we are surprised and therefore remember them. (See Ex. 3 for a few characteristic examples.) The rhythmic element is as important a contributory factor as the melodic; many of the lines have prominent feminine endings both in Hardy's poetry and, as a result, in Finzi's music. Again the effect is conversational.

Ex. 3

The purity of Finzi's word-setting has often been remarked upon. In addition to shaping his melodic contours to the rise and fall of the conversing or the reciting voice, he is thorough, probably unconsciously, in his application of the 'for every syllable a note' dictum. Indeed, apart from the early *By Footpath and Stile* songs, where he is slightly (but not much) less strict, there is only one example in all the Hardy songs of a syllable set to two notes, and that, because of the contrast, is too noticeable (it appears at the phrase 'uncloaked a star' in 'For Life I had never cared greatly'); the only other contender for melismatic status is the grace-note on the word 'pouncing' in 'Rollicum-rorum'. At the very least his mastery of word-setting guarantees him an assurance in tackling Hardy's idiosyncratic, rough-grained poetic conceits and keeping them intact which not even Britten matches – for in *Winter Words*, with the exception of the final song, 'Before life and after', the poems are chosen for their colour rather than their intellectual content. But Finzi's integrity has its dangers. One is that the vocal line can become a mere functional code, an unemotional slow recitative. Marion

Scott, reviewing the Grotrian Hall performance of *A Young Man's Exhortation* on 5 December 1933, gave the matter some thought:

> It is curious to see how the musician has reacted to the slightly non-lyric touch that checks the singing quality in so many of Hardy's poems. Mr Finzi reflects this non-lyricism by vocal lines and verbal rhythms that deviate from melody towards prosody. The process is very subtle and, at times, successful; but one wonders whether in some instances he would not have been justified in overriding Hardy with pure singing tunes that would have expressed the poems without too much deference to the spoken word values (*Musical Times* LXXV, 1934: 74).

This is a just criticism of the cycle, but the question becomes less pressing in his later works, which are more lyrical and uninhibited and, partly on account of the poetry he chooses, comparatively direct in their impact.

Yet Finzi's faithfulness to the element of acquiescent indifference in Hardy, particularly evident in his undemonstrative word-setting, does lay him open to the criticism of understatement and insipidity. His fondness for mediant and submediant chords, especially in first inversions, and his almost total avoidance of fully harmonised modulations to the dominant and subdominant, constitute symbolic harmonic renunciations which can become tedious, and certainly do in *A Young Man's Exhortation*. But in the finest songs this neutrality is used as a backcloth for the projection of a graded, positive emotional response, and it is significant that in both 'Ditty' and 'For Life I had never cared greatly' Finzi has chosen poems in which this can be achieved by a fine climax towards the last line that tilts the balance of indifference well over on to the positive side. The point about Hardy's 'For Life I had never cared greatly' is that the gradual attainment of a sense of commitment to life brings the poet not liberation but the need for careful emotional discipline; the last two lines, though admitting a vision of fulfilment, are almost grim:

> And thus re-illumed have no humour for letting
>   My pilgrimage fail.

Finzi's carefully restrained setting, one of his best, in the subdued middle range of both the piano and the baritone voice, captures the mood of control splendidly; the song never modulates, there being only one accidental, a flat 7th in the penultimate bar, but it unpretentiously explores the gentle nuances of feeling to be gleaned from a confined, diatonic D major. At the climax he uses one of his favourite chords, a cleanly ecstatic 9–8 + 4–3 appoggiatura above a supertonic bass. A similar figuration appears in the moving *pianissimo* ending of 'In years defaced', at the cycle's eponymous phrase, 'till Earth outwears' (Ex. 4).

Songs of this sort account only for a minority of Finzi's output. In most of his Hardy settings he employs an altogether more forceful mode of expression, or rather one in which more forceful expressive cells are superimposed on his basic language. The more intense aspects of his harmonic language are considerably indebted to his contemporary William Walton, and the influence of *Belshazzar's Feast* is evident in many of the songs after 1931. The dolorous, nostalgic introduction of 'In years defaced', written in April 1936, has a particularly Babylonian poignancy (Ex. 5). Equally redolent of Walton is Finzi's obsessive emphasis of tonic and dominant scale-degrees, often with the insistence of an

Ex. 4

Ex. 5

inverted pedal point and even, in the absence of complete harmony, making the scale-degree represent the dominant or tonic chord. Dominant and tonic are never confused or amalgamated, as in Britten; as in Walton, they retain their mutually balancing, traditional polar function. The function is obsessive in that it is often pared to the bare bones and focussed by appoggiaturas, particularly the strong semitonal 6–5 (Ex. 6 (a)–(c)). This formula, which in Ex. 6 (a) clearly derives from *Belshazzar's Feast* (Ex. 7) – though perhaps Walton himself took it from *The Dream of Gerontius* (Ex. 8) – is essentially instrumental, usually heightened by the simultaneous clash of the semitonal appoggiatura and its resolution; but it also gives rise to characteristic vocal phrases of emotional emphasis, as in 'I said to Love', where there is a neurotic outburst with both 6–5 (accompaniment) and 2–1 (voice part) semitonal appoggiaturas above an inverted dominant root C (Ex. 9). When the phrase *x* in Ex. 9 comes in the major, as in examples already given (see above, Ex. 4), the effect is one of controlled ecstasy.

These examples should suffice to show how apt this obsessive formula is in conjunction with Hardy's more dark-toned or rebellious comments. Hardy's formulae are equally insistent, though in his case they are elements not of language or vocabulary but of subject-matter: the mystery of the grave, the poignant crystallisation of specific memories of love, the futility of all aspiration in the face of chance. Whatever Hardy and Finzi do not have in common, they do

Ex. 6

(a) ('Ode on the rejection of St Cecilia')

(b) ('Channel firing')

(c) ('Life laughs onward')

Ex. 7

in their best moments share a clear-eyed and purposeful intensity which cannot but sustain the reader or listener. The vision is degraded only when Finzi substitutes thick harmony for spare tonic and dominant functions, which is seldom; when he does, he sounds mawkish and Hardy platitudinous (Ex. 10, from 'In five-score summers').

Ex. 8

Ex. 9

Ex. 10

The architectural basis of Finzi's Hardy settings is difficult to define, for Hardy very seldom uses the same metrical pattern twice and Finzi rarely duplicates a form. The longer songs tend to avoid sectional repetition and become *arioso* scenes whose sections are differentiated by varying rates of movement and figuration, with or without motivic cross-reference between them. 'Childhood among the ferns' is of this sort, as is 'Channel firing', but that has ritornello elements in the severe ostinato which represents the guns and closes the song as it had opened it. 'The clock of the years' involves hardly any thematic repetition. In such cases one may even feel stronger motivic links between the songs than within them, as though Finzi the craftsman works with a store of characteristically patterned musical fabrics that he cuts and sews into durable patchwork garments. Straightforward strophic form is most uncommon, apart from the satirical 'Rollicum-rorum' and 'Budmouth dears'; he normally prefers to group stanzas into some other perceptible pattern. In 'The sigh' and 'For Life I had never cared greatly' it is ABABC. In 'Ditty' each stanza has phrases which appear in the others, but there is no wholesale strophic repetition. 'Summer schemes' is essentially strophic, but the middle lines of the two stanzas are completely different. Most of the short two-stanza poems which he sets are composed to sound like a single musical paragraph with a caesura in the middle. 'It never looks like summer' is the simplest and most effective example of this type; others are 'Two lips' and 'Waiting both'.

Finzi's sense of identity with Hardy was such that, when he read a poem through, certain lines would irresistibly call up music from him. In this way he collected scraps of songs, rather like Elgar with his themes, and put them aside, having to work hard and slowly to complete them. A gratifying number of early fragments were completed in his final, comparatively prolific year, including one which he had forgotten about, as Joy recorded in her journal in February 1956:

> On reading 'It never looks like summer here' [Gerald] instantly set it. A little one but beautiful . . . Later this evening: 'It's extraordinary how the mind works – quite extraordinary.' On looking through old musical notes he came on a page with sketches for the first line of 'It never looks like summer here'. When this first line sprang instantaneously to music on reading it this afternoon, it was quite unknown to him that he had previously worked at it over 25 years ago. The line written today had the same shape and fall as the previous germ and was obviously the completed idea after 20 odd years. 'If one doesn't live long enough one can't complete the hundreds of musical lines waiting final shape.'

He also left a number of unfinished Hardy workings, ranging from 'The end of the episode', a two-bar fragment, to 'My spirit will not haunt the mound' and 'The temporary the all', both sketched in full. Nearly all these remnants are beyond completion, and with many of them only isolated lines of text were set. In several instances the text of the poem, taken either from newspaper and periodical cuttings or written out by Finzi, has survived pinned to the sketch of the music; Finzi's method was to cross out lines of text as he set them. He did not necessarily start with the first line, but with any phrase that suggested music. It is easy to see how the opening of 'June leaves and autumn' must spontaneously have inspired the answering musical lyricism (Ex. 11 – he got no further with this poem), and how his imagination was caught by the conversational rhythms of

Ex. 11

Lush   sum-mer lit the trees   to   green; ____ But__ in the ditch hard by

Ex. 12

Then, to a-bate   the mi-se-ry Of ab-sent-ness, you gave   it   me.

lines 7–8 of 'On a discovered curl of hair' (Ex. 12), which, together with the first two lines, two more (9–10), and line 13, set as a musical recapitulation of line 1, are all that he sketched. Often, as here, he crossed out matching lines of text, sometimes, as in his sketch of 'Great things', in all the stanzas of a poem, indicating that they were to be sung to the same or similar music. Frequently, as in the 'June leaves' fragment (Ex. 11), he thought of an interesting initial idea but was unable to extend it. It is a pity that Ex. 13 is all that exists of the setting of Hardy's celebrated poem 'Afterwards'. He seems only rarely to have revised his first thoughts in these incomplete sketches, for as a rule they came to him definitively, as sudden inspirations; an exception is 'Weathers', for which he made three sketches of the first half of the first stanza.

Of the two complete workings mentioned above, 'The temporary the all' was composed in 1927, but Finzi was unhappy with it, and twice attempted revisions. Both revised sketches peter out; they do not connect with the rest of the original and are stylistically disparate. Howard Ferguson rightly decided not to publish the 1927 version posthumously, since Finzi regarded it as unsatisfactory. 'My spirit will not haunt the mound', the other complete sketch, is similarly unpublishable, for apart from being an indifferent song the music is written out in two sections without a convincing join. It was to have formed the last song of his op. 11, projected in 1921 as a cycle of Hardy songs for voice and string quartet to be called *The Mound*, but only this poem, 'The subalterns' and 'The night of the dance' were sketched. Finzi did, however, leave a list of the songs he envisaged in the cycle:

> The darkling thrush
> The self-unseeing
> Postponement
> The night of the dance
> In a wood
> The subalterns
> My spirit will not haunt the mound

Ex. 13

'The self-unseeing' was finally incorporated into *Before and After Summer*, though it is doubtful whether it was actually composed as early as 1921. The opus number was eventually filled by the Romance for strings.

By Footpath and Stile, op. 2, composed in 1921–2 and published by Curwen at the composer's expense in 1925, is another essay in the medium of voice and string quartet. The whole cycle is curiously unsuccessful, and Finzi withdrew it from Curwen's catalogue in 1934 and had the stock and plates destroyed; in his own catalogue of works he aptly labels it a 'premature publication' and offers the following comments:

> A revised edition, possibly excluding some of the songs and including other new ones, has always been at the back of my mind. But until this is done, only those songs given below have been revised, or belong to the cycle. Whatever there is, should be published in score and parts (not Pf score). A miniature score should be quite enough. The original withdrawn edition should be utterly forgotten.
> 1. By footpath and stile
> 3. The oxen
> (1941, 1951: 7)

Finzi's self-criticism was always stringent, but in fact the revised versions of the first and third songs, dated 1941, do not differ radically from the originals, and still show their limitations. Those limitations are inherent in the over-disciplined style of his early period, which seldom goes beyond a repressive modality with little capacity to express the immediate emotion required by the poems. Finzi's approach to his medium here is only potentially impressive: he exploits it to the extent of building up tone pictures independent of the words in several of the songs, but he does not handle his material compellingly. In the final song of the six, 'Exeunt omnes', he recalls the themes of previous songs so that the characters whom they represent, now dead, may take their bows, but the themes themselves' are not memorable or charged with emotion.

The one other Hardy setting from Finzi's earliest period is 'Only a man harrowing clods' ('In time of "the breaking of nations"'), for baritone and small orchestra, composed in 1923 and not published. It subsequently became the third movement of the four-movement *Requiem da Camera* (1924) for choir, four soloists and chamber orchestra written in memory of Finzi's first composition teacher, Ernest Farrar. The most notable passage is the instrumental introduction, which also appears in the prelude to the *Requiem*, and in which Finzi's characteristic march of time is present as a throbbing bass (Ex. 14), but, as has already been said (above, p. 279), the song as a whole is uncommunicative.

Ex. 14

Finzi did not wish the three major song sets to be regarded as cycles, though it is not clear whether he would have made a mental exception of *A Young Man's Exhortation*, with its balancing halves and their mottos. He claimed that in grouping the songs together for publication he was merely lessening the chances of a single song's being overlooked. Certainly it increases the likelihood of performance. It also means that a weak song can survive protected by its neighbours – a dubious benefit with one or two in *A Young Man's Exhortation*, which is by far the least compelling of the three mature sets. In *Earth and Air and Rain* and *Before and After Summer*, however, the songs are of such uniform excellence that the question does not arise. But in disclaiming the status of cycles for the song sets Finzi was being unduly modest. Admittedly there are no stories running through them, and the principle of variety is more important than unity, but there is at least good evidence of their having been built up with extreme care. Only in *A Young Man's Exhortation*, however, is there an explicit theme. Rubbra, writing in 1929, stressed its unifying function:

> In the years 1926–1928 a song-cycle for tenor and piano was completed. It consists of fifteen settings of poems by Thomas Hardy. It is divided into two parts, the first dealing with various moods of youth and love, and the second with philosophical retrospect, under the shadow of age. The cycle is not to be considered as a series of separate songs but as a unity; and unity has been achieved, in spite of the diverse character of the settings (:194).

By the time of publication in 1933 the cycle had lost five of its 15 songs. These five may be among the ten incomplete manuscript sketches surviving from the 1920s; certainly the theme of 'The temporary the all' fits the cycle as described by

Rubbra. But it is more likely to have included some of the songs which were eventually published in the two posthumous sets, of which 'The market-girl' (1927), 'Two lips' (1928), 'At a lunar eclipse' (1929) and 'I say I'll seek her' (1929) are known to date from this period. 'Two lips', however, is more comfortable for a low voice, and 'At a lunar eclipse' does not really fit Rubbra's scheme, which to a certain extent still survives in the published form of two parts with five songs each, the first part headed 'Mane floreat, et transeat. Ps. 89' ('In the morning it flourisheth, and groweth up') and the second 'Vespere decidat, induret, et arescat. Ps. 89' ('In the evening it is cut down, and withereth') (= Psalm 90 verse 6 in the King James translation).

The least satisfactory aspect of the cycle is its tonal scheme. Six of the ten songs end with a different tonal centre from that of their opening; the effect is not convincing, and although one would not normally look for conscious tonal links between one song and the next in a Finzi set, the very conspicuousness of the tonal progressions within these songs, more outlandish than the unobtrusive examples in his later sets, makes one wonder whether there was not originally some overall tonal scheme which was destroyed when the cycle was reduced from 15 to 10 songs. It is more likely, however, that Finzi, whose sense of tonal cohesion was never strong, simply did not notice the weakness.

The highest tribute a song-writer can pay Hardy is not to emphasise one of his preoccupations – pessimistic philosophy, lost love, death and graveyards, the blind indifference of nature, the inexorable continuity of life, the joys of un-inhibited living or any other of his recurrent themes – but to represent the great range of his poetic conceits as broadly as possible by juxtaposing contrasted and conflicting ideas and letting the resulting antinomial structure (Hynes: 44; Marsden: 106–7) speak for itself, as it does within even the tiniest space in the individual poems. This is what Finzi achieves in *Earth and Air and Rain* and *Before and After Summer*. the first of these cycles, op. 15, for baritone and piano, was published in 1936. It looks as though 'Let me enjoy the earth' and 'I need not go' were originally also intended for the set, for they are marked in the autograph manuscripts as forming part of op. 15, but the cycle as published consists, like *A Young Man's Exhortation* and *Before and After Summer*, of ten beautifully contrasted songs. It begins and ends ambivalently. The first song, 'Summer schemes', conjures up a miraculous degree of lyrical warmth in the five bars of piano introduction, but soon reiterates the antithetical refrain

> ' – We'll go,' I sing; but who shall say
> What may not chance before that day!

Nevertheless, it is a happy song, beginning and ending in a sunny D major. The final song of the set, however, 'Proud songsters', has to bear the weight of all the shades of feeling that have passed in between, and, as it comes shortly after the grisly 'The clock of the years', that weight is considerable. It begins in the opening song's relative minor, B minor, and has a very long, deeply affective in-troduction whose yearning appoggiaturas over a syncopated pulse (recalling the cycle's centrepiece, 'The phantom') and somewhat enigmatic, inarticulately straining crotchet motives help us to realise how many contrasting moods and experiences have been projected in the cycle since the blithe expectation of 'Summer schemes'. Gradually, however, as the voice enters, the ceaseless syncopes in the accompaniment gather a more optimistic harmonic momentum: the endless cycle of life is beginning again and will continue. This thought is expressed in the final stanza, where we find ourselves back in D major:

> These are brand-new birds of twelve-months' growing,
> Which a year ago, or less than twain,
> No finches were, nor nightingales,
>   Nor thrushes,
> But only particles of grain,
>   And earth, and air, and rain.

Yet here, as so often, Hardy ends with an unresolved antithesis, and in those two last lines is expressed all the yearning of earth's perennial sorrow, as in *Das Lied von der Erde*. Within his own far smaller scope Finzi is trying to squeeze the same inexpressible longing, both pain and pleasure, out of music as Mahler (Ex. 15), and until the last chord we do not know whether the cycle will end in D major or B minor.

Ex. 15

The eighth song of the set, 'The clock of the years', is by far the largest in scope and the most powerful. It is a perfect foil to its predecessor, 'To Lizbie Browne', a prismatic miniature of an enshrined memory, for it exposes the consequences of trying to tamper with memory. It is spine-chilling, and Finzi's language is here at its most resourceful, yet it is not the sort of song with which he could have ended the cycle, for it has no philosophical depth, and is a fanciful, somewhat Gothick speculation. The almost light-hearted 'In a churchyard', with its quiet acceptance of the peace of the grave, is needed to mediate between 'The clock of the years' and 'Proud songsters'. It does so by preparing most sensitively the D major/B minor ambit as the poet reaches his attitude of atheistic acquiescence in the final stanza:

> '"Now set among the wise,"
> They say: "Enlarged in scope,
> That no God trumpet us to rise
>   We truly hope."'
>
> I listened to his strange tale
> In the mood that stillness brings,
> And I grew to accept as the day wore pale
>   That view of things.

Of the central five songs of the set, 'Rollicum-rorum', in defiance of Napoleon, originally published in *The Trumpet-Major* (1880), provides jaunty humour and light relief, especially in its refrain; it complements 'When I set out for Lyonnesse', a more subtle but no less immediately attractive ballad. 'To Lizbie Browne', in which the remembered girl is vividly described and repeatedly named, is offset by the fourth song, 'The phantom', which takes a more desolate, impersonal look at an anonymous memory, the 'ghost-girl-rider'. Yet through this distancing technique in the latter poem Hardy is in fact giving us a revealing portrait of himself, and his imperishable memory, pinpointed by Finzi's throbbing harmonies, forms the emotional core of the whole cycle:

> Not only there
> Does he see this sight,
> But everywhere
> In his brain – day, night,
> As if on the air
> It was drawn rose-bright –
> Yea, far from that shore
> Does he carry this vision of heretofore:

The theme is the converse of that of 'The clock of the years':

> . . . And though, toil-tried
> He withers daily,
> Time touches her not,
> But she still rides gaily
> In his rapt thought . . .

and the song is one of Finzi's finest.

The broad $\frac{6}{8}$ swing of 'The phantom' is followed by the satirical pastiche of an Anglican chant already mentioned; its theme of non-achievement finds a strongly contrasted expression in the remaining song, 'Waiting both', which comes third, an exquisite miniature whose tiny power makes one realise why Finzi was so anxious that such a song should not get lost or overlooked by standing on its own. The bleak, wandering counterpoint of the opening, suggestive of Holst, depicts the star's isolation, but then it looks down at the poet with hopeless sympathy expressed in a chain of quaver groups (Ex. 16) – evidently symbolic for Finzi, for he uses it again at the lines 'I send my soul through time and space / To greet you' in 'To a poet a thousand years hence'. Harmony gradually emerges with this beginning of a personal relationship, but between the verses the star is still only watching unwaveringly, with the quaver motive again in the piano. The star's question provokes from the poet an answer which in Finzi's setting shows frustra-

Ex. 16

tion, even irascibility or despair, as he acknowledges his inactivity in the face of time. But the star is unable to help: it is in the same predicament, and the counter-point of isolation returns. The quaver motive, with its absence of harmonic pro-gression, ends the song. There is no communication; still the star is watching. This is a theme similar to that of 'The comet at Yell'ham', in which the same musical techniques are employed, but less impressively.

Before and After Summer is larger in scope than *Earth and Air and Rain*. It begins in happier innocence and ends in disillusioned nihilism. Its opening and closing songs, 'Childhood among the ferns' and 'He abjures love', and the massive central 'Channel firing' (for comments on this see above, pp. 278–9), are large-scale, multi-sectional creations of great breadth. 'Childhood among the ferns' begins with a Finzi *Ur*-motive later used to represent the sun when it first appears (Ex. 17). It gives way to the equally happy sprinkling and trickling of

Ex. 17

raindrops, represented by one of Finzi's most felicitous and uninhibited accom-paniments with constant motoric movement. Yet the inevitable antithesis comes in the poem's final lines:

> I said: 'I could live on here thus till death';
>
> And queried in the green rays as I sate:
> 'Why should I have to grow to man's estate,
> And this afar-noised World perambulate?'

and by the end of the song all sense of spontaneous movement has evaporated, leaving the last word to an insistent questing dominant adumbration in the bass which produces an unsatisfying 6-4 chord (Ex. 18). The second song, from which the cycle takes its title, complements this by bewailing the passing not of child-hood and innocence but of the youthful seasons, spring and summer. Again a

Ex. 18

spontaneous quick accompanimental figuration, representing February winds and sleet, relapses into laboured movement, a typical plodding time-procession at the line 'Shadows of the October pine', but reasserts itself at the end, devoid of its joyous momentum. Already weariness has set in; joy has passed without ever being apprehended:

> For those happy suns are past,
> Fore-discerned in winter last.
> When went by their pleasure, then?
> I, alas, perceived not when.

The third song, 'The self-unseeing', begins like 'Der Doppelgänger', with ghostly and angular chord progressions depicting the disquieting search for one's own past and for its significance. This chromatic opening makes a welcome contrast to the simplistic diatonics of the first two songs (Ex. 19). Already in bar 6,

Ex. 19

however, the wandering tonality has resolved on to the inevitable dominant (heard, that is, as a dominant in G minor), with the e flat of an unresolved 2–1 appoggiatura sounding simultaneously. The obsession, in this case a vivid memory of the poet's childhood as he returns to his old home, is asserting itself. As the song progresses the memory becomes more and more sharp and animated, yet it finally collapses at the last-line antithesis, 'Yet we were looking away' – implying the paradox that the 'blessings' of the family scene were not consciously observed at the time, though imprinted on the memory long afterwards. This unresolved antithesis, the mystery of memory, is reflected in the music: after a brief reappearance of the tonally wandering introduction, the obsessive dominant returns, as a staccato bass crotchet E′ reiterated four times, but the tense 2–1 semitonal clash above it, an f, is left hanging for five bars and does not resolve: it avoids the logical e and drops finally to c.

In the next song, 'Overlooking the river', the antithesis is the opposite, namely that, after presenting exquisite memory pictures of the view of the river, the poet regrets that he was *not* looking away:

> And never I turned my head, alack,
>> While these things met my gaze
>> Through the pane's drop-drenched glaze,
> To see the more behind my back . . .
> O never I turned, but let, alack,
>> These less things hold my gaze!

What was the 'more behind my back'? It suggests a human figure, a love, hovering in the shadows, but we are not to know, and the music gives us no clue. It merely relaxes from its intense, *innig* semiquaver pattern-weaving and drifts anonymously to an insubstantial close on the chord of the supertonic.

In the cycle's centrepiece, 'Channel firing', as has already been shown, larger issues of time and destiny are at stake. One central motive which emerges is the recklessness of mankind:

> ' . . . Mad as hatters
> They do no more for Christés sake
> Than you who are helpless in such matters.'

It is perhaps deliberate that the musical figuration of these lines, impetuous dotted quavers and semiquavers in the piano right hand with the remaining semiquaver beats filled in by the left, returns in the last song of the cycle as a motivic pattern representing evil, where love, already accompanied by the motive in the first stanza, is seen as a destructive encumbrance, likewise productive of recklessness:

> Too many times ablaze
>   With fatuous fires,
> Enkindled by his wiles
>   To new embraces,
> Did I, by wilful ways
>   And baseless ires,
> Return the anxious smiles
>   Of friendly faces.

'Channel firing' is followed by 'In the mind's eye', a delightful, approachable song whose coruscating tonalities at the line 'Change dissolves the landscapes' provide welcome colourful relief from the rather excessive tonic and dominant hammerings of 'Channel firing'. The seventh song, 'The too short time', is this set's equivalent of 'Waiting both' and 'The comet at Yell'ham', in which objects of nature, here falling leaves, are depicted pictorially and then gradually merge with human consciousness, or in this case the dramatised consciousness of the leaf itself. The close of the final song is unobtrusively foreshadowed by the lines 'And night-time calls, / And the curtain falls!', but the immediate effect of the song is to reassert the theme of the continuity of the seasons, which has been lost sight of since the first two songs:

> Sunlight goes on shining
> As if no frost were here,
> Blackbirds seem designing
> Where to build next year;

This is accompanied by a flowing semiquaver figuration recalling 'Childhood among the ferns'. More light relief follows in the dance-like 'Epeisodia', in whose final section the 'rest eternal' so poignantly invoked in 'Channel firing' is presented with calm and happy acceptance, though perhaps not without a gentle pang on the penultimate chord, E flat major resolving to G major.

The last two songs must be taken as a pair; they express two different grounds for a pessimistic attitude to love. 'Amabel' registers the realisation that love is doomed not so much to deliberate cessation as to visible decay brought about by time, the 'tyrant fell'. Although this is dramatised as egocentric outrage there is also an unanswerable despair, pinpointed in the music by pathos brought about with fragmentary vestiges of traditional harmonic usage which keep stabbing through a characteristically indifferent wash of diatonic E flat: a hint of a modulation, via the dominant chord, to F minor at bar 17, heralded by a rare lyrical flat 7th on the word 'warmth'; another sharpward move to a momentary D minor chord at bar 30; finally another flat 7th in the penultimate bar. But all these are only fragments, and it is the sense of ruin which prevails. The heartless answer to this, already framed in the last stanza of 'Amabel', is again announced in the stormy opening of the final song, which follows: 'At last I put off love . . .'. The renunciation brings a tremendous sense of relief, mingling with the poet's remembrance of how he felt before ever he fell in love:

> I was as children be
> > Who have no care;
> I did not shrink or sigh,
> > I did not sicken;

but the music is bleak and fatalistic, for nothing follows love, just death and oblivion: 'the Curtain'. In this light the ending of 'Amabel' takes on ironic overtones:

> ' "Till the Last Trump, farewell,
> > O Amabel!" '

For there is no Last Trump; God has already been heard denying its probability in 'Channel firing'. Cycles these song sets may not be, musically speaking, but the thrust and counter-thrust of such ideas presented in succession builds them into powerful exegeses of Hardy's fatalistic thought.

At his death Finzi left 14 completed Hardy songs, several of them finished in a remarkable burst of song-writing in his final year, under the shadow of time running out. He had in mind at least two more Hardy sets, perhaps hoping that each would grow to ten songs like the earlier ones, but he did not complete them or specify how the songs should be put in order. Editing the posthumous material, Joy, his son Christopher and his friend and colleague Howard Ferguson wisely and sensitively grouped the songs into a set of six for low voice (*I Said to Love*) and a set of seven for high voice (*Till Earth Outwears*). The one left over, the impressive 'I say "I'll seek her " ' of 1929, constitutes the first of *Oh Fair to See*, a set to words by various authors. It is the earliest of the datable songs in which Finzi's stylistic resources are exploited to the full; the poem gains a disturbing immediacy in the setting, which rather overbalances the other songs in this set.

Till Earth Outwears is framed by two even-tempered songs. 'Let me enjoy the earth', with its codified attitude to nature, is appropriately placed first:

> Let me enjoy the earth no less
> Because the all-enacting Might
> That fashioned forth its loveliness
> Had other aims than my delight.

The set ends on a delightful note of affirmation with 'Life laughs onward', 'the first song he has written for some time . . . a good sign and one which so often happens when he is wrestling with urgent other work', Joy commented in her journal (17–18 March 1955); it marked the beginning of Finzi's final burst of song composition. Between these two complementary songs, which show Hardy nearer to a resolved view of the universe than in Finzi's earlier song sets, come three slight and two major songs. Of the latter, one is 'In years defaced', where Finzi's technique is at its most expressive and most typical; the other, 'At a lunar eclipse', is this set's equivalent of 'The comet at Yell'ham', 'Waiting both', 'At middle-field gate in February' and 'The too short time' in that it shows Hardy puzzling over the contrast or incongruity between an image of nature and a human form. The problem is stated more explicitly here than elsewhere:

> How shall I link such suncast symmetry
> With the torn troubled form I know as thine [?]

but there is no synthesis or resolution, not even a progression from the inhuman to the human. Consequently Finzi's heavy, chordal writing representing earth's shadow, reminiscent of the sombre shades of Holst's *Egdon Heath* (composed two years earlier), dominates the entire unbarred song, an effect which, though sincere and chilling, clogs very soon, although it enables the most striking verbal phrase in the poem, 'Nation at war with nation', to sink in with a most effective primeval weariness.

In *I Said to Love* the finest songs are 'For Life I had never cared greatly', discussed above (pp. 280–2), and the other undated song, 'I need not go', which opens the set. Of the others, 'Two lips' is as pure and simple as a Housman setting, and as effective, whereas 'In five-score summers', as already stated, is somewhat mawkish. Finzi was apparently not altogether happy with this poem as a song text, for Joy wrote in her journal on 16 January 1956: 'Towards end of week suddenly added to a Hardy baritone song "In five-score summers". G feels it alright as an extract from a diary but the words make it unsuitable for public performance. One verse had been written some time ago.' 'At middle-field gate in February' is a powerful song, one of those five or six in which Finzi ranges beyond the habitual confines of his musical vocabulary for some special effect. In this instance he dons Holst's Saturnine mantle for an evocative picture of wintry numbness (Ex. 20) that finally thaws into a nostalgic memory picture enshrined in his favourite *Ur*-motive, which begins the last section and closes the song (Ex. 21). The vocal tessitura drops for this final reflective section; lugubrious sentiments tended to suggest the baritone voice to Finzi, and in this instance

Ex. 20

Ex. 21

dictated a change of intention; Joy noted this on 21 February 1956: 'G finished another song – an old draft with one verse written: "At middle-field gate in February". Hoping it was going to be a tenor song it turned, in the final making, into an inevitable baritone.' The last song in the set is 'I said to Love'. Finzi interprets this as a strong, violent poem, an attempt to sweep love, the source of so many of the poet's inspirations and frustrations alike, from the board once and for all, with a far-flung gesture which will shock us. This interpretation is perhaps too histrionic: he gives the impression that the poet and love argue to the point of blind rage, acting like spoilt children, vindictively. This rather undermines our acceptance of the Olympian dimension that he sees in the poem, yet there is something apocalyptic and genuinely spine-chilling about the fiendish '*quasi cadenza*' double-octave piano passage, quite unlike anything else Finzi wrote, and although the outburst is soon over the music remains unprecedentedly intense and violent until the last lines:

> '*Mankind shall cease.* – So let it be,'
>   I said to Love.

Finzi finished the song on 12 July 1956, and two days later Joy coolly noted in her journal: 'G's 55th birthday. G went through the new five Hardy songs etc., which he has written at various times during the last few months. "I said to Love" he has just finished. More violent than some of the recent ones.' It was his last Hardy song; he died ten weeks later.

Standing off from some of Finzi's greatest songs, such as 'The phantom', 'Proud Songsters', 'He abjures love' or 'I said to Love', one perceives in them an un-canny sense of the eschatological. The poet's preoccupation with love and its ultimate cessation and the composer's assimilation of the old, dry, unadorned bare bones of three or four centuries of dominant-based western tonality are fused together in lyrical statements about love and death, time, tradition and destiny. Bearing the weight of the Romantic experience in this musical language as Hardy does in the philosophy, Finzi stands at the end of a lyrical tradition, a tradition stretching back beyond Schubert to figures such as Lawes and Pelham Humfrey. While Britten was still to build on parts of that tradition, there were vital aspects of its codification of deep, timeless emotions through the expressiveness of tonality that Finzi was perhaps the last composer fully to understand. (Ex. 22).

Ex. 22

XIV

The uses and abuses of technique

The preceding chapters have shown how a number of British composers between the wars managed to communicate personal styles and preoccupations without rejecting the Romantic tradition of the solo song – the *Lied*, in effect – and its expressive musical language. Others were less successful. Numerous young musicians in the period 1910–30 drew on the alluring harmonic legacy of Delius and his English followers and responded to the cosy sentiments of the lyrical verse still flooding off the presses in anthologies and pocket 'treasuries' – for even during the first world war it was possible to imbibe a good deal of this poetry at relatively little cost or effort. Some felt that they had something to say; others, knowing that they did not, made the most of their technical confidence and kept the market supplied with material for competitive festivals, singing lessons, broadcast recitals and the occasional *soirée*. Of the first group, the case of Charles Wilfred Orr will be examined here; of the second, Michael Head will be taken as probably the best-known representative; van Dieren, the third subject of this chapter, fits into neither group.

With Orr there is an element of 'unjust neglect' (the phrase should switch on a red warning light in the critic's mind) which caused growing embitterment in the composer:

> I can assure you that apart from two, or at the most three, I have never found any English singer manifest the slightest interest in my song efforts, and as to the BBC – until the last 18 months my average broadcasts have amounted to one every $2\frac{1}{2}$–3 years. About two years ago the BBC gave a series of twelve recitals of British Song; about 21 composers were represented, but yours truly was NOT among them. Last summer there were six recitals of songs by British composers, with a special feature of settings of Housman at each recital, but again poor C.W.O. was completely ignored. I gather that there is a faint chance (thanks to the efforts made on my behalf by a few friends) of a broadcast of some of the Housman songs coming off some time in the future, but I shall believe this when I see the announcement in the Radio Times – not before (1974–5).

A month before his death in 1976 Orr wrote similarly to Eric Sams: 'at 82 one must be prepared for death in the fairly near future, but what does get me down is the terrible disappointment of never having, and never being likely to have any recognition outside a very small circle, as a song-writer' (1961–76).

Part of Orr's problem was his isolation from the society of fellow composers. He suffered from acute eczema until middle age, and his musical studies were

301

sparse and retarded. An ill-health discharge from the Coldstream Guards in 1916 (Palmer, 1973: 690) was followed by a period of study with Orlando Morgan and a few private lessons with Edward Dent. Friendship with Warlock developed; Orr first met him whilst accompanying Beatrice and May Harrison in rehearsals of Delius's new Double Concerto, apparently in 1918 (Orr, 1961–76; Palmer, 1976: 174). Warlock arranged for Chester's to publish his first six songs (Orr, 1961–76; Copley, 1968: 12), and led him to the fringe of the Café Royal circle (see below, Appendix I). However, he stayed on the fringe and, for the sake of his health, in 1930 (Orr, 1974) he left London with his wife and resettled in his native Cotswolds in the village of Painswick, his home for the rest of his life. Deafness prevented composition from the late 1950s onwards.

This sort of career lacked self-advertisement, yet others with similarly uneventful lives, notably Finzi, grew to much larger stature and repute. In the end Orr's limitations stemmed from the same sources as his strengths, namely three overriding influences: Delius, Wolf and Housman.

Wolf he claimed as his greatest influence; Sydney Northcote wrote in 1937 that 'it is his fervent wish that he may leave "only one setting [of Housman] of which Wolf would not be ashamed"' (:355). At times the spirit of Wolf seems close enough. It is manifested in a harmonic and textural intensity which takes in the voice part instead of establishing a mass of material against it. This need for the voice to work together with the piano part for an essential homogeneity may be one of the reasons why singers have felt so little drawn to Orr's songs, although his voice parts are in no sense badly written. But Wolf's balance of elements is lacking.

Housman was more than an influence, he was an obsession:

> My first acquaintance with him came, like I dare say so many other people's did, through Graham Peel's 'In summertime on Bredon' . . . I still have the pocket edition of *A Shropshire Lad* which came out in 1914, and which I carried about with me everywhere, learning almost all of the poems by heart, and hoping against hope that one day I might be able to set some of them in a way that Wolf or Schubert might have approved. (The vanity and ignorance of youth!) (Orr, 1961–76)

Unfortunately Housman seems too often to put him in a morbid frame of mind which sinks the blithely ironic rhythmic impetus of the poetry in a glutinous sea of soulful harmony. An exception is one of his most successful songs, 'Oh see how thick the goldcup flowers', an extended essay in his style at its most typical, but with the siciliana rhythms generating enough dance-like energy to stand up against the chromatic harmony in aptly ironic opposition. Also successful is the composer's own favourite, 'The lads in their hundreds', where the poetic metre never fails to inspire music that floats upon it; but then this is true of most settings of this poem.

As for Delius, Orr first met him when he (Delius) was in London staying in Henry Wood's house; this was probably in 1918. Having followed him into Lyons' Corner House after a concert Orr, with temerity, went up to him and announced that he had made piano arrangements of works by Delius that he especially admired; surprisingly, he was well received, and became a friend (Orr, 1974; for another account see Orr, 1976: 57). The influence is not so much

Delius's harmony itself, which was so personal that no one else quite succeeded in making it their own, as the idea of harmony as an autonomous element of expression to which melody, rhythm, counterpoint and textural variety can take subsidiary places. The result is a serious loss of speed and energy in Orr's Housman settings, for he never uses declamatory methods in his vocal writing. There are further problems. Denis Browne's polemic against harmonic monomania (see above, pp. 106–7) remained directly relevant to the inter-war generation, and Orr's Housman settings are among the most obvious examples of harmony's victims. Sometimes, as with the Scottish-style melody of 'Farewell to barn and stack and tree' that so impressed Bax (Palmer, 1973: 692 and 1976: 177), to whom the song was (later?) dedicated, a broad, strong melody is in danger of losing its potency by harmonic over-writing, though in this case it struggles through. Elsewhere a song may, like some of Gurney's, begin magnificently yet drown its melodic inspiration within a few bars by discursive chromatics or rambling modulations. 'Soldier from the wars returning' is the most frustrating example of this: as soon as the 6–4 chord sounds over the subdominant at the beginning of bar 3, followed by chromatic lapses, the nobility of the opening is lost, to be wholly regained only in the final recapitulatory stanza. 'The Isle of Portland' shows a more specific niggling mannerism: the rather bland shift in the first line from one dominant 7th chord to another a tritone removed is a progression which often renders Orr's music tonally impotent. In this case the song settles after a while into the key of the second of the two dominant 7ths as though that were the tonic (Ex. 1), but periodically returns to, and finally ends in, the key of

Ex. 1

the first, or rather the key of which the first was in fact a *tonic* chord with a flat 7th added.

Part of Orr's problem is that, unlike Fauré, for instance, or even Wolf, he is incapable of suggesting harmonic nuance and not coating it with thick textural confectionery; this is what makes his Housman indigestible. 'The Lent lily', 'Oh fair enough are sky and plain', and even innately strong conceptions such as 'When smoke stood up' and 'Oh, when I was in love with you' seem to be thus impaired. Sometimes the textural overcrowding is a deliberate evocation, for instance of the rustle of spring, as in 'The Lent lily', and here, as with the recurrent cuckoo-call in 'Along the field', the model is Warlock's 'Consider', dedicated to Orr; set beside this, Orr's songs inevitably appear slightly less radiant. Orr is at his strongest when he possesses the vision to make harmonic meanderings subservient to some continuous dominant element, to an 'affection', in the baroque sense. Strange though it may seem, he achieves this least in his Housman settings, though exceptions are the melodramatic but genuinely forceful 'The carpenter's son', 'a *via dolorosa* of mounting cynicism and aggressive despair' (Palmer, 1973: 692) whose whole is imprinted with the bitter, blood-like tang of a single harmony (Ex. 2), and the beautiful setting of 'Along the

Ex. 2

field', with its breeze-blown symbolism of the gently continuing cycle of life and death in the 'rainy-sounding silver leaves' of the aspen (Ex. 3). Telling instances of such 'affections' in his settings of various authors include the persistent though sympathetic rhythmic patterns of two songs that should surely be viewed as a pair, 'The Earl of Bristol's farewell' and 'Whenas I wake', against which the exquisite vocal parts are nicely counterpointed. The former also has a well-controlled right-hand piano line constructed in a single span which gives the welcome impression of keeping the harmony on a tighter rein than usual. The care manifest in this setting brings it uncannily close to the spirit of Parry (compare his 'Take, O take those lips away'); it is a very beautiful song. 'Bahnhofstrasse' is another of Orr's best songs because of its concentrated axis of an inverted pedal (g'–g'') which, rather as in Chausson's song 'Les heures', underlines the passing of time, or more specifically here of age, with which the poem is implicitly concerned. It is a visual as well as an aural axis, for the voice part and the left hand of the piano are seen to play mockingly around it like two pendants of a mobile. Similarly, 'Tryste Noel' is kept concentrated by the judicious use of (non-inverted) pedal notes, particularly c and e flat, that anchor the familiar siciliana rhythms more firmly than usual to a harmonic discipline and are later alternated more closely to provide pleasantly mock-Elizabethan false relations. The model here is presumably Warlock's 'Balulalow'.

Ex. 3

Another redeeming feature which distinguishes a number of Orr's songs is a feeling for countermelody. In a style so completely harmonic the conscious use of unexpected or subtle melodic material within the established framework takes on considerable significance. Linking or epitaphic gestures, such as the effortless emergence of a fresh tune between the two stanzas of 'With rue my heart is laden' and the inspired piano epilogue melody of 'The Earl of Bristol's farewell', are cases in point. Others are more carefully hidden in his piano parts. The knowing little triplet figure that accompanies the wry final line, 'Never ask me whose', of 'Is my team ploughing' bears the expressive burden of the whole song if it is well performed (Ex. 4). A more complex instance occurs in 'Silent noon'. This setting,

Ex. 4

composed in full knowledge of Vaughan Williams's, which Orr said he thought sounded too much like a church voluntary, is his most intense work, although it is one of his earliest. Part of the secret of this intensity, which he rarely regained later, lies in the largely diatonic discipline of the harmony. Everywhere he savours the richness of each chord for its own sake within an unchromatic and only abstemiously modulating continuum. He is also greatly concerned with inner lines that possess an intimate life of their own yet interact exquisitely (Ex. 5). The

Ex. 5

fall of a tritone in the top line of the piano, at the words 'cow-parsley skirts . . .', onto an interrupted cadence, with the underlying g' sharp persisting in the preceding dominant 7th, counterpoints the voice particularly well. The most subtle passage, however, is an instrumental reverie in which the lovers seem to lose themselves in each other. After four bars the piano's thematic line simply melts into a series of chords, and it can be heard to trickle through them in many different ways (Ex. 6). This is the sort of multiple suggestion that Delius's harmonies at their best make possible; the endless chromatics and modulatory 7th chords which Orr and many of his contemporaries took from Delius's more peripheral characteristics are by comparison often regrettable. But whatever weaknesses of the age are to be found in Orr, more regrettable is the fact that he died knowing what his strengths had been, yet was so seldom able to hear them communicated to a public by singers that ultimately he could set no store by them in the face of overall disillusionment:

I often think that there are only two sorts of creative workers to be envied; the supreme geniuses and the 'popular' artists in words, painting or music . . . how nice to be a contented writer of garbage like Michael Head . . . without any desire to do better, and to rake in the shekels comfortably year after year. But the in-betweeners, like me and hundreds of others, who are not content with anything save that which is just out of their reach – *we* are the ones who suffer without any hope of relief. One almost wonders if it were not better to be self-deluded, and cherish the illusion that one is one of the elect, rather than to be sufficiently clear-sighted to realise that one is *not* (Orr, 1961–76).

Ex. 6

Michael Head, who also died in 1976, had avoided such alienation, for he was a singer – one of the few amongst latter-day English song composers, along with George Henschel and Liza Lehmann. He specialised in one-man performances in which he accompanied himself at the piano (like Donald Swann), and his repertoire included a number of his own songs. Most were published very soon after they were composed, and many have stayed in print. Indeed, several English competitive music festivals have a Michael Head Class for the performance of one of his songs. 'Sweet Chance, that led my steps abroad', 'The little road to Bethlehem', 'When sweet Ann sings', 'A piper' and, to a lesser extent, 'The estuary' are well known. Yet the senses in which Head can be considered a successful song composer have to be carefully limited. His fluency, which made his one-man performances possible without embarrassment, enabled him in his music to react with a surprisingly wide variety of styles and manners to his chosen poetry, but always with a certain emotional mellifluousness in which there was little room for tension. Possibly because of his unusual performing rôle, he tended as a composer to avoid any exploitation of duality (e.g. between voice part and accompaniment). The result was that he never really developed a style: there was no pressure on the notes to prove themselves in the context. The fact that his idiomatic range and literary sensibilities broadened considerably towards his last songs confirms rather than invalidates this judgement. The whole level of creative awareness in his music was somewhat lower than that of the *Lied* tradition. Style with Head was a garment, not a body tissue. Again Donald Swann provides a close parallel.

Yet it would be difficult to argue that his compositions were not art songs. They were held in that category by a highly developed sense of taste, which often covered up the fact that he had nothing to say. With this went a similarly highly developed range of techniques. He was always able to find an apt descriptive musical procedure for the poetic conceit: the chromatics of the cat's purring in 'The Matron's cat's song', the quizzically wayward minstrel's tune in 'A piper', the skylark's lyrical twitterings in 'A green cornfield', the cosy rhythms of lullabies in 'A slumber song of the Madonna' and 'Star candles', or the swell and tang of the sea in the *Six Sea Songs*. Of the latter, the first, 'A sea burthen', shows him at his most able, writing a romanticised sea shanty rather than a Romantic *Lied*. It was the attempt at combined musical and poetic conceit of any depth that nearly always failed. There was little difference of quality and potential between the Georgian poetry (e.g. Ledwidge, W. H. Davies, Drinkwater) set by Michael Head and that set by Ivor Gurney, yet Gurney often gave it depth whereas Head often trivialised it. When he tried to fill out the emotional essence of a poem he sounded stylistically insipid; see for example 'Cotwold love' and 'Sweet Chance'. Conversely, he was adept at expressing the more obvious physical implications of a poem, but not in the manner later given currency by Britten, where the vividness or subtlety of musical imagery determined the level of creative imagination of the whole; in 'Mamble', for instance, his obligingly trudging accompaniment with its tripping word-setting merely belittles Drinkwater's poem, especially at the end where, with the 'Tra la la . . .' epilogue, his sense of taste fails completely – as perhaps he acknowledges in his footnotes to the effect that part or all of the passage may be omitted. In 'Cotswold love' the poem is devalued not so much by intrinsic insipidity and sentimentality in the harmonic style as by a rather *passé* chatty colloquialism in the word-setting, maybe resulting from the inevitably confidential stance of a one-man recitalist and manifested, much as in 'Mamble', by too many gratuitous melodic contours and unpaced dotted rhythms that give the impression that the poet is uttering mere confections (Ex. 7). Songs with any rhetorical tension or sustained, emotional intensity in the vocal lines, such as 'The little dreams', are valuable exceptions. In this respect Head's technique is worlds apart from Gurney's.

One song which represents a serious attempt at something less shallow, however, and apparently 'the composer's favourite' (N. Bush: 39), is 'The estuary'. The poem, by Ruth Pitter, struggles to convey the effect on the memory of an image of a tall ship sailing up a peaceful estuary. The power of this image as a symbol is suggested by the immediate physical description of it and by the images to which it is compared:

> And silently, like sleep to the weary mind,
> Silently, like evening after day,
> The big ship bears inshore . . .

Ex. 7

Whether remembered or dreamed, read of or told,
So it has dwelt with me, so it shall dwell with me ever:
The brave ship coming home like a lamb to the fold,

But this is a weakening comparison, for it is clear from the span of the poem that the symbol is something far bigger, more archetypal, than the specific, trite images proffered. For once Head realises this, and conveys it in the music. The late Romantics understood that the secret of symbolic suggestion could lie solely in harmonic impressions, and these are what articulate Head's setting. Both Ireland and Vaughan Williams were masters of harmonic symbolism, and it is perhaps through their example that Head here begins to grasp something of the mysticism which the poem encourages. The means are simple enough: a *parlando*, dreamily gazing voice part that draws attention not to the physical elements of the scene, which are not individually explored, but to the underlying harmonic world. This includes a high ostinato, on b″ flat, f‴ and e‴ flat, representing, as it were, the 'high' level of meditation induced by 'the sleep of the afternoon'. Underneath this the developing intensity of symbolic awareness is itself symbolised by the long-term shifts of harmony, the move to the mediant chord at 'so the tide comes in' being the first example and the later G flat and D flat chords more noticeable ones. The later shift to the flat submediant at 'rolling along the fair deep channel', a similar trick of mystical intensification, is built into a cumulative passage of such modulations expressing the vital immediacy of the ship-symbol, after which the high meditative continuum is reinstated, as though emphasising the symbol's stable, lasting reality after the personal passion of recognition has passed. This reality serves to fuse the two otherwise separate worlds of past and future; similarly, at this point the music brings together, by the chromatic change from g natural to g flat, the two normally distant worlds of tonic major and minor (Ex. 8).

Ex. 8

Such analytical description may indicate what Head is attempting. Critically speaking, though, what he achieves is that virtually all of these devices, like Ruth Pitter's similes, sound hackneyed. Thus even here his affinity with the styles and methods of the other composers examined in this study is apparent rather than real.

The final composer to be examined in this chapter, Bernard van Dieren, might be easier to consider *sui generis*, but if he belongs anywhere it is to the inter-war lyrical tradition. As we have seen, Warlock and possibly Hadley came under his influence; others testified to it. He made solo settings of the English Romantic poets, including Shelley, de Quincey, Byron, Keats, Beddoes and particularly Landor, and reflected the contemporary fondness for renaissance verse in a number of his songs. Most of his music out-glimmers the Celtic twilight in sheer melancholy. Currently no more than a provisional estimate seems possible: his music is complex and little performed, and his personality repeatedly drew forth tantalising pronouncements from his devotees, particularly Sorabji, Warlock and Cecil Gray. Gray, for instance, had this to say of the *Diaphony* of 1916 for baritone and chamber orchestra (whose full score is lost):

> . . . the *Diaphony* is perhaps his most intimate and personal work . . . from the point of view of sheer constructive ability there is not one work in modern times, and indeed only the work of Bach and the Netherlanders, that could be compared with the *Diaphony*. This is not a mere statement of opinion, but a fact which can be demonstrated by means of an exhaustive analysis. There is hardly one note in the whole complicated work, lasting the best part of an hour, which does not perform some function with regard to the whole, or reveal some thematic origin (1924: 228–9).

Much was said about him as a man. To Bliss, who in his autobiography enumerated his abilities as musical performer, instrument maker, polylinguist, book-binder, chemist, and author of a book on Epstein (to which he might have added furniture-maker, photographer and electrician), he was 'the most enigmatic personality I have ever met' (:97). Howells (1974) found him abominably clever and frighteningly Satanic and was glad to have met him only once. C. W. Orr (1974) seems to have found him less daunting, but wished that he had not always spoken like a leading article in *The Times*. He was one of the few musicians for whom a similarly problematical composer, Sorabji, felt a strong affection. Sorabji (1947: 149–50) testifies with great sympathy to the suffering which van Dieren endured in the later stages of the long and painful kidney disease which afflicted him from 1913 onwards. The attendant doses of morphine should surely be taken into account in any assessment of his creative output as also, perhaps, should the fact that he seems to have been a heavy drinker (Shead: 46).

These attitudes to van Dieren beg a number of questions. Where, concerning the constructional unity that Gray finds demonstrable in *Diaphony*, does van Dieren stand in relation to the contemporary birth of serialism? If his 'constructive ability' equals that of Bach and the Netherlanders, is he as great a composer as they? Is his complexity a measure of his stature or some sort of aesthetic disease? Van Dieren needs to be scrutinised from many angles, some more relevant to the history of English song than others. The present chapter will examine one of his relatively simple compositions for voice and piano, whose stylistic premises are very similar to those of the post-Delius pastoral, chromatic school as represented by Warlock and Moeran; view it as an attempt to express personality through the setting of a poem to music; and suggest why, like the other composers discussed in this chapter, van Dieren fails to make a major contribution to the genre.

'Balow' is an anonymous 16th-century lullaby. Van Dieren sets it to music in a style which is almost conventional in England at this period, as a gentle $\frac{6}{8}$ siciliana, with plenty of dotted rhythms and a texture averaging four accompanimental parts. There is a certain amount of largely non-imitative polyphonic interest, though parts tend to come and go without regular provision of rests, and plenty of both chromatic and diatonic added-note harmony. This description fits many songs by Warlock (e.g. 'Rest, sweet nymphs' and 'Balulalow') and Moeran, as well as Orr's 'Tryste Noel', mentioned above. It differs from these three lullabies, however, in two significant ways. One is its degree of miserableness. The mother's singing to the child is a melancholy monologue in which she bewails the faithlessness of her absent husband or lover, the child's father. 'It grieves me sore to see thee weep', she sings, but we in turn are grieving to see her weep. This sustained doleful indulgence is characteristic of van Dieren and marks him off from Moeran and Warlock, for it is not the intense personal despair of *The Curlew* but a strangely drugged sorrow; it surrounds him, yet at a distance, perceived almost objectively through the morbid technical devices with which he fills the song. The other difference is the poem's length: it has five stanzas, each of the same pattern:

A
Balow, my babe, lie still and sleep,
It grieves me sore to see thee weep.
Would'st thou be quiet I'se be glad,
Thy mourning makes my sorrow sad.

B { Balow, my boy, thy mother's joy,
Thy father breeds me great annoy.
Balow, lalow.

In this first stanza van Dieren treats each line in the A section as a simple two-bar unit, with a half-bar's rest between couplets; the declamation having actually begun on the half-bar, it is back on the bar by the third line. The functional thematic thread of A is given in Ex. 9. Although it has something of the feel of a

Ex. 9

refrain, the B section actually balances A in length, numbering eight bars, with a melismatic extension on the final 'lalow'. This necessitates piecemeal declamation in order to make it last: the first line of the section is split into two with rests in between, the pacing is slower, and once again the linear continuity, comprising a new, contrasting thematic line of some distinction, is in the piano part (Ex. 10). The form of the song is as follows:

section	musical material	number of bars	key
introduction		6½	E flat
stanza I	A	8½	E flat to
	B	8 + 2	F (G flat) F
interlude		2	to
stanza II	A	8	E flat to
	B	8	G (G flat) F
		+	
interlude		4½	
stanza III	A	8½	F to
	B	8	E flat (C flat) F
		+	
interlude		3	
stanza IV	A	8 (displaced)	E flat to
	B	8 { +2	G (G flat) F
[interlude]		{ +1	to
recap. of introduction		4½	E flat
stanza V	A	8½	E flat
	B	8 { +3	F (G flat) F
interlude		{ +2	to
introduction as coda		7	E flat

Ex. 10

This tabulation indicates something of the studied mixture of regularity and irregularity permeating the structure. The elements of regularity are obvious enough on paper: eight-bar phrases, repeated thematic patterns for each stanza, and a roughly similar mode and length of transition from the melismatic ending of B back to A in each succeeding stanza. Aurally there is a very noticeable feeling of simple recapitulation from the repeat of the introduction before the fifth stanza through to the end of the song. What happens in between is more complicated, and gives glimpses of van Dieren's extraordinarily proliferative mind. In the second stanza he suddenly whittles down the texture, for the beginning of A, to two moving parts: the established melody (Ex. 9), now in the 'tenor' register of the accompaniment, and a new counterpoint for the voice. This counterpoint continues for the first two lines, but the next two enjoy new material, except for a reminiscence of Ex. 9, *x* at the end: they exploit a motive (Ex. 11, *y*) previously

Ex. 11

heard in the introduction and now couched in sequential modulations through G flat and elsewhere to arrive in G for the B section, whose melodic line (Ex. 10), still in the piano, is little changed from its statement in the first stanza except for an altered twist in its fourth bar so that it still gets to G flat afterwards, despite having begun in G. The fourth stanza, both in thematic material and in tonal structure, is a very close paraphrase of the second, thus consolidating the arch form of the whole. The third stanza has the most intricate texture, taking as its point of departure the melisma on 'lalow', the final word of each stanza. This melisma is basically a somewhat unsatisfactory vocal adornment, for it keeps getting stuck on c″, but it offers scope for proliferation in the accompaniment, first at the end of the first stanza in the form of Ex. 9, *x* working against it, and then as a preparation for the third stanza, in that it generates a continuous flow of semiquavers which persist until the second half of the stanza, although as it progresses they are increasingly relayed, *style brisé*-fashion, between the parts. This kind of scabrous generative growth, with its vague, half-imitative thematic cells of two or three types (Ex. 12), is nevertheless rhythmically much simpler here than in most of van

Ex. 12

Dieren's songs, where triplets of various kinds so often clutter and destroy rather than propel the pulse. Here the wealth of syncopated quaver figures shows some rhythmic affinity with 15th-century cadential and episodic figurations, but it lacks the harmonic control necessary in post-Romantic structures: there are nine F major imperfect cadence progressions in as many bars, giving an overall impression of stultified harmonic invention despite the intermediate chromatics.

Elsewhere in the song it is the conscious superimposition of inventive detail which provides the artistic foreground. The detail may be a matter of harmonic ellipsis, as in bars 3–4 of the introduction, to take a simple, unoriginal and un-exceptionable example, where the c natural towards which the preceding B natural wants to lead is displaced up an octave as implied by the phrasing, so that the B natural moving to the f in the bass gives the effect of an intervening harmonic step's having been left out (Ex. 13). Or it may consist of rhythmic way-

Ex. 13

wardness. Van Dieren is often overtly analytical about his rhythms; the corollary is that they often look much more interesting than they sound. An example is in the very first bar, where the left-hand part would look and sound completely un-remarkable if notated conventionally (Ex. 14). Likewise in his word-setting: there seems little point or inventive tension in the hemiola in the second stanza (Ex. 15) and the fourth; in each case the calculated result is to get the voice's metrical pacing half a bar ahead of the attendant accompanimental structure, a process

Ex. 14

Ex. 15

which detracts from the poem's and the music's lilt and makes a generally rather uncomfortable impression.

Other examples of obscure detail might be adduced. In the third stanza the quite arbitrarily bracketed echo passage, the '*non toccare*' notes at the end and, immediately after them, the exploitation of octave displacement to vary the *melos* of the interlude material – all these bespeak the debility of his invention. Perhaps the major fault in 'Balow' is its key scheme. Despite the song's relative lack of complexity, the tonal oscillations between E flat, F, and G are quite unbalanced; he seems to have no understanding of the cycle of 5ths. All his songs are tonally anarchic, which is not to say they are atonal – a distinction which van Dieren himself seems not to have appreciated.

Yet with all its oddities 'Balow' remains one of the few songs by van Dieren in which a certain touching simplicity underlies the surface detail; as one gets to know its structure, it begins to seem less introspective, more lyrically beautiful. But most of his settings remain uncommunicative. Perhaps a telling comparison can be made between Mahler's setting of 'The drunkard in spring' in *Das Lied von der Erde* and van Dieren's in his *Chinese Symphony*, written a few years later. Mahler's speaks to the world; van Dieren's lives, incommunicado, in a world of its own, the world of the solitary drinker. The Landor songs in particular, all very much alike, mark van Dieren off as a manic depressive in music. This ruling temperament becomes overwhelming in the two extended settings for voice and string quartet, de Quincey's 'Levana' rhapsody and the 'Song from *The Cenci*' of Shelley. The Shelley setting begins:

> Come, I will sing you some low, sleepy tune,
> Not cheerful, nor yet sad; some dull old thing,
> Some outworn and unused monotony . . .

The 'outworn and unused monotony' in van Dieren's style, and it *is* sad, appears at a time (if the music really dates back to 1909) when it was the aesthetic property only of members of the avant-garde such as Satie. In 'Levana' the melancholy is less narcotic and more destructive. Although rhythmically and harmonically it is much more complex than 'Balow', it is also rather more effectively written. The harmonies, particularly in the introduction and epilogue, produce a chill of diseased lethargy. An element of personal testimony seems to be revealed at the point at which he chooses to end his précis of de Quincey's text: 'These are the sorrows, all three of whom I know.' Musically the effect is due to a freer but less proliferative weft of counterpoint than in 'Balow', and to chords more Delius-like in being savoured entirely for their own sake; many of them are unprepared major 7ths and supertonic 9ths and 13ths which sometimes involve one change of key per chord.

But the monotony of this style is not easy to vindicate, and 'Levana' cannot counteract the fact that in nearly all van Dieren's songs his technique, like the temperament from which it seems to spring, is a severe barrier to communication. The only song in which his manner is simple enough not to become obstructive is the glum but compassionate setting of Bruce Blunt's memorial poem to Warlock, 'The long barrow'. Here even the words speak starkly and simply; elsewhere in his output they are set with apparently small concern for audibility. Van Dieren, whom Warlock tried to help financially, had visited him the night before his untimely death. The poem addresses the dead composer in terms of outgoing friendship; and for once van Dieren turned outwards from himself and relinquished his self-absorbed harmonies.